LINKING TRADE, ENVIRONMENT
AND SOCIAL CO...

Global Environmental Governance Series

Series Editors: Konrad von Moltke and John J. Kirton

Global Environmental Governance addresses the new generation of twenty-first century environmental problems and the challenges they pose for management and governance at the local, national, and global levels. Centred on the relationships among environmental change, economic forces, and political governance, the series explores the role of international institutions and instruments, national and sub-federal governments, private sector firms, scientists, and civil society, and provides a comprehensive body of progressive analyses on one of the world's most contentious international issues.

Also in the series

International Equity and Global Environmental Politics:
Power and Principles in U.S. Foreign Policy
Paul G. Harris
ISBN 0 7546 1735 1

Governing Global Biodiversity:
The Evolution and Implementation
of the Convention on Biological Diversity
Edited by Philippe G. Le Prestre
ISBN 0 7546 1744 0

Linking Trade, Environment, and Social Cohesion

NAFTA experiences, global challenges

Edited by

JOHN J. KIRTON
VIRGINIA W. MACLAREN
University of Toronto

Ashgate

Published by
Ashgate Publishing Limited
Gower House
Croft Road
Aldershot
Hampshire GU11 3HR
England

Ashgate Publishing Company
131 Main Street
Burlington, VT 05401-5600 USA

Ashgate website: http://www.ashgate.com

British Library Cataloguing in Publication Data
Linking trade, environment, and social cohesion : NAFTA
    experiences, global challenges. - (Global environmental
    governance)
    1. NAFTA 2. Sustainable development - North America
    3. Economic development - Social aspects - North America
    4. International trade - Social aspects
    I. Kirton, John J. II. Maclaren, Virginia White, 1953-
    338.9'2

Library of Congress Control Number: 2002100838

ISBN 0 7546 1934 6

Printed and bound in Great Britain by MPG Books Ltd, Bodmin, Cornwall

Contents

PART I: LINKING TRADE, ENVIRONMENT, AND SOCIAL VALUES: THE GLOBAL AND NAFTA EXPERIENCES

PART II: INVESTOR PROTECTION: EVALUATING THE NAFTA CHAPTER 11 MODEL

List of Tables

List of Figures

List of Contributors

Gustavo Alanís Ortega is a professor of Environmental Law at the Universidad Iberoamericana in Mexico City, and has been the president of the Mexican Environmental Law Center for the past eleven years. In addition, he is Academic Co-ordinator of the Diploma on Environmental Law and Policy at the Universidad Iberoamericana, President of the InterAmerican Association for the Protection of the Environment (AIDA), and a Fellow of Leadership on Environment and Development (LEAD), Cohort 7. He is also a columnist for the *Reforma* newspaper in Mexico City, where he writes about environmental law and environmental education. Professor Alanís received his LL.B. from the Iberoamericana University in Mexico City and holds an LL.M. in International Law from the American University, Washington College of Law, in Washington DC. LEAD is a partner institution of 'Strengthening Canada's Environmental Community through International Regime Reform' (the EnviReform project) at the University of Toronto.

Carl G. Amrhein has been dean of the Faculty of Arts and Science at the University of Toronto since November 1997. He was previously chair of the university's Department of Geography and the graduate program in planning, a position he held since 1993. He was admitted as a full member to the Canadian Institute of Planning and the Ontario Professional Planning Institute in 1997. Dean Amrhein's research concentrates on urban environmental health and spatial statistics, with a predominant focus on the quality of data. A prolific author and well-respected scholar, he has completed two terms as chair of the board of directors of the Joint Centre of Excellence for Research on Immigration and Settlement and was one of the leaders of the centre's Metropolis Project, which is examining issues of immigration and settlement in urban areas. Dean Amrhein was a principal investigator on a recently completed two-year National Health Research and Development programme grant to examine issues related to urban environmental health. Most recently, he and a colleague are working jointly with the Université Laval to support the work of the Canadian Foundation for Innovation on geographic information systems. Dean Amrhein received his B.Sc. from Pennsylvania State University in 1978 and his Ph.D. from the State University of New York at Buffalo in 1984.

Kevin Banks is Senior Labour Law Advisor at the Secretariat of the North American Commission for Labor Cooperation (CLC). He works on the Secretariat's research team on various projects, including comparative analyses of the labour laws of the three member states. Before joining the Secretariat staff, Mr. Banks practised labour, employment, human rights, and administrative law in Toronto and Ottawa as a litigator, advisor, and negotiator on behalf of various trade union and individual clients. In 1993, he served as consultant to the United States President's Commission on Labor

Law Reform (the Dunlop Commission). Mr. Banks holds a B.A. in economics and an LL.B. from the University of Toronto, and an LL.M. from Harvard Law School, where he is a candidate for a doctorate in law.

David L. Buckeridge, FRCP(C), is a member of the faculty at the Stanford University School of Medicine. He has been Research Associate with HEALNet (Health Evidence Application and Linkage Network) and a member of the Canadian Network of Centres of Excellence. His research focusses on public health informatics, that is, the collection, storage, retrieval, analysis, and dissemination of data and information relevant to the health of communities. He has a particular interest in health surveillance systems, geographical and environmental epidemiology, and human and organisational factors related to community health systems. He received his B.Sc. and M.D. from Queen's University and his M.Sc. in Epidemiology from the University of Toronto. In January 2001, Dr. Buckeridge entered the Ph.D. program in medical informatics at Stanford University.

William A. Dymond is Executive Director of the Centre for Trade Policy and Law at Carleton University in Ottawa. He has extensive experience in trade negotiation and policy. Formerly the Director-General of the Policy Planning Secretariat of Canada's Department of Foreign Affairs and International Trade, he has also served as Senior Advisor to the Trade Negotiations Office for the Canada-U.S. Free Trade Agreement, Chief Negotiator for Canada for the Organisation for Economic Co-operation and Development's Multilateral Agreement on Investment, and Chief Air Negotiator for Canada. His overseas assignments include Ambassador of Canada to Brazil, Deputy Head and Minister Counsellor for the Permanent Mission of Canada to the European Communities in Brussels, and Minister Counsellor (Commercial) at the Embassy of Canada to the United States in Washington DC. Mr. Dymond's publications include 'The MAI: A Sad and Melancholy Tale', in *A Big League Player? Canada Among Nations* (Oxford University Press, 1999); *Decision at Midnight* (co-author, University of British Colombia Press, 1994); 'Sisyphus Ascendant? Brazil and the 21st Century', in *Canadian Foreign Policy* (1997); 'Globalization and the Negotiation of International Investment Rules in a post-MAI World', in *Canadian Foreign Policy* (Winter 2000); and 'Post-Modern Trade Policy: Reflections on the Challenges to Multilateral Trade Negotiations after Seattle', in *Journal of World Trade* (June 2000). Mr. Dymond is a graduate of the University of Toronto, having received his B.A. in 1966 and his M.A. in 1967.

Sanford E. Gaines is a professor at the University of Houston Law Center, where he teaches courses in environmental law and trade law and co-directs the Law Center's Mexican Legal Studies Program in Mexico City. His recent scholarship concerns the relationships between trade and environment and the international environmental institutions in North America. He was a Fulbright Senior Scholar in Denmark in 2000 and from 1996 to 1999 was the part-time executive director of the North American Institute (NAMI), a voluntary civic organisation with members in Canada, Mexico, and the U.S. While on leave from the University of Houston from 1992 to 1994, Professor Gaines served as the Deputy Assistant U.S. Trade Representative for Environment and Natural Resources in the Executive Office of the President, responsible for environmental issues and side agreements in the negotiation of NAFTA and the Uruguay Round agreements in GATT. In 1997–99, he was a member and chair of the National Advisory Committee to the Environmental Protection Agency Administrator as the U.S. Representative to the Commission for Environmental Cooperation. He is also a member of the United Nations Environment Programme Expert Group on International Environmental Agreements and Trade, and consults occasionally with such organisations as the Commission for Environmental Cooperation, Environmental Defense, and the World Conservation Union. Professor Gaines graduated *magna cum laude* from Harvard College in 1967 and *cum laude* from Harvard Law School in 1974. He also received an M.A. from Harvard University in East Asian Regional Studies in 1974.

Jonathan Graubart is completing his Ph.D. in Political Science at the University of Wisconsin in Madison. His dissertation examines the uses made by social activists of international soft law mechanisms in areas such as labour rights, human rights, and the environment. He is a fellow at the interdisciplinary Institute for Legal Studies at the University of Wisconsin-Madison Law School. His research interests are in international relations, international law, and transnational activism. Previously, Mr. Graubart was an attorney in San Francisco practising plaintiff-side complex civil litigation. He also worked as an editorial staff member at *Tikkun Magazine*. Mr. Graubart has published articles in various journals, including *California Law Review*, *Monthly Review*, and *Consumer Reports*. He received his B.A. in 1985 from the University of Pennsylvania and his J.D. in 1989 from Boalt Hall Law School at the University of California at Berkeley.

Pierre Marc Johnson is a lawyer, physician, former Premier of Quebec, and former professor of law at McGill University. He has been Senior Counsel with the offices of Heenan Blaikie since 1996 and serves on numerous corporate boards as a director. He acts in commercial negotiations, international partnerships, and foreign investment ventures related to new information technologies, entertainment, real estate, and financial products. Vice-Chair of the National Round Table on the Environment and the Economy and Chair of its Foreign Policy Committee from 1990 to 1997, Dr. Johnson is an advisor to the Commission for Environmental Cooperation. Widely published, he is the author of 'Creating Sustainable Global Governance' in *Guiding Global Order: G8 Governance in the Twenty-First Century* (edited by John Kirton,

Joseph Daniels, and Andreas Freytag, Ashgate, 2001) as well as of *The Environment and NAFTA: Understanding and Implementing the New Continental Law* (co-author, Island Press, 1996). He holds an honorary doctorate from Claude Bernard University in Lyon, France, and is a Fellow of the Royal Society of Canada and a Grand Officier de l'Ordre de la Pleiade.

Noel Keough is co-founder and current co-ordinator of the Sustainable Calgary Society. Born in Newfoundland, he has lived in Calgary for 20 years. His academic background is in engineering and environmental science. Mr. Keough has worked and taught in the area of sustainable community development for the past 15 years in Canada, Central America, Eastern Europe, the Middle East, and Asia.

John J. Kirton is Associate Professor of Political Science, a Fellow of Trinity College, the Director of the G8 Research Group, and Research Associate of the Centre for International Studies at the University of Toronto, where he leads a team of nine scholars and seven social partners on a project on 'Strengthening Canada's Environmental Community through International Regime Reform' (the EnviReform project). He is the co-author with Alan Rugman and Julie Soloway of *Environmental Regulations and Corporate Competitiveness: A NAFTA Perspective* (Oxford University Press, 1999), and author of *Assessing the Environmental Effects of the North American Free Trade Agreement (NAFTA): Final Analytic Framework and Methodological Issues and Empirical Background* (Commission for Environmental Cooperation, 1999), *NAFTA's Environmental Institutions: Performance and Potential* (1997), and *Building a Framework for Assessing NAFTA Effects* (1996). He served as chair of the North American Environmental Standards Working Group, team leader of the Commission for Environmental Cooperation's project on NAFTA's environmental effects, a member of the Foreign Policy Committee of the Canadian Prime Minister's National Round Table on the Environment and the Economy, and a member of the Canadian Government's International Trade Advisory Committee.

Virginia W. Maclaren is Associate Professor in the Department of Geography and Program in Planning at the University of Toronto. She has participated in a number of different indicator projects in Canada over the past five years. She is currently leading a University of Toronto team that is part of a tri-university consortium providing research support to Vital Signs, a community-based indicator project for Toronto. Professor Maclaren has spoken at Porto Alegre, Brazil, and Chengdu, China, about Hamilton-Wentworth's experience in governance relating to sustainability, Vital Signs' indicators program, and the development of the local agenda VISION 2020. Her research interests include waste management, sustainable urban development, environmental assessment, and Southeast Asia. Professor Maclaren received her B.A. from Bishop's University, her M.Pl. in Regional Planning from the University of

Ottawa, and her Ph.D. in Regional Science from Cornell University. Professor Maclaren is a co-investigator in 'Strengthening Canada's Environmental Community through International Regime Reform' (the EnviReform project) at the University of Toronto.

Sylvia Ostry is Distinguished Research Fellow at the Centre for International Studies of the University of Toronto. After teaching and research at a number of Canadian universities and at the University of Oxford Institute of Statistics, she joined the Canadian government in 1964, where she served as Deputy Minister of International Trade, Ambassador for Multilateral Trade Negotiations, and the Prime Minister's Personal Representative for the Economic Summit, among other posts. From 1979 to 1983, she was Head of the Economics and Statistics Department of the Organisation for Economic Co-operation and Development in Paris. She has received the Outstanding Achievement Award of the Government of Canada and in 1990 was made a Companion of the Order of Canada; she is also a Fellow of the Royal Society of Canada. Widely published, she is author of *Who's on First? The Post-Cold War Trading System* (University of Chicago Press, 1997). Dr. Ostry has a Ph.D. in Economics from McGill University and Cambridge. She is a co-investigator in 'Strengthening Canada's Environmental Community through International Regime Reform' (the EnviReform project) at the University of Toronto.

Sarah Richardson is President of Maeander Enterprises Ltd., a Canadian company that undertakes research and analysis related to issues of trade and sustainable development. This work focusses on the question of how to conduct integrated assessments of trade liberalisation agreements and trade-related policies. Clients include the United Nations Environment Programme, the World Wildlife Fund, the International Institute for Sustainable Development, and Oxfam. Prior to heading up Maeander Enterprises, Ms. Richardson was the Program Manager for NAFTA/Environment at the Commission for Environmental Cooperation, where she was responsible for developing the framework to assess the effects of NAFTA on the environment. She has also worked as Foreign Policy Advisor at the National Round Table on the Environment and the Economy, an advisory body on sustainable development to Canada's prime minister. Ms. Richardson's background is in law and policy. She holds an LL.M. in International Law from Columbia University, an LL.B. from Dalhousie, and a B.A. (Hons.) in International Relations from the University of Toronto.

Julie Soloway is an associate with Davies Ward Phillips &Vineberg LLP, practising international trade law and competition law. She was called to the Ontario Bar in 1995 and joined the firm in 2000. Dr. Soloway previously worked as an international trade consultant associated with the Centre for International Studies and subsequently with Charles River Associates. She has advised clients on a variety of matters pertaining to international trade and investment, international dispute settlement under the North

American Free Trade Agreement and the World Trade Organization, and environmental regulation. Her clients include primarily Canadian, foreign, and international agencies. Dr. Soloway has published numerous articles on the subject of international trade, investment, and environmental regulation, and is co-author, with John Kirton and Alan Rugman, of *Environmental Regulations and Corporate Strategy: A NAFTA Perspective* (Oxford University Press, 1999). Dr. Soloway received her B.A. in Economics, her LL.B. from the University of Western Ontario, and her LL.M. (*cum laude*) in International, European, and Comparative Law from the Vrije Universiteit Brussel. She holds an S.J.D. (doctorate) in international trade law from the University of Toronto. Dr. Soloway is a collaborator on 'Strengthening Canada's Environmental Community through International Regime Reform' (the EnviReform project) at the University of Toronto.

Christopher Tollefson is Associate Professor at the Faculty of Law of the University of Victoria. His recent publications include *The Wealth of Forests: Markets, Regulation and Sustainable Forestry* (University of British Columbia Press, 1998) and *cleanair.ca: a citizen's action guide* (Sierra Legal Defence Fund, 2000). He is currently working on a manuscript funded by the Social Sciences and Humanities Research Council of Canada that considers the influence of eco-certification on forest policy in British Columbia. Professor Tollefson founded and is the Executive Director of the University of Victoria's Environmental Law Centre, home of the only clinical program in public interest environmental law in Canada. He has served on the board of the Sierra Legal Defence Fund since 1993, and was its chair from 1998 to 2001. He is also a Fellow of Leadership for Environment and Development (LEAD). The Sierra Legal Defence Fund and LEAD are partner institutions of 'Strengthening Canada's Environmental Community through International Regime Reform' (the EnviReform project) at the University of Toronto; Professor Tollefson is also an investigator with the EnviReform project.

Scott Vaughan is Head of Environment, Economy, and Trade Program of the North American Commission for Environmental Cooperation (CEC). Before joining the CEC in 1998, he worked for the World Trade Organization on trade and environment issues, and with the United Nations Environment Programme (UNEP) in Nairobi as policy advisor to the Executive Director, in New York as liaison co-ordinator for the preparatory process for the 1992 United Nations Conference on Environment and Development (UNCED), and in Geneva as head of UNEP's work on trade and finance (including its work with commercial banks and the insurance sector). Mr. Vaughan was also Senior Policy Advisor to the former Minister of the Environment, Charles Caccia, and analyst with the head office of the Royal Bank of Canada. The Commission for Environmental Cooperation is a partner institution of 'Strengthening Canada's Environmental Community through International Regime Reform' (the EnviReform project) at the University of Toronto.

Konrad von Moltke is a Senior Fellow at the International Institute for Sustainable Development. His recent work has focussed on environmental policy and international economic relations: debt, trade, investment, and development. Professor von Moltke has contributed to developing the agenda on trade and environment at global and regional levels. He is a Senior Fellow at World Wildlife Fund in Washington DC, Adjunct Professor of Environmental Studies and Senior Fellow of the Institute on International Environmental Governance at Dartmouth College, and Visiting Professor of Environmental Studies at the Free University in Amsterdam. From 1989 to 1998, he edited *International Environmental Affairs*, a journal for research and policy. Between 1976 and 1984, he was founding Director of the Institute for European Environmental Policy. He has published extensively on medieval history, comparative education and curriculum development, and international environmental policy. Professor von Moltke studied mathematics at Dartmouth College and medieval history at the University of Munich and the University of Göttingen, where he received his Ph.D. in 1970.

Serena Wilson, an attorney, co-ordinated environment and trade policy at the Environmental Protection Agency (EPA) and served as the U.S. NAFTA Coordinator for the EPA. In 1993, she was a member of the U.S. delegation that negotiated the NAFTA environmental side agreement. She later negotiated the original Article 14-15 guidelines and led the U.S. delegation during the guideline revisions. Ms. Wilson is currently a consultant and was nominated to NAFTA's Joint Public Advisory Committee in April 2000.

Preface and Acknowledgements

Forging the appropriate balance and realising the potential synergies among trade liberalisation, environmental enhancement, and social cohesion have been a challenge faced by the international community for well over a decade. Yet the two tasks are acquiring increasing urgency and importance as the twenty-first century unfolds. The failure to sustain the momentum of trade and investment liberalisation through the conclusion of the Multilateral Agreement in Investment (MAI) at the Organisation for Economic Co-operation and Development (OECD) and the delay in the launch of new round of trade negotiations by the World Trade Organization (WTO) as the twentieth century closed was due in part to intensified demands that the values and voices of the environment, labour, and, more generally, civil society be given a more integral and equal part in the new international regimes being forged. The global financial crisis of 1997–99 seemed to show that the liberalisation of finance could unleash devastating, widespread destruction of the ecological resources, material well-being, and social stability of countries around the globe, and that the previously attractive model of export-led growth provided no sure and stable route to sustainable development. In light of strong protests against the work of the International Monetary Fund (IMF) in 2000, subsequent protests in 2001 at the Summit of the Americas, European Council, and G8 Summit, and rising concerns over trade in genetically modified food, it became clear that resistance to continued trade and investment liberalisation would continue. More generally, among publics in North America, Europe, and Asia, the earlier consensus on the value of trade liberalisation began to erode as anxieties about the social impacts of globalisation grew. In the judgement of many, if the existing hard-won advances in trade liberalisation were to be preserved and extended, a better way to make trade liberalisation promote environmental enhancement and social cohesion would have to be found.

In searching for such a formula, there were good reasons to consider the experience of North Americans under the regime of the North American Free Trade Agreement (NAFTA), which had been constructed and had operated over the past decade. In many respects, those in the North American community had crafted in their NAFTA, which took effect on 1 January 1994, a set of rules and institutions that led the world in affirming ecological and social values. NAFTA had declared that among the purposes of this full free trade agreement were the promotion of sustainable development and the strengthening of environmental laws and enforcement and labour values. Moreover, alongside NAFTA had been created the North American Agreement on Environmental Cooperation (NAAEC), the North American Agreement on Labor Cooperation (NAALC), and new regional organisations for their implementation — the Commission for Environmental Cooperation (CEC) in Montreal and the Commission for Labor Cooperation (CLC) in Washington. Finally, these three agreements had given the corporate community, nongovernmental organisations (NGOs), and interested parties of civil society an unparalleled degree of direct access to these international institutions to ensure that their provisions, their member states' regulations for environmental, labour, and investment protection were upheld.

Is this pioneering North American trade-environment-labour regime a model for the global community as it seeks to move forward to secure the gains that trade and investment liberalisation can bring? There remain considerable controversy and uncertainty about the appropriate answer. Many critics felt that NAFTA would destroy social and environmental values; some have offered assessments of whether NAFTA's provisions for environmental and social protection and civil society participation have unfolded as its founders had hoped. Other critics maintain that it is still too early for an effective assessment of the ecological and social impacts of trade and investment liberalisation. Indeed, there remains uncertainty whether the North American model can serve as a framework for the international community beyond.

In order to secure better answers to these central questions, at a critical time for the global trade and environmental community, the University of Toronto Centre for International Studies mounted a conference at the Munk Centre for International Studies from 16 to 18 November 2000 on 'Strengthening Canada's Environmental Community through International Regime Reform: Twenty-First Century Challenges'. This conference and thus this book took as their focus the central issues of the contemporary trade-environment-social cohesion debate.

This was the inaugural annual conference of the EnviReform project, an innovative partnership between scholars from a broad range of disciplines and social partners from an array of communities across Canada. The project's mission is to identify ways for Canadians to participate more cohesively and directly in the international trade and finance systems that affect their natural environment, food, health, and safety. It analyses the social and environmental impacts on Canadians of existing trade liberalisation through the WTO, NAFTA, and other regimes, and explores new strategies for regulation and risk assessment, environmental information, standard setting, voluntary activities, sustainability assessments of trade agreements, and participation by civil society in international trade, finance, and environmental institutions. These strategies aim at equipping Canadians to participate in more effective and unified ways in shaping international trade and finance regimes that enhance environmental quality, social cohesion, and sustainable development at home and abroad.

This book, as with the conference on which it is based, has five primary purposes. The first is to identify how the general process of, and debate about, globalisation on a global scale impacts upon and is informed by the NAFTA-centred experience and concerns of North Americans in their home region. The second is to assess the current record of the NAFTA regime in integrating trade, environment, and social concerns, and place this record in the context of major efforts at the global level. The third is to determine how well the NAFTA institutions have fulfilled their promise of providing direct civil society participation and done so in ways that promote environmental and social values. The fourth is to explore how well the NAFTA regime has assessed the environmental and social impacts it has brought, given the state of the art for monitoring environmental quality and the environmental impacts of trade liberalisation at the local, regional, and global levels. The fifth is to identify ways in which the NAFTA model might be improved to better meet sustainable development goals and how it can contribute to meeting trade-related challenges faced by the broader international community.

To address these issues, the volume has assembled the analyses from leading scholars and practitioners from all countries in North America, as well as representatives from the CEC and CLC, and other stakeholders. Most of the chapters included in this volume were first presented as papers at Toronto in November 2000, and have been extensively revised as a result of the dialogue at the conference and subsequent research. Added to them is John Kirton's chapter 'Winning Together: The NAFTA Trade-Environment Record', which reflects some of the early research sponsored by the project and was first presented in Vancouver in October 2000, at 'Rethinking the Line: The Canada-U.S. Border', a conference sponsored by the Policy Research Institute. Also added is John Kirton's chapter on 'Embedded Ecologism and Institutional Inequality: Linking Trade, Environment, and Social Cohesion in the G8', a revised version of a paper first presented at the annual conference of the International Studies Association in Chicago in February 2001. Most of the papers presented at the EnviReform conference are available on the project's Web site at <www.envireform.utoronto.ca>.

Acknowledgements

It is impossible to produce a volume such as this without the support and contributions of a great many people. We are, of course, grateful to our colleagues on the EnviReform team: Stephen Clarkson, University of Toronto; Harriet Friedmann, University of Toronto; Peter Hajnal, University of Toronto; Sylvia Ostry, University of Toronto; Louis Pauly, University of Toronto; Christopher Tollefson, University of Victoria; Michael Trebilcock, University of Toronto; Alan Rugman, Indiana University; and Julie Soloway, Davies Ward Phillips and Vineberg LLP. We are also grateful to our social partners — Canadian Auto Workers, le Centre patronal de l'environnement du Québec, Commission for Environmental Cooperation, Foodshare, Leadership for Environment and Development (LEAD) Canada, Pollution Probe, and the Sierra Legal Defence Fund.

We are especially thankful to the conference sponsors: the Centre for International Studies, Collaborative Master of Arts in International Relations, the Institute for Environmental Studies, and the Munk Centre for International Studies at the University of Toronto, and the Social Sciences and Humanities Research Council of Canada, without which none of this would be possible.

Producing a conference as well as a book requires the hard work of many people. We owe a debt of gratitude to Mary Lynne Bratti, Munk Centre for International Studies, Joan Golding, Collaborative Master of Arts in International Relations, and Diane Granato and Tina Lagopoulos, Centre for International Studies. We wish also to thank Anju Aggarwal, Vanita Goela, Brendan Heath, Petra Kukacka, Marilena Liguori, Klaudyna Osika, and Bob Papanikolaou for their research assistance. Our debt extends to the co-ordinator of the project, Gina Stephens, the Web manager, and Rob Roy McGregor, as well as to Madeline Koch, the managing editor of the Global Environmental Governance series. We also appreciate the contributions and criticisms of the many people who participated in the first annual EnviReform conference, both as speakers and as delegates.

Finally, we acknowledge the understanding, patience, and support of our families as we laboured to convert raw drafts into published text.

John J. Kirton and Virginia W. Maclaren
December 2001

List of Abbreviations

AFA	Association of Flight Attendants (United States)
AFL-CIO	American Federation of Labor-Congress of Industrial Organizations
AIT	Agreement on Internal Trade
ANAD	Asociación Nacional de Abogados Democráticos (National Association of Democratic Attorneys)
APEC	Asia-Pacific Economic Cooperation
ASSA	Asociación Sindical de Sobrecargos de Aviación (Association of Flight Attendants)
BIS	Bank for International Settlements
BIT	bilateral investment treaty
CAL-OSHA	California Occupational Safety and Health Agency
CAT	Committee on Agricultural Trade
CEC	Commission for Environmental Cooperation
CEDF	Canadian Environmental Defence Fund
CEROI	Cities Environment Reports on the Internet
CIESIN	Centre for International Earth Science Information Network
CJM	Coalition for Justice in the Maquiladoras
CLC	Commission for Labor Cooperation
CPRN	Canadian Policy Research Network
CQDE	Centre québécois du droit de l'environnement
CSRM	Committee on Standards-Related Measures
CTM	Confederación de Trabajadores de México (Mexican Labour Confederation)
CUPW	Canadian Union of Postal Workers
CWA	Communications Workers of America
DDT	dichlorodiphenyltrichloroethane
DFAIT	Department of Foreign Affairs and International Trade (Canada)
ECE	Evaluation Committee of Experts
EIA	environmental impact assessment
ENGO	environmental nongovernmental organisation
EPA	Environmental Protection Agency (United States)
ERG	Emergency Response Group
EWG	North American Working Group on Environmental Enforcement and Compliance Cooperation
FAT	Frente Auténtico de Trabajo (Authentic Workers Front)
FDC	Frente Democrático Campesino (Democratic Farm Workers Front)
FDI	foreign direct investment

FIPA	foreign investment protection and promotion agreement
FTA	(Canada-U.S.) Free Trade Agreement
FTAA	Free Trade Agreement of the Americas
G7	Group of Seven
G8	Group of Eight
G10	Group of 10
G20	Group of 20
GATS	General Agreement on Trade in Services
GATT	General Agreement on Tariffs and Trade
GDP	gross domestic product
GIS	geographic information system
GNP	gross national product
GPI	genuine progress indicator
ICSID	International Centre for the Settlement of Investment Disputes
IISD	International Institute for Sustainable Development
ILO	International Labour Organization
ILRF	International Labor Rights Fund
IMF	International Monetary Fund
INE	Instituto Nacional de Ecología
INM	Inspection and Maintenance
INS	Immigration and Nationalization Service (United States)
IRC	Independent Review Committee
JPAC	Joint Public Advisory Committee
LPA	Labor Planning Association (United States)
LTRAP	Long-Range Transboundary Air Pollution
LULU	locally undesirable land use
MAI	Multilateral Agreement on Investment
MDBs	multilateral development banks
MEA	multilateral environmental agreement
MMT	methylcyclopentadienyl manganese tricarbonyl
MNC	multinational corporation
MOU	memorandum of understanding
MTBE	methyl tertiary butyl ether
NAAEC	North American Agreement on Environmental Cooperation
NAALC	North American Agreement on Labor Cooperation
NAC	National Advisory Committee
NAFTA	North American Free Trade Agreement
NALC	National Association of Letter Carriers (United States)
NAO	national administrative office
NAPRI	North American Pollutant Release Inventory
NGO	nongovernmental organisation

NIMBY	not in my back yard
NLRB	National Labor Relations Board (United States)
OCAW	Oil, Chemical, and Atomic Workers
ODA	official development assistance
OECD	Organisation for Economic Co-operation and Development
OPEC	Organization of the Petroleum Exporting Countries
PAN	Partido Acción Nacional
PCBs	polychlorinated biphenyls
PRI	Partido Revolucionario Institucional
PROFEPA	Procuraduría Federal de Protección al Ambiente
QOL	quality of life
SCOPE	Scientific Committee on Problems of the Environment
SCWM	Support Committee for Workers in the Maquiladoras
SEA	strategic environmental assessment
SETO	Southeast Toronto coalition
SIA	sustainability impact assessment
SOC	state of the city
SOE	state of the environment
SOW	state of the watershed
SPS	Sanitary and Phytosanitary Measures
STRM	Sindicato de Telefonistas de la República Mexicana (Union of Mexican Telephone Workers)
SUTSP	Sindicato Unico de Trabajadores de la Secretaría de Pesca (Single Union of Workers of the Fishing Industry)
TBT	Technical Barriers to Trade
TRIMs	trade-related investment measures
TRIPs	trade-related aspects of intellectual property
TWGP	Trilateral Working Group on Pesticides
UE	United Electrical, Radio, and Machine Workers
UFW	United Farm Workers (United States)
UNCED	United Nations Conference on Environment and Development
UNCITRAL	United Nations Commission on International Trade Law
UNCTAD	United Nations Conference on Trade and Development
UNCTC	United Nations Centre on Transnational Corporations
UNEP	United Nations Environment Programme
UNFCCC	United Nations Framework Convention on Climate Change
UNT	Unión Nacional de Trabajadores (National Union of Workers)
USTR	United States Trade Representative
WTO	World Trade Organization
WWF	World Wildlife Fund

Chapter 1

Forging the Trade-Environment-Social Cohesion Link: Global Challenges, North American Experiences

John J. Kirton and Virginia W. Maclaren

Global Problems, North American Solutions

Linking trade liberalisation, environmental protection, and social cohesion in mutually supportive ways has long been a challenge for the global community. The connection among these three realms was first forged in practice almost a century ago with the emergence of the first multilateral environmental agreements with trade-restrictive provisions. It was identified in principle three decades ago when the Stockholm Conference of 1972 first advanced a series of environmental precepts distinctively different from those at the heart of the traditional multilateral trade regime. By the late 1970s, the Group of Seven (G7), now Eight (G8), major industrial democracies began to articulate the principles by which potential tensions among trade, the environment, and their social dimensions should be governed. In the ensuing decades, the General Agreement on Tariffs and Trades (GATT) and its successor, the World Trade Organization (WTO), have also taken up the task of identifying the ways environmental values could be protected within the ongoing process of trade liberalisation (Esty and Institute for International Economics 1994).

The decade and a half following the 1987 publication of *Our Common Future*, known as the Bruntland Report, saw a major expansion of the effort to forge an acceptable link (World Commission on Environment and Development 1987). The G7 and the United Nations (UN) developed a rich normative framework through which to link trade liberalisation and environmental protection, while incorporating a wide range of social considerations. The Organisation for Economic Co-operation and Development (OECD) devised a methodology for assessing the environmental impacts of trade and a broad array of environmental indicators by which to measure the changing state of the global environment. Within North America, the North American Free Trade Agreement (NAFTA), which took formal force on 1 January 1994, offered a pioneering, new regional free trade regime that included extensive environmental provisions and an accompanying organisation to help give them effect (Mayer 1998; McKinney 2000; Cameron and Tomlin 2000).

Despite this considerable progress, however, very few would claim that the challenge of forging an appropriate trade-environment-social cohesion link has now been adequately met. At the global level, the sustainable development principles articulated by the G7/8 have been translated most imperfectly into the ongoing practices of the international institutions governing the world's trade regimes. The WTO, beginning work in 1995, contained only rudimentary environmental and social provisions in its governing agreements and ongoing work (Sampson 2000; Sampson and Chambers 1999; Schrecker and Dalgleish 1994). Attempts to produce stronger ones as part of a new comprehensive round of multilateral trade negotiations were delayed by resistance from many developing countries at the WTO ministerial meeting in late 1999. They were aided by some civil society protesters, who claimed that trade liberalisation itself was antithetical to the environmental and social values they held dear. At the regional level within North America, despite some successes, efforts to deepen the environmental and labour provisions of the NAFTA regime and extend them to similar and related free trade arenas on a wider geographic plane, across the Pacific in the Asia-Pacific Economic Cooperation (APEC) forum or across the Americas through the prospective Free Trade Agreement of the Americas (FTAA) have proven difficult indeed.

Citizens throughout the global community have now come to see trade liberalisation as the core of a profound and proliferating process of globalisation that has reached into their daily lives, and that can cause, or has already caused, widespread environmental and social costs through processes that they can neither fully comprehend nor control (Deardorff and Stern 2000). Indeed, visible and effective opposition to trade and investment liberalisation from civil society and from the streets has mushroomed. It has followed from the defeat, led by nongovernmental organisations (NGOs), of the OECD's effort to create the Multilateral Agreement on Investment (MAI) in 1997, through ever larger and more violent protests at the Seattle WTO ministerial in 1999, the United Nations Conference on Trade and Development (UNCTAD) in Bangkok and the International Monetary Fund (IMF) in Washington and Prague in 2000, and the Quebec City Summit of the Americas, the European Council at Gotenberg, Sweden, and the G8 in Genoa, Italy, in 2001. This proliferation of violent protest has left many wondering whether globalisation or its critics have gone too far (Rodrik 1997).

Within this cascading confrontation over the effects of globalisation, the debate about the links among trade, the environment, and social cohesion has had a central place. While the concept of social cohesion has been invested with many meanings, it focusses here on how trade liberalisation and its link with environmental protection can either contribute to or detract from the propagation of shared values, democratic participation, and equal opportunities for all citizens of a country, across its many regional, linguistic, economic, generational, and gender divides.

The failure to sustain the momentum of trade and investment liberalisation through the conclusion of a multilateral agreement on investment at the OECD and the WTO's launch of the Millennium Round of trade negotiations as the twentieth century closed was due in part to intensified demands that the values and voices of the environment, labour, and, more generally, civil society be given a more integral and equal part in the new international economic regimes being forged. The global financial crisis of 1997–99 seemed to show that the liberalisation of finance could unleash devastating, widespread destruction on the ecological resources, material well-being, and social stability of countries around the globe, and that the previously attractive model of export-led growth provided no sure and stable route to sustainable development (Kaiser, Kirton, and Daniels 2000). The sometimes violent protests against the work of the IMF at its ministerial meetings in 2000 and mounting concerns over trade in genetically modified food showed that the resistance to continued trade and investment liberalisation was by no means ephemeral. More generally, among publics in North America, Europe, and Asia, the earlier consensus on the value of trade liberalisation began to erode as anxieties about the social and environmental impacts of globalisation grew. In the judgement of many, if the existing hard-won advances in trade liberalisation were to be preserved and extended, a better way to make trade liberalisation promote environmental enhancement and social cohesion would have to be found (Pettigrew 1999; Hockin 2001).

At the start of the twenty-first century, then, the challenge of designing regimes for global governance that simultaneously enhance trade liberalisation, environmental protection, and social cohesion has acquired a compelling claim. In taking up this task, there are good reasons for scholars and policy makers alike to conduct a close and critical examination of the experience of North Americans under the NAFTA regime. In many respects, those in the North American community had crafted in their NAFTA a set of principles, norms, rules, decision-making procedures, and institutions that led the world in affirming ecological and social values and linking them to the far-reaching trade, investment, and finance liberalisation it brought (Kirton 1996; Johnson and Beaulieu 1996; Audley 1997). While NAFTA was by no means initially conceived as an instrument for advancing sustainable development, when the core text was finally negotiated in 1992 it declared that the purposes of this full free trade agreement included promoting sustainable development and strengthening environmental laws and enforcement (North American Free Trade Agreement 1994, 1). It gave life to these principles by placing several innovative environmental and social norms and rules throughout its lengthy text. Moreover, it came with two parallel and interlinked accords — the North American Agreement on Environmental Cooperation (NAAEC) and the North American Agreement on Labor Cooperation (NAALC) — that extended these links and created new regional organisations for their implementation — the Commission for Environmental Cooperation (CEC) in Montreal and the Commission for Labor Cooperation (CLC) in Washington. Perhaps most important, these three agreements gave the corporate community, NGOs, and interested parties of civil society an unparalleled degree of direct access to, and a role in, these international institutions and organisations to ensure that their provisions and their member states' regulations for environmental, labour, and investment protection were upheld. With its pioneering links among trade, environment, and society, with its unprecedented creation of regional organisations in North America to govern two of the richest and most powerful countries in the world together with a leading developing country, and with its path-breaking provisions for civil society participation, NAFTA appeared to have much to offer the wider world.

Is this distinctive North American trade-environment-labour regime in fact a model for the global community as it seeks to move forward to secure the gains that trade and investment liberalisation can bring? Or does it — more modestly — contain valuable lessons, learned over almost a decade of often difficult and controversial operation, about what and what not to do? As the NAFTA regime approaches the end of its first decade in operation, considerable controversy and uncertainty continue about the appropriate answers to these key questions.

On the oppositional side, there were many who felt, as NAFTA was being negotiated, that it would destroy social and environmental values. Those criticisms continue to this day. Others have focussed on how NAFTA has operated in practice, but offer widely varying assessments of, and often profound disappointment about, whether its innovative provisions for environmental enhancement, social protection, and civil society participation have unfolded as its founders and promoters had hoped. These critics say that if NAFTA has not worked and cannot be made to work for people and their habitat, it should be replaced by new governance arrangements that can. Still others have argued that too little is known about how to assess accurately the multifaceted, complex, cumulative, long-term ecological, and social impacts of trade and investment liberalisation. They thus argue that more adequate analytical frameworks, indicators, and information must be devised at the international, national, and local levels. Following a political version of the precautionary principle, they are reluctant to replicate this — still unfolding and uncertain — NAFTA experiment in other geographic domains. Other observers doubt that the North American model, even if it works well enough in its home region, provides a realistic or appropriate framework for the broader international community, with its very different circumstances and constituents. And even if it does so in theory and practice, there could well be severe practical difficulties in having it accepted politically by other countries in other regions, with much different levels of development, economic, and legal traditions, and far less attachment to democracy, rule of law, and a politically empowered and engaged citizenry.

Yet NAFTA's defenders have a strong case as well. Almost a decade since it formally took effect, they claim that among the world's many trade and investment liberalisation agreements, NAFTA remains a lonely high watermark of respect for environmental and social values and the incorporation of those values. Similarly, they argue that it stands out as a unique innovator of transparency and public participation, at a time when the global demand for such processes is proliferating. Indeed, they suggest that among the world's actual operating trade and investment regimes, for devotees of sustainable development there is 'nothing but NAFTA' to inspire or to build and improve upon.[1] Moreover, NAFTA's defenders point out that its environmental, social, and participation provisions are being replicated in large part in many of the numerous bilateral free trade agreements signed by Canada and the United States within the western hemisphere and beyond. In this sense, citizens of Chile, Costa Rica, Central America, Jordan, and prospectively of the Caribbean, have — along with Americans, Canadians, and Mexicans — already said 'yes' to the NAFTA model.

Perhaps most strikingly, at a time when doubts and dissent about globalisation have burgeoned around the world, most North Americans have come to accept their NAFTA as it has actually operated and evolved. At the most minimal level, the annual ministerial meetings of NAFTA's trade and environment ministers have attracted none of the protests and the violence that such political level gatherings of other multilateral and regional institutions now routinely do. Americans are now supportive both of NAFTA and of trade liberalisation, but demand that the latter have strong environmental and social protections built in (Kirton 2000; Program on International Policy Attitudes 2000). Canadians in particular, who were highly negative about NAFTA at the start and who remain regionally divided on so many issues within their diverse country, now express a surprisingly strong degree of support for NAFTA (Mendelsohn and Wolfe 2001; Parkin and Centre for Research and Information on Canada 2001). A February 2001 national poll found that almost two thirds of Canadians support NAFTA, down from the peak of 70 percent in 1999, but substantially higher than the 29 percent who were in favour of it in 1993 during negotiations over the agreement (Tuck 2001; Gallup Canada 1993). That Canadians have also been highly unified for well over a decade about the need to put global environmental protection in first place when they look abroad (Gherson 1998) suggests that they may see in the realised NAFTA — as opposed to the rhetorical NAFTA — an instrument for doing real environmental good.

Yet even if most Americans and Canadians have come to accept their NAFTA, to varying degrees, several elements of this consensus are profoundly clear. First, it is not so much trade itself but the broader process of globalisation and the values it affects that concern citizens. Second, it is the impact of trade on those other values, above all environmental quality, rather than its consistency with neoliberal precepts or its ability to raise job prospects and incomes, that cause the most consternation. Third, the consensus over NAFTA is neither automatically nor easily transposable to the other bilateral, regional, plurilateral, or multilateral trade liberalisation projects in which the United States, Canada, and Mexico are engaged. And the consensus on the home continent may itself disappear if NAFTA should fail to provide the promised and desired environmental and social goods. In short, NAFTA, with its pioneering provisions and performance, cannot be taken for granted by citizens of North America or by those in the wider world.

To address these concerns, and the core issues they create, this book explores the experience of the North American region under NAFTA in linking trade, environment, and social cohesion, within the context of a rapidly globalising world. Its central purpose is to assess, on the basis of the best and most current analysis and evidence, just how effective the NAFTA regime has been after almost a decade in operation in integrating and promoting trade, environment, and social values in ways that realise the shared sustainable development ideal in a globalising world. To fulfil this purpose, it takes up five specific tasks.

The first is to identify how the general process of, and debate about, globalisation on a world scale has an impact upon and is informed by the NAFTA-centred experience of North Americans in their home region. There is likely to be a great amount of overlap between these global and regional processes and anxieties. Many of the concerns about the social and ecological impact of trade, investment, and finance liberalisation featured in the NAFTA debate of the early 1990s are those that have now arisen globally. Since 1996, G7 policy makers have taken up the growing anxieties about globalisation and scholars have asked the basic question: Has globalisation gone too far (Rodrik 1997)? With far-reaching provisions for the liberalisation of foreign direct investment (FDI), and ones that the broader multilateral community could not secure in the OECD with an MAI, NAFTA could serve the global community as a leading indicator — some might say a regional canary in the globalisation mineshaft — of what to do or what not to do in the investment field. The NAFTA experience could say much about where the global community might want to go, particularly along the highly and long integrated border between countries so similar and yet so different as Canada and the United States. In any event, the three North American countries are large enough, in economic weight, territorial expanse, ecological capital, international institutional influence, and social, cultural, and linguistic reach, that their own extensive experiment is likely to have a global impact, whatever the outside world intends. At the same time, through NAFTA's pioneering integrated trade-environment-labour provisions and institutions, North Americans are doing things regionally in a very different fashion than other regional communities or the global community have done thus far. There may thus be much to learn from North America about how to proceed in the twenty-first century.

The second task is to assess the current record of the NAFTA regime in integrating trade, environment, and social concerns, and to compare it to major efforts at the global level (in the WTO and G7/8) in this regard. After almost a decade, just how well have the NAFTA regime and its institutions fulfilled their promise of producing the economic benefits of trade, investment, and finance liberalisation in ways that promote environmental and social values and also empower citizens? With at least three years of anticipation and almost ten years of formal operation, the NAFTA regime, its additions, and its mid-course corrections are ready to be thoroughly reviewed, not only for their immediate impact, by also for their delayed, long-range, and complex, cumulative interactive effects. Even major disturbances from within or without — the Mexican peso devaluation of 20 December 1994, periodic drought, or the 1997–99 Asian-turned-global financial crisis (Kaiser, Kirton, and Daniels 2000) — cannot cloud what NAFTA itself has brought. Indeed, they help demonstrate, as the years pass, how robust the regime is at its core in delivering its declared results. Moreover, as these years accumulate, they allow for greater confidence that some of the initial fears, or 'ticking time bombs' — such as the commercial export of bulk water from Canada to the United States, or the abolition of Canada's publicly funded healthcare or educational system — are not inevitable products of a comprehensive, and novel agreement the effects of which were partly unknown. These years permit a dynamic comparison with an outside world that has now had the time needed to learn about and from, and catch up with, the North American experiment. Indeed, 1994 — the year NAFTA formally took effect — also saw the launch of full free trade commitments in the entire Americas, and the broader APEC forum, as well as the acceptance of the Uruguay Round agreements and creation of the WTO. That year also witnessed the launch of a 'political' P8 alongside the initial G7, and the establishment of a regular annual forum for G7 environment ministers alongside the G7's trade ministers' Quadrilateral that had operated since 1982. Almost a decade later, it is possible to ask how well NAFTA has done in the sustainable development race, compared to its regional, plurilateral, and global competitors.

The third task is to explore in detail the distinctive features and accumulated results of NAFTA's pioneering provisions to give civil society a direct role in the intergovernmental institutions of international governance. Nowhere was NAFTA more innovative and prescient than in its major moves to give a wide range of civil society actors a part to play in its ongoing operations. Industry representatives and other experts were involved in the many functional committees created by NAFTA (Kirton and Fernandez de Castro 1997). The environmental side agreement's CEC included the Joint Public Advisory Committee (JPAC), and the National Advisory Committee (NAC) (Kirton 1996). But the most innovative step, and that of greatest interest ever since, has been the creation of three processes for giving civil society actors direct access to intergovernmental dispute resolution. The first was the core NAFTA's Chapter 11 investment provisions, under which corporations could directly secure a panel under the auspices of the International Centre for the Settlement of Investment Disputes (ICSID) or the United Nations Commission on International Trade Law (UNCITRAL) to investigate allegations that national governments had infringed their rights. The second was the NAAEC's Article 14-15 citizen submission process, under which any 'interested party' could charge that their government was failing to enforce its own environmental laws effectively. And the third was the NAALC's similar procedure for ensuring labour rights were upheld. By establishing these three processes, NAFTA succeeded where the broader multilateral community subsequently failed in the investment and environmental fields. It was here that NAFTA responded to the emerging demand for civil society participation in, and the democratisation of, global governance. It was here, too, that NAFTA's new values and rule of law took their greatest toll on the old principles of the unfettered sovereignty of national and sub-federal states. The other more traditional components of NAFTA's array of dispute settlement mechanisms, such as those for antidumping, subsidy/countervailing, and general complaints, have been dealt with extensively, and are left outside the analysis here (Hart 2000).

The fourth task of this volume is to investigate innovative tools and approaches for assessing what is known, analytically and empirically, about the environmental and social effects of trade liberalisation agreements as they unfold at the global, regional, national, and local levels. The NAFTA regime itself recognised the need for these types of methodological advances when it charged the CEC, as a mandatory provision of the NAAEC, with the role of assessing NAFTA's environmental effects on an ongoing basis. Fulfilling this mandate, and thereby keeping the faith with the many North American environmentalists and citizens who gave the new NAFTA the initial benefit of the doubt, proved to be a difficult mission. It required not only transcending ongoing political resistance but also conducting the broader analytical task of designing and applying an appropriate framework and method to meet this new need (Kirton et al. 1999), in ways that responded to the particular characteristics and values of the North American region. Parallel to the efforts of the CEC, other international organisations were developing similar frameworks and indicators to assess the impacts of bilateral, regional, plurilateral, and multilateral trade liberalisation agreements. Even at the community level in North America, a burgeoning interest in indicators of community sustainability has produced new tools for tracking changes in local environmental, economic, and social conditions (Maclaren 1996). These community indicators may provide insight into the impacts of trade liberalisation at the local level.

The fifth task is to make some modest suggestions, based on this foundation, about the next generation of research about, and policy innovation within, the embryonic but rapidly growing and ever-evolving NAFTA-governed North American community. This includes the internally oriented task of identifying ways for improving the NAFTA model to meet its sustainable development goals more effectively. It also embraces the outward-oriented task of identifying if and how the existing North American experience and improvements built on it might assist the broader international community in the challenges it now faces.

At the heart of these five purposes, and thus of this volume, is the task of determining how the values of trade liberalisation, environmental protection, and social cohesion have been and can continue to be linked in international regimes that embrace integrated national communities, across the old north-south divide. This task and the task of evaluating the record of the North American region under NAFTA are large subjects. Only key aspects can be dealt with here. Yet even such a selective exploration requires that the concept of 'trade' be extended much more broadly than has traditionally been the case. As does NAFTA itself, this volume thus deals not only with trade in its classical definition, but also with the foreign direct investment with which North American and global trade is now integrally linked, the integrated production systems, business alliances, and corporate strategies that lie behind such investment, and the governmental regulations that constitute 'behind the border' trade barriers and corporate instruments alike. It similarly adopts a broad conception of the 'environment', dealing with the major ambient media of air, water, land, and living things, the stresses on and supports for them, the regulatory and institutional systems that protect them, and the complex processes by which they change.

In addition, a central feature of this analysis is the central place given to the societal dimension of the trade-environment debate. This volume thus focusses on the impact of civil society actors in NAFTA and global institutions, and the broader value of democratisation in global governance. It is concerned with labour as well as with environmental aspects of trade liberalisation, the broad social impacts of trade liberalisation and environmental protection, and the place of social values in sustainability assessments at the international, regional, and local levels. Above all, it is concerned with the relationship of trade liberalisation and environmental protection to social cohesion, particularly to the cohesion of the national communities involved in the NAFTA pioneering experiment.

As an analysis with NAFTA at its core, this volume embraces the challenges of linking trade, environment, and social cohesion within the United States, Canada, and Mexico. But its primary focus at the national and sub-national levels is on Canada. Canada began its NAFTA voyage as one of the most internationally open countries in the world across the dimensions of trade, investment, the environment, and demography. While all three NAFTA members had internal strains in 1994, it was only in Canada that the very unity of the country was seriously at stake as a result of the forthcoming 1995 referendum on the separation of Quebec. And it was in Canada that the unifying value of global environmental protection exerted its greatest claim (Kirton 2000, 52). The Canadian experience thus speaks poignantly to the challenges and the choices the rest of the world faces in a globalising age.

Each author in this volume inevitably identifies these challenges in a distinctive fashion, even as all embrace, in some way in their analysis, the trade, environmental, and social domains. Yet all share an overarching concern with the common evaluative referent of sustainable development. While this concept also embraces many meanings and causes much controversy, it is taken here to mean development in which the values of trade/investment liberalisation, environmental enhancement, and social cohesion are fully integrated, accorded equal value, and are mutually reinforcing.

To achieve these goals, this volume has assembled the contributions of 18 leading scholars and practitioners from all three countries of North America. They bring analyses grounded in the disciplines of political science, law, geography, economics, and medicine, and the fields of international relations, regulation, environmental studies, and public health and epidemiology. Their analyses are enriched by the practical experience many contributors have acquired through past or present service in key trade and environment positions in, or in working with, the Canadian and U.S. governments, major environmental NGOs such as the World Wildlife Fund, the Sierra Legal Defence Fund, the Mexican Centre for International Law, Leadership for Environment and Development Canada, the Sustainable Calgary Group, as well as the CEC and CLC Secretariats, and the CEC's Joint Public Advisory Committee. These authors include those who were among the very first to call for an environmental agreement and institutions of the NAAEC and CEC kind, who helped give them political life by working outside and inside government, and who have been engaged in operating and improving them to this day. In particular, ten of the authors have participated in various ways over six long years to develop and apply the CEC's framework for assessing NAFTA's environmental effects. The authors' contributions are thus infused with a historical perspective of previous realities, initial hopes, disappointed expectations, and unintended consequences, as well as a realistic understanding of what, amidst all the constraints, has been accomplished and what remains to be done.

With this rich array of disciplinary and experiential starting points, the authors have explored their subjects free from the confines of a single interpretative framework, analytic tradition, theory, or model, or overall consensus about what NAFTA's record has been or could be in the realisation of sustainable development. Instead, each author has focussed on the empirical domain in which he or she is most interested, and, in virtually all cases, in which he or she has had first-hand professional involvement. Here the authors have mobilised their core disciplinary skills and contributed to a critical analysis and forward-looking conclusion. In some cases, where they have addressed the same subject through similar methodologies, the results of each have been retained so that sometimes subtle differences of interpretation and understanding can be brought to light. The cumulative result is a wide array of diverse judgements that reflect much of the ongoing disagreement about NAFTA and the broader issues of globalisation, social cohesion, and sustainable development in the real world.

The Analyses

This volume examines in turn the overall record of NAFTA in its global context, the record of its investment, environmental, and labour institutions to which civil society actors have direct access, and the various ways to assess the impact of international trade agreements at the global, regional, national, and local levels. This latter section is of vital concern to those in the environmental community, and to citizens as a whole, who want to know just what the environmental and social impacts of trade-investment liberalisation as pursued thus far has been. It is of equal interest to the trade-investment community, which needs to make the case that liberalisation agreements have been or can be done in ways that promote ecological and social values for a broad array of citizens in their daily lives. Knowing what these existing effects are, how better to assess and monitor them, and how better to realise them through improved rules and institutions could well be central to meeting the trade and investment liberalisation challenges that lie ahead.

The book thus begins in Part I with 'Linking Trade, Environment, and Social Values: The Global and NAFTA Experiences'. This section outlines the broad challenges of globalisation, sustainable development, and social cohesion on a world scale, and relates them to the particular innovations brought by NAFTA to the region of North America. It features divergent perspectives about how well, and even whether, the link between trade liberalisation and sustainable development should be forged regionally and globally, and whether NAFTA or the G8, as a flexible leader for the global community, is in the vanguard of forging the link.

This exploration opens in Chapter 2 with Pierre Marc Johnson's 'From Trade Liberalisation to Sustainable Development: The Challenges of Integrated Global Governance'. This chapter begins with the causes of the failure of the Seattle WTO meeting and identifies the major components and consequences of the new process of 'globalisation'. Johnson considers the consequent challenges for global environmental governance and the contributions made by NAFTA's environmental regime. He concludes with an assessment of the NAFTA regime's record and the lessons learned from the experience.

Johnson argues that globalisation came to a crossroads at Seattle. The failure there was not merely of one particular ministerial meeting but of the liberalisation project of preceeding decades to command the continued confidence and consent of the world's citizenry. As globalisation has intensified and expanded the movement of goods, capital, people, and ideas, it has increased the divide between rich and poor, allowed room for new actors to enter the international political arena, and empowered transnational firms and NGOs in particular. Giving NGOs and broader civil society, and the environmental values they forward, a greater place in the trade regime is necessary if the global community is to meet the intensifying environmental threats it now faces. Here the NAFTA trade-environment regime can help, as it provides an interesting model and a source of inspiration for the WTO system. On the whole, its record has been a positive one, in addressing the trade and environment nexus, engaging civil society in a constructive dialogue, and strengthening environmental co-operation. It is less than certain, however, whether this model can be replicated in other trade regimes. But civil society can clearly be a constructive force if it is meaningfully engaged in processes of trade liberalisation. It also demonstrates that addressing sustainability issues in a trade agreement benefits both the trade and environmental communities, and that a broader agenda for environmental co-operation is a key strategy to ease trade and environment tensions when countries with different levels of development liberalise trade among themselves. What is now needed, in keeping with these NAFTA lessons, is a 'new deal' at the global level, if globalisation is to be sustained in sustainable ways.

In Chapter 3, 'The New Interface Agenda among Trade, Environment, and Social Cohesion', William A. Dymond offers a more sceptical analysis of what lies ahead. He agrees that the trade and investment agenda of the WTO and OECD and the controversy over NAFTA's investor state dispute settlement procedures are at the centre of many of the current concerns about globalisation and whether that agenda can be made to serve the needs of society. He also asks whether the integration of trade and investment liberalisation with environmental and social concerns is necessary if globalisation is to proceed. Is this project desirable in its own right? He asserts that the evidence suggests that the answer to both questions might well be a resounding no.

Dymond argues that the trade liberalisation agenda for Canada has been largely completed and that the presumption that there is broad public concern with the impacts of trade liberalisation suffers from a lack of evidence. Equally doubtful is the claim that civil society protest was responsible for the failure to produce an MAI. Rather, the object of trade policy has been transformed from trade liberalisation through trade barrier reductions to positive rule making, making the negotiating issue no longer trade liberalisation but global governance. This new 'interface agenda' exceeds the policy and institutional competence of the WTO. It produces a natural tendency away from negotiation toward litigation as a dispute settlement procedure. Viewed in this light, NAFTA's Chapter 11 process has been operating largely as intended, and should essentially be left alone. Governments should concentrate on ensuring that the international obligations they undertake are consistent with sound public policy and should not look for ways to narrow the range of potential litigants.

In Chapter 4, 'Embedded Ecologism and Institutional Inequality: Linking Trade, Environment, and Social Cohesion in the G8', John J. Kirton explores the effort of the G7 major industrial democracies to fuse trade, environment, and social concerns in balanced and mutually supportive ways. He surveys the principles and norms that have been articulated collectively by the G7/8 in the key areas of trade, the environment, and social cohesion since its establishment in 1975. He specifies the priority assigned to each, the intersections identified among these realms, and the balance offered for the governance of this integrated domain. Kirton concentrates on the content and strength of the G7's initial consensus, how that consensus might have eroded, and how a new consensus might have emerged. On that basis, he suggests, largely inductively, the sources of such ideological consensus and change as have occurred. In particular, he identifies moves to or from the articulation of a normative order based on the sustainable development ideal in which environmental enhancement, trade liberalisation, and social cohesion are tightly integrated and equally balanced. In creating such a combination, such moves generate a foundation for what might be termed a modern 'embedded ecologism' that extends and reinforces the embedded liberalism of old.

This analysis reveals that since 1975 the G7 has continually asserted and progressively developed a doctrine of embedded ecologism. This doctrine has defended the employment and social welfare values at the core of the 1945 consensus on embedded liberalism, while reinforcing them with a new array of ecological values, totally absent in 1945, which the G7 has integrated into the spheres of employment and trade in protective and proactive ways. While the elements of embedded ecologism were evident at the G7's outset, the G7 came to adopt a conception of trade liberalisation that was more aggressively far-reaching than that of 1945 and 1975, added investment and finance (if not also capital account) liberalisation to it, and entrenched its new conception in the powerful institution of the WTO that the G7 did much to create. Moreover, prompted by the OECD, during the 1980s the G7 turned from a macroeconomic trade- and growth-based conception of employment to one that privileged market-oriented structural policies. In both cases, the weight of these economic and trade-focussed international organisations generated an institutional imbalance in the G7's evolving consensus in ways that assigned ecological and social values a subordinate place. Yet at the start of its fourth seven-year cycle in 1996, the G7 moved, in advance of the 1997–99 global financial crisis and the 1999 civil society assaults on trade, investment, and finance liberalisation, to address the challenges of globalisation and restore the balance of earlier years. This task proved to be easier in the trade-labour realm, where the G7/8 could readily mandate the WTO to work with the International Labour Organization (ILO), than in the trade-environment realm, where no similar world environmental organisation existed.

Kirton's conclusions at the global level are reinforced by his examination of the efforts to fuse trade and environment considerations at the regional level. In Chapter 5, 'Winning Together: The NAFTA Trade-Environment Record', Kirton takes a close empirical look at how the new NAFTA trade-environment regime has operated in practice. Kirton takes up the central issue in the debate between NAFTA's defenders and critics through a comprehensive exploration of how the advent of NAFTA and its institutions altered the process and outcomes in the full universe of 84 cases of 'environmental regulatory protection'. He first defines environmental regulatory protection and then examines the new conditions of 'complex institutional responsiveness' that give rise to a growing number of trade-environment cases. He examines the process for handling these cases and the resulting outcomes, exploring in particular how the balance of outcomes changes across issue areas and industry sectors, from the pre-NAFTA to post-NAFTA periods and as the NAFTA institutions — particularly the CEC rather than NAFTA's trade institutions — are involved. Kirton also considers the overall record of the cases in two key institutional domains: those taken to the Chapter 11 and Article 14-15 dispute settlement mechanisms. The chapter concludes with a consideration of the record of environmental regulatory protection in general and Chapter 11/Article 14-15 cases in particular. It does so in reference to recent analyses and findings about NAFTA's environmental effects as they relate to domestic regulation in Canada and the United States.

Kirton's analysis reveals that there has been a proliferation of cases of environmental regulatory protection in North America from the 1980s to the NAFTA era of the 1990s. However, in resolving such cases, the three North American governments have tended to find solutions that generate both higher and more convergent environmental regulations, as well as greater trade and investment liberalisation. Despite the overwhelming economic power of the United States in the NAFTA region, and the trade-investment community within it, the outcomes of such cases move toward equality among the member countries and between their trade and environment communities as the NAFTA era arrives, and as the NAFTA institutions in general, and the CEC in particular, assume consequential roles. Despite the controversies over a few high-profile cases and the need for some reforms, both the Chapter 11 and Article 14-15 processes, which give societal actors direct access to international tribunals, contribute to these more balanced results. NAFTA thus has the potential to serve as a model and foundation for building a more equitable and socially sensitive trade-environment regime on a wider regional as well as global scale.

In Part II, 'Investor Protection: Evaluating the NAFTA Chapter 11 Model', attention focusses on the most advanced and most controversial of NAFTA's three major mechanisms that give civil society actors direct access to international dispute settlement forums. This analysis starts in Chapter 6, with 'The Masked Ball of NAFTA Chapter 11: Foreign Investors, Local Environmentalists, Government Officials, and Disguised Motives' by Sanford E. Gaines. Here Gaines first summarises the core elements of Chapter 11, including both the substantive disciplines on government action and the procedural devices for raising and resolving investor claims. He then examines the complex aspects of the environmental, political, and business competition dimensions of the three major environment-related Chapter 11 cases that have resulted in obligations to pay compensation. He next analyses the common circumstances and legal conclusions leading to compensation in these cases, and the case of *Methanex v. United States*, which may give important new definition to the investment-environment relationship. He concludes with an overall assessment of Chapter 11 and its potential threat to environmental regulation.

Gaines argues that the environmentalist alarm about Chapter 11 springs from mistaken identity about the interests that were really taking the lead during the complicated decision-making process. Government regulatory decisions turn out to have little environmental legitimacy, but serve domestic commercial or political interests well. Despite official claims, mistreatment of foreign investments or restrictions on them are not always derived from decisions that act for the benefit of the environment. Indeed, the weight of the evidence in these cases suggests that by disciplining arbitrary government action, the three Chapter 11 awards — far from inhibiting governments from protecting the environment — will indirectly benefit domestic environmental regulation as well as properly compensate foreign investors wounded in domestic political crossfire.

A similar legal analysis and conclusion is offered by Julie Soloway in Chapter 7, 'Environmental Expropriation under NAFTA Chapter 11: The Phantom Menace'. Soloway first reviews the international law of expropriation to determine the broad framework of international law within which NAFTA Chapter 11 decisions are taken and against which their process and results can be judged. She then examines the early, pioneering cases that considered the expropriation provisions of NAFTA. She ends with a synthesis of what these early decisions suggest for NAFTA's investment regime, the debate about its reform, and its utility as a model elsewhere.

Soloway argues that current environmentalist concerns over the expropriation provisions of NAFTA are unfounded. Indeed, she claims that based on the jurisprudence to date, the view that the expropriation provisions of NAFTA would ignite an environmental disaster is without merit. Rather than an expansive and novel interpretation of these provisions, 'conservatism' describes the concrete application of Article 1110 in the first three cases that have ruled on expropriation. The tribunals in these cases have given member-governments significant latitude in which to regulate economic activity within their borders, and to do so without taking action that was deemed to constitute expropriation. Furthermore, the tribunals have suggested that the degree of government interference in each case was the key to their decisions.

Also taking issue with the current environmentalist critique of Chapter 11 is Konrad von Moltke. In Chapter 8, 'Investment and the Environment: Multilateral and North American Perspectives', von Moltke begins by noting how past efforts to establish an international investment regime have been fraught with failure. He then outlines an approach to the problem, pursued in environmental agreements, that is problem driven, with the institutional response deriving from the particular structure of the problem in question. He concludes by offering, on this basis, ways in which investors and environmentalists can come together to create a common regime that meets the needs of both.

Von Moltke argues that the widespread attitude in the environmental community that an investment agreement is a bad thing is a fundamental mistake. All environmental agreements are fundamentally investment agreements, in that they are aimed at inducing microeconomic change. The fatal flaw thus far has been to model prospective international investment agreements after agreements for trade in goods, where the nature of the problem is very different. A much superior approach is to follow the model of environmental agreements, and indeed, embed investment protections within such environmental agreements. Offering investment protections within a new climate change agreement could produce a combined regime that would meet the pressing political and substantive needs of both the investment and environmental communities.

Part III, 'Environmental Protection: Evaluating the NAFTA Commission for Environmental Cooperation Model', takes up the parallel and in some respects balancing NAFTA mechanism for direct civil society access to dispute settlement — the citizen submission process of the NAAEC's Article 14-15. In Chapter 9, 'Stormy

Weather: The Recent History of the Citizen Submission Process of the North American Agreement on Environmental Cooperation', Christopher Tollefson explores the history, operation, and potential of the Article 14-15 process from a legal perspective. He first provides an introduction to the citizen submission process, and considers the key legal and institutional issues that have emerged in the administration of the submission process by the Secretariat. Particular attention is devoted to the uncertainties associated with defining the legal rights and responsibilities contemplated by the NAAEC, and to the institutional tensions that the process has created. He concludes with some observations on how the legal uncertainties and institutional tensions relate to the broader rationale of, and purposes served by, the submission process.

Tollefson argues that for many within civil society, the submission process will continue to have real value — even though it does not yield binding recommendations or results, let alone entail the imposition of sanctions. Yet this is only as long as the process offers the prospect of spotlighting deficient domestic enforcement practices. Were the process to lose its ability to perform this spotlighting function credibly and neutrally, civil society support for the submission process would dissipate rapidly. Moreover, with respect to two of the key objectives of the citizen submission process — its contribution to effective enforcement of environmental laws and its longer term impact on environmental protection and enhancement — the evidence needed to evaluate how effectively the process is working is not readily available. In terms of the objective of providing civil society with the means to participate more effectively in government environmental decision making, however, one can tentatively conclude that the process is working and enjoys a conditional legitimacy within the sector it is intended to benefit.

In Chapter 10, 'Public Participation within NAFTA's Environmental Agreement: The Mexican Experience', Gustavo Alanís Ortega examines the Cozumel case against the Mexican government. It was the first to go through the entire Article 14-15 process, concluding with the first factual record, published in October 1997. Alanís considers in turn the process that was followed, the impact that the process and decisions had, and the lessons that were learned from this seminal case.

Alanís argues that the Cozumel case was fraught with much uncertainty and harsh accusations. Nonetheless, it had several environmentally beneficial effects, in a variety of ways. He identifies nine as most important. He also identifies several lessons that can be drawn from the process that unfolded in the case, 13 of which warrant close attention in the ongoing effort to improve the Article 14-15 process. Thus, although the Cozumel case had a major positive impact on environmental quality and civil society participation in Mexico, and benefited the NAFTA process as a whole, there is much further work to be done.

In Chapter 11, 'Article 14-15 of the North American Agreement on Environmental Cooperation: Intent of the Founders', Serena Wilson provides a brief but valuable American perspective on the creation and subsequent operation of Article 14-15.

She examines the origins, the negotiations, and the record of Article 14-15 and the subsequent effort to revise the guidelines for Article 14-15 submissions.

Part IV, 'Worker Protection: Evaluating the NAFTA Commission for Labor Cooperation Model', takes up the third major mechanism for direct civil society access to NAFTA dispute settlement — the public communication process under the CLC. In Chapter 12, 'Civil Society and the North American Agreement on Labor Cooperation', Kevin Banks explores the relationship among civil society, national governments, and international organisations under the NAALC. He first reviews the structure of the agreement and the channels for public participation that it creates. He then examines the NAALC's public communications — or complaints — filed under the agreement during its first seven years. Finally, he considers the use of complaint-driven strategies to bring about social and political change, and whether there may be opportunities under the NAALC for a more expanded form of civil society participation and transnational politics, and ones in which the CLC should have a role.

Banks concludes that it is difficult to evaluate the effectiveness of an agreement like the NAALC, in part because it is difficult to attribute causation in diplomatic processes. The timing of events may suggest that changes shortly following a public complaint were not merely coincidental. But publicly at least, governments may prefer to present them as an extension of existing policy rather than a concession to international pressure. Moreover, factors other than the complaint itself may have proven decisive behind the scenes. The bulk of public participation under the agreement appears thus far to have been almost exclusively driven by complaints. This is, in some respects, a natural development. However, there may be limits to this model, given the type of systemic problems and complex political issues raised by the submissions filed under the agreement, particularly with the added complexity of dealing with these kinds of problems across national borders. It could well be time to look for less litigious alternatives.

A further analysis, and a more conclusively optimistic assessment of the CLC's record, comes in Chapter 13, 'Giving Teeth to NAFTA's Labour Side Agreement'. Jonathan Graubart notes the debate surrounding the value of the CLC and the need to examine these competing claims from the perspective of soft law. He then examines in detail the submissions filed under the NAALC from a bottom-up perspective that focusses on the efforts of cross-border coalitions of labour movements and labour rights activists to give the complaint channel substance.

Graubert concludes that despite low initial expectations, the NAALC submission process has proven efficacious in practice. During its first eight years, 23 submissions have been filed. Virtually all have been filed by labour movements, labour advocates, or human rights groups. These submissions have often shown considerable political and legal sophistication, with a few involving as many as 40 co-submitters from all three countries, including the major labour federations. Submitters have creatively boosted the political punch of these channels through careful legal argumentation, targeting specific companies, proposing systematic remedies, and incorporating the submissions into a multi-pronged effort to advance a broader cause. Several have received favourable media coverage, exposed questionable labour practices to public scrutiny, and, in the case of Mexico, opened up public debate on the government's historic practice of discriminating against independent unions — those not affiliated with Mexico's long-ruling party, the Partido Revolucionario Institucional (PRI). A few complaints have even prompted changes in behaviour by the complained-of government or private company.

Part V, 'Assessing Environmental Effects: Local, North American, and Global Perspectives', turns to the broader issue of how to assess the environmental effects of trade agreements at the regional and global levels. It also investigates the challenges of developing environmental and sustainability indicators at the local level and the extent to which these indicators are relevant for assessing the environmental effects of trade in urban areas. While the previous three sections focussed on how key civil society actors could access, influence, and use the NAFTA institutions and rules for their investment, environmental, and social purposes, this section asks how civil society can and should influence the development of tools to monitor and evaluate the environmental and broader sustainability effects of trade liberalisation regimes.

In Chapter 14, 'Understanding the Environmental Effects of Trade: Some Lessons from NAFTA', Scott Vaughan begins by noting the evidence on increasing income disparity and increasing concern about the social costs of globalisation, and by specifying the similar central issues in the debate over NAFTA. He then notes the move toward more sophisticated analyses of the environmental effects of trade liberalisation, and the CEC's contribution to this effort. He next reviews the findings of the CEC's recent step in the ongoing effort to assess NAFTA's environmental effects — the North American Symposium on Assessing the Environmental Effects of Trade, held in October 2000 at the World Bank in Washington DC.

Vaughan argues that there has been considerable progress in the development and application of analytic tools to assess the environmental and social impacts of trade liberalisation, even if much more remains to be done. In the case of NAFTA, the papers presented at the symposium suggest a mixed record. Although there is no evidence that many of the greatest initial fears have been realised, there are clear negative environmental impacts in particular locales, processes, and sectors. Above all, despite the increased work done on assessing the environmental effects of trade agreements in recent years, the policy implications of these effects remain unclear. Clearly, policies need to be shaped that mitigate negative environmental effects and maximise positive environmental outcomes. However, the long-standing debate continues over where policy interventions should occur.

In Chapter 15, 'Sustainability Assessments of Trade Agreements: Global Approaches', Sarah Richardson reviews efforts at the global level to develop and apply assessment frameworks, and in particular the question of at what stage in the trade liberalisation progress such assessments should occur. She identifies the reasons for the upsurge in international interest in sustainability assessments of trade agreements, the elements common to all approaches, the assessments conducted at the national level in Canada and the U.S., those done at the plurilateral or regional level in the OECD and European Union, and those undertaken at the multilateral level in the United Nations Environmental Programme (UNEP).

Richardson concludes that there is a great deal of work in progress in what is a very dynamic field. Some work remains to be done on the interaction with the trade policy-making process, and how the results of the assessment will be taken into account in order to make them an integral part of trade liberalisation negotiations. Public participation is now a given, as the authors of assessments increasingly rely on stakeholders to assist in scoping out the problem, to provide ideas, and to shape the direction of assessments. There is no 'one size fits all', particularly as assessment is extended to apply to developing countries.

In Chapter 16, 'Concern for the Environmental Effects of Trade in Canadian Communities: Evidence from Local Indicator Reports', Virginia W. Maclaren conducts a bottom-up analysis of the sustainability impacts of trade agreements. She notes that in the ever growing debate about the environmental effects of free trade, the existence and influence of such effects in urban areas and local communities seem to have been neglected, amidst the widespread concern with global, regional, national, and provincial effects. In order to connect the global to the local level, she explores a potentially important source for tracking these impacts and community concern surrounding them — the local or community indicator report. She thus searches the 200-plus local indicator reports in North America for evidence of community concern with the environmental effects of trade in local communities. She also assesses the extent to which the environmental information and analysis found in local indicator reports can contribute to a better understanding of the environmental effects of trade at the local level. She begins by comparing the different kinds of local indicator reports and their goals, and then proceeds to investigate their environmental content and inclusion of trade-related variables.

Maclaren discovers that there are several different types of assessments employed at the local level, and that the goals of these exercises vary according to the type employed. While only three local indicator reports make specific mention of NAFTA or its organisations, some local indicator reports do address pollution trade problems. For the most part, they do not attempt to make a link between pollution trade and liberalised trade regimes. They are not so much concerned with the causes of international pollution as with the effects. There is, however, a growing interest in the indicator of ecological footprint, which is the only indicator in these local assessments of pollution from trade.

In Chapter 17, 'Using Indicators to Engage the Community in Sustainability Debates', Noel Keough reports the results of one of the most advanced North American efforts to conduct local sustainability assessments that are related to trade — developed in Canada's sixth largest city, Calgary, on the outskirts of which the 2002 G8 Summit will be held. He discusses the process, outcomes, and future directions for the Sustainable Calgary indicators project. He also considers what insights these local experiences have to offer the debate on international trade regime reform.

Keough concludes that there are signs of wear in the fabric of Calgary's community life. To be sure, tentative steps are being taken to address resource consumption; Calgarians enjoy a relatively healthy natural environment, and their education and healthcare systems are still among the best in the world, even if showing some signs of stress. But, economically, the city's prosperity still rests on the lucrative but finite resources of the oil and gas industry, and masks intolerable inequities. Given global trends represented by indicators such as the ecological footprint, and Calgarians' current energy- and resource-intensive lifestyle, Calgary cannot be considered sustainable. Looking ahead and upward, Keough identifies three particular areas where local community sustainability indicators projects can contribute to the discussion of environmental reform of global trade: the need for a more democratic process in globalisation, a questioning of the mythology of economic growth, and a redefinition of the concept of progress.

In Chapter 18, 'Development and Usability of a System for Environment and Health Indicators: A Case Study', David L. Buckeridge and Carl G. Amrhein provide a second case study of a local indicators project, focussed on environmentally related health concerns in Canada's largest city, Toronto. They seek to identify the issues that influence indicator development and the use of indicators for decision making through a case study of a project aimed at improving access to community health information. They describe the evolution of a community/university collaboration underlying the case study and provide an overview of the system's development. They discuss issues in the development and use of the system of health and environment indicators.

Buckeridge and Amrhein end this chapter with suggestions to assist the development of environment and health indicator systems for communities. They argue that geographic information systems (GISs), and information systems in general, have the potential to be powerful resources for integrating and presenting health and environment indicators. Yet there are several obstacles to their development and use. They recommend, first, that methodologies that facilitate user involvement be designed to recognise the effort required to maintain user involvement in the design process. Second, those governmental and nongovernmental organisations that create and keep data should seek to improve the accessibility and usability of health data. Third, there is a need for research into methods for optimising the use of population health data.

Part VI, 'Concluding Reflections', takes a final look at the implications of the NAFTA experience in meeting the challenges of linking trade liberalisation, environmental protection, and social cohesion on a global basis. In Chapter 19, 'Fix It or Nix It? Will the NAFTA Model Survive?', Sylvia Ostry contends that NAFTA is not a model for other regional agreements. She questions whether any such model exists given the current division between the North and the South over the provisions of the current trading regime. A key issue of concern in the South is the inclusion of environmental and labour standards in trade agreements. Ostry laments the lack of international leadership on this issue. She calls for new leadership to break the post-Seattle stalemate that puts the very legitimacy and credibility of the WTO at stake. In her view, the critical question is not whether the NAFTA model will survive or work elsewhere, but whether the rules-based multilateral system can be 'fixed' before it is 'nixed'.

In the conclusion, in Chapter 20, Virginia W. Maclaren and John J. Kirton summarise how the chapters in this volume have helped to answer the five questions posed in this introduction. They present a more optimistic appraisal of NAFTA's relevance, the indicators effort, and the way both can help meet the challenges faced by the global community as a whole. They maintain that the NAFTA regime has set valuable precedents for other trade liberalisation agreements while providing useful lessons about what to avoid.

Much progress is being made in developing indicators and other tools for assessing the environmental effects of trade, although the pace and applicability of this work are stronger at the regional and global levels than they are at the local level. NAFTA's institutions have made great strides toward achieving meaningful civil society participation in their deliberations, but increased empowerment of civil society is still possible and warranted. Kirton and Maclaren conclude that, after a decade of experience, and despite its faults, the NAFTA experiment is a bold one that has succeeded in many ways and has had a far-reaching influence on other trade liberalisation agreements.

The diversity of views expressed by the authors in this volume is a powerful reminder of how contentious the trade liberalisation debate has become and how difficult it is to assess the effects of trade. Much work remains in order to forge more equitable trade, environment, and social cohesion links under NAFTA and for trade liberalisation in general. It is to be hoped that this volume helps point the way toward achieving these improvements and realising a more sustainable future.

Note

1   While other regional or plurilateral agreements such as Mercosur and APEC have different approaches and some superior elements, they lack the full range of NAFTA's environmental, social, and public participation provisions and institutions. The European Union remains a very special supranational case, and thus one of limited utility for a world not wanting to proceed to Europe's prospective unified end state.

References

Audley, John J. (1997). *Green Politics and Global Trade: NAFTA and the Future of Environmental Politics*. Georgetown University Press, Washington DC.

Cameron, Maxwell A. and Brian W. Tomlin (2000). *The Making of NAFTA: How the Deal Was Done*. Cornell University Press, Ithaca.

Deardorff, Alan V. and Robert Mitchell Stern (2000). *Social Dimensions of U.S. Trade Policies*. University of Michigan Press, Ann Arbor.

Esty, Daniel C. and Institute for International Economics (1994). *Greening the GATT: Trade, Environment, and the Future*. Institute for International Economics, Washington DC.

Gallup Canada (1993). '46% Oppose Free Trade Deal, Poll Suggests'. *The Globe and Mail*, 30 August. p. A11.

Gherson, Giles (1998). 'Canadians Are Activists at Heart, New Poll Finds'. *Ottawa Citizen*, 24 April. p. A5.

Hart, Michael (2000). 'The Role of Dispute Setlement in Managing Canada-U.S. Trade and Investment Relations'. In M. A. Molot and F. O. Hampson, eds., *Vanishing Borders: Canada among Nations 2000*. Oxford University Press, Toronto.

Hockin, Thomas A. (2001). *The American Nightmare: Trade Politics after Seattle*. Lexington Books, Lanham.

Johnson, Pierre Marc and André Beaulieu (1996). *The Environment and NAFTA: Understanding and Implementing the New Continental Law*. Island Press, Washington DC.

Kaiser, Karl, John J. Kirton, and Joseph P. Daniels, eds. (2000). *Shaping a New International Financial System: Challenges of Governance in a Globalizing World*. Ashgate, Aldershot.

Kirton, John J. (1996). 'Commission for Environmental Cooperation and Canada-U.S. Environmental Governance in the NAFTA Era'. *American Review of Canadian Studies* vol. 26 (Autumn), pp. 1–14.

Kirton, John J. (2000). 'Deepening Integration and Global Governance: America as a Globalized Partner'. In T. Brewer and G. Boyd, eds., *Globalizing America: The USA in World Integration*. Edward Elgar, Cheltenham.

Kirton, John J. and Rafael Fernandez de Castro (1997). *NAFTA's Institutions: The Environmental Potential and Performance of the NAFTA Free Trade Commission and Related Bodies*. Commission for Environmental Cooperation, Montreal.

Kirton, John J. et al. (1999). *Assessing Environmental Effects of the North American Free Trade Agreement (NAFTA): An Analytic Framework (Phase II) and Issue Studies*. Commission for Environmental Cooperation, Montreal.

Maclaren, Virginia (1996). *Developing Indicators of Urban Sustainability: A Focus on the Canadian Experience*. ICURR Press, Toronto.

Mayer, Frederick (1998). *Interpreting NAFTA: The Science and Art of Political Analysis*. Columbia University Press, New York.

McKinney, Joseph A. (2000). *Created from NAFTA: The Structure, Function, and Significance of the Treaty's Related Institutions*. M.E. Sharpe, Armonk, NY.

Mendelsohn, Matthew and Robert Wolfe (2001). 'Probing the Aftermyth of Seattle: Canadian Public Opinion on International Trade, 1980–2000'. *International Journal* vol. 56 (Spring), pp. 234–260.

North American Free Trade Agreement (1994). *NAFTA Text*. CCH Incorporated, Toronto.

Parkin, Andrew and Centre for Research and Information on Canada (2001). 'Trade, Globalization, and Canadian Values'. The CRIC Papers, April. <www.cric.ca/pdf/cahiers/cricpapers_april2001.pdf> (December 2001).

Pettigrew, Pierre S. (1999). *The New Politics of Confidence*. Stoddart, Toronto.

Program on International Policy Attitudes (2000). 'Americans on Globalization: A Study of U.S. Public Attitudes'. Program on International Policy Attitudes. <www.pipa.org/OnlineReports/Globalization/contents.html> (December 2001).

Rodrik, Dani (1997). *Has Globalization Gone Too Far?* Institute for International Economics, Washington DC.

Sampson, Gary P. (2000). *Trade, Environment, and the WTO: The Post-Seattle Agenda.* Overseas Development Council, Washington DC.

Sampson, Gary P. and W. Bradnee Chambers (1999). *Trade, Environment, and the Millennium.* United Nations University Press, Tokyo.

Schrecker, Ted and Jean Dalgleish (1994). *Growth, Trade, and Environmental Values.* Westminster Institute for Ethics and Human Values, London, ON.

Tuck, S. (2001). 'Fewer Canadians Support Free Trade'. *The Globe and Mail*, 5 February. pp. A1, 6.

World Commission on Environment and Development (1987). *Our Common Future.* Oxford University Press, Oxford; New York.

PART I
LINKING TRADE, ENVIRONMENT, AND SOCIAL VALUES: THE GLOBAL AND NAFTA EXPERIENCES

From Trade Liberalisation to Sustainable Development: The Challenges of Integrated Global Governance

Pierre Marc Johnson

The Seattle Shock

Seattle, or the post-Seattle period, is sometimes referred to as the end of globalisation.[1] Whatever perceptions circulate about the meaning of the 1999 Seattle conference, where the effort to launch a new round of multilateral trade liberalisation failed amidst violent protests on the streets, it is indeed reasonable to suggest that it constitutes a turning point in globalisation (Bayne 2001; Ullrich 2001; Hockin 2001). Yet deriving its impacts or meaning for the globalisation process remains a considerable analytical challenge for specialists and policy makers. Trade liberalisation has slowed down in the post-Seattle environment, and it will probably remain this way for some time. However, the post-Seattle world is still a world in which the globalisation process is proceeding, because globalisation is about much more than strict trade liberalisation.

Several factors can explain the Seattle failure. First of all, there are circumstantial causes. One very technical change that happened during Seattle relates to the so-called Green Room, where heads of the technical delegations get together before the ministers fly into town and approve the negotiated texts (Cohn 2001). The Green Room process never took place in Seattle because too many people in the streets prohibited diplomats from getting in touch with one another to conduct this work. So when the ministers flew into town, they had to cope with an agenda that was longer than usual, was more complex than expected, and contained major unresolved issues.

The U.S. presidential campaign also interfered with the negotiation process. Bill Clinton's declaration about the need for trade sanctions to enforce environmental and labour standards — a comment designed to appeal to the domestic electorate — infuriated developing countries. They helped derail the process by walking out of the room or simply keeping their arms crossed. The demonstrations and violent clashes in the streets sent a shock wave through many politicians. Some realised that they had been propelled by a bureaucratic process that had captured them. Suddenly and almost brutally, it appeared to them profoundly disconnected from some of their own constituencies.

Secondly, there were substantive reasons for Seattle's failure. The scope of the new round was obviously too broad to realise at that time. Negotiations tried to address the issue of agriculture, a highly politically sensitive issue, especially in the trade relationship between the United States and the European Union. The equitable sharing of the benefits of the new round between rich member countries of the Organisation for Economic Co-operation and Development (OECD) and developing countries also created significant distrust and animosity. Most developing countries consider that the Uruguay Round has never delivered its results in terms of increased market access and increased development. Furthermore, labour and environment issues were in the minds of some OECD countries, while many developing countries considered the incorporation of these items to be a Trojan horse for disguised protectionism.

Thirdly, procedural issues emerged. Seattle made it clear for public opinion in OECD countries to view the process as tainted with a lack of transparency and an obfuscation of the consequences of the negotiations, as revealed by a frustrated civil society. Inadequate participation by developing countries and many unresolved implementation issues also became apparent. Indeed, many developing countries still struggle to comply with the Marrakech Agreement, which established the World Trade Organization (WTO) in 1994, within the timeframe it provided for.

Understanding these very important causes of Seattle's failure is only a first step toward a broader analysis of the process of globalisation at the dawn of this new century. The deep underlying cause of the events at Seattle is an unbalanced globalisation process that is too focussed on trade, and that is effectively governed by institutions that lack effective participation from civil society and developing countries. As trade and other economic regimes are gradually built into globalisation's new constitutional framework, citizens in OECD countries fear the real or perceived impacts of globalisation on their communities and on their daily lives. They raise, in vociferous ways, procedural issues such as transparency, accountability, and participation, as well as substantive social, environmental, and human rights issues that trade negotiations obviously do not address.

Globalisation came to a crossroads in Seattle. In the streets, as in domestic media subsequently, the trade process started being criticised as never before. It must now integrate and address some of these environmental, human rights, and social equity issues — even if they are often ill defined or stridently expressed. Otherwise, it will face increasing hostility from the population of OECD countries as well as of other parts of the world. Such hostility will continue to be a drag on economic globalisation as it is expressed in international fora. It will result in diminishing political support for trade and financial liberalisation in elective institutions and in public opinion. This situation constitutes a source of great concern for the fundamental economic interests of a country such as Canada, which is constantly looking for a predictable and stable rules-based international system in which it can evolve comfortably as it exports more than 40 percent of its gross domestic product (GDP).

The Multidimensional Nature of Globalisation

The Components of Globalisation

Globalisation is fundamentally a multidimensional phenomenon about movement: the movement of goods, capital, people, and ideas. These four aspects can be described with a few simple figures.

First, the new movement of goods is evident in the fact that international trade represented 14 percent of the world's GDP in 1998, whereas it was only 6 percent in 1950. In the decade from 1987 to 1997, the share of trade in global GDP jumped from 10 percent to 15 percent. Trade currently represents on average 19 percent of the GDP of OECD countries, and more than 40 percent of Canada's GDP. The rising importance of trade means in practice that communities are facing new opportunities. But they also confront new challenges, as they can be more sensitive to foreign export markets and must face increased competition from foreign-produced goods and services in their domestic markets.

Second, globalisation is also about the movement of capital. Total portfolio investments in 1970 amounted to a daily US$10 billion to US$20 billion on the exchange rate market. Today, more than US$1500 billion is exchanged everyday in anonymity, nonaccountability, and increased volatility. Foreign direct investment (FDI) has also become tremendously more important, both in developed and developing countries. Total FDI reached US$644 billion in 1998 — a gain of 39 percent over the previous year. It was driven by cross-border mergers and acquisitions. FDI flows have become much more important than official development assistance (ODA) to developing countries, although FDI is highly concentrated in only a few emerging economies such as China. As FDI becomes the major engine of economic development, it has an important conditioning impact on the economy and on the development of communities. The establishment of appropriate legal frameworks for foreign direct investment is therefore of the highest importance in order to ensure that FDI has positive economic, social, and environmental impacts (Rugman 1999).

Third, globalisation is about the movement of people. The world population reached 6 billion in October 1999. Eighty million people, or the equivalent of today's united Germany, are added to the global population every year. Every year, 42 million people migrate temporarily and 6 million migrate permanently. World-wide, approximately 140 million legally registered migrants live permanently outside their country of origin. There are 4 million internal refugees and 15 million external refugees on the planet. These movements of population are unprecedented in human history. The sheer increasing mass of humans using the planet's resources with an unprecedented consuming appetite poses an enormous challenge in itself. Here, technology will play a fundamental role in finding solutions. These demographics lead to reciprocal interdependencies and linkages amongst groups across borders that are changing the world's social fabric.

The final component of this unprecedented change is the movement of information. The information revolution has induced a fundamental shift in economic, social, and political realities. The number of television sets per thousand people doubled between 1980 and 1995. In 1990, 33 billion minutes of international telephone communication were held, and that figure had more than doubled by 1996. There were 260 million internet users in 1999; this number should increase to 700 million by 2002. These expanding networks carry unprecedented volumes of information and increase the circulation of ideas, connecting people all across the world in real time. A good example of the power of that communication was the extraordinary success of the opposition to the Multilateral Agreement on Investment (MAI), which was blocked by an unprecedented international mobilisation of civil society.

The Consequences of Globalisation

This multidimensional process of globalisation has several consequences. One process accompanying globalisation is an increased divide in which the richest fifth of the world's population now controls 86 percent of world GDP and 82 percent of world exports. This privileged top fifth is responsible for 92 percent of FDI outflows and receives 68 percent of FDI inflows. The poorest fifth accounts for less than 1 percent of these indicators. Relative disparities between the world's richest and poorest fifth of the world population have increased from 30 to 1 in 1960 to 74 to 1 in 1997. Many indicators are also announcing a technological and digital divide, with the OECD countries representing 17 percent of the world's population and having 74 percent of telephone lines and 88 percent of the internet subscribers. In the high-technology sector, in 1993 OECD countries accounted for 84 percent of global research and development expenditures and possessed 97 percent of the world's patents. From this divide also emerges, in the fields of health and agriculture, a drug divide and genome divide. These figures and underlying disparities are a source of great concern for those who are seeking an equitable development model.

Another phenomenon accompanying globalisation is the emergence of more room for more new actors. Nation-states have suffered a vertical loss of power and sovereignty in the globalised world. This vertical loss of power results in part from the downward delegation of power in OECD countries to local governments in their fight against deficits. It also results from an upward loss of power in favour of international regimes and regional institutions, with trade and finance liberalisation pushing nation-states to abandon portions of their sovereignty to international agreements. This delegation of power to international regimes fosters a very interesting phenomenon: what many have called the constitutionalisation of trade and finance liberalisation regimes, with its accompanying impact on political systems, social change, and the nation-state's role in general (Cerny 1995; Clarkson 1998).

This new context allows for new actors to emerge, the two most important being the multinational corporations (MNCs) and nongovernmental organisations (NGOs). MNCs have become the main drivers of FDI and world trade. In 1970, there were about 700 MNCs. In 1998, there were 60 000 MNCs with 500 000 foreign affiliates. MNCs accounted for 25 percent of the world's GDP and one third of world exports in 1997.

NGOs have also become influential actors. They have developed into a highly organised and diversified web of organisations, creating a truly global civil society. There were a mere 176 international NGOs in 1909. By 1993, there were 28 900. While MNCs are the drivers and main actors of economic globalisation, organised civil society represents the emerging voice of an evolving global democracy. Although in terms of accountability and responsibility, NGOs and MNCs differ from nation-states as actors in the global system, neither can be ignored. Their power, influence, and relevance, at the local and international levels, demand that they be linked into various formal processes of globalisation.

Globalisation and the Challenges of Environmental Governance

Among all the issues that are related to globalisation, one imposes itself as clearly one of the highest concerns for citizens across the world: the environment. Scarcities caused by pollution, the exhaustion of natural resources, and the destruction of ecosystems pose an enormous challenge to economic growth and development. Climate change, ozone depletion, loss of biodiversity, freshwater scarcity, deforestation, and desertification have all become global issues in the past 20 years. They demand international responsiveness, and often global governance.

There are currently 216 effective multilateral environmental agreements (MEAs) in the world. About 10 major global and multilateral agreements have been signed since 1985. These agreements are part of the global governance system and constitute an important component of what globalisation is about. The existence of this rapidly developing environmental regime creates a need for consistency and coherence in governance. This has been lacking thus far.

Trade regimes must be adapted to nontrade governance regimes. As the centre of world trade governance, the WTO cannot escape these new challenges. First, environmental protection and related competitiveness issues are fundamental aspects of the process of multilateral trade liberalisation. There is also an unresolved north-south issue about market access and protectionism. Developing countries are concerned about environmental protection because their perception is that environmental regulations are one more means for OECD countries to restrict access to their markets.

These matters pertaining to the consistency of the trade and environmental agenda contributed to the Seattle failure. They must now be addressed if the new round of trade liberalisation is to succeed. Key issues that need to be addressed in the trade and environment nexus are environmental regulations and market access; the trade-related aspects of intellectual property (TRIPs) and their relationship to biodiversity and technology transfers; the relationship between the WTO regime and MEAs; the application of the precautionary principle; and the elimination of trade-distorting and environmentally damaging subsidies. Lastly, improved transparency and participation from civil society and improved means of participation for developing countries should emerge as necessary procedural improvements. Seattle destroyed any hope for a quick start of a new round of multilateral trade liberalisation. The WTO now needs to broaden its agenda and strengthen its links and relations with multilateral environmental institutions as it moves ahead.

NAFTA's Environmental Regime

The trade and environment regime centred within the North American Free Trade Agreement (NAFTA), developed since 1993, could provide an interesting model or a source of inspiration for the WTO system (Johnson 1999; Johnson and Beaulieu 1996; Rugman, Kirton, and Soloway 1999; Hockin 2001). NAFTA was presented in 1994 as the 'greenest' trade agreement ever made, because it has five specific provisions that integrate sustainable development concerns. First, NAFTA's preamble includes a commitment to implement the treaty in a manner consistent with environmental protection and conservation, as well as commitments to sustainable development and the enforcement of environment laws and regulations. Second, the agreement establishes the principle of paramountcy of a list of environmental treaties over itself. Third, Chapter 7 and Chapter 9, on sanitary and phytosanitary measures, allow for countries to have the level of protection that they consider best as long as these measures do not constitute disguised restrictions to trade. Fourth, the question of pollution havens is addressed by the rejection of the concept of lowering environmental standards as a method of attracting investment, although this does not give way to true sanctions but only to consultations. And, fifth, the trade dispute settlement system within NAFTA places the burden of proof in favour of maintaining environmental legislation against a legal challenge rather than on the reverse approach under the system created by the General Agreement on Tariffs and Trade (GATT) and the WTO.

In addition to these environmental provisions included within NAFTA itself, the North American trade and environment regime also offers the parallel North American Agreement on Environmental Cooperation (NAAEC), which established the North American Commission for Environmental Cooperation (CEC). The CEC is a trinational organisation headed by the environment ministers of Canada, Mexico, and the United States. Its secretariat, located in Montreal, conducts a series of activities that concentrate on five main areas. The first is research and knowledge development, which allows the CEC to assemble resources and expertise to collect data and develop knowledge on a region-wide continental basis over a wide range of environmental issues. The agreement also provides that the CEC can initiate independent investigations into issues that it identifies. It has done so three times in its first seven years.

The second stream is public outreach and awareness. The CEC is a unique organisation in its openness to civil society from all sectors or regions in the three member countries of the United States, Canada, and Mexico. It has engaged civil society in a substantive and constructive dialogue over its seven years in operation through the development of mechanisms for public participation. It has also developed an extensive Web site and a listserv communication system. Part of the CEC is also an innovative institution called the Joint Public Advisory Committee (JPAC), which has been instrumental in fostering this dialogue. The JPAC consists of 15 members, five from each of the countries in NAFTA, who come from NGOs, the private sector, and academia. It is responsible for conducting public consultations and providing advice to the ministers on any issue within the mandate or work program of the CEC.

Capacity building, which is a key issue when dealing with developing countries, is a third stream of the CEC's work. Particular attention has been given to enhancing capacities for pollution prevention, environmental monitoring, and law enforcement in Mexico. Elements of capacity building are present in various forms in almost every CEC project, through initiatives that include sharing data, training, and exchanging best practices.

A fourth and central stream is effective law enforcement, which is a pivotal element in efforts to prevent environment-related disputes from arising between trading partners. Not surprisingly, the effectiveness of the enforcement of environmental laws is at the core of the NAAEC. Not only is it an important component of the CEC's work but the agreement requires the three countries to produce an annual report on the fulfilment of their enforcement obligations. In addition, in cases of persistent patterns of failure to enforce environmental laws, Part V of the agreement provides for government-to-government consultations and outlines a mechanism for dispute resolution. These articles have not yet been invoked by any party.

A unique aspect of the NAAEC is that it allows citizens or groups to file submissions with the secretariat of the CEC alleging that a party is failing to enforce its environmental law. Such a process of direct public petitioning is rare in international institutions. Under the NAAEC, it can lead eventually to the drafting of a factual record on the alleged non-enforcement. This record can be made public. Ultimately, there are no legally binding obligations imposed on the country that is the object of the petition denouncing alleged non-enforcement of domestic environmental legislation. Yet the process facilitates the application of public pressure on that country, by making officials uncomfortable, and thus may prevent similar cases from arising in the future. Public pressure can also move countries to anticipate a complaint or possible factual record and modify behaviour accordingly. From 1995 to November 2000, 28 petitions had been filed: nine against Canada, eleven against Mexico, and eight against the U.S. Only one factual record had been publicly released.

Finally, a fifth stream of the work of the CEC is a systematic effort within the commission to strengthen environmental co-operation in such fields as the joint management of shared resources, biodiversity, and pollutants control, to give only a few examples. Many people see the CEC experience in environmental co-operation as a model that could be used in developing full hemispheric environmental co-operation.

Assessing NAFTA's Environmental Regime

NAFTA's environmental regime was an ongoing experiment during its first seven years. In many regards, this experience has been a positive one, in terms of addressing the trade and environment nexus, engaging civil society in a constructive dialogue, and strengthening environmental co-operation. It is less than certain, however, that this model could be replicated in other trade regimes. Given the present context of the WTO as well as the Free Trade Agreement of the Americas (FTAA), with the extraordinary diversity of interests across the world and across the western hemisphere and the number of actors involved in these processes, applying this model would constitute a daunting challenge. Nonetheless, many of its elements could serve as an inspiration to integrate nontrade issues in furthering trade-centred globalisation. A first step should be to assess the results of NAFTA's environmental regime after seven years in existence.

The model could certainly be improved by the establishment of a permanent dialogue between the CEC and the trade commissions of NAFTA. Also, since 1999 serious concerns over the impacts of NAFTA's Chapter 11 investment provisions on governments' capacity to regulate for environmental protection have been raised. Howard Mann (2001) has shown in his research and analysis that the 'polluter pays' principle is gradually being reversed, in the context of Chapter 11, with a 'pay the polluter' principle. The ability of the regime to adapt to this new challenge will be key to its credibility.

New multilateral environmental agreements to which the three countries are parties should also be added to the list of treaties protected by the paramountcy clause. Furthermore, Articles 14 and 15 remain subject to great political controversy as they constitute a pivotal element of the CEC's system of public participation through its direct citizen's petitioning approach. This process should be strengthened and improved. Last, reaching out to remote or isolated communities has been a problem for the CEC. It can certainly be said that the ongoing dialogue established between the commission and civil society institutions has done much to maintain support for trade liberalisation within the environmental community in North America.

Lessons Learned from the NAFTA Experience

There are several lessons to be learned from NAFTA experience thus far. First, in the post-Seattle world, civil society can be a constructive force if it is meaningfully engaged in processes of trade liberalisation. This means that one must balance democracy, transparency, and effectiveness in negotiations. Second, addressing sustainability issues in a trade agreement is not a zero-sum game. It benefits both the trade and environmental communities. Third, establishing an agenda of broader environmental co-operation is a key strategy to ease trade and environment tensions when countries with different levels of development liberalise trade amongst themselves.

All have to face the fact that the WTO negotiations will not go very far if OECD governments feel they lose support on the domestic front in order to proceed with a trade liberalisation agenda. Addressing nontrade issues is therefore a key strategy for building support for new trade agreements within OECD countries. In this context, therefore, Canada must make every effort to bring to the table issues of environment, social equity, and cultural differentiation into the FTAA and WTO negotiations.

International institutions work slowly, with no real visible or transparent accountability process in their negotiations. Thus, adapting international institutions to the new challenges of broader global governance becomes a very difficult task. The only way to foster the necessary adaptation process in the international system is for a limited number of economies of a significant size to play a leadership role. Canada can initiate such activities, particularly in the G20 process (Johnson 2001; Kirton 2001).

The G20 comprises members of the G8, major developing countries of the world, and international financial institutions. This organisation, led by ministers of finance, represents 80 percent of the world's production and 65 percent of the world's population. It has the potential to be tremendously influential in global governance. Until now, the G20 has concentrated on dealing with financial stability issues, but it has shown an interest in expanding this mandate to broader issues, as the G7 did in the 1980s. If the ministers of finance and the heads of state of the G20 can get closer to broadening their perspectives and addressing other key issues, such as the sharing of growth in the context of liberalised trade, they could lay down the basis of a new deal that includes developed and developing countries.

Such a new deal would consist of OECD countries transferring more aid and more technology, and giving more access to their markets to developing countries more quickly than is now provided for under the WTO. On the part of developing countries, the deal would consist of a commitment to address environmental and human rights issues, as well as the implementation of the various international instruments to which they are a party. If the world can strike such a deal between the developed and developing countries, then perhaps it will have a better integrated globalisation that more strictly addresses trade and financial concerns and that responds to some concerns of civil society, communities, and citizens all across the globe.

Note

1 This chapter builds on the keynote address to the first Annual EnviReform conference in November 2000, and on Pierre Marc Johnson (2001).

References

Bayne, Nicholas (2001). 'The G7 and Multilateral Trade Liberalisation: Past Performance, Future Challenges'. In J. J. Kirton and G. M. von Furstenberg, eds., *New Directions in Global Economic Governance: Creating International Order for the Twenty-First Century*, pp. 171–187. Ashgate, Aldershot.
Cerny, Philip G. (1995). 'Globalization and the Changing Logic of Collective Action'. *International Organization* vol. 49, no. 4, pp. 595–625.
Clarkson, Stephen (1998). 'Fearful Asymmetries: The Challenges of Analyzing Continental Systems in a Globalizing World'. *Canadian-American Public Policy* vol. 35, pp. 1–6.
Cohn, Theodore H. (2001). 'Securing Multilateral Trade Liberalisation: International Institutions in Conflict and Convergence'. In J. J. Kirton and G. M. von Furstenberg, eds., *New Directions in Global Economic Governance: Creating International Order for the Twenty-First Century*, pp. 189–218. Ashgate, Aldershot.
Hockin, Thomas A. (2001). *The American Nightmare: Trade Politics after Seattle*. Lexington Books, Lanham.
Johnson, Pierre Marc (1999). 'Five Windows for the Future of NAFTA's Environmental Commission'. *Policy Options* vol. 20, no. 5 (June), pp. 27–32.
Johnson, Pierre Marc (2001). 'Creating Sustainable Global Governance'. In J. J. Kirton, J. P. Daniels and A. Freytag, eds., *Guiding Global Order: G8 Governance in the Twenty-First Century*, pp. 245–282. Ashgate, Aldershot.
Johnson, Pierre Marc and André Beaulieu (1996). *The Environment and NAFTA: Understanding and Implementing the New Continental Law*. Island Press, Washington DC.
Kirton, John J. (2001). 'The G20: Representativeness, Effectiveness, and Leadership in Global Governance'. In J. J. Kirton, J. P. Daniels and A. Freytag, eds., *Guiding Global Order: G8 Governance in the Twenty-First Century*, pp. 143–172. Ashgate, Aldershot.
Mann, Howard (2001). *Private Rights, Public Problems: A Guide to NAFTA's Controversial Chapter on Investors Rights*. International Institute on Sustainable Development and World Wildlife Fund, Winnipeg.
Rugman, Alan M. (1999). 'Negotiating Multilateral Rules to Promote Investment'. In M. R. Hodges, J. J. Kirton and J. P. Daniels, eds., *The G8's Role in the New Millennium*, pp. 143–157. Ashgate, Aldershot.
Rugman, Alan M., John J. Kirton, and Julie A. Soloway (1999). *Environmental Regulations and Corporate Strategy: A NAFTA Perspective*. Oxford University Press, Oxford.
Ullrich, Heidi K. (2001). 'Stimulating Trade Liberalisation after Seattle: G7/8 Leadership in Global Governance'. In J. J. Kirton and G. M. von Furstenberg, eds., *New Directions in Global Economic Governance: Creating International Order for the Twenty-First Century*, pp. 219–240. Ashgate, Aldershot.

Chapter 3

The New Interface Agenda among Trade, Environment, and Social Cohesion

William A. Dymond

This chapter addresses three distinct, central elements of the public debate on Canadian international trade and investment policy. The first is the dichotomy between public protests over this policy exemplified at the Quebec City Summit of the Americas in April 2001 and public policy exemplified by the Canadian government's continuing enthusiastic pursuit of multilateral and bilateral trade and investment agreements. The second is the fundamental change in the structure of international trade rules and the associated challenges posed to domestic and international governance of the trade system. And the third is the increasingly central role that dispute settlement has come to play in the management of international trade relations.

These elements are drawn together by globalisation, conceived of here less as the rapid integration of national economies into a global borderless economy and more as the growing public concern with the capacity of national governments to regulate the environmental and social impacts of globalisation. It is thus important to the globalisation debate to ask whether trade and investment agreements need to be integrated with environmental and social policy objectives. The evidence suggests that the answer lies in the evolution of the broader framework of international governance.

The Dichotomy between Public Protest and Public Policy

Public protest over the evolution of the international trade system erupted in Canada in 1996 after a long hiatus following the conclusion of the Canada-United States Free Trade Agreement (FTA) in 1988. The spark was provided by the negotiations within the Organisation for Economic Co-operation and Development (OECD) for the Multilateral Agreement on Investment (MAI). It occurred at a time when the trade liberalisation agenda for Canada had been largely completed except for a few sectors such as supply-managed agriculture and textiles and clothing. At that time, all the good and bad effects of 50 years of trade liberalisation in the General Agreements on Tariffs and Trade (GATT) and the FTA had already worked their way through the Canadian economy and society.[1] The MAI negotiations, which failed in 1998, and the Seattle ministerial conference of the World Trade Organization (WTO), which failed in 1999, were posited on an agenda that had little to do with classic trade liberalisation. It focussed instead on the interface between national governance and the dynamics of the global economy.

The presumption that noisy public protest represents broad public concern with the impacts of trade liberalisation suffers from a lack of evidence. For many years, nationalists, labour unions, environmentalists, human rights advocates, and social justice groups have been trying to persuade Canadians that global trade and investment liberalisation is emasculating governments, destroying the environment, and subordinating human rights and social justice to the greed of corporations. Street theatre in Seattle, Quebec City, and Genoa, where the Group of Seven and Group of Eight (G7/8) Summit was held in July 2001, is one thing. The verdict of the voters is quite another thing. In the United States, the antiglobalisation vote — garnered by Ralph Nader — amounted only to 3 percent of the total in the U.S. presidential election in 2000. In Canada's general election in 2000, the pro–free trade, proglobalisation parties won nearly all the seats in the House of Commons and most of the votes cast by Canadians. Even the New Democratic Party, where concerns about trade liberalisation should normally reside, limited itself to a few liturgical references to corporate greed from the old hymn book. It hardly waged a war on trade and investment liberalisation as a central part of its campaign. In Mexico, the historic election of Vincente Fox as president can also be seen as an endorsement of the North American Free Trade Agreement (NAFTA), liberalised trade policies, and a more open economy and polity in general.

The contention that public agitation was the major factor in the failures of the MAI and the Seattle ministerial is scarcely more credible. The root cause of both failures was the lack of a central policy purpose for a multilateral investment agreement among OECD countries or a new round of trade liberalisation (Rugman 1999; Dymond 1999). The MAI, intended to be an investment protection agreement among the countries of the OECD, would have added no additional benefits for foreign investors since these countries already guarantee high standards of treatment for foreign investment from all countries. When serious protest emerged, there were no persuasive countervailing arguments to support the MAI. In the case of Seattle, there was no consensus among the major trading countries on the object and purpose of a new round of multilateral trade negotiations. This was particularly the case between countries, such as the United States, which sought a narrow, tightly focussed agenda and others, such as the European Union, which wanted a comprehensive agenda. Furthermore, developing countries came to Seattle deeply disaffected with the slim benefits flowing from the WTO. They were disinclined to embrace a new agenda, for example on environmental and social issues. Little help from the street was necessary to ensure a failure: WTO members were entirely capable of failing without any help.[2]

In retrospect, the alleged victory of the protesters has been hollow indeed. While the prospect of completing the new round of WTO negotiations remains problematic, the G8 countries continue to express strong support for multilateral negotiations.[3]

There has been, moreover, an explosion of regional and bilateral free trade initiatives both within Latin America, the Caribbean, and the Asia-Pacific region and between countries in these regions and the EU, Canada and latterly the U.S. (see Scollay 2001). Notwithstanding the protests at Quebec City, the government presided over the issuance of a summit declaration, which imparted new momentum to the negotiations for free trade in the Americas. On the day following the summit, Canada and Costa Rica signed a free trade agreement. Canada is currently pursuing a free trade agreement with Honduras, Nicaragua, El Salvador, and Guatemala, as well as with Singapore, and remains committed to free trade with the EU and the European Free Trade Association (Department of Foreign Affairs and International Trade [DFAIT] 2001b).[4] An independent observer could come to no other conclusion but that the government is confident, and with strong reason, of strong public and parliamentary support for its international trade policy.

Fundamental Changes in the Trade Rules

How did the trade liberalisation agenda become transfigured into what might be termed the 'interface' agenda?[5] The post-war model of multilateral trade policy — enshrined within the 1948 General Agreement on Tariffs and Trade (GATT) — sought to foster the expansion of world trade through the reduction of tariffs and other barriers to trade and the elimination of discriminatory treatment in international commerce (Hart 1998). The rights and obligations of the GATT, which give expression to this object and purpose, consist of an interlocking set of negative prescriptions by which governments undertake self-denying ordinances disciplining their capacity to impose trade barriers and to discriminate among their trading partners. With the entry into force of the WTO, there has been a fundamental shift of the centre of gravity in the object and purpose of international trade policy from the negative prescription of trade-barrier reductions to positive rule making. The negotiating issue is no longer trade liberalisation but global governance. The new focus of trade negotiations has profound implications for the political economy of international trade. What are these implications?

The first is a change in the balance of economic benefits of trade rules. The prime objectives of seven rounds of multilateral trade negotiations, from Geneva to the Tokyo Round, were the reduction and elimination of barriers to trade imposed at the border. The economic benefits of such negotiations flow from the exploitation of comparative advantage made possible by the more efficient employment of capital, labour, and natural resources. These are widely distributed to all economic actors. The shift into rule making aims principally at the harmonisation of the regulatory framework of trade. While global economic efficiencies flow from eliminating barriers that arise from different regulatory structures, the distribution of benefits among economic actors, including countries participating in such rules, is far less clear. Indeed, in certain cases economic costs will be incurred. For example, enhanced intellectual property protection rules produce economic benefits for the owners of intellectual property rights but costs for the users without corresponding benefits in terms, for example, of greater export opportunities.

Second, positive rule making changes the basic bargain by changing the relationship between trade rules and domestic governance. The construction of trade rules based on negative prescription, principally affecting border measures, leaves domestic governance basically intact. The shift into positive rule making inserts international rules and procedures into domestic governance and brings areas of public policy hitherto immune from international rules within the ambit of international rule making and global governance. Furthermore, differences in economic regulation may have little to do with the economic need for protection against imports but rather may have deep historical or social roots or reflect strongly held public opinion.[6] One important example is the requirement to base food safety standards upon scientific examination as provided for in the Sanitary and Phytosanitary Agreement, rather than a requirement that decisions by governments be held accountable to their electorates.

The third change is in the political management of trade rules and trade negotiations. Prior to the Uruguay Round, trade negotiations fell within the ambit of a small number of ministries: essentially those responsible for trade, finance, and agriculture. In countries, these issues are typically the exclusive domains of the federal level of government. The constituencies affected by the negotiations were confined to goods-producing industries competing with imports or for export markets. The shift to positive rule making introduces a new universe of public policy issues and economic sectors for negotiation within the context of a trade agreement. It also brings to the scene a new cast of players in terms of ministries with interests that are directly engaged, sub-federal levels of government with jurisdictions that are affected, and a broader and more diverse range of constituencies for which support, opposition, or indifference will be crucial to the outcome of negotiations. More importantly, positive rule-making intrudes deeply into domestic policy and raises critical issues of governance in terms of the power of democratic governments to control economic development and influence the distribution of its benefits across various groups in society. For example, the General Agreement on Trade in Services (GATS) prohibits an economic needs test as a condition for licensing service providers, thereby depriving national governments of the capacity to reserve certain economic activities for certain regions or groups or to control the number of service providers.

The fourth change is from negotiation to litigation as the principal currency of trade relations management. A trade agreement erected upon a set of self-denying ordinances produces a natural momentum toward negotiation as a means of managing trade relations. The source of trade relations problems will typically be the level of trade barriers maintained by a country that frustrates the export ambitions of its partners; the solution will be found in negotiations to reduce and eliminate such barriers. In contrast, a trade agreement erected upon positive rule making produces a natural momentum toward litigation because the source of problems lies not in trade barriers intended to protect domestic industry but in differences in the policies and practices of domestic regulation. In such litigation, the economic gains that flow from the trade-barrier reduction that may be employed to justify such reductions politically, such as lower prices to consumers, are more indirect and difficult to document. Economically and politically, the change to accommodate the interests of a partner presents itself as a loss and thus is only available through litigation.

Dispute Settlement

The controversy over dispute settlement, in particular the investor state procedures of NAFTA, crystallises the public debate over the international trade system. It arises in large measure because of the success of the dispute settlement systems in the WTO and NAFTA. Both systems emerged from a consensus that the largely informal ad hoc system of the GATT had outlived its usefulness and that the complexity of the global economy and the increasing scope and depth of international trade agreements required reinvigorated dispute settlement procedures. The result in the WTO has been a system that has generated some 234 notifications of complaints involving 180 distinct issues, of which only 51 to date have proceeded to adjudication.[7] In the first six years of NAFTA, from 1994 to 2000, the investor-state procedures generated 17 cases, of which five been concluded.[8] Many critics (Mann 2001) assert that dispute settlement, especially investor-state arbitration with its potential for monetary remedies, has a chilling effect on the making and administering of policy and regulation owing to the risk of challenge. Such critics ignore the fact that the purpose of trade agreement obligations enforced through dispute settlement is, indeed, to have a chilling effect on the capacity of governments to interfere with the flows of trade and investment.

A strong argument can be made that the public controversy over the NAFTA Chapter 11 rights of private foreign investors to arbitration of disputes arising out of alleged breaches of trade agreement obligations is largely misplaced. The key issue in the first major case, that of Ethyl Corporation against the Canadian ban on the gasoline additive methylcyclopentadienyl manganese tricarbonyl (known as MMT), was not the identity of the litigant or the procedure followed but the action taken by Canada on environmental grounds that could not be sustained. In the subsequent case of S.D. Myers, Inc., the principal judgement of the panel was that the Canadian government's ban on the cross-border movement of hazardous wastes constituted discrimination against a foreign investor in order to protect a domestic facility. Indeed, it could be argued that public controversy would have been more intense had the U.S. government, rather than a U.S. investor, challenged the Canadian government on the grounds that the U.S. would have then been attacking the environmental measures of another sovereign government.[9] The argument that the U.S. government would not have challenged Canada for fear of exposing its own practices is scarcely convincing in light of U.S. past practice that respects political pressures to launch cases more than embarrassing precedents in terms of its own practices.[10] Whether the U.S. government would have taken the case or not, it is indisputable that the absence of investor-state procedures would not, and in fact does not in the WTO, constitute an argument that governments should treat their international obligations with impunity.

The task of governments ought to be to ensure that the international obligations they undertake are consistent with sound public policy and not to look for ways to narrow the range of potential litigants. In this sense, it is highly appropriate that the Canadian government has taken the lead within NAFTA to seek clarification of certain substantive provisions of Chapter 11 in order to ensure that these provisions comply with the public interest.[11] Any attempt to narrow the rights of litigation of private parties would be marginal to the central policy issue.

Conclusion

A consequence of the nature of the global economy is a vertical loss of authority by national governments, downward to local authorities and upward to international rules and institutions in the WTO, regional agreements, as well as related institutions such as the International Monetary Fund (IMF) (Johnson 2001). Less commented upon but equally important is the endorsement by electorates in both industrialised and developing countries of the progressive deregulation and privatisation of the national economy and surrender of sovereign decision making over increasing areas of domestic governance. Although governments retain the full panoply of constitutional powers to recapture these losses of sovereignty and to reassert burdensome economic regulation, there is a virtual absence of political legitimacy for any such programme.

It is within this context that the consideration of environmental and social consequences of globalisation must take place. Such consideration needs to begin not with the alleged shortcomings of international trade agreements in these areas, but rather with an assessment of the existing rules and institutions of international governance. These are arguably less effective than the trade rules, but it cannot be asserted that they do not exist. Multilaterally in the United Nations, regionally in NAFTA, for example, and bilaterally in numerous Canada-U.S. environment agreements, there is a host of environmental agreements and institutions to govern state conduct. On social issues, the International Labour Organization (ILO) founded in 1919 has produced hundreds of conventions governing almost every aspect of labour conditions. In 1998, the ILO adopted the Declaration of Fundamental Principles and Rights at Work (ILO 2001), which made implementation of eight core conventions an obligation binding upon its members by virtual of membership in the organisation.[12]

Further progress to broaden and deepen international governance over environmental and social issues can obviously proceed only as fast as international consensus permits. The untimely and fundamentally flawed intervention of U.S. president Bill Clinton on the eve of the Seattle ministerial calling for the application of economic sanctions to address breaches of environmental and social rules poisoned an already difficult discussion between developed and developing countries on these issues. Developing countries contend, not without reason, that the pressure from industrialised countries for a consideration of environmental and social issues within the WTO is a guise for protectionism intended to deprive them of access to world markets. Creating the trust and confidence necessary to resolve such issues will not be easy. However, the reconstruction of the broad international consensus on the object and purpose of the international trade system requires an understanding of how to handle such issues. Without such an understanding, developed countries will be unwilling to engage on issues of importance to developing countries, and the environmental and social agenda will remain unfulfilled.

The question of whether it is necessary to integrate environmental and social issues into trade and investment agreements must be rephrased: How can the capacity of existing international governance in such areas be enhanced in order to acquire the status and authority of the trade and investment rules?

Notes

1 While the bilateral trade relationship with the United States is defined by the North American Free Trade Agreement (NAFTA), the major economic impacts were the result of the FTA. The economic impact of NAFTA is slight.
2 This is in contrast to those, such as Pierre Marc Johnson in Chapter 2 of this volume, who argue that the protests prevented the Green Room process from operating efficiently. Given the host of unresolved fundamental issues confronting ministers when they arrived in Seattle, the prospect of any agreement emerging from any process was exceedingly slight.
3 See, for example, paragraph 10 of the final communiqué at Genoa (G8 2001).
4 See also the Regional and Bilateral Agreements section of the Department of Foreign Affairs and International Trade's Web site at <www.dfait-maeci.gc.ca/tna-nac/reg-e.asp>.
5 This section draws on William Dymond and Michael Hart (2000).
6 The WTO beef hormone case is an example. Whatever the scientific justification of a ban on the imports of hormone containing meat, European public opinion is by all appearances solidly opposed (Glasgow 2001).
7 The WTO Web site contains information on dispute settlement proceedings and reports of the panels and Appellate Body findings on the cases adjudicated to date at <www.wto.org/english/tratop_e/dispu_e/dispu_e.htm>.
8 See Howard Mann (2001) for a summary of the cases, albeit from a critic's perspective.
9 Documentation on these and other Chapter 11 cases to which Canada is or has been a party can be found at <www.dfait-maeci.gc.ca/tna-nac/nafta-e.asp> (December 2001).
10 In the current as well as past countervailing duty cases against Canadian softwood lumber exports, the existence or otherwise of U.S. subsidies to its lumber industry plays no role in

the U.S. decision to initiate proceedings or in the manner in which those proceedings are conducted or eventually adjudicated through dispute settlement.

11 The first fruit of persistent efforts to persuade the U.S. and Mexico of the need for clarification was harvested with an agreement on enhanced transparency. See DFAIT (2001a).

12 See William Dymond (2001) for a discussion of the ILO declaration.

References

Department of Foreign Affairs and International Trade (Canada) (2001a). 'Pettigrew Welcomes NAFTA Commission's Initiatives to Clarify Chapter 11 Provisions'. News release 116, 1 August. <198.103.104.118/minpub/Publication.asp?FileSpec=/Min_Pub_Docs/104441.htm> (December 2001).

Department of Foreign Affairs and International Trade (Canada) (2001b). 'Trade Liberalization with European Union Could Bring Economic Gains'. News release 86, 21 June. <198.103.104.118/minpub/Publication.asp?FileSpec=/Min_Pub_Docs/104322.htm> (December 2001).

Dymond, William A. (1999). 'The MAI: A Sad and Meloncholy Tale'. In F. O. Hampson, M. Hart, and M. Rudner, eds., *A Big League Player? Canada among Nations 1999*, pp. 22–54. Oxford University Press, Toronto.

Dymond, William A. (2001). 'Core Labour Standards and the World Trade Organization: Love's Labour Lost'. *Canadian Foreign Policy* vol. 8, no. 3 (Spring), pp. 99–114.

Dymond, William A. and Michael Hart (2000). 'Post-Modern Trade Policy: Reflections on the Challenges to Multilateral Trade Negotiations after Seattle'. *Journal of World Trade* vol. 34, no. 3 (June), pp. 21–28.

G8 (2001). 'Communiqué'. 22 June, Genoa. <www.g7.utoronto.ca/g7/summit/2001genoa/finalcommunique.html> (December 2001).

Glasgow, Laurette (2001). Deputy Head of the Canadian Mission to the European Union. Interview with author, Brussels. September.

Hart, Michael (1998). *Fifty Years of Canadian Tradecraft: Canada at the GATT 1947–1997.* Centre for Trade Policy and Law, Ottawa.

International Labour Organization (2001). 'ILO Fundamental Declaration of Principles and Rights at Work'. <www.ilo.org/public/english/standards/decl/declaration/text/index.htm> (December 2001).

Johnson, Pierre Marc (2001). 'Creating Sustainable Global Governance'. In J. J. Kirton, J. P. Daniels and A. Freytag, eds., *Guiding Global Order: G8 Governance in the Twenty-First Century*, pp. 245–282. Ashgate, Aldershot.

Mann, Howard (2001). *Private Rights, Public Problems: A Guide to NAFTA's Controversial Chapter on Investors Rights.* International Institute on Sustainable Development and World Wildlife Fund, Winnipeg.

Rugman, Alan M. (1999). 'Negotiating Multilateral Rules to Promote Investment'. In M. R. Hodges, J. J. Kirton and J. P. Daniels, eds., *The G8's Role in the New Millennium*, pp. 143–157. Ashgate, Aldershot.

Scollay, Robert (2001). 'Regional Trade Negotiations in the Asia-Pacific Region: Assessment of Current Trends and Implications for the FTAA and the WTO'. Working paper prepared for the Inter-American Development Bank.

Chapter 4

Embedded Ecologism and Institutional Inequality: Linking Trade, Environment, and Social Cohesion in the G8

John J. Kirton[1]

Amidst the vibrant contemporary debate over globalisation, there are few elements that command such consensus among proponents and critics alike as the assumption that this multidimensional and contested process has at its core a foundational ideology of neoliberalism. This ideology is seen as having arisen during the turbulent 1970s, acquired policy dominance in the 1980s under the impact of Margaret Thatcher and Ronald Reagan, and achieved practical implementation in the 1990s as the end of the cold war and the triumph of free market ideals took hold. As it grew from an initial 'Ronald Thatcherism', through a policy-oriented 'Washington consensus' (Williamson 1993, 1990; Birdsall and de la Torre 2001), to a full-blown 'disciplinary neo-liberalism' (Gill 2000), it seems to have transformed and then replaced the prior ideological foundation of 'embedded liberalism' constructed by the victorious World War Two allies as the core of the institutionalised order created in 1945 (Ruggie 1983; Ikenberry 1998/99, 2001). That liberal order had combined external multilateral liberalisation of traded goods and trade finance with fixed but adjustable exchange rates, various forms of capital controls, and, above all, a large sphere for state intervention to achieve employment and broader social objectives in a protected national sphere. In its place has now allegedly come a celebration of internationally free markets for goods, services, direct and portfolio investment, and intellectual property, a celebration of the need for domestic privatisation and deregulation, and a celebration of the virtues of constricting the domestic role of the economic and social regulatory state. The new ideology and processes, it is charged, '[tend] to atomise human communities and [destroy] the integrity of the ecological structures that support all life', thereby generating a 'crisis of social reproduction on a world scale, a crisis that is ecological as well as social' (Gill 2000, 1).

Such an ideological revolution is seen as all the more powerful and permanent for having been institutionalised in the international organisations at the centre of the global political economy. The International Monetary Fund (IMF), once the guardian of embedded liberalism, has seen its preference for fixed and pegged exchange rates swept away, to be replaced in the late 1990s by an embrace of the virtues of market-driven floating, capital account liberalisation, and a routine prescription that countries receiving financial assistance must withdraw from state intervention in wide reaches of the economy long under government control. In the trade system, the exception-ridden rules of the old General Agreement on Tariffs and Trade (GATT) have been replaced, effective 1 January 1995, by those of the new World Trade Organization (WTO), featuring a single undertaking with wide-ranging disciplines on goods, services, investment, and intellectual property, an effective legalised dispute settlement mechanism, regular review of national trade policies, a more robust secretariat, built in processes of further liberalisation, and periodic ministerial oversight (Keohane, Moravcsik, and Slaughter 2000; Goldstein and Martin 2000). And at the centre of disciplinary neoliberalism is said to stand the G7 major industrial democracies, acting, along with the international financial institutions, in the 1980s and 1990s in a 'deliberate and strategic manner' (Gill 2000, 21; Gill 1999).

As the twentieth century passed into the twenty-first, however, this process of proliferating finance and trade liberalisation and the consensus on neoliberalism that fuelled it came under severe, sustained, and successful short-term attack. Here the major events were the defeat of the Multilateral Agreement on Investment (MAI) at the Organisation for Economic Co-operation and Development (OECD), the protests of 50 000 demonstrators on the streets of Seattle at the WTO's failed December 1999 ministerial meeting to launch the Millennium Round, and the equally energetic demonstrations at the United Nations Conference on Trade and Development (UNCTAD) in Bangkok, at the IMF meetings in Washington and Prague, and at the World Economic Forum in Davos in the following years, as well as the up to 200 000 protesters at the Genoa G8 Summit in July 2001.[2] This cadence of complaint and conflict showed that the faith in neoliberalism, or at least its incarnation in Anglo-American liberalism or the Washington consensus, was being assaulted, arrested, and even potentially abandoned. It was also being adjusted, as the leaders of both the IMF and WTO proclaimed their acceptance of the values of the protestors and proceeded with programs of often far-reaching institutional reform (Kaiser, Kirton, and Daniels 2000; Kirton, Daniels, and Freytag 2001).

Are the G7 and now G8 indeed at the deliberate and strategic centre of constructing and enforcing a so-called disciplinary neoliberalism and of mounting the necessary defences, in part by making the marginal adjustments to allow this ideology to continue amidst major systemic change and these new voices of dissent? Those who see such a major transformation in the reigning ideology of global governance are right to suspect that the G7 would lie at the heart of such change. It is, after all, at the G7 and its companion institution with Russia included, the G8, that the leaders and ranking ministers of the world's most powerful market democracies regularly assemble to deliberate, set new directions, and make decisions on a wide range of finance, trade, and social issues, to articulate new principled and normative visions of the interrelationship among these issues, and to implement their visions through instructions to and reforms of the established international organisations (Hajnal 1999). To be sure, some dismiss the G7/8 as a soft law institution of little consequence (Goldstein et al. 2000b, 2000a; Abbott et al. 2000) or as a body rendered ineffective by the post–cold-war globalisation of the 1990s (Bergsten and Henning 1996; Whyman 1995; Smyser 1993). Yet others have claimed that it has become an increasingly effective centre of global governance in the new era, for better (Kirton 1999; Bayne 1999) or for worse (Helleiner 2001; Gill 1999). Even those who see it more modestly as a lightly institutionalised caucus, or as a 'ginger group' for the rich and powerful, agree that the principles and norms it promulgates can have important governance effects (Hodges, Kirton, and Daniels 1999; Baker 2000).

Among those who regard the G7/8 as a consequential centre of global governance, the global financial crisis of 1997–99 and the succession of civil society protests aroused by subsequent efforts at liberalisation spawned a debate among three schools of thought. The first, 'conservative' reinforcement school suggested that the G7/8, in the face of crisis, had largely and properly maintained the new neoliberal emphasis and produced a market-friendly international institutional reform effort to reinforce a now contested core (Sally 2001; Freytag 2001; Donges and Tillman 2001; Theuringer 2001; Dluhosch 2001). The second, 'superficial adjustment' school, argued that the G7 and the IMF had, amidst compounding crisis, altered their rhetoric at the margin, while maintaining their longstanding neoliberal commitments (Gill 2000; Dallaire 2001; Thérien and Dallaire 1999). The third, 'responsive leadership' school, asserted that neither reinforced neoliberalism nor marginal adjustment but a genuine move to a new normative consensus on socially sustainable globalisation was what the 1997–99 crisis and the G7's effective global governance in response had brought (Kirton, Daniels, and Freytag 2001). None of these competing schools of thought, however, grounded its argument in a detailed examination of the core principles, norms, and commitments of the G7/8 in order to identify its seminal values, how those values might have changed in subsequent decades, and what new directions the 1997–99 crisis might have brought.

This chapter conducts such an examination. It surveys the principles and norms that the G7/8 has collectively articulated since its 1975 establishment in the key areas of trade, the environment, and social cohesion, to identify the priority it has assigned to each, the intersections it has identified among these realms, and the balance it has offered for the governance of this increasingly integrated domain. It concentrates on the content and strength of the G7/8's initial consensus, when and how that consensus might have eroded, and when and how a new consensus might have emerged. On that basis, it suggests, largely inductively, the sources of such ideological consensus and change that may have occurred. In particular, it identifies moves toward or away from the articulation of a normative order based on the sustainable development ideal in which trade liberalisation, environmental enhancement, and social cohesion are tightly integrated, equally balanced, and mutually supportive. In creating such a combination, such moves generate a foundation for what might be termed a modern 'embedded ecologism' that reinforces and extends the 'embedded liberalism' of old.

This focus on the normative order that governs the trade-environment-social cohesion interface is justified on several grounds. Most generally, it is in the trade realm where the liberalisation justified by embedded liberalism began, and where in the 1990s the new WTO extended liberalisation to a degree even beyond that which the IMF proved able to accomplish for finance. Second, it was the demand for social and employment protection, grounded in full and stable employment and welfare programs, that justified the claim for nation-state intervention and control of capital accounts by the consensus of embedded liberalism in 1945 and by the civil society protesters at present. Third, one of the important reasons for the 1999 failure to launch the Millennium Round and for the strength of subsequent protests was the demand of environmentalists that the new trading system take far greater account than did the old GATT and new WTO of the environmental and social impacts of the system, and of the way in which trade liberalisation could serve as a proactive instrument of ecological enhancement, social cohesion, and sustainable development on a global scale. And, finally, since its start the G7/8 has always dealt with trade, employment, and environmental issues (broadly defined to include energy) as part of its core agenda (Kirton 1989, 1990; Kirton and Richardson 1995; Bayne 2001). It secured high compliance by member countries with the trade and environment energy commitments it reached (von Furstenberg and Daniels 1991; Kokotsis 1999; Juricevic 2000). At the same time, the G7/8 remains a 'hard case' for finding the emergence of a new normative order in which trade liberalisation, environmental enhancement, and social cohesion are tightly integrated, equally balanced, and mutually supportive, given the G7's apparent creation as an economic summit, its alleged dominance by the U.S. and its leadership (Putnam and Bayne 1987), its creation of a ministerial forum for trade liberalisation (in 1981) long before that for the environment (in 1992–94), and its status as the bastion of neoliberalism in the judgement of its critics (Gill 1999).[3]

This analysis reveals that since its 1975 inception, the G7/8 has developed progressively and has regularly asserted a doctrine of embedded ecologism.[4] This doctrine has defended the employment and social welfare values at the core of the 1945 consensus on embedded liberalism, while reinforcing them with a new array of ecological values, totally absent in 1945, that the G7/8 has integrated into the employment and trade spheres in protective and proactive ways. In its fully developed form, the doctrine of embedded ecologism asserts that employment and social cohesion, and the democratic practices and polities they sustain, are fundamental to the G7/8's mission, that environmental protection as well as trade liberalisation foster such objectives, and that trade liberalisation should take place only insofar as it protects and promotes environmental and labour values.[5] External liberalisation is thus bounded both by domestic and global welfare and ecological concerns.

Although the elements of embedded ecologism were evident at the G7 Summit's outset, the effort to elaborate the edifice encountered two major challenges. First, during its first quarter century, the G7 adopted a conception of trade liberalisation that was far more aggressively far reaching than that of 1945 and 1975, and added investment and finance (if not capital account) liberalisation to it; it entrenched its new conception in the powerful institution of the WTO that it did much to create. Second, prompted by the OECD, during the 1980s the G7 turned from a macroeconomic trade- and growth-based conception of employment to one privileging market-oriented structural policies. In both cases, the weight of these economic and trade-focussed international organisations generated an institutional imbalance in the G7's evolving consensus of embedded ecologism in ways that assigned a subordinate place to ecological and social values. Yet at the start of its fourth seven-year cycle in 1996, in advance of the 1997–99 global financial crisis and the 1999 civil society assaults on trade, investment, and finance liberalisation, the G7 moved to address the challenges of globalisation and restore the balance of earlier years. This task proved to be easier in the trade-labour realm, where the G7/8 could readily mandate the WTO to work with the International Labour Organization (ILO) to extend and implement the principles struck by the G7. In the trade-environment realm, however, the G7 was left to affirm the principles of equality and integration, and cast increasing doubt on the WTO's record in realising them, without moving to address the more fundamental institutional imbalance created by the absence of a world environmental organisation.

Affirming the Trilogy: The Rambouillet Foundation, 1975

For an apparently economic summit focussed on replacing the international finance regime that had died at U.S. hands on 15 August 1971, at the first gathering at Rambouillet, France, in November 1975 the G7 gave considerable and prominent attention to trade, social, and environmental matters in its brief, but seminal, concluding communiqué.[6] What might be considered the 'Rambouillet Charter' of the G7 opened with the statement that the institution's ultimate concern was with the 'human, social and political implications' of 'economic problems common to our countries' (G7 1975). It declared: 'We are each responsible for the government of an open, democratic society, dedicated to individual liberty and social advancement.' It pledged 'to reduce the waste of human resources involved in unemployment', to make 'new efforts in the areas of world trade', and to 'avoid resorting to measures by which they could try to solve their problems at the expense of others, with damaging consequences in the economic, social and political fields'. It also promised 'to reduce our dependence on imported energy through conservation and the development of alternative sources'.

It is noteworthy that social concerns were identified as the overriding value and were the first to be listed among the trade-environment-society trilogy. In this social realm, social advancement joined individual liberty as the two ultimate values. Society was thus viewed and valued as a collectivity that was more than an amalgam of competing individuals each pursuing his or her own self-interest. The first identified challenge to social advancement was unemployment, portrayed as a social problem arising from poor overall growth. Trade arose as a defensive concern directed elsewhere, with the emphasis on combating protectionism and on its direct negative social consequences in foreign societies. Furthermore, it is striking that an environmental value was included from the start. It was, however, the traditional, narrow one of conservation, portrayed as an instrument rather than a value in its own right and given equal weight to development of alternative sources in a communiqué that celebrated growth. Moreover, it was not directly linked to the trade or the social domains.

Thus at the start the G7 set social advancement as well as individual liberty as its two overarching values, saw trade as fostering the social cohesion that would be damaged by the unemployment bred by protectionism, and considered energy conservation as an instrumental priority in its effort to restore economic growth. All three values — social cohesion, trade liberalisation, and environmental protection — were there from the very start, with social cohesion occupying the top spot, and the trade-employment-social cohesion link clearly drawn.

Forging the Trade-Environment Link: The First Cycle, 1975–1981

During the next several years, this seminal set of principles was reaffirmed and reinforced. Unemployment remained the major problem identified by the summit, although inflation had a large and increasingly equal place. The solution to the unemployment problem lay in non-inflationary growth and trade, which came again by resisting protectionism and increasingly now by launching new trade liberalisation negotiations and opening markets. Environment, first as resource conservation and then as environmental protection in the energy sector, remained a value. And, in 1979, ecological values were linked directly and positively to the trade domain (see Appendix 4-A).

Thus, 1977 saw unemployment labelled the most urgent problem, with youth unemployment singled out for special concern (G7 1977). In 1978, the communiqué noted that unemployment 'hits hardest at the most vulnerable section of the population' and that 'its economic cost is high and its human cost higher still' (G7 1978). The 1979 'oil shock' summit asserted that energy price increases would lead to more unemployment (G7 1979), while 1980 declared that increasing employment to be the goal (G7 1980). In 1981, the communiqué said reducing unemployment along with inflation was the highest priority (G7 1981). But, in a preview of the 1980s, the 1981 Summit — Ronald Reagan's first and Margaret Thatcher's third — also signalled that the answer lay primarily not in growth alone but in higher investment and domestic structural change.

During this phase broader social concerns appeared regularly. The 1976 communiqué called for 'partnership among all groups within our societies' (G7 1976), while that of 1977 spoke of the 'continuing strength of our societies and the proven democratic values that give them vitality' (G7 1977). In 1978, the declaration declared a determination to use social policy to help sectors in difficulty (G7 1978). In 1979, it stated that oil price increases had very serious social consequences and would endanger stability (G7 1979). In 1980, it affirmed the 'ability of our democratic societies, based on individual freedom and social solidarity' to meet the challenges they faced and called for 'continuing dialogue among the social partners' (G7 1980).

During these years, the emphasis on trade expanded from defensively combating protectionism to offensively securing greater liberalisation of trade and then capital. The initial pledge against protectionism moved to ever more detailed promises to 'avoid the imposition of new trade barriers' (G7 1976), to stand still and roll back, and to strengthen the multilateral trade system, while stating directly that protectionism would cause unemployment (G7 1977). By 1979, it began to extend its vision, calling for the 'removal of impediments to the international flow of trade and capital' (G7 1979). The G7 also became increasingly specific and ambitious in calling for the conclusion of the Tokyo Round, and by 1981 in calling for the ministerial conference that would lead to the launch of a new round.

Yet the environment was the area where the greatest expansion took place. While the topic disappeared briefly from the 1976 communiqué, by 1977 energy conservation had returned. By Bonn 1978, the approval of energy efficiency and renewables was accompanied by the first appearance of the environment itself in the generic pledge: 'In energy development, the environment and human safety must be safeguarded with greatest care' (G7 1978). By 1979, in response to the second oil shock, the G7 reaffirmed the value of energy conservation; it also offered its first trade-environment norm in its pledge 'to increase as far as possible coal use, production, and trade, without damage to the environment' (G7 1979). This linkage, while affirming the connection and value of the environment to trade, was still specific to the coal sector, reactive, protective, and unbalanced, in that it allowed trade to expand if it could be done while holding environmental quality constant.

This link was then joined by a proactive, preventive one that was surprisingly prescient in regard to the future issue of climate change. It read: 'We need to expand alternative sources of energy, especially those which will help to prevent further pollution, particularly increases of carbon dioxide and sulphur oxides in the atmosphere' (G7 1979). In 1980 the G7 added building standards, fuel-efficient vehicles, standards for automobile fuel efficiency, and public transport as desirable measures. And 1981 culminated with the expansive economy-wide, if protective, vision: 'In shaping our longterm economic policies, care should be taken to preserve the environment and the resource base of our planet' (G7 1981). Thus, by the end of its first cycle, the G7 had forged the trade-environment link, accorded protective equality to the environment, called for a preventive approach, singled out central issues, specified microeconomic, sector-specific measures, and made environmental preservation integral to economic development as a whole.

Trade for Environment: The Second Cycle, 1982–1988

The second summit cycle, from 1982 to 1988, saw unemployment move from a macroeconomic to a market-oriented microeconomic issue, and a broader and deeper emphasis on trade liberalisation arise. Yet it also saw, after an early downgrade, a major expansion of ecological values by the cycle's end. The first two elements of this shift are consistent with the advent of a new neoliberal consensus rather than embedded liberal one, as first Margaret Thatcher and then Ronald Reagan acquired prominence within the G7. However, even here social values continued to be affirmed in a body in which the continental European socialists of Germany's Helmut Schmidt and France's François Mitterrand were influential. Moreover, environmental values proliferated in breadth and depth as Germany's Helmut Kohl and Canada's Brian Mulroney entered in 1983 and 1985 respectively, and the otherwise much maligned Bonn 1985 Summit proved to be a watershed. Finally, by 1987–88 the trade-environment link was established in ways that protected environmental and other social values as comprehensive trade liberalisation proceeded, and in ways that mobilised trade and investment liberalisation and technology transfer as instruments for environmental goals. The North American Free Trade Agreement (NAFTA) principle of 'trade for the environment' was thus introduced.[7] Even as the 1988 Toronto Summit recognised the 'globalization' of markets, it endorsed the concept of sustainable development and declared that trade liberalisation should assist in the achievement of a broad range of social and environmental goals (G7 1988).

In the social domain, the 1982 Summit, hosted by Mitterrand, began with the declaration that full employment was the objective, and added preserving the 'cultural heritage of our peoples' as a further goal (G7 1982). Williamsburg in 1983 highlighted youth unemployment and cultural development and introduced labour market policies as a way of creating employment (G7 1983). In 1984, London elaborated a wide range of measures for the latter, including facilitating the mobility of labour and capital (G7 1984). At Bonn in 1985, the declaration began by proclaiming the goals of increasing job opportunities and reducing social inequalities, while adding higher employment, 'maintaining appropriate social policies for those in need', and creating new, permanent jobs especially for the young and combating social inequality (G7 1985). Tokyo in 1986 noted, in a curious reversal, that high unemployment could impair growth and called in response for a full range of structural adjustment policies, high technology, small business promotion, and a strengthening of market-oriented incentives for employment (G7 1986). At Venice in 1987, the G7 continued the emphasis on employment and structural adaptation, specifying measures such as the functioning of international financial markets for the latter (G7 1987). In 1988, the communiqué added that structural reforms would continue 'while mitigating adverse effects on social groups' (G7 1988).

In the trade field, the G7 began its second cycle with ambitious objectives, reinforced by the Quadrilateral Trade Ministers forum created by the leaders at the G7 Summit in 1981. The 1982 leaders' communiqué began by asserting that the growth of world trade was a necessary element for growth and the employment and stability they would bring, that freer flows of trade and capital would create them, and that trade in new technologies was desirable (G7 1982). In 1983, the communiqué spoke of expanding trade with developing countries, while 1984 asked reciprocally for developed countries to open their markets to developing countries and for an early decision on a new negotiating round (G7 1983, 1984). The communiqué in 1985 began with an overall goal of halting protectionism, declared open multilateral trade essential, and called for an early and substantial reduction of barriers to trade, a growth in exports, and a more balanced expansion of international trade (G7 1985). In 1986, the communiqué asked for an early launch of a new round, specified that it should include services, intellectual property, and foreign direct investment (FDI), and demanded action on agriculture, while recognising 'the importance of agriculture to the wellbeing of rural communities' (G7 1986). The 1987 communiqué called for improvements to the functioning of the GATT, an appeal emphasised even more strongly in 1988 and one that eventually led to the birth of the WTO (G7 1987).

In the field of environment, the G7 started slowly. The 1982 communiqué spoke only in passing of the need to economize on energy (G7 1982); 1983 endorsed energy conservation and added: 'We have agreed to strengthen cooperation in protection of the environment, in better use of natural resources' (G7 1983). In 1984, the communiqué recognised 'the international dimension of environmental problems and the role of environmental factors in economic development' (G7 1984). It asked for a working group to identify the need for research on the air, water, and ground media, and relevant industrial co-operation.

The year 1985 marked a watershed. The German-hosted G7 Summit placed 'the preservation of natural resources' in an equal first place with 'the future of the world economy' as the ultimate responsibility of the G7 (G7 1985). It declared essential new approaches 'to anticipate and prevent damage to the environment', added the problems of acid deposition, climactic change, soils, fresh water, and the seas (particularly regional seas), and promised that 'We shall develop and apply the "polluter pays" principle more widely'. It also called for measurement, co-operation with developing countries, and co-operation among G7 environment ministers *within* existing international bodies, especially the OECD. There was, notably, no environmental parallel to the 1987 and 1988 calls for strengthening the functioning of the GATT. In 1986, the environment was confined to a single paragraph that added nothing new (G7 1986). Yet the 1987 G7 called on the United Nations Environment Programme (UNEP) for action on measurement (but not trade), and added endangered species and tropical forests as key concerns (G7 1987).

Most importantly, the 1987 Venice Summit added two direct trade-environment principles — the first since the fragile 1979 beginning. The first read: 'The long-term objective is to allow market signals to influence the orientation of agricultural production, by way of a progressive and concerted reduction of agricultural support, as well as by all other appropriate means, giving consideration to social and other concerns, such as food security, environmental protection and overall employment' (G7 1987). The second pledged: 'We also intend to examine further environmental issues such as ... promotion of international trade in low-pollution products, low-polluting industrial plants and other environmental protection technologies'. Toronto in 1988 reaffirmed and reversed the causal flow of the connection in the agriculture field, putting the ecological and social objectives at the top. The declaration read: 'More market-oriented agricultural policies should assist in the achievement of important objectives such as preserving rural areas and family farming, raising quality standards and protecting the environment' (G7 1988). It added that in doing so 'ways should be developed to take account of food security and social concerns'.

Thus by the time the second cycle ended, and the age of more comprehensive, globalisation-driven trade and investment liberalisation and market-oriented employment policies began, the essential elements of embedded ecologism had been firmly put in place. The trade-environment-social cohesion link had been directly and comprehensively forged, in the broad and important domain of agriculture. It was recognised that employment and a wide range of social values (from cultural diversity to family farming) were central, would be affected by, and must be protected or compensated in trade liberalisation and the move to market-oriented labour policies. The same was true for the environment (including food security). Moreover liberalisation, in agriculture and in trade, investment, and technology more generally, was called upon to be a proactive instrument for the fulfilment of ecological objectives. The principle of using trade liberalisation for the higher goal of environmental enhancement had arrived.

Completing the Triangle and Institutionalising Imbalance:
The Third Cycle, 1989–1995

These principles provided a foundation for a major expansion and deepening of the G7's concern with trade, employment, social, and environmental values during its third cycle. During this time all three component areas saw a large increase in their range, detail, and ambition. Moreover, the summit began regularly to generate a set of direct trade-environment and employment-environment linkages, which, when joined with the earlier trade-employment linkage, completed the integrated triangular conception. Indeed, by the end of the cycle, the G7 had directly linked all three values together. And while the third cycle witnessed an increase in the G7's liberalisation demands, employment — now joined by environmental integrity — assumed pride of place.

The third cycle also saw an important transformation at its end, especially in the trade-environment domain, for the evolving cadence of affirming ever tighter, more balanced, and reciprocal relationships among trade-environment and trade-labour was broken in 1994. That year, the G7 chose the old OECD and the new WTO as the bodies to develop and operationalise the connections. In 1995, as the WTO began its first year of operation, the G7 explicitly mandated continued trade liberalisation as the overriding parameter for the trade-environment and trade-labour balances being struck.

The 1989 Paris Summit, the greenest in G7 history, began by affirming the urgent need to create jobs, promote social justice, and protect the environment. It also forged the first direct environment–social cohesion link, by declaring: 'Such environmental degradation endangers species and undermines the well-being of individuals and societies' (G7 1989). Indeed, it recognised the G7's responsibilities for social protection by pledging co-operation to preserve a 'healthy and balanced global environment in order to meet shared economic and social objectives and to carry out obligations to future generations'. It also added the most comprehensive, far-reaching, and balanced trade-environment link to date, stating: 'Environmental protection is integral to issues such as trade, development, energy, transport, agriculture, and economic planning. Therefore, environmental considerations must be taken into account in economic decision-making. In fact good economic policies and good environmental policies are mutually reinforcing'.

The 1990 Houston Summit opened by affirming the trilogy of a 'skilled and motivated labor force whose fundamental rights are protected', an 'open system of international trade and payments', and 'an environment safeguarded for future generations' (G7 1990). However, it only noted the social and not environmental impacts of agricultural trade liberalisation, and dealt only indirectly with trade-environment links, through its endorsement of voluntary environmental labelling.

London 1991, however, forged a direct, broad, and now operational link. At the regional level, it offered integration and balance by asking for a new European energy charter 'to promote free and undistorted energy trade' and 'to protect the environment' (G7 1991). Yet multilaterally, when it offered in its trade section a second trade-for-environment precept, it began the process of reinforcing institutional imbalance by investing responsibility for elaborating the trade-environment link in the economic and trade institutions alone. It stated: 'Open markets help to create the resources needed to protect the environment. We therefore commend the OECD's pioneering work in ensuring that trade and environment policies are mutually supporting. We look to the General

Agreement on Tariffs and Trade (GATT) to define how trade measures can properly be used for environmental purposes'. A new balance was thus struck in the growth-mediated, 'trickle down' linkage and in investing the responsibility for forging the link analytically to an economic organisation and operationally to an trade organisation, with no recognition that any environmental institution should play a role.

The 1992 Munich Summit said nothing about trade-environment or environment-employment linkages. This was perhaps in part because the United Nations Conference on Environment and Development (UNCED) in Rio was trusted to deal with the issue. It may also have arisen from the fact that the G7 had assigned the issue to the OECD and WTO the previous year, and because environmental issues were treated by the G7's first ever meeting of ministers of the environment, held in the spring. Yet 1993 opened with the now traditional trilogy of jobs, trade, and the environment as defining values, and stated that an open multilateral trading system was good for employment. It also forged two employment-environment links. It declared international co-operation on the environment and environmental policies should offer opportunities for employment. On trade and environment, vis-à-vis developing countries, it stated 'To this end, we will pursue a comprehensive approach, covering not only aid but also trade [and] investment ... and taking environmental aspects into account' (G7 1993).

The 1994 Naples Summit brought all three relationships together. It asked that structural employment policies protect the environment, and created the employment-environment link by declaring: 'Environmental policies can contribute to employment' (G7 1994). In the first passage combining all three values in parallel, it again affirmed — this time more strongly — its faith in the GATT/WTO to forge by itself both the trade-environment and now trade-labour links. It stated: 'We welcome the work on the relation between trade and environment in the new WTO. We call for intensified efforts to improve our understanding of new issues including employment and labour standards and their implications for trade policies.'

This trend toward the WTO capturing the responsibility for implementing the trade-environment and trade-labour links was reinforced a year later. Halifax 1995 reaffirmed that environmental protection as well as trade created long-term employment. Yet the shift to a trade-first approach was apparent in its statement that: 'Consistent with the goal of continued trade liberalization, we will pursue work on ... trade and environment to ensure that rules and policies in these different areas are compatible' (G7 1995). Continuing trade liberalisation was now added as the parameter within which all linkage efforts must take place.

Restoring the Balance: The Fourth, 'Globalization' Cycle, 1996–Present

The fourth summit cycle, starting in 1996, unfolded amidst the process of, and anxieties about, globalisation. Globalisation formed the major thematic preoccupation of the

G7/8 itself, and subsequently bred a focus on the Asian-turned-global financial crisis of 1997–99 and its accompanying social trauma. The fourth cycle also saw the full incorporation of the Russians into the new G8 forum, to which the G7's environment agenda migrated. It further witnessed the deepening and broadening of the new generation of domestic ministerial G7/8 fora that had begun with employment and the environment in 1994. During this time, the G7 embraced globalisation, social cohesion, and sustainable development with equal ardour. The G7's embedded ecologism, only recently subject to institutionalised trade capture, was quickly restored and extended, first normatively within the G7 and subsequently institutionally in the centres preferred by the G8. In a rare display of the G7/8's prescience and proactiveness, the shift took place from the start, before the global financial crisis arrived.

The 1996 Lyon Summit began with a celebration of how globalisation offered the benefits of 'an unprecedented expansion of investment and trade' and the 'proliferation of skilled jobs' (G7 1996). It also underscored the need to ensure more and better jobs as well as the sustainability of members' social security systems, and to 'prevent and fight against social exclusion'. It recognised the need to address 'the relationship between trade and internationally recognized core labour standards' and to promote these and the protection of the environment in its relations with developing countries. In the trade-environment field, it restored an earlier balance and added a challenge to the WTO:

> Global liberalization of trade and a high level of environmental protection should be mutually supportive. It will be important, for example, to ensure that WTO rules and multilateral environmental agreements and ecolabelling programs are complementary. The Singapore Ministerial Conference of the WTO will be an important opportunity to demonstrate the ability and willingness to integrate environmental protection and thus sustainable development concerns into the multilateral trading system (G7 1996).

The year 1997 saw sustainable development restored to the list of defining values, the concern with social inclusion continued, and a demand for the full integration of environment, economic, and social policies added. It affirmed the value of food security and the need to harness the information revolution for sustainable development in Africa, to protect vulnerable groups, and to prevent social conflict. It added a new trade-environment commitment that moved into the realm of finance, while maintaining the G7's faith in the OECD. Under the heading 'Environmental Standards for Export Credit Agencies', the communiqué stated:

> Private sector financial flows from industrial nations have a significant impact on sustainable development worldwide. Governments should help promote sustainable practices by taking environmental factors into account when providing financing support for investment in infrastructure and equipment. We attach importance to the work on this in the OECD, and 'will review progress at our meeting next year' (G7 1997).

The communiqué from the 1998 Summit opened with the trilogy of safeguarding the environment, trade liberalisation, and 'combating social exclusion' (G8 1998). It called for inclusion throughout the world and to this end approved the implementation of core labour standards and the continued collaboration between ILO and WTO secretariats, in accordance with the proposals of both organisations. While striking an institutional balance in the trade-labour realm, it forged no new trade-environment links, perhaps in part because its easy trade-labour formula was not institutionally available in the trade-environment realm.

The 1999 Summit saw a major expansion of trade-environment linkages, as part of its creation of a new 'Cologne consensus' on socially sustainable globalisation (Kirton, Daniels, and Freytag 2001). It emphasised the value of social inclusion and the need to 'provide social safety nets that support employment' (G8 1999). Moreover, for the first time ever, it produced a section on 'Strengthening Social Safeguards', in which it declared that 'social security policies, including social safety nets, must be strong enough to encourage and enable individuals to embrace global change and liberalization and to improve their chances on the labor market, while enhancing social cohesion'. It thus made the social dimension a necessary foundation in order for the liberalisation project to continue, and declared the enhancement of social cohesion to be a new and proactive goal. It further stated that respect for 'core labor standards are further indispensable prerequisites for social stability' and stressed the importance of co-operation between the WTO and the ILO on the social dimensions of globalisation and trade liberalisation.

In the trade-environment realm, the 1999 Summit was similarly far reaching. It established four trade-environment principles or commitments, in both the environmental and trade sections of the communiqué. It set a deadline for the completion of the OECD export financing work. More importantly, it signalled a loss of confidence in the WTO efforts to date and expanded the *problèmatique* to include social welfare. It stated: 'We will also seek a more effective way within the WTO for addressing the trade and environment relationship and promoting sustainable development and social and economic welfare worldwide' (G8 1999). Moreover, it moved beyond the WTO alone as the institutional forum for the linkage effort by urging 'greater cooperation and policy coherence among international financial, economic and labour organizations'. Most ambitiously and broadly, it declared 'environmental considerations should be taken fully into account in the upcoming round of WTO negotiations. This should include a clarification of the relationship between both multilateral environmental agreements and key environmental principles, and WTO rules'. It was now key environmental principles (left unspecified) rather than specific provisions that had to be fully taken into account in a revised WTO.

By 2000, after the global financial crisis had ended, and as the summit hosting moved to Japan, the new Cologne consensus remained. Amidst a general emphasis on strengthening social safety nets, the Okinawa Summit offered three trade-labour/social linkages. It again asked for effective WTO-ILO co-operation on the social dimension of globalisation and trade liberalisation, and offered more open markets to developing countries with sound social policies, while affirming that the multilateral trade system had brought social progress.

In the trade-environment domain, Okinawa drew three links. It endorsed the OECD work on export credit policies, broadened it to involve the multilateral development banks, and reaffirmed the commitment to develop common environmental guidelines. It promised to combat illegal logging as part of a sustainable forest management approach. Most broadly, it declared that among the objectives of its desired new round of multilateral trade negotiations would be to 'ensure that trade and social policies, and trade and environment policies are compatible and mutually supportive' (G8 2000). The need for integration, equality, and mutual support in both domains had been accepted.

The 2001 Genoa Summit increased and expanded this trade-environment commitment. Early pledges that trade and environment should be mutually supportive and that the environment should be taken fully into account in the next trade round were transformed into an obligation to 'ensure that the new Round supports sustainable development' (G7 2001). For the first time, it included the pledge that 'WTO should continue to respond to the legitimate expectations of civil society'. And it mobilised a new instrument in the integrative task by calling on the 'MDBs [multilateral development banks] to provide support for global public goods, such as fighting infectious diseases, facilitating trade, fostering financial stability and protecting the environment'.

Conclusion: Causes of Normative Continuity and Change

What accounts for the relative continuity and progressive elaboration of the doctrine of embedded ecologism in the G7/8, for the adjustments in response to the ambitious trade liberalisation and market-oriented labour market policies of the 1980s, and for the move from 1996 onward to a deeper and broader consensus on socially sustainable globalisation? Although no conclusive answers can be offered from this analysis, some suggestions based on an inductive foundation can be offered.

The continuity can be attributed to the close connection between employment and social cohesion and the common democratic principle at the heart of the G7/8, and to the character of the forum as one directly delivered by popularly elected leaders uniquely sensitive to the concerns of their publics, and, in the foundational years of the first generation of leaders, to the memories of the depression and the inflation that had brought Hitler to power and led to the tragedy of the World War Two. These features of the concert equality model of summit co-operation (Kirton and Daniels 1999) are reinforced by the fact that several member countries, rather than just the

U.S., contributed to building the edifice of embedded ecologism during the years when they hosted the summit.

At the same time, no single country or leader hosting more than one summit proved to be consistent, either in advancing the consensus or in mounting the two counter-assaults that eroded it for a time. Germany was active in 1985 and 1999, Italy in 1987, and Canada in 1988; yet each failed to maintain the momentum of trade-environment leadership in, respectively, 1992, 1994, and 1995. And the arrival of neither Margaret Thatcher nor Ronald Reagan adequately accounts for the beginning of the aggressive trade liberalisation and market-oriented labour policies.

Nor is the prevalence of a common political orientation a convincing explanation. The major exception is the dominance of socialist and liberal governments in the late 1990s. This, together with the hosting of the 1999 Summit by Germany's red-green coalition, had some impact in generating the Cologne consensus on socially sensitive globalisation that year.

Crisis, broadly conceived, offers only a limited explanation. The second oil shock of 1979 did contribute to a trade-environment linkage, but the recessions of 1981–82 and 1990–91 did not. Indeed, the first began a move to market-oriented labour policies, and the second a move toward a privileging of trade liberalisation. Most important, the move toward restoring and enriching embedded ecologism as part of the focus on globalisation began in 1996, two years before the 1997–99 global financial crisis struck. And while the Mexican financial/economic meltdown of 1994–95 constituted a crisis for the United States and Canada, it did not for the other members of the G7.

A more promising explanation lies in the broader arena of international institutions within which the G7 operates, and in the imbalances favouring economics and trade in this domain. In particular, the analytic work of the OECD (Bernstein 2000) and the operational efforts of the WTO, organisations founded and dominated by the G7, skewed the work of a G7 with no comparable capacity of its own. Indeed, the failure of the UNCED in 1992 to produce an environmental organisation of comparable stature to that established by the WTO in 1995 fuelled the imbalance of the early and mid 1990s, until the WTO's failure to strike an balance that accorded with the G7's carefully constructed principles of embedded ecologism became clear. Even then, the presence of the ILO in the broader multilateral community made it easier for the G7 to find a way to restore the desired balance in the social domain.

The causal consequence of institutional imbalance is evident within the G7/8's own institutional structure as well. Here the weight of the Quadrilateral Trade Ministers forum established in 1981 and meeting several times a year, compared to an environmental ministers forum created in 1992 but institutionalised only in 1994 and meeting only once a year, provided an institutional imbalance from the start. An analysis of the trade-environment provisions of the G7/8 environment ministers forum, listed in Appendix 4-B, confirms the activism of the latter institution in forging the trade-environment link.[8] Its trade-environment passages centre on recommendations for the WTO to incorporate environmental concerns more fully within its trade liberalisation framework. The 1996 and 1999 G7 environment ministerials, preceding the major international negotiations of the Kyoto Protocol on Climate Change and the Seattle WTO meetings respectively, contain the most extensive and robust statements linking trade and environment. More broadly, from 1994 to 1999 the summit communiqués promoted the principles of trade liberalisation and environmental protection as intrinsically interlinked and mutually beneficial. After successive communiqués firmly established this relationship, in 1999 the environment ministers proceeded to promote specific policy recommendations, notably the relationship between multilateral environmental agreements (MEAs) and WTO rules, and a closer relationship between the WTO and other environmental entities such as the UNEP. The 1999 environment ministerial also declared for the first time that states should be able to implement health and environment standards stronger than international standards without discrimination. From 1999 on, the communiqués also showed an increased awareness of the concept of, and concomitant need for, sustainable development in the developing world. As a remedy, the 1999 and 2000 communiqués supported increased capacity building on trade and environment issues in developing countries. The 2001 ministerial most explicitly expanded the trade-environment paradigm into a sustainable development triad, maximising the synergies among trade, environment, and social cohesion in the next round of WTO liberalisation negotiations.

The model of democratic institutionalism has long argued that the presence of strong institutions in the G7/8 system and in the broader multilateral community (under G7/8 control) generates compliance among G7/8 members with their collective G7 commitments (Kirton and Daniels 1999; Kokotsis 1999). This analysis suggests that such G7/8 institutions may well be equally consequential in determining the content of those commitments, and the principles and norms that guide them. Strong G7/8 institutions may be important not only in faithfully implementing G7/8 leaders' concrete commitments, but also in catalysing and constructing them, as well as the broader principles and epistemes on which they rest and those that come to predominate in the international community as a whole.

Notes

1   This chapter is based in part on a paper prepared for a panel on 'New Directions in Global Trade Governance: Competition, Consensus, and Coherence' at the annual meeting of the International Studies Association in Chicago 20–24 February 2001. The author gratefully acknowledges the comments of Jeffrey Hart, the research assistance of Anju Aggarwal and Vanita Goela, and the financial support of the Social Sciences and Humanities Research Council of Canada through the project on 'Strengthening Canada's Environmental Community through International Regime Reform' (the EnviReform project).

2   The G7 major industrial democracies was founded in 1975 as an annual institutionalised summit of the leaders of the United States, Japan, Germany, France, Britain, and Italy, with Canada joining physically in 1976, and the European Union starting to attend in 1977. In 1997, the 'Denver Summit of the Eight' added Russia as a virtually full member, a move rendered permanent through the creation of the institutionalised 'G8' in 1998. The G7 continues to meet separately and issue a distinct declaration, usually just in advance of the full G8 meeting at the annual summit, thus creating a G7/8 system.

3   This analysis, focussed on the G7/8 and the incorporation of ecological and social values into its economic 'norm complex', is thus the empirical opposite of those who focus on global environmental institutions and norms and the emergence of a 'compromise of liberal environmentalism' (Bernstein 2000, 2001). It is an easy case to make only in the sense that as an institution not bound by an international law-encoded charter and delivered by national leaders, it has flexibility in setting new normative directions that the 1945 generation of charter-constrained and bureaucratically based international organisations lack. This flexibility, however, can be exercised equally easily in any of the three ways the competing schools of thought suggest.

4   This is not to suggest that the G7 was created as an institution with an ecological purpose as conceived today or at the time of the 1972 Stockholm Conference. Indeed, its initial treatment of the environment was in the context of the energy crisis that helped catalyse its creation. The G7 was, however, centrally created to combat the 'crisis of governability', and thus the social challenge that lay at the core of this crisis.

5   Among the rich array of multiple meanings ascribed to the term 'social cohesion', in this analysis it is used in three, increasingly expansive ways. Most narrowly, it is equated with labour and the principle that 'labour', along with 'land' (the natural ecology across all ambient media) should be accorded equal value to 'capital' (the third factor of production) in government policies and welfare outcomes. Secondly, it refers to the presence within a polity of strong social capital (Putnam, Leonardi, and Nanetti 1993), sufficient to offset atomisation (Kornhauser 1966) and the crisis of reproduction generated by globalisation (Gill 2000). Thirdly, it refers to the absence of cleavages, across land-labour-capital, mass populace–elite, and other (ethnic, religious, regional, linguistic, gender) divides sufficient to destroy a G8 country's character as a democratic polity or its national unity and thus its continuation as a country.

6   Unless otherwise indicated, the declaration referred to is the comprehensive document issued by the G7 or G8 leaders at the conclusion of their annual summit. They are available at <www.g8.utoronto.ca>.

7   For an analysis of the environmental principles in the NAFTA regime see Alan Rugman, John Kirton, and Julie Soloway (1999).

8   The author is grateful to Anju Aggarwal for her assistance with this paragraph.

References

Abbott, Kenneth, Robert Keohane, Andrew Moravcsik, et al. (2000). 'The Concept of Legalization'. *International Organization* vol. 54, no. 3, pp. 401–420.

Baker, Andrew (2000). 'The G-7 as a Global "Ginger Group": Plurilateralism and Four Dimensional Diplomacy'. *Global Governance* vol. 6 (April-June), pp. 165–190.

Bayne, Nicholas (1999). 'Continuity and Leadership in an Age of Globalisation'. In M. R. Hodges, J. J. Kirton and J. P. Daniels, eds., *The G8's Role in the New Millennium*, pp. 21–44. Ashgate, Aldershot.

Bayne, Nicholas (2001). 'The G7 and Multilateral Trade Liberalisation: Past Performance, Future Challenges'. In J. J. Kirton and G. M. von Furstenberg, eds., *New Directions in Global Economic Governance: Creating International Order for the Twenty-First Century*, pp. 171–187. Ashgate, Aldershot.

Bergsten, C. Fred and C. Randall Henning (1996). *Global Economic Leadership and the Group of Seven*. Institute for International Economics, Washington DC.

Bernstein, Steven (2000). 'Ideas, Social Structure, and the Compromise of Liberal Environmentalism'. *European Journal of International Relations* vol. 6, no. 4, pp. 464–512.

Bernstein, Steven (2001). *The Compromise of Liberal Environmentalism*. Columbia University Press, New York.

Birdsall, Nancy and Augusta de la Torre (2001). 'Washington Contentious'. *Politica Internazionale* vol. 29 (January-April), pp. 97–104.

Dallaire, Sébastien (2001). 'Continuity and Change in the Global Monetary Order'. In J. J. Kirton and G. M. von Furstenberg, eds., *New Directions in Global Economic Governance: Managing Globalisation in the Twenty-First Century*, pp. 95–111. Ahsgate, Aldershot.

Dluhosch, Barbara (2001). 'The G7 and the Debt of the Poorest'. In J. J. Kirton, J. P. Daniels and A. Freytag, eds., *Guiding Global Order: G8 Governance in the Twenty-First Century*, pp. 79–92. Ashgate, Aldershot.

Donges, Juergen and Peter Tillman (2001). 'Challenges for the Global Financial System'. In J. J. Kirton and G. M. von Furstenberg, eds., *New Directions in Global Economic Governance: Managing Globalisation in the Twenty-First Century*, pp. 33–43. Ashgate, Aldershot.

Freytag, Andreas (2001). 'Internal Macroeconomic Policies and International Governance'. In J. J. Kirton and G. M. von Furstenberg, eds., *New Directions in Global Economic Governance: Managing Globalisation in the Twenty-First Century*, pp. 21–32. Ashgate, Aldershot.

G7 (1975). 'Declaration of Rambouillet'. 17 November, Rambouillet. <www.library.utoronto.ca/g7/summit/1975rambouillet/communique.html> (December 2001).

G7 (1976). 'Joint Declaration of the International Conference'. 28 June, San Juan. <www.library.utoronto.ca/g7/summit/1976sanjuan/communique.html> (December 2001).

G7 (1977). 'Declaration: Downing Street Summit Conference'. 8 May, London. <www.library.utoronto.ca/g7/summit/1977london/communique.html> (December 2001).

G7 (1978). 'Declaration'. 17 July, Bonn. <www.library.utoronto.ca/g7/summit/1978bonn/communique/index.html> (December 2001).

G7 (1979). 'Declaration'. 29 June, Tokyo. <www.library.utoronto.ca/g7/summit/1979tokyo/communique.html> (December 2001).

G7 (1980). 'Declaration'. 23 June, Venice. <www.library.utoronto.ca/g7/summit/1980venice/communique/index.html> (December 2001).

G7 (1981). 'Declaration of the Ottawa Summit'. 21 July, Ottawa. <www.library.utoronto.ca/g7/summit/1981ottawa/communique/index.html> (December 2001).

G7 (1982). 'Declaration of the Seven Heads of State and Government and Representatives of the European Communities'. 6 June, Versailles. <www.library.utoronto.ca/g7/summit/1982versailles/communique.html> (December 2001).

G7 (1983). 'Williamsburg Declaration on Economic Recovery'. 30 May, Williamsburg. <www.library.utoronto.ca/g7/summit/1983williamsburg/communique.html> (December 2001).

G7 (1984). 'London Economic Declaration'. 9 June, London. <www.library.utoronto.ca/g7/summit/1984london/communique.html> (December 2001).

G7 (1985). 'The Bonn Economic Declaration Towards Sustained Growth and Higher Employment'. 4 May, Bonn. <www.library.utoronto.ca/g7/summit/1985bonn/communique/index.html> (December 2001).

64   *Linking Trade, Environment, and Social Cohesion*

G7 (1986). 'Tokyo Economic Declaration'. 6 May, Tokyo. <www.library.utoronto.ca/g7/summit/
1986tokyo/communique.html> (December 2001).

G7 (1987). 'Venezia Economic Declaration'. 10 June, Venice. <www.library.utoronto.ca/g7/
summit/1987venice/communique/index.html> (December 2001).

G7 (1988). 'Toronto Economic Summit Economic Declaration'. 21 June, Toronto.
<www.library.utoronto.ca/g7/summit/1988toronto/communique/index.html> (December
2001).

G7 (1989). 'Economic Declaration'. 16 July, Paris. <www.library.utoronto.ca/g7/summit/
1989paris/communique/index.html> (December 2001).

G7 (1990). 'Houston Economic Declaration'. 11 July, Houston. <www.library.utoronto.ca/g7/
summit/1990houston/communique/index.html> (December 2001).

G7 (1991). 'Economic Declaration of the G8 Summit'. 17 July, London. <www.library.utoronto.ca/
g7/summit/1991london/communique/index.html> (December 2001).

G7 (1993). 'Economic Declaration: A Strengthened Commitment to Jobs and Growth'. 9 July,
Tokyo. <www.library.utoronto.ca/g7/summit/1993tokyo/communique/index.html>
(December 2001).

G7 (1994). 'G7 Communiqué'. 9 July, Naples. <www.library.utoronto.ca/g7/summit/1994naples/
communique/index.html> (December 2001).

G7 (1995). 'Halifax Summit Communiqué'. 16 June, Halifax. <www.library.utoronto.ca/g7/
summit/1995halifax/communique/index.html> (December 2001).

G7 (1996). 'Economic Communiqué: Making a Success of Globalization for the Benefit of
All'. 28 June, Lyon. <www.library.utoronto.ca/g7/summit/1996lyon/communique/
index.html> (December 2001).

G7 (1997). 'Confronting Global Economic and Financial Challenges. Denver Summit Statement
by Seven.' 21 June, Denver. <www.g7.utoronto.ca/g7/summit/1997denver/confront.htm>
(December 2001).

G7 (2001). 'G7 Statement'. 20 July, Genoa. <www.g7.utoronto.ca/g7/summit/2001genoa/
g7statement.html> (December 2001).

G8 (1998). 'Communiqué'. 15 May, Birmingham. <www.library.utoronto.ca/g7/summit/
1998birmingham/finalcom.htm> (December 2001).

G8 (1999). 'G8 Communiqué Köln 1999'. 20 June, Cologne. <www.library.utoronto.ca/g7/
summit/1999koln/finalcom.htm> (December 2001).

G8 (2000). 'G8 Communiqué Okinawa 2000'. 23 July, Okinawa. <www.g7.utoronto.ca/g7/
summit/2000okinawa/finalcom.htm> (December 2001).

Gill, Stephen (1999). 'Structural Changes in Multilateralism: The G-7 Nexus and the Global
Crisis'. In M. Schecter, ed., *Innovation in Multilateralism*. St. Martin's Press, New York.

Gill, Stephen (2000). 'The Constitution of Global Capitalism'. Paper presented at the annual
convention of the International Studies Association, 15 March. Los Angeles.

Goldstein, Judith, Miles Kahler, Robert Keohane, et al. (2000a). 'Introduction: Legalization
and World Politics'. *International Organization* vol. 54, no. 3, pp. 385–399.

Goldstein, Judith, Miles Kahler, Robert Keohane, et al. (2000b). 'Legalization and World
Politics'. *International Organization* vol. 54, no. 3.

Goldstein, Judith and Lisa Martin (2000). 'Legalization, Trade Liberalization, and Domestic
Politics: A Cautionary Tale'. *International Organization* vol. 54, no. 3, pp. 603–632.

Hajnal, Peter (1999). *The G7/G8 System: Evolution, Role, and Documentation*. Ashgate,
Aldershot.

Helleiner, Gerald (2001). 'Markets, Politics, and Globalization: Can the Global Economy Be
Civilized?' *Global Governance* vol. 7, no. 3, pp. 243–263.

Hodges, Michael R., John J. Kirton, and Joseph P. Daniels, eds. (1999). *The G8's Role in the
New Millennium*. Ashgate, Aldershot.

Ikenberry, John (1998/99). 'Institutions, Strategic Restraint, and the Persistence of American Postwar Order'. *International Security* vol. 23 (Winter), pp. 43–78.

Ikenberry, John (2001). *After Victory: Institutions, Strategic Restraint, and the Rebuilding of Order after Major Wars.* Princeton University Press, Princeton.

Juricevic, Diana (2000). 'Controlling for Domestic-Level Commitments: An Analysis of the Authoritative National Commitments Made in Canada and the United States from 1995 to 2000'. 7 November. <www.g7.utoronto.ca/g7/scholar/juricevic2000/juricevic.pdf> (December 2001).

Kaiser, Karl, John J. Kirton, and Joseph P. Daniels, eds. (2000). *Shaping a New International Financial System: Challenges of Governance in a Globalizing World.* Ashgate, Aldershot.

Keohane, Robert, Andrew Moravcsik, and Anne-Marie Slaughter (2000). 'Legalized Dispute Resolution: Interstate and Transnational'. *International Organization* vol. 54, no. 3, pp. 457–488.

Kirton, John J. (1989). 'Contemporary Concert Diplomacy: The Seven-Power Summit and the Management of International Order'. Paper presented at the annual convention of the International Studies Association, 29 March–1 April, London.

Kirton, John J. (1990). 'Sustainable Development at the Houston Summit'. Paper prepared for the Foreign Policy Committee, National Round Table on the Environment and the Economy, 6 September.

Kirton, John J. (1999). 'Explaining G8 Effectiveness'. In J. J. Kirton and J. P. Daniels, eds., *The G8's Role in the New Millennium*, pp. 45–68. Ashgate, Aldershot.

Kirton, John J. and Joseph P. Daniels (1999). 'The Role of the G8 in the New Millennium'. In M. Hodges, J. J. Kirton and J. P. Daniels, eds., *The G8's Role in the New Millennium*, pp. 3–17. Ashgate, Aldershot.

Kirton, John J., Joseph P. Daniels, and Andreas Freytag, eds. (2001). *Guiding Global Order: G8 Governance in the Twenty-First Century.* Ashgate, Aldershot.

Kirton, John J. and Sarah Richardson (1995). *The Halifax Summit, Sustainable Development, and International Institutional Reform.* National Round Table on the Environment and the Economy, Ottawa.

Kokotsis, Eleanore (1999). *Keeping International Commitments: Compliance, Credibility, and the G7, 1988–1995.* Garland, New York.

Kornhauser, William (1966). *The Politics of Mass Society.* Free Press, Glencoe, IL.

Putnam, Robert and Nicholas Bayne, eds. (1987). *Hanging Together: Co-operation and Conflict in the Seven-Power Summit.* 2nd ed. Sage Publications, London.

Putnam, Robert, Robert Leonardi, and Raffaella Nanetti (1993). *Making Democracy Work: Civic Traditions in Modern Italy.* Princeton University Press, Princeton.

Ruggie, John (1983). 'International Regimes, Transactions, and Change: Embedded Liberalism in the Postwar Economic Order'. In S. Krasner, ed., *International Regimes.* Cornell University Press, Ithaca.

Rugman, Alan M., John J. Kirton, and Julie A. Soloway (1999). *Environmental Regulations and Corporate Strategy: A NAFTA Perspective.* Oxford University Press, Oxford.

Sally, Razeen (2001). 'Looking Askance at Global Governance'. In J. J. Kirton, J. P. Daniels and A. Freytag, eds., *Guiding Global Order: G8 Governance in the Twenty-First Century*, pp. 55–76. Ashgate, Aldershot.

Smyser, W. R. (1993). 'Goodbye , G-7'. *Washington Quarterly* vol. 16 (Winter), pp. 15–28.

Thérien, Jean-Philippe and Sébastien Dallaire (1999/2000). 'Nord-Sud: une vision du monde en mutation'. *La revue internationale et stratégique* vol. 36 (Winter), pp. 21–35.

Theuringer, Martin (2001). 'International Macroeconomic Policy Co-operation in the Era of the Euro'. In J. J. Kirton, J. P. Daniels and A. Freytag, eds., *Guiding Global Order: G8 Governance in the Twenty-First Century*, pp. 173–187. Ashgate, Aldershot.

von Furstenberg, George M. and Joseph P. Daniels (1991). 'Policy Undertakings by the Seven "Summit" Countries: Ascertaining the Degree of Compliance'. *Carnegie-Rochester Conference Series on Public Policy* vol. 35, pp. 267–308.

Whyman, William E. (1995). 'We Can't Go on Meeting Like This: Revitalizing the G-7 Process'. *Washington Quarterly* vol. 18 (Summer), pp. 139–165.

Williamson, John (1990). *The Progress of Policy Reform in Latin America.* Institute for International Economics, Washington DC.

Williamson, John (1993). 'Democracy and the "Washington Consensus"'. *World Development* vol. 21, pp. 1329–1336.

Appendix 4-A: Trade-Environment Links in the G7/8 Communiqués, 1975–2001

1979: 'to increase as far as possible coal use, production, and trade, without damage to the environment' (para. 3).

1987: 'The long term objective is to allow market signals to influence the orientation of agricultural production, by way of a progressive and concerted reduction of agricultural support, as well as by all other appropriate means, giving consideration to social and other concerns, such as food security, environmental protection and overall employment' (para. 18).

1987: 'We also intend to examine further ... promotion of international trade in low pollution products, low polluting industrial plants and other environmental protection technologies' (para. 30).

1988: 'Market oriented agricultural policies should assist in the achievement of important objectives such as preserving rural areas and family farming, raising quality standards and protecting the environment'. It added that in doing so 'ways should be developed to take account of food security and social concerns' (para. 12).

1989: 'Environmental protection is integral to such issues as trade, development, energy, transport, agriculture, and economic planning. Therefore, environmental considerations must be taken into account in economic decision-making. In fact good economic policies and good environmental policies are mutually reinforcing' (para. 37).

1991: 'Open markets help to create the resources needed to protect the environment. We therefore commend the OECD's pioneering work in ensuring that trade and environment policies are mutually supporting. We look to the General Agreement on Tariffs and Trade (GATT) to define how trade measures can properly be used for environmental purposes' (para. 15).

1993: 'To this end, we will pursue a comprehensive approach, covering not only aid but also trade, investment ... taking environmental aspects into account' (para. 13).

1994: 'We welcome the work on the relation between trade and environment in the new WTO. We call for intensified efforts to improve our understanding of new issues including employment and labour standards and their implications for trade policies' (para. 4).

1995: 'Consistent with the goal of continued trade liberalization, we will pursue work on ... trade and environment to ensure that rules and policies in these different areas are compatible [and on] trade, employment and labour standards' (para 43).

1996: 'Global liberalization of trade and a high level of environmental protection should be mutually supportive. It will be important, for example, to ensure that WTO rules and multilateral environmental agreements and ecolabelling programs are complementary. The Singapore Ministerial Conference of the

WTO will be an important opportunity to demonstrate the ability and willingness to integrate environmental protection and thus sustainable development concerns into the multilateral trading system' (para. 23).

1997: Environmental Standards for Export Credit Agencies: 'Private sector financial flows from industrial nations have a significant impact on sustainable development worldwide. Governments should help promote sustainable practices by taking environmental factors into account when providing financing support for investment in infrastructure and equipment. We attach importance to the work on this in the OECD, and will review progress at our meeting next year' (para. 24).

1999: 'We will also seek a more effective way within the WTO for addressing the trade and environment relationship and promoting sustainable development and social and economic welfare worldwide' (para. 9).

1999: 'We also urge greater cooperation and policy coherence among international financial, economic, labor and environmental organizations' (para. 10).

1999: 'We agree that environmental considerations should be taken fully into account in the upcoming round of WTO negotiations. This should include a clarification of the relationship between both multilateral environmental agreements and key environmental principles, and WTO rules' (para. 31).

1999: 'We will work within the OECD towards common environmental guidelines for export finance agencies. We aim to complete this work by the 2001 G8 Summit' (para. 32).

2000: 'We are firmly committed to a new round of WTO trade negotiations with an ambitious, balanced and inclusive agenda, reflecting the interests of all WTO members. We agree that the objective of such negotiations should be to enhance market access, develop and strengthen WTO rules and disciplines, support developing countries in achieving economic growth and integration into the global trading system, and ensure that trade and social policies, and trade and environment policies are compatible and mutually supportive' (para. 36).

2000: 'We will also examine how best we can combat illegal logging, including export and procurement practices' (para. 67).

2000: 'Export credit policies may have very significant environmental impacts. We welcome the adoption of the OECD work plan to be completed by 2001. We reaffirm our commitment to develop common environmental guidelines, drawing on relevant MDB [multilateral development bank] experience, for export credit agencies by the 2001 G8 Summit' (para. 68).

2001: 'The WTO should continue to respond to the legitimate expectations of civil society, and ensure that the new Round supports sustainable development' (para. 8).

2001: 'We call on the MDBs to provide support for global public goods, such as fighting infectious diseases, facilitating trade, fostering financial stability, and protecting the environment ...' (para. 13).

Appendix 4-B: Trade-Environment Links in the G7/G8 Environment Ministers Communiqués, 1994–2001

1994: 'Sound environmental and trade policies can be mutually supportive. Environment regulation is not harmful to trade. In fact, environmental regulation that internalizes environmental costs into the price structure is essential if gains from trade liberalization are to be assured. On the other hand, expanded trade is not intrinsically harmful to the environment insofar as using environmental resources more efficiently is the key to pollution prevention'.

1995: No direct reference to trade or globalisation.

1996: 'Trade liberalisation and environmental protection are equally important objectives. Provided that the right policy framework is in place, they should be mutually supportive in favour of sustainable development. The removal of trade obstacles should contribute to achieving a more efficient use of the Earth's natural resources in both economic and environmental terms [and] to lessening pressures on the environment. However, the environmental benefits of trade liberalisation are not automatic. They can only be derived if appropriate environmental policies and sustainable development strategies are implemented nationally and internationally. If this condition is not met, trade liberalisation can act as a magnifier of policy and market failures'.

1996: 'The work of the WTO Committee on Trade and Environment (CTE) is particularly important. This committee is emerging as a major forum to address the interlinkages between trade and environment, especially in the view of the fact that it can make recommendations on whether any modifications to the provisions of the multilateral trading system are required' (para. 28).

1996: 'The Singapore Ministerial Conference will be a first test of the ability of the WTO to integrate environmental protection and sustainable development concerns into the multilateral trading system. We must ensure that any agreements do not weaken environmental policies' (para. 28).

1996: 'We consider that the WTO should be supportive of efforts to promote a positive framework to acknowledge the importance of greater internalization of environmental costs. We call upon the WTO to examine the relationship between the trade rules and environmental principles, including the polluter-pays principle (PPP) and the precautionary principle' (para. 29).

1996: 'To make sure that they encourage industry to operate in a more ecologically-aware fashion, we shall work to ensure that the WTO rules, and in particular those on technical barriers to trade, do not hinder the development of voluntary ecolabelling schemes based on life-cycle analysis, but on the contrary further their utilization and effectiveness by encouraging the use of instruments to promote transparency and consultation, while avoiding trade protectionism' (para. 30).

1996: 'It is particularly important to devise effective solutions to prevent conflicts between the WTO rules and MEA's [multilateral environmental agreements) and to ensure that trade measures pursuant to MEA's find accommodation within the WTO system ... WTO members should fulfill the terms of the agreement establishing it which recognize that parties should conduct their trade and economic relations while allowing for the optimal use of the world's resources in accordance with the objective of sustainable development, seeking to protect and preserve the environment' (para. 31).

1997: 'The globalization of trade and a high level of environmental protection should be mutually supportive in favour of sustainable development. We should seek to avoid conflict between the international trade system and international environmental law. The WTO must give practical expression to the objectives of sustainable development and environmental protection as contained in the Rio Declaration and in the preamble to the agreement instituting the WTO, and it should serve as a framework for the assessment of trade agreements.'

1998: 'Internationally we must maintain the momentum by making progress at Buenos Aires on the outstanding issues left by Kyoto. Flexible mechanisms such as international emissions trading, joint implementation and the clean development mechanism shall be supplemental to domestic action. They can play an essential role in achieving our commitments cost effectively. Defining the relevant principles, modalities, rule and guidelines to ensure that these mechanisms provide real environmental benefits is a priority. It is important that these flexibilities, in particular trading, should help us to achieve greater overall abatement of greenhouse gases than would otherwise occur. The rules must ensure an enforceable, accountable, verifiable, open and transparent trading system'.

1999: 'We want to ensure that "trade and environment" is incorporated as a key issue into the next WTO negotiations, including the following issues to be addressed:
  • preserve the integrity of multilateral environmental agreements and clarify the relationship between multilateral environmental agreements and WTO rules
  • undertake environment and/or sustainable development reviews of the new round
  • strengthen co-operation between WTO and UNEP as well as other international environment related organisations and secretariats of multilateral environmental agreements'.

1999: 'We reaffirm our determination that the next WTO negotiations must contribute to the achievement of sustainable development. "Trade and Environment" is a key issue to be included and it is important that environmental concerns be fully taken into account across the WTO agreements ...We will individually or, as appropriate, collectively with other interested WTO members, conduct environment and/or sustainable development reviews of the next WTO negotiations beginning at an early stage. We will undertake to continue integrating policy formation between trade/economic, development and environment ministries and encourage all WTO members to do so.

1999: It is also necessary to intensify capacity building efforts to deal with new trade and environment challenges. While working towards a more environmentally responsive WTO, we stress the need to preserve the integrity of multilateral environmental agreements. We consider that the relationship between multilateral environmental agreements and the WTO rules should be clarified. We must respect the right of nations to set protective standards for health and safety, the environment and biodiversity, even when they are stronger than international standards, avoiding arbitrary or unjustifiable discrimination and consistent with our multilateral obligations' (para. 6).

1999: 'Labelling, environmental principles, liberalisation of environmental goods, services and technologies, and the co-operation between WTO and UNEP, as well as other international environment related organisations and MEA secretariats, are important trade and environment issues. We are open to consider further trade and environment issues of concern for other countries, in particular developing countries. The world-wide liberalisation of trade and a high standard of environmental protection should be mutually supportive' (para. 6).

2000: 'In the wake of the World Trade Organization's Ministerial Conference held in November 1999 in Seattle, we recall our commitments from our meeting in Schwerin in 1999. We need to work with our trade colleagues to advance the trade and environment agenda. It is important that environmental concerns be fully taken into account in the context of the multilateral trading system, in particular in the next Trade Round. We also need to examine what we, as Environment ministers, can do to advance the trade and environment agenda outside the WTO. In particular, we support practical international efforts to build capacity on trade and environment issues in developing countries, particularly those which bring together officials from both the trade and environment fields and foster policy integration supportive of sustainable development' (para. 28).

2001: 'Furthermore, we underline that environmental considerations should be taken into account throughout the negotiations of the next WTO round with a view to achieving by the end of the round an overall outcome which respects global and regional environmental commitments and contributes to the advancement of sustainable development. The new round should maximise the potential for positive synergies between trade liberalization, environmental protection and economic and social development, including through the phasing out of environmentally harmful subsidies' (para. 22).

Chapter 5

Winning Together:
The NAFTA Trade-Environment Record

John J. Kirton[1]

Within North America, throughout the long history of the intense northern bilateral relationship between Canada and the United States, environmental and trade issues have recurrently been at the centre of controversy and conflict (Nye 1976). They have equally been at the centre of co-operative steps, including the construction of pioneering bilateral institutions such as the International Joint Commission and those created or catalysed by the Canada-United States Free Trade Agreement (FTA) of 1988 (Spencer, Kirton, and Nossal 1981). Moreover, many of these controversies — for example, the *Arctic Waters Pollution Prevention Act* of 1970 and the FTA itself — and the co-operative initiatives and institutions that have arisen to govern them, have inherently involved tradeoffs and other linkages between trade and investment on the one hand and, on the other, the environment and associated social values (Munton and Kirton 1996).

Yet it was only in the 1990s, with the advent of trilateral co-operation — through the North American Free Trade Agreement (NAFTA), the accompanying North American Agreement on Environmental Cooperation (NAAEC), and the first regional organisation, the Commission for Environmental Cooperation (CEC) — that trade and environment became formally fused in a single regional regime encompassing Canada and the United States (Kirton 1998b, 1997; Munton and Kirton 1996; Magraw and Charnovitz 1994; Lowry 1992). It is paradoxical that these two countries, with the largest two-way trading relationship in the world and with vast borders that combine their massive ecological capabilities and vulnerabilities, should have waited until the arrival of Mexico and the trilateralism it brought to forge a direct international trade-environment link. It is even more paradoxical that these world-leading G7 trade and environmental powers and pioneers of broad multilateral trade and environment institutions in the 1990s, notably the World Trade Organization (WTO) and institutions created by the 1992 United Nations Conference on Environment and Development (UNCED) at Rio, should not have crafted and used such multilateral institutions as important instruments to address the trade-environment relationships within their continental home. But with few exceptions, it is the trilateral NAFTA regime, rather than available bilateral or multilateral alternatives, that is defining how trade and environment are being fused within the North American region.

After more than seven years in operation, and three years in serious anticipation, this consequential and revolutionary NAFTA regime remains the subject of considerable controversy over what its impact has actually been (Abbott 2000; Groetzinger 1997; Kirton et al. 1999; Grossman 2000; Jansen 2001; Rugman and Kirton 1998). Those examining the NAFTA trade-environment regime in general terms, from realist, liberal institutionalist, and constructivist perspectives, have concluded that it is very limited in its degree of institutionalisation and effectiveness relative to that of the European Union (Steinberg 1997), and that its rules and decision-making procedures are not supported by any genuine change in underlying norms or principles (Audley 1997; Mayer 1998). Indeed, some scholarly observers and NAFTA's many critics argue that NAFTA's new environmental institution, the CEC, has done little to fulfil what they see as its core purpose of ensuring the effective enforcement of national environmental regulations (Mumme and Duncan 1996; Public Citizen 1995; Economic Policy Institute 1997).

Yet other assessments are more favourable to the basic argument of liberal-institutionalist theory that international regimes have an autonomous impact in altering the behaviour in co-operative dimensions, if not in altering the underlying interests and identities, of their competing member governments. Perhaps the most popular claim is that NAFTA's powerful trade and investment regime, with its far-reaching rules for liberalisation, has had an independent impact in unleashing a more intense round of competition among the countries and companies of North America. Here the argument is that the free trade, foreign direct investment (FDI), and intensified competition brought by NAFTA has led to a 'race to the bottom' in regulation and industrial relocation, to regulatory chill in the face of rising environmental problems, awareness, and demands, to restraint on the ability of national and sub-federal governments to regulate freely to supply the demanded environmental protection, and to a result in which a strong trade community and a strong U.S. benefit at the expense of a weaker environmental community and the smaller Canadian and Mexican neighbours. In particular, attention has focussed on the way NAFTA's Chapter 11 investment dispute settlement mechanism has rewarded U.S.-based multinational corporations (MNCs) at the expense of Canadian and Mexican environmental regulations, whereas the counterpart Article 14-15 citizen complaint process in the NAAEC, instituted to ensure governments enforce their existing environmental laws and regulations, has offered little balance (Mann and von Moltke 1999).

In contrast, others more faithful to liberal-institutionalist claims take seriously the fact that NAFTA was not only a pioneering trade and investment agreement, but also a historic environment agreement, and thus a trade-environment one as well. They point to the innovative and potentially powerful environmental principles, rules, and norms at the core of NAFTA and to its environmental side agreements, to the 50 or more institutions these agreements inspired, and to the unique creation of a regional organisation — the CEC — that the trade component of the overall NAFTA regime lacks. Some see the capacity and early record of the CEC as pointing to an institution with considerable potential (Munton and Kirton 1996; Johnson and Beaulieu 1996; Abbott, F. 1996; Johnson 1999). Others view the NAFTA rules and institutions more broadly as engendering effective environmental co-operation among the parties in several instances, as well as constraining national and sub-federal environmental regulations that serve as barriers to trade (Rugman, Kirton, and Soloway 1997, 1999; Rugman and Kirton 1999, 1998; Kirton and Fernandez de Castro 1997; Kirton and Rugman 1999; Kirton 1998b, 1997; Weintraub 1997). And on this foundation of prospective regime effectiveness rests the possibility that NAFTA might, over time, affect the underlying interests and even identities of its governments, corporate communities, and civil society and citizens, in ways that enable a new trade-environment balance to emerge in North America and provide a model for the wider world.

What does the record actually reveal? To answer this question, this chapter reports the results of a comprehensive exploration of how the advent of NAFTA and its institutions has altered the process and outcomes in the full universe of 84 cases of broadly defined 'environmental regulatory protection' involving at least two of the three NAFTA member countries from 1980 to mid 1998.[2] To do so, it first defines the phenomenon of environmental regulatory protection and examines how emerging conditions of 'complex institutional responsiveness' affect the ability of U.S., Canadian, and Mexican governments to take environmental or trade actions that have an impact on the prevailing behaviour in the other domain. It then examines the process through which these cases are handled and the outcomes that result, exploring in particular how the balance of outcomes changes across issue areas and industry sectors, from the pre-NAFTA to post-NAFTA periods, as the NAFTA institutions and the CEC, rather than NAFTA's trade institutions, are employed. It next explores the overall record of the cases in two key institutional domains — those taken to the Chapter 11 and Article 14-15 dispute settlement mechanisms. The results of the actual operation of these innovative NAFTA provisions for direct societal actor access lie in many ways at the heart of the current debate over NAFTA's environmental regulatory effects. The chapter concludes by considering the record of environmental regulatory protection in general and Chapter 11–Article 14-15 cases in particular in reference to recent analyses and finding about NAFTA's environmental effects as they relate to domestic regulation in Canada and the United States.

This analysis reveals, in the first instance, that there has been a proliferation of cases of environmental regulatory protection in North America from the 1980s to the NAFTA era of the 1990s. This suggests, consistent with realist claims, that NAFTA-ensconced governments in the U.S., Canada, and Mexico have by no means had a diminished appetite or ability to regulate for environmental protection in ways that restrict trade and that provoke intergovernmental action in response, or to pursue their distinctive national preferences through whatever new as well as old fora they can find. However, in resolving such cases, the three North American governments have tended to find solutions that generate both higher and more convergent environmental regulations, as well as greater trade and investment liberalisation. Despite the overwhelming economic power of the United States in the NAFTA region, and the trade-investment community centred in it, the outcomes of such cases move toward equality among the member countries and between their trade and environment communities as the NAFTA era arrived, and as the NAFTA institutions in general, and the CEC in particular, assumed consequential roles. Despite the controversies over a few high-profile cases and the need for some reforms, both the Chapter 11 and Article 14-15 processes, where societal actors have direct access to international tribunals, contribute to such results.

In short, relative to the previous regime and available alternatives, NAFTA has provided an incentive and an instrument for governments in Canada, the U.S., and Mexico to regulate more aggressively and successfully in order to secure higher levels of environmental protection, through a more equal process of mutual adjustment yielding outcomes that more equally benefit each of the region's three countries and its environment and trade communities. In particular, NAFTA has given the United States and its smaller regional partners both a reason to recognise and a regime to respond to the new trade opportunities and ecological vulnerabilities that the trilateral community brings, and to do so in ways that benefit all. And the opening up of international institutions to allow direct access and meaningful influence for corporations and citizens has strengthened the equalising and community-building effects of the innovative NAFTA trade-environment regime. Despite the influence of traditional instincts and interests, it thus has the potential to serve as a model and foundation for building a more equitable and socially sensitive trade-environment regime on a wider regional, and even global, scale.

The Record of Environmental Regulatory Protection in North America

NAFTA's trade and tightly related investment liberalisations were particularly important for smaller firms from smaller countries, such as Canada and Mexico, which depend on access to the larger U.S. market for much of their trade and, in Canada's case, for much of its gross national product (GNP). They were also important for a steadily internationalising U.S., which has Canada and Mexico as its top-ranked trade partners and has more than 30 percent of its trade with them (United States Trade Representative 1997). Yet in moving to seize these new opportunities in the NAFTA marketplace, such firms confronted emerging conditions of complex institutional responsiveness, which brought a new array of barriers to foreign market access and brought new vulnerabilities for internationally oriented firms and their governments. The conditions of complex institutional responsiveness consist of a three-component complex of a new generation of environmental regulations at the national and sub-federal level (Esty and Geradin 1997), a growing dependence on international sales and production in an era of internationally integrated production, and the advent of international regimes, such as NAFTA, with powers of trade liberalisation and environmental regulation (Rugman and Kirton 1999). These have produced a far more complex environment in which firms must operate.

This more complicated environment was not resolved by firms demanding and their governments accepting the need for reduced or stagnant environmental regulations in order to seize the new NAFTA-wide market opportunities. Rather, it was resolved by an upsurge in both trade-investment and environmental regulations, with the NAFTA institutions called upon to help governments solve the conflicts and seize the co-operative opportunities that resulted. The degree and form of this trade-environment link, and the environmental regulation that lay behind it, can be seen by examining the cases of environmental regulatory protection that have arisen in North America since 1980.

Environmental regulatory protection is defined as government action at the sub-federal, national, or international level that is directed at affecting trade liberalisation or environmental protection, but that has clear, direct, substantial, and recognised implications for activities and values in the other domain. It thus embraces activity aimed at environmental protection that influences trade, as with national regulations that impede (or enhance) market entry for foreign firms, or international action to create region-wide environmental regulations (at any level) that lower transactions costs and thus facilitate trade. Furthermore, it embraces activity aimed at trade liberalisation that affects environmental protection and quality, in either positive or negative ways.

Such cases can be initiated by government action at the sub-federal, national, or international level. At the international level, it embraces initiatives taken by the secretariats of intergovernmental institutions themselves. Such government action may arise in response to firm behaviour or pressure, or as a result of a independent government initiative. Moreover, such cases can encompass the full spectrum, from those marked by high conflict to those embracing full co-operation. The research universe thus runs the range from reactive, conflictual cases, in which new environmental regulations create trade barriers, to proactive co-operative ones, in which governments actively create region-wide environmental or trade rules in advance of any conflicts occurring. Finally, unlike the original Keohane-Nye conception, which was limited to conflict cases that reached the attention of the U.S. president, the current study includes cases from the high-political to the low-functional level (Nye 1976; Keohane and Nye 1977).

An application of these criteria yields 84 cases of intergovernmentally managed environmental regulatory protection involving at least two of the three North American national governments or their sub-federal units between 1980 and mid 1998. An examination of these cases suggests several trends.

In the first instance, the new politically grounded conditions of complex institutional responsiveness have led to an upsurge in the frequency of environmental regulatory protection. Those hoping that NAFTA would issue in a new era of transborder commercial harmony devoid of environmental regulatory impediments have good reason to be disappointed with the record. There have been substantially more trade-environment issues involving at least two North American countries that have arisen in the five years since NAFTA took formal effect than in the five years when the Canada-U.S. Free Trade Agreement (FTA) operated (1989–1993), and in the preceding five years when the three countries of North America could look only to the distant General Agreement on Tariffs and Trade (GATT) for international relief (see Appendix 5-A).

There has been a similar post-NAFTA expansion in the range of environmental regulatory protection, seen in the broad range of sectors that have been affected by it. Such issues abound in the automotive sector (at the heart of the North American manufacturing economy), in the environmentally rich natural resource sectors of agriculture, fisheries, and forestry, in other manufacturing industries and service industries such as trucking, and, paradoxically, in the new sector of environmental services. Indeed, no sector of a modern, internationally engaged economy is likely to escape the impact of environmental regulatory protectionism in its future operations.

This upsurge in environmental regulatory protection is taking place in the long-opened U.S.-Canada relationship as well as in the newly NAFTA-opened U.S.-Mexico one. The cases have arisen not only across the U.S.-Mexican border, as the U.S. debate over NAFTA assumed. They have arisen equally voraciously along the rhetorically 'undefended' Canada-U.S. border as well. A home-base location in a highly developed, internationally integrated country with high degrees of environmental consciousness and regulations is thus unlikely to allow firms to escape facing the impact of environmental regulatory protection from abroad. Indeed, there are good reasons for expecting that even in such relationships, characterised by high degrees of intra-industry trade, trade liberalisation will lead individual firms to seek protection, including through different and higher environmental regulation ever more strongly (Gilligan 1997; Weintraub 1994). As trade liberalisation agreements such as NAFTA eliminate border barriers, newly exposed shelter-seeking firms will seek alternative forms of protection by demanding different, usually higher, forms of behind-the-border environmental regulation in the face of low-cost competition from firms in less developed countries with lower costs of production. Firms on the other side of the newly exposed border may well respond in kind, leading to a protectionist environmental regulatory 'race to the top'. This phenomenon of administered protection, well known to scholars of economics and management studies, offers an offsetting logic and dynamic as powerful as the 'race to the bottom' hypotheses focussed on by concerned environmentalists. It appears to be alive and abundant in the Canada-U.S. relationship of the NAFTA age.

This upsurge in the overall frequency, sectoral range, and geographic spread of environmental regulatory protectionism could theoretically be generated by ever more aggressive export-oriented firms assaulting even more intensely long-existing and even relaxed environmental regulation, in a lust to win in an intensified competitive race. But a detailed examination of the 84 cases suggests it arises primarily from the first of the three particular conditions of 'complex institutional responsiveness' — the rise of environmental regulations. This process has several components.

First, the spread of mass public environmental concern in the three NAFTA countries, partly induced by NAFTA, has generated a growing demand for and thus a governmental supply of such regulations. Both sub-federal and international governmental bodies have joined national governments in meeting this demand (Orbuch and Singer 1995). And the advent of NAFTA itself has changed environmental issues from being considered fully domestic to a matter of international concern.

Second, environmental regulatory protectionism has now become much more entrenched. As is evident in the cases of herring-salmon and softwood lumber, several of these issues go through multiple stages, with outcomes at a particular moment leading not to enduring solutions but only to temporary respites before an offspring of the dispute erupts to impede or close the border again. Moreover, such disputes, once centred in the traditional trade domain of antidumping and countervailing duties, have now spread laterally to involve general trade disputes, FDI disputes, and issues involving the domestic enforcement of federal and sub-federal environmental regulations.

Third, the new tenacity of environmental regulatory protectionism has a deeper domestic base, grounded ultimately in 'green and greedy coalitions', than merely the protectionist-seeking firms, employees, suppliers, and surrounding communities of old. The rise of mass public environmental concern has enormously increased the number, resources and political influence of environmental nongovernmental organizations (ENGOs), not only in the United States, but also in Canada and now Mexico. The new generation of environmental regulations, with provisions for expanded public participation (as in the NAAEC's Article 14-15 process at the international level), and the activism of sub-federal governments have increased the access and power wielded by such groups. It has consequently also increased their opportunities to identify compatible or common interests with industries seeking protection, and to forge active alliances of so-called green and greedy coalitions to secure such outcomes (De Sombre 1995). Governments seeking to keep their borders open must now face the self-interested claims of a particular firm or industry promising jobs, as well as the often nation-wide, highly attractive pleas of not-for-profit groups claiming to represent the public good.

Such coalitions exist in abundance in North America. Indeed, in many cases they can be identified as a force that has held the trade-restricting environmental regulation in place. Moreover, such coalitions exist, operate, and prevail not only in the United States; they now exist in Canada and Mexico, too. Also of note is the broad array of groups that have joined these coalitions. Industry groups and their environmental allies are now often joined by the sub-federal governments where an industry is concentrated, as well as consumer groups, and, as in the Chapter 11 MMT case, religious groups. When, as in the MMT case, they are supported by sub-federal governments, they have the full resources of government and constitutional law in federal systems behind them (Soloway 1999). The very diversity of groups and motives is what often make such coalitions, once formed, difficult to counter and dislodge, as are the new and high environmental regulations those coalitions press for and protect.

Fourth, environmental regulatory protectionism is now more complex in the content and character of the regulations that industry must face. Regulations address not merely the nature of their product, but also their after-sales services (as the cases of California newsprint recycling and Ontario beer show), their harvesting production processes (as with the herring-salmon, softwood lumber, and ecolabelling cases), and with the components of the materials used by consumers to operate their products (as with the MMT and other automotive fuel additive cases). Industry must now too be concerned about such issues. The scientific evidence required to challenge regulations is becoming more subtle and complex, as the MMT case indicates. And regulatory politics now confront major issues of co-ordination and burden sharing among powerful industries such as automobiles and petroleum in the case of automotive emissions, and between the chemicals and railroad industry in the case of halogenated organic chlorides.

Fifth, such complexity is a direct result of a further condition of complex institutional responsiveness — the new generation of environmental regulation. In particular, regulations now often express the environmentalists' core values of full life-cycle environmentalism and, as in the MMT case, the precautionary principle. This has increased the backward and forward linkages that regulations embrace, and made the task of using sound science to challenge regulations more difficult. Moreover, the move to a 'total systems' approach to environmental control, as in the automotive industry, raises major issues of inter-industry and economy-wide co-ordination.

Sixth, and final, environmental regulatory protectionism is now more costly for the firms that face it. As the experience of Lactel in the case of UHT milk shows, the cost and time of process protectionism can impose major competitive costs — destroying a firm's entire export market — even when its claims are ultimately accepted as legally valid by a foreign government. As the experience of British Columbia in the case of California newsprint recycling demonstrates, small regulatory changes can put major export markets at risk, even for some of the world's major multinational enterprises (notably, MacMillan Bloedel). Such was also the case for Ethyl Corporation, which faced the complete termination of its ability to export to Canada as a result of one regulatory change.

While not all or even most of this new environmental regulatory protection and the aims of the coalition partners behind it are consciously protectionist in intent, they are often protectionist in impact. Regardless of the motives of the originators, such protection severely compromises the competitiveness of most firms having to operate under new business conditions.

Several conditions of complex institutional responsiveness have generated these increased costs. Most generally, trade and investment liberalisation has made domestic firms and home-based exporters vulnerable to competitors from abroad and raised the protectionist impact of regulatory arbitrage (Leyshon 1992). As the automotive industry shows, the spread and speed of new technology, and the move to integrated production and the just-in-time inventory it allows, require rapid, unimpeded, and costless access to foreign markets (Kirton 1998a). The emergence of international business alliances, as in the automotive industry, reinforces the need for integrated international production. Meanwhile the move to global markets and competition means even large firms from large countries, such as the big three of the North American automobile industry, need a seamless regional home base on which to build the scale required to compete in world markets.

It is thus the cost of regulation itself, as well as — or rather than — the competitive pressures brought by trade and investment liberalisation that will lead firms to seek strategic solutions. And among the alternative strategies, relocation or lobbying for reduced regulation is only one of many that are available, that have been employed, and that have met with success (Rugman, Kirton, and Soloway 1999).

Patterns and Sources of Regime-Governed Outcomes

It is an analytically and empirically challenging task to identify how firms and their governments actually respond to this dilemma of rising environmental regulatory protection, when and why they use the new international institutional instruments offered by NAFTA, and when and why these institutions are successfully employed to balanced benefit. The NAFTA regime has been in operation for only a short time. Many of the cases dealt with under it are still in progress. Some of the issues resolved immediately prior to NAFTA taking formal effect were done so in anticipation of and thus under the influence of the NAFTA, as a calculated consequence of how countries and firms would be better off by moving to particular solutions. Most importantly, in many of these cases several instruments worked together to produce an outcome, making it somewhat artificial to single out and score each in operation alone. Nonetheless, after a half decade of operation of the NAFTA regime itself, there is a sufficiently strong empirical foundation to allow confident judgements about the emerging patterns to be made.

To begin this analysis, it is necessary to score the outcome of those cases that have been resolved, under NAFTA's influence or not. In keeping with the initial Keohane-Nye conception for scoring outcomes of Canada-U.S. disputes and variants based on it, outcomes are scored as to whether these cases, once resolved, conform to the initial preferences of each of three countries (Nye 1976; Leyton-Brown 1976; Norton 1998). However, in an extension of this method, they include the co-operative, positive-sum possibility of joint or mutual gains, in which outcomes reflect the initial preference of both or all parties (as distinct from the original Keohane-Nye 'compromise' possibility of 'tied' outcomes equidistant between the initial preferences of each). A further extension allows a scoring of cases according to whether the positions, interests, and values of the transnational trade or environment communities were realised in the outcomes.

As Appendix 5-A and Table 5.1 indicate, 50 of the 84 cases have come to an effective resolution where such outcomes can be scored. Ten did so in the pre-NAFTA period, and 40 have done so in the post-NAFTA period or in the immediate leadup to and under the conscious anticipation of NAFTA.

One of the most striking findings is how the outcome of cases of environmental regulatory protectionism have benefited the United States, which has won 58 percent of the time. Of the 50 cases effectively resolved, the United States and its firms have won 29, Canada 8, and Mexico 7, while 8 have been resolved to the mutual benefit of two or three of the North American partners. Such a pattern would appear to be a further testament to the realist presupposition that in this bargaining domain, as in so many others, the United States with its overwhelmingly superior power (based on having at least ten times as much economic capability as Canada and at least 20 times as much as Mexico) is bound to prevail.

However, this first-order conclusion needs immediate qualification. The impact of complex institutional responsiveness is to equalise outcomes in a trade-liberalising and environmentally enhancing manner.

Table 5.1   Outcomes of North American Environmental Regulatory Protection by Country and Issue (Post-NAFTA)

Case	No. of Cases	U.S.	Canada	Mexico	Equal/All
Trade cases	42 (29)	27 (17)	4 (2)	5 (4)	6 (6)
Automotive emissions	6 (6)	6 (6)	–	–	–
Automotive fuels	3 (2)	3 (2)	–	–	–
Agriculture inspections	15 (14)	9 (8)	1 (1)	4 (4)	1 (1)
Manufacturing recycling	4 (1)	3 (–)	–	–	1 (1)
Fisheries conservation	6 (1)	4 (1)	1 (0)	1 (0)	–
Forestry conservation	3 (1)	1 (0)	1 (0)	–	1 (1)
Environmental services	1 (1)	–	–	–	1 (1)
Dangerous goods	2 (2)	–	–	–	2 (2)
Other	2 (1)	1 (0)	1 (1)	–	–
Environment cases	8 (8)	2 (2)	3 (3)	2 (3)	2 (3)
Pesticides	4 (4)	(1)	2 (2)	–	1 (1)
Environmental information	1 (1)	–	–	1 (1)	–
Environmental science	2 (2)	–	–	1 (1)	1 (1)
Environmental enforcement	1 (1)	1* (1)	1* (1)	–	–

* Both the U.S. and Canada are scored as successful in the Cozumel case.

First, the U.S. wins far less frequently than its relative economic weight suggests it should. On a GNP basis, the United States commands about 85 percent of the overall economic capability within the North American region. This is far more than its 58 percent success rate actually delivered. (It remains for further research to develop a calculus of economic vulnerability and ecological capability and vulnerability, and assess the overall record of success against these referents.)

Second, in keeping with an issue-structure model, the degree of U.S. success varies widely across issue areas, according to the relative size of the home-based firms that dominate each (Keohane and Nye 1977). Thus, the United States enjoys complete success (prevailing in all nine cases) in the area of automotive emissions and fuels, an area dominated by the U.S.-owned Big Three (including DaimlerChrysler) assemblers and U.S.-owned parts suppliers. It has a success rate of 75 percent in manufacturing recycling and 67 percent in fisheries conservation. But it has only 60 percent in agricultural inspection, where the Canadian and especially Mexican industries (based on home-based exporters) loom relatively large. Moreover, the United States has a success rate of only 33 percent in forestry conservation, an area in which Canadian companies were particularly strong. It is worth noting that these natural resources sectors of fisheries and forestry (along with agriculture) are the ones that concern environmentalists most about the stress on ecosystems, and of trade and NAFTA's environmental effects.

Third, in many of the cases, notably in the areas of automotive emissions, U.S. dominance arises because of its national environmental leadership — it is the first to recognise an environmental problem and take regulatory action. Canadian and Mexican compliance with these regulations is not a case of acquiescence after significant resistance but a case of these two partner countries coming to support the initial U.S. action to produce an environmentally superior result. This process, often with attendant convergent national adjustments, involves the exercise of structural and other forms of power, but may be best seen as a form of beneficent rather than coercive hegemony, based in part on the superior scientific resources of the United States. In some cases, it is a matter of NAFTA operating in a world where states have no fixed preferences but acquire their interests through the process of interaction inspired and guided by NAFTA. Propelling this process is the dominance of U.S.-owned MNCs, and an empowered North American public demanding better environmental solutions. More recently, it has led to a process of environmental regulatory leapfrogging, especially in the automotive and related air-quality domains, where Canadian jurisdictions have moved to introduce new environmental regulations and standards that are more stringent by many measures than those of neighbouring U.S. states and the U.S. as a whole (Kirton 1998a, 1999).

Fourth, in the domain of trade-related environmental cases there is an almost perfect equality of outcome, and a complete absence of U.S. dominance. In contrast to the environmentally related trade issues, where the United States is successful in 64 percent

(27 of 42) of the cases, in the domain of trade-related environmental cases it prevails in only 25 percent. In this latter realm, success is shared equally among the U.S. with 25 percent, Canada with 38 percent, Mexico with 25 percent, and all three with 25 percent. This sharp shift toward balanced outcomes can be attributed to two factors. The first is the superior ecological capability of Mexico and especially Canada, manifested in a vulnerability for the United States that has been expanded by NAFTA economic liberalisation. To contain this new vulnerability, the United States is forced to co-operate and accept balanced outcomes, as the cases of pesticides and environmental information suggest. The second is the presence in the trade-related environmental area of a strong international institution — the CEC — which, unlike those institutions in the trade area, possesses an international organisation with a single secretariat, substantial budget and staff, and considerable powers of autonomous investigation (Kirton 1997; Housman 1994).

The autonomous power of international institutions is further seen by examining the outcome of the cases according to their non-NAFTA or NAFTA-affected resolution. Here it is clear that the NAFTA era makes an equalising difference. As Table 5.2 displays, in the ten resolved pre-NAFTA cases (with the U.S. directly involved in all), the United States prevailed in eight cases or 80 percent of the time. Canada, directly involved in ten, won in two, for a success rate of 20 percent overall and 20 percent in the issues of direct engagement. Mexico was not directly involved in any cases. This distribution is very close to the overall distribution of economic capability in the region, with Canada's somewhat larger than predicted score (20 percent rather than 10 percent) traceable to the presence of the bilateral FTA. Mexico's score reflects a still relatively autarkic Mexico, carefully choosing the issues on which it ventured to confront the United States. Equally striking, in this pre-NAFTA era none of the cases resulted in an equal outcome.

In sharp contrast, in the much larger set of 40 cases in the NAFTA era, the distributions are dramatically different. The rate of success for the United States alone, directly involved in all cases, has dropped from 80 percent to 50 percent. Canada's has remained relatively constant, moving from 20 percent to 13 percent in all cases and 19 percent in the 26 cases

Table 5.2   Outcomes of Resolved Cases of North American Environmental Regulatory Protection (Pre- and Post-NAFTA)*

Winner	Overall		Pre-NAFTA		Post-NAFTA	
			All	Direct	All	Direct
U.S.	29	58%	10 77%	(13) 77%	19 51%	(37) 51%
Canada	7	14%	2 15%	(11) 18%	5 14%	(22) 23%
Mexico	7	14%	1 7%	(2) 50%	6 16%	(29) 21%
Both/equal	8	16%	– –	– –	8 22%	(14) 57%

* Number of cases of direct involvement.

in which it is directly involved (as a disputant or through the NAFTA trilateral institutions). Mexico's has increased substantially to 18 percent over all cases and to 23 percent in the 30 issues in which it is directly involved. And outcomes that benefit both or all of the countries and their involved firms have risen from zero to 20 percent. Indeed, 57 percent or more than half of the cases involving all three NAFTA countries are resolved according to the preferences of all three.

From these figures it is clear that the NAFTA era works for the United States. It still wins half of the issues in the region. It further shares in the additional 20 percent of joint gains, to produce an overall success rate of 70 percent. The NAFTA era also works for Canada, as its success rate holds at 19 percent in the issues in which it is directly involved, and it records an overall success rate of 39 percent. The greatest beneficiary of the NAFTA era, however, is the region's weakest member — Mexico — with a success rate that has risen to an encouraging overall level of 38 percent. Over the dramatically expanded number of issues in which it is directly involved, it records a success rate relative to the pre-NAFTA period of 23 percent against a still much stronger United States, with which it is now much more intensely involved. Above all, the NAFTA era works for the common North American community, as all three members benefit equally in 20 percent of the issues, and do so in 50 percent of those cases in which all three are directly involved. The world of three competitors struggling for relative gains is clearly giving way to a single integrated community in which all members participate and profit equally.

The importance of the NAFTA era can be further seen by examining the outcomes of those resolved cases in the post-NAFTA era that have been dealt with through the NAFTA institutions, either by its trade domain or from its environmental domain. Here it is clear that the NAFTA institutions make an equalising difference. As Table 5.3 shows, of the 40 resolved cases in the post-NAFTA era, the NAFTA institutions attracted almost half the traffic. Nineteen, or 48 percent, were resolved through the NAFTA institutions (even if other instruments of firm strategy ultimately proved decisive in securing particular outcomes). Of these 19 cases, the United States prevailed in 47 percent, Canada in 22 percent, Mexico in 21 percent, and all three countries equally in 21 percent. These are still clearly the United States' NAFTA's institutions, as the U.S. is the sole beneficiary of their use to a greater degree than the other partner countries. Indeed, if one takes its individual and collective gains together, the United States wins through the NAFTA institutions 68 percent of the time. However, the autonomous impact of international institutions is evident in the greater equality of outcomes when issues are processed through the NAFTA bodies. Here Canada's success rate rises from 19 percent to 32 percent, and Mexico's from 18 percent to 21 percent. Most strikingly, when individual and common gains are taken together, the NAFTA institutions deliver a distribution of outcomes that is vastly more equal than power ratios among countries in North America: United States 68 percent, Canada 53 percent, Mexico 42 percent.

Table 5.3 Resolved Cases of Post-NAFTA North American Environmental Regulatory Protection Dealt with through the NAFTA Institutions*

Case	Regulatory initiator	Challenger (supporter)	Outcome closer to institution objectives	International institution
A. Environmentally related trade issues				
Automotive fuels				
MMT	Canada	U.S. (Ethyl)	U.S. (Ethyl)	NAFTA 11
Agriculture Inspections				
Tomatoes, 1992–97	U.S.	Mexico	U.S.	NAFTA 19
Stone fruits, 1997	Mexico	U.S.	U.S.	NAFTA SPS
Sweet cherries	Mexico	U.S.	U.S.	NAFTA
Pork, 1997	U.S.	Mexico	Mexico	NAFTA SPS
Citrus canker	Mexico	U.S.	U.S.	NAFTA SPS
Mangoes	U.S.	Mexico	U.S.	NAFTA SPS
Supply management	Canada	U.S.	Canada	NAFTA 20
Dangerous Goods Transportation				
Small packages	All	(All)	Equal	CSRM
Truck spills (ERG)	All	(All)	Equal	CSRM
Other				
Trucking	U.S.	Mexico	Canada	NAFTA FTCC
B. Trade-related environmental issues				
Pesticides				
PCBs	All	All	All	CEC TWGP
DDT	U.S. (Canada)	Mexico	U.S. (Canada)	CEC TWGP
Chlordane	Canada (U.S.)	Mexico	Canada (U.S.)	CEC TWGP
Mercury	All	All	Canada (U.S.)	CEC TWGP
Environmental information				
NAPRI, 1997	CEC	All	Mexico	CEC
Environmental science				
Silva Reservoir	CEC	Mexico	Mexico	CEC

* See page xxiii for a list of abbreviations.

The remaining imbalance points to the legacy of U.S. power and highly active environmental movement, and also to Canada's particular historic skill at diplomacy through international institutions. However, the autonomous importance of international organisation and the environmental intervulnerabilities that underlie it are again apparent. The NAFTA environmental institutions make a difference that does more than create an equal or common community. In the 11 cases where NAFTA's trade institutions served as a nest for resolution, the outcomes were distributed as follows: United States 55 percent, Canada 18 percent, Mexico 9 percent, and all 18 percent. In the eight cases where NAFTA's environmental institution — the CEC — served as the nest, the outcomes were Canada 38 percent, the United States 25 percent (including the joint win with Canada on Cozumel), Mexico 25 percent, and all 25 percent.

At the level of the firm, the importance of effective international institutions is again seen in the particular form in which the NAFTA bodies were fashioned. Of particular importance is their open architecture, allowing firms to have direct access to the work of these institutions and involvement in that work. Firms are involved in the CEC through the Joint Public Advisory Committee (JPAC) and many of its working groups. This direct industry involvement was a critical element in producing the mutually beneficial outcomes through regulatory convergence in the Trilateral Working Group on Pesticides (TWGP). Within the NAFTA trade institutions, industry involvement is less direct. The mechanism for industry involvement, through the joint meetings of the Committee on Standards-Related Measures (CSRM) with trilateral industry bodies, is a facilitator of success.

Direct Societal Access under NAFTA Chapter 11 and NAAEC Article 14-15

Perhaps of greatest importance is the right provided by the NAFTA regime for firms and environmentally concerned organisations and individuals to initiate and pursue processes of dispute settlement over trade-related environmental issues, without having to face the barrier of first securing often unavailable or unenthusiastic government support at home. Indeed, among the most innovative features of the NAFTA trade-environment regime, and a truly prescient pioneering step given the current crescendo of demands for improved civil society participation in global governance, were the two major mechanisms that NAFTA constructed to allow societal actors (multinational firms and NGOs and interested citizens) direct access to international dispute settlement procedures.[3] For firms that felt discriminated against by government environmental and other regulations in a foreign country, including regulatory action that was 'tantamount to expropriation', NAFTA's Chapter 11 offered the ability to take their claim for compensation to one of two multilateral dispute settlement mechanisms. The NAAEC's Article 14-15 citizen submission process, in a balancing provision, allowed NGOs and citizens to pursue claims that national and sub-federal governments were not adequately enforcing their own environmental laws and regulations (Markell 2000). Each innovation was the subject of considerable criticism, hope, and speculation about its impact at the time of its birth. Now, after almost seven years in operation, it is possible to identify empirically what the actual record, and its probable impact on regulatory behaviour, has been.

Chapter 11

During this time, there have been 14 known cases initiated under Chapter 11 (Mann 2001; Hufbauer et al. 2001; Mann and von Moltke 1999; Soloway 1999; Wagner 1999).[4] There was one in 1995, four in 1996, none in 1997, six in 1998 (the peak year), two in 1999, and one in the first six months of 2000. This average of only two cases a year does not suggest that firms are rushing to use this new mechanism to an extent that its existence and availability deter regulators. This is even more evident in light of the increasingly large numbers of firms involved in FDI, the number of North American governments eager to regulate, and the number of regulations that have been generated. At the same time, there are enough cases to suggest that there would be far more if firms felt compelled to challenge such regulations, as the first step of the 'race to the bottom' hypothesis suggests.[5]

In a surprise to those who crafted Chapter 11 to counter classic cases of expropriation and FDI discrimination, 8 of the 14 cases have involved challenges to environmental regulations as an explicit part of the petitioning firm's claim. Often such claims have involved claims regarding the economic damage in projected sales or other aspects as a consequence of regulatory change, rather than more direct forms of expropriation of property located in a foreign jurisdiction. Yet it is important to note that these environmental cases have involved challenges to new and often far-reaching forms of government environmental regulation, suggesting that any NAFTA-induced chill has had a much less potent effect. Governments continue to raise the level and sophistication of environmental regulations, whatever the cadence of Chapter 11 cases. It is true that the Canadian government's out-of-court settlement of the Ethyl MMT claim in July 1998 was followed by an outburst of environmentally related cases in quick suggestion, suggesting copycat behaviour by firms beginning to act in ways, and with a frequency, consistent with the race-to-the-bottom hypothesis. Yet this outburst was short lived, and since the Methanex case filed in June 1999 no environmentally related cases have arisen.

As Chapter 11 was introduced primarily to protect U.S. investors in Mexico from the traditional forms of discriminatory treatment they had long suffered there, it was surprising that only a minority of the 14 cases involved U.S. firms petitioning against regulatory action by governments in Mexico.[6] U.S. firms did initiate 9 of the 14 cases, with Canadian firms responsible for four and Mexican firms one (a pattern fully explained by the number and size of foreign direct-investing firms based in each of the three NAFTA countries). However, the Mexican government served as the defendant in only five of the cases, a level equalled by Canada with five and the U.S. with four (including most of those cases in the most recent period). On a pairwise basis, the five claims of U.S. firms against Mexico were closely followed by the four of the U.S. against Canada and the four of Canada against the United States (with a Mexican claim against Canada accounting for the remaining one).

This pattern shows that Chapter 11 has become predominantly an instrument for bilateral Canada-U.S. trade/investment-environmental diplomacy. Yet it is inconsistent with the fear that Chapter 11 provides an instrument for U.S. firms to use against the relatively small and weak but environmentally inclined Canadian and Mexican governments. The fact that Canadian firms have used it against the U.S. government as often as the reverse, in a perfect balance, refutes this argument of nationally based discrimination. Furthermore, the classic race-to-the-bottom hypothesis does not explain why Canadian and U.S. firms would concentrate their investment, regulatory, and legal attention on each other's rich and highly regulated jurisdictions (including California) rather than on Mexico, where the sucking sound was supposed to lead them and where pollution havens are presumed to exist.

Finally, in almost seven years, the Chapter 11 process has yielded two clear outcomes in addition to the Ethyl MMT case, which was settled out of court before the NAFTA-generated panel could rule. In these two cases, both involving U.S. firms' claims against Mexico, the Mexican regulators won the first (Desona) and the U.S. investors the second (Metalclad). Even if two or three resolved cases are sufficient to generate widespread 'chill' calculations on the part of firms and governments throughout the region, the perfect equality of the outcomes provides no basis for an assumption that a chill conclusion will result. Moreover, the fact that Metalclad received a far lower level of compensation sought by the firm (and one that covered only direct physical property costs) and the fact that Canada settled in the Ethyl MMT case only after its regulatory actions were declared illegal under domestic Canadian law suggest that the compounding Chapter 11 case law and precedents will dispense any fears that might lead to chill.

Even with this record, there remains a respectable case for an interpretative statement and for greater transparency in the Chapter 11 proceedings (Hufbauer et al. 2001; Mann and von Moltke 1999). However, the burden of the reform effort should be redirected at replacing the inherited multilateral nests for dispute settlement (International Centre for the Settlement of Investment Disputes [ICSID] and the United Nations Commission on International Trade Law [UNCITRAL]) with a new, all-NAFTA institution. Such a NAFTA creation would be more sensitive to the trade and ecological conditions and regulations within the region, and to the NAFTA regime and its moves to balance trade and environmental considerations within the NAFTA architecture.

Article 14-15

In one of many important and innovative provisions to offset the trend toward liberalisation-induced chill, the NAFTA regime created a provision under NAAEC's Article 14-15 for any interested party to initiate direct action against governments felt not to be enforcing their own environmental regulations. With 28 cases in NAFTA's first six and a half years, this mechanism has generated twice the volume of activity as Chapter 11, and more than three times as much if only Chapter 11's environmental cases are included. In sharp contrast, the government-to-government Part V mechanism, designed to serve a similar purpose but reliant on the governments themselves to initiate such cases, had no cases during this time. With two Article 14-15 cases in 1995, three in 1996, eight in 1997 (including one refiled case), six in 1998, three in 1999, and six in the first six months of 2000, the level of activity rapidly rose to a relatively high and sustained level (despite the one-time dip of 1999).

The cases initiated under Article 14-15 have featured very good overall balance in the spotlight it casts, with the U.S. attracting eight challenges, Canada nine, and Mexico eleven. Indeed, given the widespread perception that Mexico lacked the will and ability to regulate and enforce, and the reality of restricted resources following the December 1994 financial crisis, it is remarkable that so much effort — 17 of the 28 cases — has been directed at ensuring that Canadian and U.S. enforcement remains at the relatively high level long specified by their legislation. At the same time, the imbalance is not sufficiently great to suggest that the region's NGOs have been directing their Article 14-15 activity on the basis of an assumption that chilled U.S. and Canadian jurisdictions are the ones requiring priority remedial action. Indeed, the particular nature of the cases, particularly some of the most high-profile ones, does not relate to behaviour that predated the advent of NAFTA.

Moreover, the chill hypothesis cannot account for the particular temporal pattern of cases, with the initial emphasis on the U.S. and Canada as the defendants, being soon replaced by a focus on Canada and Mexico (which received all eight complaints in 1997), and subsequently on the U.S. and Mexico. The chill hypothesis would suggest a consistent pattern of litigation against the United States and Canada by NGOs fearful that firms would flee to (especially post-crisis) Mexico, and that their home governments would relax enforcement to keep them at home.

Article 14-15 operates, as intended, as an instrument for NGOs concerned with environmental quality and related social concerns. A full 22 of the 28 cases have been filed by NGOs, with four by individuals. In 1999–2000, firms began to file actions, but the two mounted were declined on the grounds that they were already the subject of action under NAFTA's Chapter 11. Article 14-15 has thus remained a pure instrument for environmental protection, rather than being mobilised by firms and foreign investors to forward their ultimately commercial concerns. It is also accessible to individuals, who have used it in conjunction with an NGO.

Of the 28 cases brought to the CEC under Article 14-15, 13 have been terminated, withdrawn or diverted (to an Article 13 investigation), or deferred, leaving 15 to proceed through the review process. Of those 15, two have resulted in a factual record, the CEC's Council of Ministers has declined the recommendation that a record by prepared in a further case, and the remainder are in various stages of review (including two where the preparation of a factual record has been recommended). Of the two that have been settled, the factual record upheld the submitters' cases against Mexican government action (in the case of the Cozumel pier) and the Canadian government (over failure to enforce the *Fisheries Act* at hydro dams in British Columbia). In neither case was remedial action specified.

The production of only two factual records after six and a half years, the long and lengthening time it has taken to produce the two that have emerged, and the government's willingness to veto production of a factual record all suggest that Article 14-15 is a less effective instrument to ensure environmental enforcement than had been intended. Yet these derogations do not arise as a result of regulatory chill. The chill hypothesis would predict that the U.S. and Canada would be the subject of such actions, rather than Canada and Mexico against which a factual record has been released. Moreover, in both these cases, it was not the advent of NAFTA that caused the lack of enforcement that was highlighted. The Cozumel case featured tourism rather than trade in goods, and actions that predated the advent of NAFTA. Similarly, the Canadian case dealt with a pattern of enforcement behaviour that existed long before NAFTA took effect, when any NAFTA competitiveness link was highly indirect (reduced costs for hydro that would benefit all firms and residents in British Columbia and potentially, under deregulated electricity trade, those in the U.S. and Mexico).

Although the Article 14-15 record suggests that regulatory refugee and chill behaviour is not at work, there remain good general and trade-related grounds for significantly improving the mechanism. At a minimum, as a basic matter of good governance, democratically elected governments and their citizens all have a strong interest in ensuring that their existing laws and regulations are fully respected and enforced. Furthermore, the accumulating evidence suggests that both governments and their firms have a strong interest in moving rapidly to high environmental standards to reap the full competitive advantages offered by the NAFTA marketplace and to thrive as North Americans in the single global market that is rapidly emerging (Kirton 1999).

Conclusion

There is a legitimate concern that the competitive dynamics unleashed by NAFTA trade and investment liberalisation in the 1990s, and perhaps the similarly deep liberalisation to come under the World Trade Organization in the coming decade, will create regulatory refugees as firms seek pollution havens where environmental standards are lax, where regulatory chill exists as their home governments relax regulations and standards in order to retain those firms, and where international legal and institutional restraints inhibit the freedom of national and sub-federal governments to regulate as their local conditions and citizens demand. Yet the accumulating evidence uncovered by analyses conducted from several vantage points suggests that there is little support for such fears and much to indicate they are false.

At one end of the spectrum, patterns of FDI and firm location and expansion suggest decisively that there is no physical race to the bottom, and that the consequential cases of firm relocation are not caused by differential environmental regulations and enforcement (Kirton 1998c; Cole and Ensign 1997). Similarly, the observed improvement in general conditions of environmental quality in the major ambient media throughout much of the region, in the face of strong economic growth, suggests that refugees, regulatory relaxation and chills, and international restraints do not exist to any meaningful extent (Hufbauer et al. 2001; Jones, Griggs, and Fredricksen 2000). An examination of firm incentives, strategies, choices, and experiences in the new era of complex institutional responsiveness suggests that among the rich array of alternatives available to cope with rising environmental regulatory protection, environmentally enhancing solutions are preferred (Rugman, Kirton, and Soloway 1999). It is hardly surprising that the general and sectoral case studies conducted as part of the development of the CEC's analytic framework for assessing NAFTA's environmental effects, and the 14 studies conducted most recently to apply the framework, found very little to support and much to refute the hypothesis of regulatory refugees, relaxation and restraint (Kirton et al. 1999).[7]

The more detailed analysis of the full set of cases of environmental regulatory protection in North America confirms these conclusions. Conditions of complex institutional responsiveness have generated a proliferating number of cases in North America in which actions in the trade and environmental protection spheres intersect and influence each other. Given the profound imbalance in capability among the three countries of the region, the historical absence of trilateral interaction, and the very recent advent of regional international organisation, it seems unlikely that the NAFTA trade-environment regime, despite its pioneering provisions, could exercise an autonomous impact in altering the pattern of outcomes from those predicted by power and interest, in which powerful U.S. multinational investors and free traders would have their way over the weaker Canadian and Mexican governments and environmental regulators throughout the region.

Yet an analysis of 84 cases of environmental regulatory protection from 1980 to mid 1998 demonstrates that this regional regime is effective in giving smaller countries and environmental values a more equal place. Although more cases have arisen as the 1980s have given way to the 1990s, there has been a distinct move toward equality of outcomes, and joint gains, as the NAFTA era has progressed, as the NAFTA institutions have been employed and as NAFTA's environmental organisation, the CEC, has been used as the locus for action. Similarly, the records of NAFTA Chapter 11's 14 cases and NAAEC Article 14-15's 28 cases suggest a reasonable equality in process and outcomes among the three countries, and one in which the values of trade and investment liberalisation are well balanced by environmental ones.

At a minimum, future research on the regulatory refugees, relaxation, and restraint hypothesis will need to specify much more clearly and fairly which particular behaviours they predict, and generate reliable interview-based research with regulators and firms that can demonstrate that the hypothesised calculations and resulting causally related behaviours actually exist. At a maximum, perhaps the time has come to stop approaching the important task of modernising the NAFTA architecture with a focus on solving this essentially nonexistent problem, and start redesigning it so it serves the needs of both trade liberalisers and environmental protectors better in the face of the fierce global competition and challenges that lie ahead.

Notes

1   This is a revised version of a paper entitled 'Canada-U.S. Trade and the Environment: Regimes, Regulatory Refugees, Races, and Results', presented at the conference on 'Rethinking the Line: The Canada-U.S. Border', 23–25 October 2000, The Waterfront Centre Hotel, Vancouver, British Columbia, sponsored by the Policy Research Secretariat. The author expresses his gratitude for the contribution of Alan Rugman and Julie Soloway, who collaborated in the initial research on which this paper is substantially based, and of Gina Stephens, who assisted with the empirical updates. This research forms part of the research conducted under a strategic grant from the Social Sciences and Humanities Research Council of Canada for a project on 'Strengthening Canada's Environmental Community Through International Regime Reform' (EnviReform), based at the Centre for International Studies at the University of Toronto.
2   This section and that which follows are based heavily on Chapter 11 of Alan Rugman, John Kirton, and Julie Soloway (1999).
3   The importance of the direct access granted by Chapter 11 is seen in the Ethyl MMT case, in which the petitioning firm, Ethyl, did not have its case taken up by its home (U.S.) government when it filed under the traditional trade law provisions contained in NAFTA's Chapter 20.
4   As only Canada makes public records of Chapter 11 proceedings that involve it, it is possible that there are additional cases, including those settled in ways that generate environmentally regulatory chill. However, the year-by-year pattern of cases initiated suggests this is unlikely.
5   The 'race to the bottom' hypothesis, in its integrated form, suggests that firms in less stringent and now open jurisdictions will threaten their local home governments with relocation if those governments do not relax, freeze, or raise to a less than required degree their own environmental regulations. This thus induces governments to comply with these threats (thereby creating regulatory chill) and also induces firms to relocate if they do not. In turn, these two channels induce a regulatory race to the bottom among home governments and would-be host jurisdictions of the relocating firm. While this hypothesis is capable of disconfirmation, it requires much more precise specification, as various forms of government behaviour (lowered, frozen, and raised-less-than-demanded regulations) and firm behaviour

(actual relocation and remaining in place under a chilled home government) all currently qualify as supporting evidence.
6 The counter-argument that the mere existence of Chapter 11 led to a regulatory chill that obviated the need for any Chapter 11 action is refuted by the large increase in Mexican government regulation and enforcement since NAFTA took effect.
7 Texts of all 14 studies, prepared for a symposium in Washington DC on 10–11 October 2000, are available on the CEC Web site at <www.cec.org>.

References

Abbott, Frederick M. (1996). 'From Theory to Practice: The Second Phase of the NAFTA Environmental Regime'. In R. Wolfrum, ed., *Enforcing Environmental Standards*, pp. 451–478. Springer-Verlag, Berlin.

Abbott, Frederick M. (2000). 'NAFTA and the Legalization of World Politics: A Case Study'. *International Organization* vol. 54, no. 3, pp. 519–548.

Audley, John J. (1997). *Green Politics and Global Trade: NAFTA and the Future of Environmental Politics*. Georgetown University Press, Washington DC.

Cole, Elizabeth and Prescott Ensign (1997). 'An Examination of United States Foreign Direct Investment into Mexico and Its Relation to the North American Free Trade Agreement: Towards a Balanced Understanding of the Effects of Environmental Regulation and Factor Endowments That Affect Location Decisions'. Paper presented at the annual convention of the Academy of International Business, 8–12 October. Monterrey.

De Sombre, Elizabeth (1995). 'Baptists and Bootleggers for the Environment: The Origins of United States Unilateral Sanctions'. *Journal of Environment and Development* vol. 4 (Winter), pp. 53–75.

Economic Policy Institute (1997). *The Failed Experiment: NAFTA at Three Years*. Economic Policy Institute, Washington DC.

Esty, Daniel C. and Damien Geradin (1997). 'Market Access, Competitiveness, and Harmonization: Environmental Protection in Regional Trade Agreements'. *Harvard Environmental Law Review* vol. 21, no. 2, pp. 265–336.

Gilligan, M. (1997). 'Lobbying as a Private Good with Intra-Industry Trade'. *International Studies Quarterly* vol. 41, no. 3, pp. 455–474.

Groetzinger, Jon (1997). 'Nafta's Environmental Provisions: Are They Working as Intended? Are They Adequate?' *Canada-United States Law Journal* vol. 23, pp. 401–428.

Grossman, Perry (2000). 'Globalization and the Linkage of Trade and Environmental Issues: A Comparative Analysis of the Canada-United States and North American Free Trade Agreements'. Ph.D. diss. New York University, New York.

Housman, Robert (1994). 'The North American Free Trade Agreement's Lessons for Reconciling Trade and Environment'. *Stanford Journal of International Law* vol. 30, pp. 379–422.

Hufbauer, Gary Clyde, Daniel C. Esty, Diana Orejas, et al. (2001). *NAFTA and the Environment: Seven Years Later*. Institute for International Economics, Washington DC. <www.iie.com/publications/publication.cfm?pub_id=322&source=none> (December 2001).

Jansen, Heinz (2001). 'Induced Institutional Change in the Trade and Environment Debate: A Computable General Equilibrium Application to NAFTA with Endogenous Regulation Setting'. *Environmental and Resource Economics* vol. 18, pp. 149–172.

Johnson, Pierre Marc (1999). 'Five Windows for the Future of NAFTA's Environmental Commission'. *Policy Options* vol. 20, no. 5 (June), pp. 27–32.

Johnson, Pierre Marc and André Beaulieu (1996). *The Environment and NAFTA: Understanding and Implementing the New Continental Law*. Island Press, Washington DC.

Jones, Laura, Laura Griggs, and Liv Fredricksen (2000). *Environmental Indicators*. 4th ed. Fraser Institute, Vancouver.

Keohane, Robert and Joseph Nye (1977). *Power and Interdependence: World Politics in Transition*. Little, Brown, Boston.

Kirton, John J. (1997). 'The Commission for Environmental Cooperation and Canada-U.S. Environmental Governance in the NAFTA Era'. *American Review of Canadian Studies* vol. 27, no. 3, pp. 459–486.

Kirton, John J. (1998a). 'The Impact of Environmental Regulation on the North American Automotive Industry in the NAFTA Era'. In S. Weintraub and C. Sands, eds., *The North American Auto Industry under NAFTA*. Center for Strategic and International Studies Press, Washington DC.

Kirton, John J. (1998b). 'NAFTA's Trade-Environment Institutions: Regional Impact, Hemispheric Potential'. Center for International Relations, University of Southern California, Columbia International Affairs Online. <www.ciaonet.org/srchfrm.html> (December 2001).

Kirton, John J. (1998c). 'NAFTA, Foreign Direct Investment, and Economic Integration: A Canadian Approach'. In Organisation for Economic Co-operation and Development, *Migration, Free Trade, and Regional Integration in North America*, pp. 181–194. Organisation for Economic Co-operation and Development, Paris.

Kirton, John J. (1999). 'Successful Strategies for Environmental Regulation in the North American Automotive Industry under NAFTA'. Paper prepared for the project on 'The North American Automotive Industry under NAFTA', Center for Strategic and International Studies. Washington DC.

Kirton, John J. and et al. (1999). *Assessing the Environmental Effects of the North American Free Trade Agreement (NAFTA): Final Analytic Framework and Methodological Issues and Empirical Background*. Commission for Environmental Cooperation, Montreal.

Kirton, John J. and Rafael Fernandez de Castro (1997). *NAFTA's Institutions: The Environmental Potential and Performance of the NAFTA Free Trade Commission and Related Bodies*. Commission for Environmental Cooperation, Montreal.

Kirton, John J. and Alan M. Rugman (1999). 'Regional Environmental Impacts of NAFTA on the Automotive Sector'. *Canadian Journal of Regional Science* vol. 21 (Summer), pp. 227–254.

Leyshon, A. (1992). 'The Transformation of Regulatory Order: Regulating the Global Economy and Environment'. *Geoforum* vol. 23, pp. 249–267.

Leyton-Brown, David (1976). 'The Multinational Enterprise and Conflict in Canadian-American Relations'. In A. B. Fox, A. Hero and J. Nye, eds., *Canada and the United States: Transnational and Transgovernmental Relations*, pp. 140–161. Columbia University Press, New York.

Lowry, Andrew (1992). 'North American Free Trade and the Environment'. *Business America* vol. 113, no. 21, pp. 22–24.

Magraw, D. and Steve Charnovitz (1994). 'NAFTA's Repercusions: Is Green Trade Possible?' *Environment* vol. 36, no. 2, pp. 14–27.

Mann, Howard (2001). *Private Rights, Public Problems: A Guide to NAFTA's Controversial Chapter on Investors Rights*. International Institute on Sustainable Development and World Wildlife Fund, Winnipeg.

Mann, Howard and Konrad von Moltke (1999). *NAFTA's Chapter 11 and the Environment: Addressing the Impacts of the Investor-State Process on the Environment*. International Institute for Environment and Development, Washington DC.

Markell, David L. (2000). 'The Commission for Environmental Cooperation's Citizen Submission Process'. *Georgetown International Environmental Law Review* vol. 12, no. 3, pp. 565–574.

Mayer, Frederick (1998). *Interpreting NAFTA: The Science and Art of Political Analysis.* Columbia University Press, New York.

Mumme, Stephen and Pamela Duncan (1996). 'The Commission on Environmental Cooperation and the U.S.-Mexico Border Environment'. *Journal of Environment and Development* vol. 5 (June), pp. 197–215.

Munton, Don and John J. Kirton (1996). 'Beyond and Beneath the Nation-State: Province-State Interactions and NAFTA'. Paper presented at the annual convention of the International Studies Association, 17 April. San Diego.

Norton, Roy (1998). 'Posture and Policymaking in Canada-U.S. Relations: The First Two Multroney and Chrétien Years'. *Canadian Foreign Policy* vol. 5 (Winter), pp. 15–36.

Nye, Joseph (1976). 'Transnational Relations and Interstate Conflicts: An Empirical Analysis'. In A. B. Fox, A. Hero and J. Nye, eds., *Canada and the United States: Transnational and Transgovernmental Relations*, pp. 367–404. Columbia University Press, New York.

Orbuch, Paul and Thomas Singer (1995). 'International Trade, the Environment, and the States: An Evolving State-Federal Relationship'. *Journal of Environment and Development* vol. 4 (Summer), pp. 121–144.

Public Citizen (1995). *NAFTA's Broken Promises.* Public Citizen, Washington DC.

Rugman, Alan M. and John J. Kirton (1998). 'Multinational Enterprise Strategy and the NAFTA Trade and Environment Regime'. *Journal of World Business* vol. 33, no. 4, pp. 438–454.

Rugman, Alan M. and John J. Kirton (1999). 'NAFTA, Environmental Regulations, and International Business Strategies'. *Global Focus* vol. 11, no. 4.

Rugman, Alan M., John J. Kirton, and Julie Soloway (1997). 'Canadian Corporate Strategy in a North American Region'. *American Review of Canadian Studies* vol. 27 (Summer), pp. 199–219.

Rugman, Alan M., John J. Kirton, and Julie Soloway (1999). *Environmental Regulations and Corporate Strategy: A NAFTA Perspective.* Oxford University Press, Oxford.

Soloway, Julie A. (1999). 'Environmental Trade Barriers under NAFTA: The MMT Fuel Additives Controversy'. *Minnesota Journal of Global Trade* vol. 8, no. 1, p. 55.

Spencer, Robert, John J. Kirton, and Kim Richard Nossal (1981). *The International Joint Commission Seventy Years On.* Centre for International Studies, Univeristy of Toronto, Toronto.

Steinberg, Richard (1997). 'Trade-Environment Negotiations in the EU, NAFTA, and WTO: Regional Trajectories of Rule Development'. *American Journal of International Law* vol. 91, no. 2, pp. 231–267.

United States Trade Representative (1997). 'Study on the Operation and Effect of the North American Free Trade Agreement'. 1 July. United States Trade Representative.

Wagner, J. Martin (1999). 'International Investment, Expropriation, and Environmental Protection'. *Golden Gate University Law Review* vol. 29, nos. 1–3, pp. 465–538.

Weintraub, Sydney (1994). 'Current State of U.S.-Canada Economic Relations'. *American Review of Canadian Studies* vol. 24 (Winter), pp. 473–488.

Weintraub, Sydney (1997). *NAFTA at Three: A Progress Report.* Center for Strategic and International Studies, Washington DC.

Appendix 5-A: Cases of North American Environmental Regulatory Protection[a]

Case	Regulatory initiator	Challenger (supporter)	Outcome closer to institution objectives	International institution
A. *Environmentally related trade issues (60)*				
Automotive emissions (6)				
Oxides of sulphur	U.S.	(Mexico)	U.S.	
Oxides of nitrogen	U.S.	(Mexico)	U.S.	
Ozone	U.S.	(Canada, Mexico)	U.S.	
Particulates	U.S.	(Canada, Mexico)	U.S.	
Onboard diagnostic systems	U.S.	(Canada, Mexico)	U.S.	
INM	U.S.	(Canada)	U.S.	
Automotive fuels (4)				
Lead[b]	U.S.	(Mexico)	U.S.	
MMT	Canada	U.S. (Ethyl)	U.S. (Ethyl)	NAFTA 11
Sulphur	U.S.	(Canada)	U.S.	
Benzene	U.S.	(Canada)	Ongoing	
Agriculture inspections (24)				
Apples, 1989–98	Mexico	U.S.	Mexico	NAFTA 19
Avocados, 1914–97	U.S.	Mexico	Equal	
Beef 1, 1991–98	U.S.	Canada	Ongoing	NAFTA SPS
Beef 2, 1994–97	Mexico	U.S.	Mexico	—
Blueberries, 1991–93	U.S.	Canada	U.S.	FTA
Christmas trees 1, 1994–98	Mexico	Canada	Ongoing	NAFTA SPS
Christmas trees 2, 1994–98	Mexico	U.S.	Ongoing	NAFTA SPS
Citrus canker, 1991–97	Mexico	U.S.	U.S.	NAFTA SPS
Global wheat trade	All	All	Ongoing	NAFTA CAT
Mangoes, 1993–95	U.S.	Mexico	U.S.	NAFTA SPS
Pork, 1997	U.S.	Mexico	Mexico	NAFTA SPS
Potatoes, 1995–96	U.S.	Canada	Ongoing	
Poultry 1	U.S.	Mexico	Ongoing	
Poultry 2	Mexico	U.S.	Ongoing	—
Seed potatoes	Mexico	Canada	—	NAFTA SPS
Sorghum, 1997–98	Mexico	U.S.	Ongoing	NAFTA SPS
Strawberries, 1996	U.S.	Mexico	U.S.	—
Stone fruits, 1991–97	Mexico	U.S.	U.S.	NAFTA SPS

Supply management	Canada	U.S.	Canada	NAFTA 20
Sweet cherries, 1991–97	Mexico	U.S.	U.S.	NAFTA
Tomatoes, 1937–98	U.S.	Mexico	U.S.	NAFTA 19
UHT milk, 1987–95	U.S.	Canada	U.S.	FTA 18
Wheat 1, 1995–98	Mexico	U.S.	U.S.	—
Wheat 2, 1995–97	U.S.	Mexico	Mexico	NAFTA SPS
Manufacturing recycling (4)				
Newsprint[b], 19	U.S.	Canada	U.S.	—
Beer cans 1, 1988[b]	Canada	U.S.+EU	U.S.	GATT
Beer cans 2, 1992[b]	Canada	U.S.	U.S.	GATT
Beer cans 3, 1992	Canada	U.S.	Equal	—
Fisheries conservation (6)				
Lobsters[b], 1989–	U.S.	Canada	U.S.	FTA
Tuna[b], 1979–82	U.S.	Canada	Canada	GATT
Herring-salmon 1[b], 1988	Canada	U.S.	U.S.	GATT
Herring-salmon 2[b], 1989	Canada	U.S.	U.S.	FTA
Pacific salmon, 1998	Both	Canada	U.S.	—
Tuna-dolphin, 1993	U.S.	Mexico	Mexico	GATT
Forestry conservation (4)				
Lumber 1[b], 1986–	U.S.	Canada	U.S.	
Lumber 2[b], 1992	U.S.	Canada	Canada	FTA
Lumber 3, 1998	U.S.	Canada	Ongoing	—
British Columbia forestry, 1998	EU	Canada	Equal	—
Environmental services (4)				
PCB exports[b], 1995	Canada	U.S.	Equal	
Metalclad	U.S.	Mexico	Ongoing	NAFTA 11
Desona	U.S.	Mexico	Ongoing	NAFTA 11
USA Waste	U.S.	Mexico	Ongoing	NAFTA 11
Dangerous goods transportation (5)				
Small packages	All	(All)	Equal	CSRM
Large containers	All	—	Ongoing	CSRM
Halogenated organic chlorides	All	—	Ongoing	NAFTA CSRM
Truck spills (ERG)	All	(All)	Equal	CSRM
Rail cars	All	—	Ongoing	NAFTA CSRM
Other (2)				
Asbestos[b]	U.S.	Canada	U.S.	—
Trucking	U.S.	Mexico	Canada	NAFTA FTCC

B. Trade-related environmental issues (25)
Pesticides (4)

PCBs	All	All	All	CEC TWGP
DDT	U.S. (Canada)	Mexico	U.S. (Canada)	CEC TWGP
Chlordane	Canada (U.S.)	Mexico	Canada (U.S.)	CEC TWGP
Mercury	All	All	Canada (Mexico)	CEC TWGP

Environmental information (1)

NAPRI, 1997	CEC	All	Mexico	CEC

Environmental science (3)

Silva Reservoir	CEC	Mexico	Mexico	CEC 13
LRTAP	CEC	All	Equal	CEC 13
San Pedro	CEC	U.S.-Mexico	Ongoing	CEC 13

Environmental enforcement (17)

Biodiversity, 1995	U.S.	U.S.	Terminated	CEC 14-15
Sierra Club, 1995	U.S.	U.S.	Terminated	CEC 14-15
CPRN, 1996	Mexico	Mexico	Canada/U.S.	CEC 14-15
Aage Tottrup, 1995	Canada	Canada	Terminated	CEC 14-15
Oldman River, 1996	Canada	Canada	Terminated	CEC 14-15
SW Biodiversity, 1996	U.S.	U.S.	Terminated	CEC 14-15
BC Aboriginal Fisheries, 1997	Canada	Canada	Proceeding	CEC 14-15
Rio, 1997	Canada	Canada	Proceeding	CEC 14-15
CQDE, 1997	Canada	Canada	Proceeding	CEC 14-15
CEDF, 1997	Canada	Canada	Terminated	CEC 14-15
Animal Alliance, 1997	Canada	Canada	Terminated	CEC 14-15
Oldman River, 1997	Canada	Canada	Proceeding	CEC 14-15
IDA, 1997	Mexico	Mexico	Proceeding	CEC 14-15
IDA, 1998	Mexico	Mexico	Proceeding	CEC 14-15
Martinez, 1998	Mexico	Mexico	Terminated	CEC 14-15
Planet Earth, 1998	Canada	U.S.	Proceeding	CEC 14-15
Sierra Club, 1998	Canada/U.S.	Canada/U.S.	Proceeding	CEC 14-15

a See page xxiii for a list of abbreviations.
b Denotes non-NAFTA cases, defined as those effectively resolved prior to NAFTA and whose resolution was unaffected by calculations about the onset of NAFTA.

PART II
INVESTOR PROTECTION:
EVALUATING THE
NAFTA CHAPTER 11 MODEL

Chapter 6

The Masked Ball of NAFTA Chapter 11: Foreign Investors, Local Environmentalists, Government Officials, and Disguised Motives

Sanford E. Gaines

Environmental laws and regulations can have important effects on economic behaviour, so the liberalised investment regime established in Chapter 11 of the North American Free Trade Agreement (NAFTA) could be expected to intersect on occasion with domestic environmental policy decisions. But no one expected that more than half (10 of 17) of the investor-state arbitration claims under Chapter 11 in the first six years would seek compensation for actions by the respondent government related to risks to public health or to the protection and conservation of natural resources (Mann 2001). Suddenly, Chapter 11 is seen as (another) trade-based threat to environmental protection. Obscure company names in four cases — Ethyl Corporation, Metalclad, S.D. Myers Inc., Methanex — have become code words for environmental advocates and governments at this latest front of the trade-environment war. The advocacy for dismantling or reforming Chapter 11 gains energy from the nature of the products made or handled by the four companies: methylcyclopentadienyl manganese tricarbonyl, or MMT (Ethyl), hazardous waste (Metalclad), polychlorinated biphenyls, or PCBs (S.D. Myers), and methyl tertiary butyl ether, or MTBE (Methanex). One environmentalist sees in these cases the danger of 'a wholesale overturning of the regulatory state, which took 100 years to build' (California Lawyer 2000). Even moderate voices in the environmental community express grave concern about Chapter 11 (Mann and von Moltke 1999).

But when the facts and behaviours in specific cases are introduced, those truths prove to be elusive and their implications not at all so obvious. Surely citizens want their governments to have a free hand in protecting them from the health risks of exposure to such toxic-sounding materials. There is, then, a legitimate cause for concern that the environment and human health are in jeopardy if governments have to compensate foreign companies for the economic losses caused by controls on human exposure to these nefarious materials. The concern is only heightened when the compensation payments are being ordered by obscure, secretive tribunals. These 'truths' of conflict between environmental protection and investor protection seem self-evident.

This chapter presents one environmentalist's revisionist view that the public alarm about Chapter 11 springs from mistaking the identity of the interests that were really taking the lead during complicated decision-making minuets. Government decisions publicly dressed in green turn out, once unmasked, to have little environmental legitimacy. Domestic commercial or political dancers at the masked ball, lurking in the shadows, were well served by putatively environmental decisions taken at the expense of foreign guests. At the very least, a look behind the masks of the figures in the news serves as a cautionary reminder that restrictions on or mistreatment of foreign investments come cloaked in many disguises (Gudofsky 2000). Public policy is poorly served by naive acceptance at face value of every official claim to be acting for the benefit of the environment. The argument in the chapter goes further, asserting that the weight of the evidence in these cases better supports an environmentally contrarian conclusion: the two Chapter 11 awards (*Metalclad v. United Mexican States, S.D. Myers, Inc. v. Canada*) and the one settled case (*Ethyl Corporation v. Canada*), by disciplining arbitrary government action, benefit domestic environmental regulation as well as properly compensate foreign investors wounded in domestic political cross-fire.

The chapter begins with a brief synopsis of the core elements of Chapter 11, including both the substantive disciplines on government action and the procedural devices for raising and resolving investor claims. It then recounts each of the three major environment-oriented Chapter 11 cases that have resulted in obligations to pay compensation as of early 2001. The discussion of these three cases will identify the environmental, political, and business competition aspects of each case, which are more tightly intertwined than news media accounts would suggest. It next analyses the common circumstantial factors and the common legal conclusions leading to compensations in these cases. With this analysis of the three resolved cases, the following section examines the pending case of *Methanex v. United States*, which may give important new definition to the investment-environment relationship. The chapter concludes with an overall assessment of Chapter 11 and its potential threat to environmental regulation.

Overview of NAFTA Chapter 11

Although thought by many to be a NAFTA innovation (Alvarez 2000), Chapter 11 in fact applied established U.S. and Canadian investment policy to the new trinational economic relationship (Gantz 2001; Price 2000a; Van Duzer 1997; Abbott 2000). Throughout the 1980s and 1990s, the United States negotiated bilateral investment treaties (BITs) with developing countries around the world, while pressing for the first multilateral disciplines on investment regulations through the World Trade Organization's Agreement on Trade-Related Investment Measures (TRIMs). Canada followed a similar approach in a dozen foreign investment protection and promotion agreements (FIPAs) with developing countries. Like many parts of NAFTA, Chapter 11 builds in particular on the Canada-U.S. Free Trade Agreement (FTA), which had similar core liberalisation disciplines on investment restrictions, national treatment of investors, and protection of investors from direct or indirect expropriation of their investments. As with the more familiar rules on trade in goods, the agreed disciplines in Chapter 11 circumscribe in specific ways each nation's freedom to determine internal policies affecting economic behaviour. In Mexico's case, for example, the international norms of NAFTA Chapter 11 supersede the long-cherished Calvo doctrine, under which Mexico rejected the application of international law to its internal actions affecting investors (Lee 2001; Enriquez 2000).

Violations of the Chapter 11 disciplines can give rise to claims for compensation by foreign investors alleging that they are being treated in unfair or discriminatory ways or that the government has effectively expropriated their investment. Of course, investors can always pursue legal remedies against government measures under the laws of that country. In the ordinary course of trade agreements such as the FTA, a violation of an agreement provision would also be resolved through state-to-state consultations or dispute resolution. The dispute settlement provisions of NAFTA Chapter 11 take a different approach for investor claims. Tracking the U.S. BITs with developing countries, which seek to reinforce investor protection in countries where local administrative or judicial remedies may not be reliable, Chapter 11 provides the option for investors to bring their claims against a state directly to international arbitration through the procedures and services of several international arbitration entities (Trakman 2001).

Substance

Article 1101 of NAFTA declares the broad scope of the chapter: 'This Chapter applies to measures adopted or maintained by a Party relating to' investors or investments of another Party. 'Measure,' defined in Article 201(1), is 'any law, regulation, procedure, requirement or practice'.[1] The term 'investment,' defined in Article 1139, encompasses virtually every conceivable form of investment, including enterprises themselves, equity or debt securities in enterprises, loans, rights to a share of profits, real estate and tangible and intangible property, and contractual or other interests associated with capital commitments. Only claims to money, sales of goods and services, or credit associated with such sales are specifically excluded.[2]

Articles 1102 and 1103 establish the familiar core trade obligations of national treatment (nondiscrimination between domestic and foreign investors) and most-favoured-nation treatment (nondiscrimination between foreign investors from different countries). Chapter 11 also assures a minimum standard of treatment for foreign investors. Article 1105 obliges the governments to comply with international law, 'including fair and equitable treatment and full protection and security'. This is understood to encompass, among other matters, minimum standards of administrative and judicial due process (Wallace 2000). Another important substantive rule, Article 1106, protects foreign investors and investments against 'performance requirements', such as minimum export sales, local sourcing of raw materials or supplies, or minimum 'domestic content' requirements. There are, however, exceptions embedded within Article 1106. A country may require the use of a particular technology 'to meet generally applicable health, safety or environmental requirements' on a nondiscriminatory basis. Moreover, the rules against local sourcing and domestic content requirements are subject to an exception for measures 'necessary to protect human, animal or plant life or health' or 'necessary for the conservation of living or non-living exhaustible natural resources'.

Article 1110 sets forth the important rule against uncompensated expropriation. Expropriation itself is not forbidden, by NAFTA or by any rule of international law. What Article 1110 prohibits is direct or indirect nationalisation or expropriation or any 'measure tantamount to nationalization or expropriation' of the investment of an investor of another country unless the expropriation is:

a)   for a public purpose;
b)   on a nondiscriminatory basis;
c)   in accordance with due process of law and Article 1105(1); and
d)   on payment of compensation in accordance with paragraphs 2 through 6.[3]

Note that all four conditions must be satisfied. That is, even a national measure for a public purpose applied through due process of law and without discrimination may give rise to a claim for compensation if its result is tantamount to expropriation. The key interpretive question about Article 1110(1) thus becomes the meaning of expropriation and the phrase 'measure tantamount to ... expropriation' (Gudofsky 2000). Julie Soloway, in Chapter 7, discusses these questions in more detail.

A final note is in order about Article 1114, touted as one of NAFTA's 'green' provisions. Article 1114(1) provides that 'Nothing in this Chapter shall be construed to prevent a Party from adopting, maintaining or enforcing any measure *otherwise consistent with this Chapter* that it considers appropriate to ensure that investment activity in its territory is undertaken in a manner sensitive to environmental concerns' [emphasis added]. Article 1114 was included as an explicit reservation of the sovereign right, already implicit, to adopt laws or policies of general application controlling or regulating or restricting investments so as to preserve or protect the environment. This broad right covers everything from environmental impact assessment requirements to pollution control requirements to generally applicable restrictions on land use or prohibitions on the production of certain chemicals. But the italicised phrase is critically important. The environment-related investor-state disputes thus far all involve claims that the government environmental measures in question were taken in ways inconsistent with the substantive provisions of Chapter 11 outlined above.

Procedure

The procedures under Chapter 11 have become as controversial as its substantive disciplines on government action. In a step that is seen to diminish the power of governments vis-à-vis private investors, Chapter 11 makes provision for investor-state arbitration of investor grievances (Mann 2001). Arbitration gives foreign investors a degree of procedural protection against abusive actions by the host government by offering investors the option to pursue any grievance against the government through arbitration in an impartial forum rather than in the national administrative or judicial tribunals (Price 2000b). Investor-state arbitration is neither exclusive nor mandatory; it is initiated at the option of an investor in one of the NAFTA parties, either on behalf of that individual or on behalf of an enterprise, when that investor has a claim that a NAFTA government breached one of the substantive rules described above and that the investor has thereby incurred loss or damage (Pearce and Coe 2000).[4] The investor-state arbitration provisions of NAFTA build on a process first established by the World Bank in 1965 and subsequently incorporated into many bilateral investment treaties of the United States and Canada (Gantz 2001).

There is a three-year statute of limitations on bringing a claim under this process. NAFTA Article 1118 imposes an obligation on both sides to attempt first to settle the claim through negotiation or consultation (Pearce and Coe 2000). In submitting a claim under Article 1120, the investor must consent to the arbitration procedure, and must waive the right to initiate or pursue any administrative or judicial process involving the same claim. One NAFTA claim has been dismissed for failure clearly to waive these rights.[5]

Once a claim is submitted to arbitration, the case proceeds under one of three international systems, at the choice of the investor.[6] All three systems are managed by the International Center for the Settlement of Investment Disputes (ICSID), housed in the World Bank (DePalma 2001; Alvarez 2000). Under any of these systems, the disputants first seek agreement between themselves on the composition of the three-person arbitral tribunal. Typically, each side nominates one arbitrator, and the two arbitrators so selected agree on the third arbitrator, often a national of a non-NAFTA country. If the parties cannot reach agreement, the ICSID will make appointments. In the NAFTA cases to date, tribunals have comprised a distinguished practitioner or scholar from each of the disputing countries and an eminent scholar or expert from a third country, typically a European.

Environmentalists have an acute concern about the inherently secretive nature of investor-state arbitration. There is no formal or public process for notification that an investor has filed a notice of intent to submit a claim, or that such a claim has been submitted. Even environmental officials and trade officials in the federal governments may not know until well after the fact that a claim has been brought, thwarting any opportunity to invoke the intergovernmental consultation procedures on trade-environment issues under Article 10(6) of the North American Agreement on Environmental Cooperation (NAAEC). Once a tribunal has been appointed, the representations of the parties are handled confidentially and the deliberations of the tribunal take place behind closed doors. There is not even a requirement that the tribunal's decision be made public. The information available about these cases comes from voluntary releases of information or documents, typically by the private investors, or the rudimentary information about claim status available from the U.S. government under the *Freedom of Information Act* for claims involving the United States.

The secrecy of the process raises serious public policy questions (Abbott 2000), but it is in some respects more apparent than real. In an interim procedural ruling, the arbitral tribunal in *Metalclad v. United Mexican States* ruled that neither NAFTA nor the international arbitration rules impose any restriction on public disclosures by a party to the arbitration, so any party is free to publicise many details. The full texts of arbitral awards and of many briefs by the parties have become available through these informal channels, often immediately. The private parties have also made active use of the media to get out at least their own side of the story. However, the *Metalclad* tribunal cautioned the parties to act with restraint, noting that one of the hallmarks of arbitration is settlement of disputes outside the glare of publicity.

In the case of *Methanex v. United States*, nongovernmental organisations (NGOs) are pressing for another opening in the veil of secrecy.[7] The International Institute for Sustainable Development (IISD), a Canadian organisation, and Friends of the Earth (in the U.S.) have separately petitioned for the opportunity to file *amicus curiae* briefs.[8] Chapter 11 and the international arbitration rules are silent on the question of *amicus* briefs. The *Methanex* tribunal asked all three governments to file their comments on these requests and issued an interim ruling in January 2001. In their comments to the tribunal, the United States and Canada expressed support in some degree for the acceptability of the briefs. The tribunal found that there is no bar to such briefs, but postponed until a later stage the question of whether it would accept such briefs in the particular case (DePalma 2001; Fracassi 2001).

The closed nature of the arbitration process may also interfere with the effective representation of the real parties in interest. Because state/provincial and local government actions may give rise to an investor's claim, whereas the federal government is always the responding party, the states and localities are not able to fight their own battles to protect their environmental actions against foreign investors. It should be noted, however, that provincial or state governments in the arbitrations resolved to date have not raised public complaints against their federal representatives. In the *Methanex* case, the State of California is reported to be pleased so far with the level of co-ordination between the state government and the federal officials representing the United States.

The trade ministers of the NAFTA parties addressed some of the secrecy and transparency issues in a recent 'clarification' (Free Trade Commission 2001). The ministers agreed that all documents submitted to or issued by a tribunal should be made public, subject only to confidentiality limits or 'the relevant arbitral rules, as applied'. They also clarified that the national governments may share all information about an arbitral proceeding, including confidential information, with state or provincial officials.

Environmental Issues in Chapter 11 Arbitrations

There is inherent tension within NAFTA or any other trade framework between the sovereign authority of local or national governments to set environmental rules and the agreed right of a foreign investor to be secure in its investments against expropriation or discriminatory or arbitrary treatment. In reality, this trade-environment tension is rarely presented in stark terms. Rather, it appears in circumstances complicated by commercial and political considerations. The three environment-related claims in which the investors have received or been awarded compensation give some evidence to judge how the trade-environment tensions have been resolved under NAFTA Chapter 11.[9]

Ethyl Corporation v. Canada

The Ethyl case presents a particularly complex set of facts (Soloway 1999; Wagner 1999). Ethyl Corporation, a U.S. company, manufactures the gasoline additive MMT. An octane booster that enhances fuel efficiency, MMT has been widely used since the phaseout of lead in gasoline. The additive contains manganese, which raised significant concerns about health effects from manganese oxides in tailpipe emissions and interference by manganese with the onboard diagnostic systems that are a key pollution control component in automobiles. In 1994, Canada's minister of the environment announced her intention to have MMT removed from Canadian gasoline by August 1995, apparently motivated to respond to public health concerns. The Chapter 11 case arose out of her resort to a restriction on trade to reach her avowed health-protection goal.

At just the time of Canada's initiative to ban the use of MMT, the U.S. Environmental Protection Agency (EPA) was being required by court order to lift its restrictions and allow the production and use of MMT in the U.S. The U.S. court noted that the EPA no longer claimed interference with emission controls, which had until then been a valid ground for its regulation of the fuel additive under the *Clean Air Act*, and was relying instead on alleged health effects, which the court found were outside the scope of the agency's limited statutory authority to regulate fuel additives. There are legitimate hypotheses about the possible effects of inhalation of manganese compounds from MMT combustion, but a number of scientific studies conducted in both Canada and the United States to validate or refute those hypotheses were inconclusive. Thus, the EPA lacked adequate scientific support for a health-based ban under other sections of the *Clean Air*

Act. Similarly, the Canadian environment minister concluded that, under the Canadian *Environmental Protection Act*, the scientific evidence of health effects was insufficient to allow her to use federal administrative authority to impose a ban on MMT.

Lurking in the background of the scientific controversy over MMT in both countries are two economic struggles. First, the mineral-based MMT competes against alternative fuel additives such as ethanol (which is aggressively advocated by corn growers and processors) or petroleum-derived additives. Second, automobile manufacturers joust with fuel suppliers, each seeking to be sure that it does not end up with the main burden of meeting ever more demanding automotive pollution control standards. In Canada, these economic conflicts took on interprovincial aspects, pitting western grain- and fuel-producing provinces such as Alberta against the automotive-industry–centred Ontario.

Looking for a means to control MMT other than a health-based prohibition on its use, the federal government submitted a bill in Parliament in 1995 to ban the importation and interprovincial sale of manganese-based products. Ethyl Corporation, a U.S. company, was the sole supplier of MMT to the Canadian market. Through a Canadian subsidiary, Ethyl blended MMT in Ontario and then sold it to refiners in other provinces. Given this arrangement of its business, the bill would effectively prevent Ethyl from continuing to sell MMT in Canada. The 1995 bill died, but was resubmitted to a new Parliament a year later, and the ban on trade in MMT under Bill C-29 ultimately took effect in June 1997. Ethyl immediately filed a claim under NAFTA Chapter 11.

While Ethyl's NAFTA claim was pending, the Province of Alberta initiated a domestic challenge to the interprovincial trade ban under Canada's Agreement on Internal Trade (AIT). The panel that heard that dispute ruled in Alberta's favour in June 1998. The panel recognised that protection of public health is a legitimate objective that could justify an internal restriction on trade and it did not directly question the public health purposes of the measure. Nonetheless, it found the MMT ban an undue burden on internal commerce in Canada not justified by health concerns because there was no urgency to them, so the federal government could have met its legitimate objective through less trade-restrictive means.

A month after the AIT ruling, the Canadian government amended Bill C-29 to remove the trade ban and settled Ethyl's Chapter 11 claim for a reported US$13 million to cover Ethyl's legal expenses and for lost profits during the year of the trade ban. As part of the settlement, the government publicly declared that there was no scientific basis to prohibit MMT on health grounds. The terms of this settlement clearly and officially contradict the argument that Ethyl's challenge to the Canadian trade ban constituted a serious threat to Canadian environmental policy, and help explain why the Canadian government chose to settle this case rather than pursue the arbitration on the merits.

Metalclad

Many facts of this case are controverted, but the basic story is as follows.[10] A Mexican company, Coterin, was authorised by the Mexican federal government to build and operate a hazardous waste transfer facility in a valley within the municipal limits of Guadalcazar (but about 70 kilometres from the city), and operated that transfer facility starting in 1990. In 1993, Metalclad, a U.S. company, took an option to buy Coterin just as it was seeking construction and operating permits for a full-fledged hazardous waste landfill on the same site. After the federal environmental authorities assured Coterin that it would receive the construction and operating permits, and after the State of San Luis Potosí gave a land-use permit for the project, Metalclad exercised its option and bought the company. Shortly thereafter, however, the governor of San Luis Potosí began to oppose the facility. Meanwhile, the municipality of Guadalcazar insisted that Coterin needed a municipal permit. Coterin applied for such a permit, but the municipality failed to act on it. After consulting with the federal environmental agency Procuraduría Federal de Protección al Ambiente (PROFEPA) and despite persistent local protest actions, Metalclad/Coterin completed the construction of the facility under a federal permit. Local protestors, however, prevented the site from operating. In 1995, federal authorities audited the completed facility and negotiated an agreement (*convenio*) with Metalclad under which Metalclad would be allowed to operate the facility if it undertook certain remediation actions to clean up waste remaining on the site from its earlier use by Coterin. Metalclad also agreed to establish an environmental buffer zone around the facility and to undertake some community-related activities.

After the federal environmental authorities and Metalclad concluded this agreement, the municipal council of Guadalcazar, without any notice to Metalclad or opportunity for it to be heard, voted to deny the long-pending municipal construction permit. Some two years later, after various inconclusive legal proceedings involving the municipality and Metalclad, and after Metalclad had filed its notice of intent to initiate arbitration under Chapter 11, the governor of San Luis Potosí, just before leaving office, issued an ecological decree declaring a 600 000-acre zone for the protection of rare cactus species (see Public Citizen 1998). This zone surrounds and includes the Metalclad facility site, and effectively precludes Metalclad from operating the facility.

There are three possible explanations for what happened, none of which should be imagined as legitimate exercises of environmental authority. One possibility is that the local and state officials were acting in a xenophobic way, or for the benefit of a competing Mexican-owned enterprise. Having tolerated a Mexican-owned operation at the site in question, they were perhaps determined not to allow a so-called foreign company to take over. One of the purposes of Chapter 11 is to shield investors against such discrimination based on their nationality.

Another scenario is that Metalclad confronted a NIMBY (not in my back yard) mentality at the local level that conflicted with Mexico's widely recognised national need for modern hazardous waste disposal capacity. The issue then becomes one of the relationship between local and federal control under Mexican law. Mexico may, if it wishes, legally empower local communities to reject unwanted facilities, but the tradition in Mexico and the current law (apparently) assigns to federal authorities the legal authority to make final decisions on facilities such as this. Investors have a reasonable right to be shielded from actions by local officials that are contrary to or outside of their authority under national law, regardless of the virtue of the sentiment motivating such behaviour.

The third possibility — also a likely factor, especially with respect to the governor's actions — is that there was a personality or political power struggle going on between the state/local officials on the one hand and the federal authorities on the other. In this respect as well, Mexico is free to establish whatever allocation of authority it prefers between federal and state/local jurisdictions. Mexico could, for example, arrange its affairs along the Canadian model, giving the states broad powers with only weak and limited powers at the federal level. But that is not its current practice or historical preference. On the contrary, centralised power is the norm. Metalclad dealt with the central authorities and was apparently assured by them (and had every reason to believe) that they had full power to authorise the construction and operation of the landfill. If Mexico wishes to allow the state governor, nonetheless, to declare an ecological zone that has the effect of preventing the facility's operation, that is Mexico's prerogative, but it should not ask the foreign investor, after having made an investment in good faith, to suffer that last-minute change in the law without compensation for its sunk costs.

A Chapter 11 counter-example should, in any event, reassure environmental interests about potential abuses of investor protections in cases involving waste disposal in Mexico. In the very first final Chapter 11 arbitral award, a tribunal turned down the compensation claim of certain American investors who complained that their contract for waste collection services had been improperly cancelled by a Mexican municipality. The claimants had pursued their claim first in Mexican courts. The courts ruled that the municipality had acted within the scope of its authority under a valid federal law. The arbitral tribunal said that it was not its role to act as a court of appeal from a domestic court. It thus reframed the Chapter 11 question as one of whether the Mexican court's decision was somehow contrary to the Article 1105 obligations of fair and equitable treatment. It concluded that there was no evidence that the court had breached the Chapter 11 standards, and therefore the investors' claim failed (Gallaird 2000).

S.D. Myers, Inc. v. Canada

Like the Ethyl case before it, the claim of *S.D. Myers, Inc. v. Canada* presents a situation in which environmental policy and economic policy decisions in both the United States and Canada converged and diverged in ways that did economic damage to a plan by a U.S. company to compete for business in Canada through an associated Canadian company.

S.D. Myers, based in Ohio, is an electrical equipment repair and maintenance company that in the 1980s developed, as an outgrowth of its core business, a separate business of remediation of PCB contamination through the destruction of PCBs. By 1990, S.D. Myers was not only a leading company in U.S. PCB disposal, but also had established operations in Australia, Mexico, and South Africa. Eastern Canada, with a considerable inventory of PCB-contaminated equipment but no local disposal capacity, was another attractive opportunity for the company. But there was an obstacle: even though the terms of the bilateral agreement on hazardous waste between the U.S. and Canada allowed for cross-border movement of waste for environmentally sound disposal, EPA regulations pursuant to the U.S. *Toxic Substances Control Act* virtually banned importation of PCBs into the United States. In 1993, S.D. Myers began a concerted effort to overcome this obstacle and obtain the Canadian business. It incorporated a separate company, Myers Canada, and began lobbying both U.S. and Canadian environmental officials for a relaxation of the ban on movements of PCBs from Canada to the United States. It was supported in this effort by many eastern Canadian firms, which believed that disposal of their PCBs by S.D. Myers in Ohio would be less expensive than working with the only available Canadian service provider, Chem-Security in Swan Hills, Alberta.

The U.S. EPA began public consideration of S.D. Myers's request for a relaxation of the import ban in early 1995. Canadian environmental officials, as well as Chem-Security, monitored these developments closely. In July 1995, before final EPA action, the Canadian minister for the environment responded to a parliamentary question by enunciating a government position that, 'the handling of PCBs should be done in Canada by Canadians'. Subsequently, on 26 October 1995, the EPA issued S.D. Myers a written notice of 'enforcement discretion' under which it would allow import of PCBs from Canada for disposal (by destruction) in the United States between 15 November 1995 and 31 December 1997.

No sooner had the EPA announced its policy than Chem-Security wrote to the minister of the environment urging a quick Canadian response to the U.S. opening of the border to trade in PCBs. On 16 November 1995, one day after the border was 'opened' under the U.S. EPA policy, the minister signed an interim order that had the effect of closing the border from the Canadian side by amending Canada's PCB Waste Export Regulations to prohibit the export of Canadian PCBs. This interim order was confirmed by Canada's Privy Council on 28 November 1995, and made into an Order in Council of the Governor General on 26 February 1996. One year later, in February 1997, Canada reversed the closed-border policy, amending the PCB Waste Export Regulations to allow PCB shipments to the United States.[11]

This bare-bones chronology underscores the strong commercial pressures at work in both the United States and Canada throughout this episode. But it also shows the relative weakness of environmental claims on either side that transboundary movements of PCB wastes for disposal constitute an undue environmental risk. At a time when

Canada allowed export of PCBs, S.D. Myers lobbied actively to get the EPA to remove or relax its import ban, which dated from the mid 1970s. The shift in United States policy was justified by EPA determinations that the environmental risk of shipment from Canada to Ohio for PCB disposal was negligible, and that S.D. Myers ran an environmentally responsible operation for the destruction of PCBs through incineration. No sooner had the company succeeded in its effort with the EPA, however, than its only Canadian competitor secured a change to Canada's export regulations that nullified the EPA action, keeping Canada's inventory of PCB wastes in Canada.

The Canadian environment minister claimed that the export ban was based on environmental policy, in particular the Basel Convention on the Control of Transboundary Movements of Hazardous Wastes and Their Disposal (1999). That convention has two relevant provisions. Article 4(2)(b) calls on parties to 'ensure the availability of adequate disposal facilities, ... to the extent possible', within its own boundaries. Article 4(2)(d) commits governments to 'ensure that the transboundary movement of hazardous wastes and other wastes is reduced to the minimum consistent with the environmentally sound and efficient management of such wastes'. Notwithstanding the Basel Convention, Canada had long observed a policy of allowing PCB waste exports to the United States, a policy in accordance with the consistent advice of senior officials in Environment Canada that the allowance of PCB waste exports was consistent with Canada's interpretation of the Basel Convention, with Canada's bilateral Agreement on the Transboundary Movement of Hazardous Wastes with the United States, and with an objective assessment of the relatively smaller environmental risks of shipment of PCB wastes from eastern Canada to nearby Ohio as compared to distant Alberta. Canada had also consistently expressed the view in international negotiations that Article 4(2) should not be construed to bar environmentally sound transboundary movements of waste. Viewing 'the documentary record as a whole,' the arbitral tribunal found that it 'clearly indicates that the Interim Order and the Final Order were intended primarily to protect the Canadian PCB disposal industry from U.S. competition'. It also found that 'there was no legitimate environmental reason for introducing the ban'.

The strongest environmental policy argument for the Canadian export ban is the Basel obligation to assure adequate domestic disposal capability. If Canada allowed its inventory of PCB wastes to be shipped to Ohio, Chem-Security might have been left with an insufficient volume of waste to sustain its continued operation. On this point, the tribunal simply asserted that Canada's objective 'could have been achieved by other measures'. Such an argument is firmly rooted in the law in all jurisdictions for evaluating trade restrictions applied in the name of environmental policy. In Canada itself, as well as in the United States and the European Union, trade restrictions in pursuit of environmental goals are not allowed to pose undue burdens on the free movement of goods and services or to impose economic costs disproportionate to the environmental gain to be achieved. The government's burden of justification is particularly heavy where the economic effect of its action falls on a single firm. The scrutiny is heightened further when that single firm happens to be foreign.

An Analytical Framework for Assessing Chapter 11 Cases

Investor-state arbitration has no institutional or theoretical framework to bring coherence to the judgements of the arbitral tribunals. Each tribunal is unique, and there is scant reference in any award decision to the reasoning of other arbitral tribunals. Such a system works quite well in a commercial context, where continuity of business relations in each case is more important than uniform application of abstract rules. But the investor-state context demands a more consistent, rules-based approach in order to create predictability of awards on issues that can have a significant influence on government behaviour. Absent a structured institutional or juridical context for consistency from arbitration to arbitration, the system will depend on a common law–style accumulation of decisions to develop a coherent body of law. One source of law that the NAFTA negotiators expected to apply and that Chapter 11 tribunals have drawn on to some extent is the corpus of international arbitration awards in investor-state cases, including the many cases decided by the Iran-United States Claims Tribunal (Gudofsky 2000; Price 2000a; Trakman 2001). Soloway delves into that body of law in Chapter 7. One settlement and two arbitral awards have been reached under Chapter 11 compensating investors for the effects on their investments of government decisions that were, on their face, meant to protect the environment. This provides enough experience to begin the first, tentative outlines of a Chapter 11 jurisprudence on the investment-environment relationship.

As a first approach to these three cases, the next section first derives a framework for a fact-based analysis relating the circumstances of the three cases to the outcomes. It identifies five characteristics of fact situations and explains how those characteristics pertain to the legal and policy issues at stake in Chapter 11. The section then takes a second step in outlining a Chapter 11 jurisprudence, examining the tribunals' reasoning on the major legal issues of unfair treatment and expropriation to see how they are construing these key aspects of investor protection.

Circumstantial Characteristics of the Cases

Ex Post Actions

The first notable characteristic of the government action in each of the above cases is that it was *ex post* regulation rather than *ex ante*. That is, the government changed the environmental rules after the investor had made the investment. This characteristic is both obvious and important. If the regulations had been *ex ante,* the government actions would have fallen under NAFTA Article 1114, which expressly reserves the right of governments to set environmental conditions on investments through measures consistent with Chapter 11. A foreign investor should have no ground for complaint about expropriation or unfair treatment if the local legal conditions governing the investment are fixed and knowable in advance of the investment.

Ex post facto legal regulation, on the other hand, is problematic because it surprises the investor and may thwart the investor's reasonable expectations about the value of the investment on which the investment decision was based (Rose 2000). To be sure, nothing in NAFTA or international law precludes governments from adopting and applying new environmental rules *ex post* to existing investments. It is the very essence of the law-making function of governments to set new policies or revise earlier policies, and many such changes will have some effect on the profitability of existing businesses in general or businesses in certain sectors. For example, a government may increase a tax or impose a new tax. A government may also set new requirements for environmental performance, such as in the control of air pollution. For the most part, however, such new legal requirements alter the terms of competition for all firms in a particular business sector, and reductions in the economic value of existing investments stemming from such changes are modest in proportional terms even though they may have severe consequences for financially vulnerable enterprises.

But *ex post* legal changes should come under closer scrutiny when the new rules apply specifically to particular investments. Two major questions arise under NAFTA Article 1110. First, does the new measure have a public purpose? Second, does it result in an expropriation, meaning a total or nearly total loss of value for an affected person or enterprise? If the measure lacks a public purpose or if the measure destroys all or nearly all of an investor's value, then the last question is what compensation the government owes for the lost economic value. When *ex post* rules changes are proposed or made in the domestic context, they usually provoke political and legal efforts by the newly regulated entities to overturn or block or delay the new rule, or for special exemptions or some other form of relief. In comparison to their domestic counterparts, foreign investors are at a distinct disadvantage in such political contests, and local courts may also be less inclined to accept their view if an issue goes to litigation (Brower and Steven 2001). Moreover, as these cases show, *ex post* decisions can be made on very narrow grounds to promote or defeat specific activities, increasing the possibility of arbitrary or legally unsound decisions. An important purpose of NAFTA Chapter 11 and other investment treaties is to shield foreign investors from just such arbitrary, discriminatory, or unfair action by host governments.

The Actions Affected Only a Single Foreign Investor

New public policies that affect a single existing firm or product are not unheard of. Nevertheless, the fact that each decision at issue in these Chapter 11 cases was specific to a single investor rather than a matter of environmental policy affecting many parties is a relevant factor for consideration. Trade policy frequently distinguishes between measures of general effect and measures that benefit or restrain a particular firm or industry. In the context of protection of foreign investors from discriminatory or unfair treatment, the fact that the single affected investor was foreign should heighten the level of scrutiny about whether the government action was truly environmental, or whether it was motivated more by political considerations or a desire to protect local competitors of the foreign investor.

Decisions taken to protect the public health from exposure to toxic chemicals present a special challenge in this regard because they tend to be specific rather than generic. Such regulation properly proceeds chemical by chemical through scientific evaluation of the risks each chemical or each phase in its life cycle may present. Canada's decisions to control distribution of MMT or to prevent export of PCBs for disposal, then, are not exceptional for focussing on specific products. What does make them exceptional is that each measure was not a restriction on the production or use of the chemical, but on its shipment across provincial or international boundaries. Such trade measures do not protect well against health or environmental risks and have a high likelihood of affecting economic competition. In the *Ethyl* and *S.D. Myers* cases in particular, it seems more than coincidental that the economic cost of each decision fell entirely on a foreign investor. In the *Ethyl* case there was no Canadian producer of MMT; in the *S.D. Myers* case, in the case of PCBs there was a competing Canadian PCB disposal service provider that actively lobbied the Canadian government in support of the challenged decision.

The *Metalclad* case involved the siting of a hazardous waste landfill, a locally undesirable land use (LULU). Siting and permitting of LULUs is notoriously contentious, and government decisions relating to a particular facility are ineluctably specific rather than generic. No investor, foreign or domestic, can justly make a claim for compensation if it failed to obtain the necessary site-specific permits and approvals unless such permits or approvals were unreasonably withheld (Gantz 2001). In the *Metalclad* case, the tribunal concluded that the refusal of the municipality to grant a local construction permit was not fair and equitable because the decision was reached in a nontransparent manner. The judge of the British Columbia Supreme Court that heard Mexico's appeal from the tribunal award determined on legal grounds that transparency of process is not part of the international law meaning of the fair and equitable treatment to which foreign investors are entitled. Nevertheless, he upheld the tribunal's award on the basis that the supervening last-minute declaration of an ecological zone surrounding the completely built waste facility effected an expropriation of Metalclad's investment.[12]

Personal Executive Decisions

A third characteristic of each case to date, as well as the pending claim of Methanex, is that it was triggered by a controversial decision by a high-level executive official. The *Ethyl* and *Metalclad* cases involve other government decision makers as well (Parliament and the municipal council, respectively) but executives initiated the critical decisions. In the *S.D. Myers* case, the minister of the environment acted in her executive capacity, although her decision did require endorsement by the Privy Council. Methanex is challenging an executive order by the governor of California.

Underscoring the personal nature of the executive decisions in two cases — *S.D. Myers* and *Metalclad* — the professional federal environmental staff, more insulated from politics, counselled against the executive actions that were later challenged. The *S.D. Myers* record, in particular, contains numerous internal documents from Environment Canada supporting *on environmental grounds* the option of disposal of Canadian PCBs in the United States. The environment minister elected to ignore that expert staff advice.[13] Although the record in *Metalclad* is more obscure, a consistent pattern appears of decisions by federal environmental officials to allow the construction and the operation of the Metalclad facility, reinforced by apparent encouragement from them to Metalclad to persist in its construction activities despite signs of local opposition and the lack of a local construction permit. In the end, the definitive action that led to a compensation award for Metalclad was the executive declaration of a broad ecological zone around the site by the governor of the state of San Luis Potosí.[14]

National environmental legal systems depend on broad executive discretion to take steps to protect the environment. Nevertheless, the risk of abuse of executive authority always exists, so domestic legal systems create opportunities for legislative or judicial reviews of executive action or legislative avenues to countermand executive decisions. When the situation involves an executive decision in favour of certain local interests at the expense of a foreign investor, however, such political and judicial review devices serve poorly to control executive abuse because no domestic interest will argue against the abuse. Investment treaty provisions such as Chapter 11 fill this remedial gap by giving the investor a neutral forum to seek redress from allegedly arbitrary government action (Price 2000b, 2000a).

Conflicting Judgements within the Government about the Environmental Rationale for the Action

Scientific controversy about the need for or form of government action surrounds most environmental regulation decisions, so it is altogether unremarkable that the environmental cases under Chapter 11 are also wrapped in reasonable disagreements among the various affected interests about the need for the government action in question. In these three cases, however, the disagreements over science and policy go deeper than usual. Substantial, open disagreements *within* the government about the proper course of conduct from an environmental point of view appear in each case. This situation is a corollary to the previous point about executive decisions. In each case, an executive official took definitive action without regard to the substantial internal environmental policy conflicts.

In the two cases in which Canada was the respondent, the federal government officially disavowed any environmental basis for the challenged action in settling the *Ethyl* claim, and the government reversed the challenged decision on its own initiative after one year in the *S.D. Myers* case (Mann 2001). Moreover, the settlement with Ethyl may have been prompted by the domestic determination, in which Ethyl itself did not participate directly, that the challenged legislation was inconsistent with Canada's Agreement on Internal Trade because the health concern was not sufficiently urgent to warrant interference with trade (Soloway 1999).

In *Metalclad*, the federal environmental agency repeatedly and consistently approved Metalclad's project. The state and local political officials who, with equal persistence, disagreed with and tried to counteract the federal environmental determinations, did so without directly contradicting the federal permitting decisions. The governor's declaration of an ecological zone to protect some rare species of cactus in a large region bore only a tangential relationship to environmental hazards from hazardous waste landfilling.

In the pending *Methanex* case, it is interesting to observe the absence so far of any disagreement within the California government about the decision to ban MTBE, although some scientists and others dispute the merits of the scientific studies on which the governor based his executive order.

Objective Evidence of Non-environmental Issues Influencing Government Action

The internal conflict within the governments about the proper environmental decision to be made in each instance casts doubt on the assertions that the rules being applied to the foreign investor were *bona fide* manifestations of environmental policy. But it would be wrong to suspect that the environmental rationale was concealing some other reason for the government's behaviour without evidence of other influences. Characteristically, each Chapter 11 case shows evidence of active government consideration of economic and political factors.

The *Ethyl* case arose because the environment minister, unable to regulate MMT as a health risk under Canadian law, insisted on deploying trade-restrictive legislation as a way of targeting MMT. Substantial dispute within the government over this policy and subsequent domestic challenges to the legislation revealed important regional differences over the MMT policy, differences springing from a blend of economic concerns and partisan political differences.

In the *S.D. Myers* case, the arbitral tribunal's award describes active lobbying of government officials by Myers's Canadian competitor, Chem-Security. Moreover, the environment minister herself cast repeated public statements of her PCBs policy in terms of competitiveness — disposal of Canadian PCBs in Canada *by Canadians*. In light of consistent advice to the minister from Environment Canada staff that an export ban on PCBs was not advisable as a matter of environmental policy, the goal of having PCBs disposal done by Canadians must be seen to express a commercial rather than an environmental protection objective. The tribunal reached precisely that conclusion.

The record in *Metalclad* strongly suggests a web of political and perhaps personal differences between the federal officials on the one hand and the state and local leaders on the other. Counsel for Metalclad also adduced evidence that the governor of San Luis Potosí had connections with a Mexican competitor of Metalclad, though the arbitral award does not mention this aspect of the case.

At their core, trade agreements such as NAFTA, including their investment provisions, seek above all to discipline government policy decisions taken to favour domestic economic interests over the foreign producer of goods, provider of services, or investor. Objective or circumstantial evidence that government decisions intended to confer economic benefit on domestic constituents at the expense of foreign interests, therefore, has an important bearing in determining whether those decisions are inconsistent with the reciprocal, mutually agreed treaty disciplines against economic protectionism.

The Key Legal Issues: Unfair Treatment and Expropriation

Three arbitral awards delve into the law on unfair treatment and expropriation: the *Metalclad* award, the partial award in *S.D. Myers*, and an interim ruling in the matter of *Pope & Talbot*. Because Canada settled with Ethyl before an arbitral award on the merits, one can draw, at best, only weak inferences about how the parties viewed each other's legal arguments in that case. The constraints of space preclude a thorough legal analysis of the rulings to date; this section will simply sketch the outlines of an emerging NAFTA jurisprudence on these questions. Chapter 7 offers a more detailed analysis of the law on expropriation.

Fair and Equitable Treatment and Nondiscrimination

Both the *Metalclad* and the *S.D. Myers* awards give considerable attention to the obligation on governments to afford investors 'fair and equitable treatment' enunciated in Article 1105. *S.D. Myers* also addresses the separate nondiscrimination obligations, in particular the obligation to afford treatment to foreign investors no less favourable than the treatment for domestic investors 'in like circumstances'.

The arbitral tribunal in *Metalclad* found that the manner of the municipal decision denying the local construction permit — in a hastily convened meeting without notice to the applicant or opportunity to appear — was deficient under international law notions of due process implicit in fair and equitable treatment. The *S.D. Myers* tribunal concluded that the language of Chapter 11 sets the standard of fair and equitable treatment standard as one specific aspect of a more general obligation to treat foreign investors 'in accordance with international law'. On the one hand, this means that even if a domestic investor were without remedy against such arbitrary government behaviour, the foreign investor is assured of an international minimum standard of fairness. On the other hand, governments are not required to provide treatment that goes beyond international norms, even if the resulting treatment might strike some as unfair or inequitable.

Justice David Tysoe, in his decision on the appeal of the *Metalclad* tribunal award, fully endorsed the opinion of the *S.D. Myers* tribunal that the fair and equitable standard should be interpreted in light of the more general obligation to provide the foreign investors with treatment in accordance with international law. He then disagreed with the *Metalclad* tribunal's conclusion that transparency is implicit in the international law of fair and equitable treatment. In his view, there was no basis in Chapter 11 or in international law generally to consider transparency of process as a matter of fair treatment.[15] In the process, he also took issue with two other constructions of fair and equitable treatment that would impose more demanding procedural requirements on governments. A separate arbitrator's opinion in *S.D. Myers* argued for an expansive interpretation of the term 'international law' to include norms not yet accepted as a matter of customary international law. The justice took the view that international law should be given its 'usual and ordinary meaning'. In the *Pope & Talbot* partial award, the tribunal adopted an interpretation of Article 1105 that would add 'fairness elements' to the international law of minimum due process. The justice again hewed to a stricter construction that took the phrase 'in accordance with international law' to refer to settled principles and practices shorn of any added elements.[16]

The *S.D. Myers* award puts one further gloss on Article 1105 that is both unnecessary and erroneous. The *S.D. Myers* tribunal unanimously agreed that Canada in this case violated the national treatment obligation of Article 1102, giving disparate treatment to a national investor and a foreign investor that were in 'like circumstances'. In a further analysis with which one of the tribunal disagreed, the majority then determined that the violation of Article 1102 in this case 'essentially establishes a breach' of the broader fair treatment obligation of Article 1105. The tribunal did not need to find a violation of Article 1105 to award S.D. Myers compensation; the Article 1102 violation would have been sufficient. The tribunal member who dissented on this point has the better of the argument: breach of another NAFTA provision is not, by itself, a foundation for a conclusion that the treatment has failed to meet the fair and equitable requirements of international law. Whether the government's actions violate Article 1105 must be separately determined. The NAFTA trade ministers authoritatively expressed this view in their clarification on Chapter 11, stating simply that a breach of another NAFTA provision or another international agreement 'does not establish that there has been a breach of Article 1105(1)' (Free Trade Commission 2001).

Expropriation and 'Tantamount to Expropriation'

Two points about NAFTA Article 1110 are reasonably clear, although they only reframe the interpretive challenge. First, among the important sources of international law are common principles of law accepted by many countries and national judicial decisions. On the question of government measures that are tantamount to expropriation, the U.S. constitutional jurisprudence on uncompensated takings under the Fifth and Fourteenth Amendments to the U.S. Constitution is a rich source, one referred to on occasion by international tribunals in expropriation cases (Wagner 1999; American Law Institute 1987). Second, under international law as well as U.S. constitutional law, regulatory exercises of the police power of the government are in principle excluded from the notion of expropriation (Wagner 1999).[17] That still leaves the question of defining whether a particular environmental measure is or is not within the scope of that power. In short, evaluation of compensation claims based on environmental regulatory expropriations of investments under NAFTA Chapter 11 is likely to be just as fractious and legally complex as the decisions on claims for just compensation for environmental regulatory takings in U.S. law, and will turn on the same core issues. This is thorny territory even for U.S. lawyers, and much more so for foreign lawyers and arbitrators (Rose 2000).[18] Daniel Price (2000a), who was the U.S. negotiator on Chapter 11, recalls in this context that the negotiators considered trying to 'draw a bright line in the text' between regulation that was legitimate and regulation that would be expropriatory: 'We quickly gave up that enterprise. If the United States Supreme Court and arbitral tribunals could not do it over 200 years, it was unlikely that the negotiators were going to do it in a matter of weeks with one line in a treaty'.

The *Metalclad* tribunal examined whether the actions of Guadalcazar in denying the construction permit and the governor of San Luis Potosí in declaring the ecological zone were tantamount to expropriation under Article 1110. The tribunal explained its judgement as follows:

> By permitting or tolerating the conduct of Guadalcazar in relation to Metalclad which the Tribunal has already held amounts to unfair and inequitable treatment breaching Article 1105 and by thus participating or acquiescing in the denial to Metalclad of the right to operate the landfill, notwithstanding that the project was fully approved and endorsed by the federal government, Mexico must be held to have taken a measure tantamount to expropriation in violation of NAFTA Article 1110(1).

The tribunal here recites certain facts without explaining how those facts connect legally with its conclusion that expropriation occurred. It is worth exploring elements of the apparent rationale.

The awkward language just quoted leaves the impression that the tribunal was equating the violation of the fair and equitable treatment standard of Article 1105 with an expropriation under Article 1110. Neither the NAFTA language nor logic would support such an interpretation. As noted above, Articles 1102 and 1103 establish the core trade law obligations of national treatment and most-favoured-nation treatment. Violation of those obligations can give rise directly to a claim for compensation if the investment of the investor has lost value or income as a result. Similarly, Article 1105 establishes an independent and self-sufficient standard that the foreign investor must be afforded fair and equitable treatment under principles of international law. A violation of this standard, too, can be a sufficient basis for a claim for compensation. As the partial award in *S.D. Myers* explains more clearly, a violation of Articles 1102 or 1105 does not necessarily support the proposition that the government measure is an expropriation within the terms of Article 1110.

Article 1110 requires either a direct expropriation of the investment or a measure tantamount to expropriation. 'Tantamount to expropriation', the *S.D. Myers* tribunal noted, has been interpreted by the *Pope & Talbot* tribunal to mean equivalent to expropriation (indeed, the French and Spanish versions of NAFTA use their respective cognates for 'equivalent'), which in turn conforms to the international law concept of creeping expropriation. Measures equivalent to expropriation may fall short of a direct seizure of the investment or operate by some indirect control of the investment, but such indirect action must have an effect on the investment and its operation equivalent to a direct expropriation. U.S. takings jurisprudence also recognises the functional equivalence between a physical appropriation of the property and a regulation that deprives an owner of all or nearly all use of the property. The *S.D. Myers* tribunal found no expropriation in that case, but made an award in an undetermined amount nevertheless based on violations of Articles 1102 and 1105.

From the paragraphs that follow the quoted statement in the *Metalclad* award, though, an analysis of the case can be derived that makes a legitimate connection between the unfair treatment and the expropriation in that case. It appears that the tribunal determined that Metalclad's investment was made in reasonable expectation that it had legal permission to construct and to operate the facility if the construction met federal environmental standards. If Guadalcazar had acted correctly and within its clear authority in withholding the construction permit, thwarting Metalclad's operations would not have been expropriation because Metalclad would have lacked any foundation for its belief that it was making its investment within the pre-existing framework of local law. Only because Guadalcazar's action in withholding the construction permit was contrary to Mexican law can it be said that it thwarted Metalclad's reasonable investment-backed expectations, making the bar to operation tantamount to expropriation. Similarly, if Metalclad had invested in the facility without construction and operating permits in hand from the federal authorities, or had failed to meet the known requirements of those permits, then a denial of its right to operate would not have been tantamount to expropriation, but rather an appropriate exercise of environmental enforcement power to prevent a violation of federal environmental law. Put another way, Metalclad would have had no legitimate investment to be protected from expropriation if it had behaved in disregard of or with indifference to the established domestic legal requirements governing its investment. But with clear permission at every stage from the federal authorities, the unexpected developments that then thwarted Metalclad's reasonable investment-backed expectation that it could operate the site become tantamount to an expropriation (Laird 2001).

The appeal decision by Justice Tysoe of the British Columbia Supreme Court allows scope for the argument sketched out just above for a connection between an Article 1105 violation and an Article 1110 expropriation in matters where there may be such a clear case of a government acting contrary to its own national law in thwarting the investor's reasonable investment expectations that it rises to a level considered unacceptable by international law. In the *Metalclad* case itself, though, the justice concluded that, 'the Tribunal did not simply interpret the wording of Article 1105. Rather it misstated the applicable law to include transparency obligations and it then made its decision on the basis of the concept of transparency'. Such a misstatement of the law, in the justice's view, took the tribunal beyond the scope of the submission to it because the supposed transparency obligation is not within the scope of Chapter 11.

Some have commented with concern on another paragraph of the *Metalclad* tribunal's award. In opening its discussion of the question about tantamount to expropriation, the tribunal paraphrases the Article 1110 language as follows: 'Thus, expropriation under NAFTA includes not only open, deliberate and acknowledged takings of property ... but also covert or incidental interference with the use of property which has the effect of depriving the owner, in whole or in significant part, of the use or reasonably-to-be-expected economic benefit of property'.

If one focusses in isolation on the phrase 'incidental interference with property', then there would be cause for consternation. Governments act in many ways that result in incidental interference with property, and it would be alarming to think that every such action might give rise to a claim for compensation from a foreign investor under Chapter 11. Justice Tysoe, for example, wonders whether this 'extremely broad definition' would not bring 'legitimate rezoning of property' within the scope of an expropriation. From the context of the quoted phrase, it does seem clear that the tribunal has not opened such a loophole. The reference to incidental interference with property goes inseparably with the following qualification: 'which has the effect of depriving the owner, in whole or significant part, of the use or reasonably-to-be-expected economic benefit of property'. This reading brings the *Metalclad* award back within the realm of fairly well-accepted understandings of expropriation, as confirmed in the Chapter 11 context by the interim and partial awards in *Pope & Talbot* and *S.D. Myers*.

Where Do We Go from Here?

Perhaps because of the early high-profile *Ethyl* case, Canada shows particular sensitivity to Chapter 11. Even if the awards to date can be justified by the unusual facts of the cases, Canadian analysts express alarm that the federal trade authorities are already using the awards and the publicity surrounding the awards in an educational campaign that may intimidate local and provincial officials in the exercise of their authority to protect health or to manage natural resources. The nature of the binding, international arbitration process contributes to this atmosphere of anxiety; because provinces and municipalities are not directly involved in dispute settlement over their measures, they have no assurance that the federal officials representing Canada, including trade officials, will vigorously advocate their interests. The lack of direct access by sub-federal governments is compounded by the fact that the arbitration proceedings can be secretive and the records are not publicly accessible through regular channels.

Reacting to these concerns, Canada has asked Mexico and the United States to work with it to develop a consensus interpretive statement on the most controversial provisions — the indirect or 'tantamount to' expropriation language of Article 1110 — that would bind the decisions of future arbitral tribunals. Thus far, however, the other NAFTA parties have shown no official interest in such a strategy (Gantz 2001).

From the U.S. perspective, the United States alone among the NAFTA countries has constitutional law doctrines about takings of property that have been construed in some cases to require compensation to domestic property owners when environmental protection measures are adopted (Wagner 1999; Rose 2000). To that extent, American officials are not particularly discomfited by the Chapter 11 outcomes thus far. Ironically, though, the argument by environmentalists and many Canadians is precisely that NAFTA Chapter 11 should not be allowed to extend U.S. takings doctrine to the treatment of foreign investors throughout North America. There is also a fear that arbitral tribunals will be tempted to go beyond the U.S. doctrine and protect investors even further against impairment of their businesses by local regulators. Chapter 11 has certainly given foreign investors, through self-serving interpretations of Chapter 11, an opening to create a NAFTA takings law much broader than anyone realised when NAFTA was being negotiated.

Environmentalists fear Chapter 11 as an avenue for business attack on environmental regulations and thus a threat to aggressive environmental protection policies, especially at the local and state/provincial levels. By the same token, however, if businesses and other investors see insufficient protections for foreign investors in Chapter 11, important investment flows in environmental services and technology could be inhibited, with potential adverse environmental consequences. The *Metalclad* case is one example of these cross-currents. After the actions of Guadalcazar and the governor of San Luis Potosí prevented it from operating its hazardous waste landfill, Metalclad announced that it was discontinuing all operations in Mexico. Since that announcement, at least six major foreign environmental investment projects in Mexico have been either delayed or discontinued. Environmental advocates, however, fear that such pressure from foreign investors will cause the Mexican government to soften its environmental policy responses in order to appease foreign investors and avoid future legal battles. State and local governments may be pressured by the federal government to do the same.

As a deliberate national and international policy choice agreed among the partner countries of North America, Chapter 11 of the NAFTA seeks to improve the climate for foreign direct investment by giving foreign investors certain protections against unfair treatment by host governments. There is no inherent conflict between freer movement of goods, more security for foreign investments, and national and international actions to protect public health and the environment and wisely manage natural resources. There is an inherent conflict, however, between the economic interest of specific individuals or firms in resources and in activities that generate and release contaminants and pollutants on the one hand and on the other the vast majority of environmental protection measures, which intentionally impinge on those activities and interests. In meshing their economic and their environmental policies, governments show a predictable tendency to protect strong interests and allow weaker, disenfranchised interests to be sacrificed in the choices they make. For any national or sub-national government, foreign investors, by their very foreignness, tend to fall into the politically vulnerable class of the weak and disenfranchised. Politically expedient avenues of environmental protection at the expense of foreign investors may be narrowed or blocked by Chapter 11. Chapter 11 also curtails government behaviour targeting foreign investors that seek to advance local economic or political interests under disingenuous claims of environmental protection.

As Canada, Mexico, and the United States continue their quests for means to advance environmental protection in their three independent federal political systems while embracing a continent-wide integrated economy, there is ample room for discussion and disagreement about the proper point of balance between the legitimate economic interests of foreign investors and the legitimate local or national interests in implementing and strengthening environmental protection measures. The debate will only lead toward more effective policies for North America, if it proceeds from a clear-eyed and unprejudiced analysis of the multiple competing considerations.

Notes

1   The full text of NAFTA is available at <www.nafta-sec-alena.org/english/index.htm>.

2 *S.D. Myers, Inc. v. Canada*, 2000.
3 Paragraphs 2 through 6 have to do with details of calculation such as interest charges and exchange rates.
4 Usually under international trade agreements only a national government can bring a suit in front of an international tribunal and the only remedy is to impose corrective or punitive tariffs or quotas on products from the violating nation. Under NAFTA, for example, most trade disputes are to be resolved through government-to-government procedures set forth in Chapter 20 of the agreement. There is one other exception to this general approach — the provision in NAFTA Chapter 19 for binational panels to review final national decisions on the application of antidumping or countervailing duties in lieu of judicial review in the courts of the nation that made the decision.
5 *Waste Management (Acaverde) v. Mexico (No. 1)*, described in Howard Mann (2001).
6 The three systems are the World Bank's International Center for Settlement of Investment Disputes (ICSID), the ICSID's Additional Facility, and the United Nations Commission on International Trade Law (UNCITRAL). Because the ICSID requires both parties to be members and neither Canada nor Mexico have agreed to it, that option is not currently available. Under the Additional Facility provisions, however, much the same process is available when one party has agreed to the system, and thus can be selected if the U.S. is either the respondent or the home of the claimant. The UNCITRAL process is open for all NAFTA disputes.
7 *Methanex v. United States,* Decision of the Tribunal on Petitions from Third Persons to Intervene as 'Amici Curiae'. 15 January 2001.
8 In an *amicus curiae* brief, a party or organisation interested in an issue participates in the argument in a case in which that party or organisation is not one of the litigants.
9 Not discussed here are one other major proceeding and one minor one by U.S. companies against Canadian actions related at least indirectly to environmental policy — *Pope & Talbot v. Canada* and *Sunbelt, Inc. v. Canada* — and two claims by U.S. investors against Mexico relating to solid waste disposal that were dismissed, one on procedural grounds, one on the merits. There are also two pending Canadian claims against the U.S., one related to a land-development scheme and one related to fuel additives regulation. This last case, *Methanex v. United States*, is discussed later in this chapter.
10 This section draws on two cases: the award of the tribunal in *Metalclad v. United Mexican States* in 2000 (available at <www.pearcelaw.com/metalclad.html> and *United Mexican States v. Metalclad* (2001). British Columbia Supreme Court (Tysoe J.), 2001 B.C.D. Civ. J. 1708.
11 This window of commercial opportunity for S.D. Myers was closed for a good five months later by a U.S. court decision that the 1995 enforcement discretion from the EPA was contrary to the *Toxic Substances Control Act.*
12 *United Mexican States v. Metalclad Corporation*, 2001.
13 *S.D. Myers, Inc. v. Canada*, Partial Award, 13 November 2000.
14 *United Mexican States v. Metalclad Corporation*, 2001.
15 Compare this judgement with the following views of one of the negotiators of Chapter 11: 'The fair and equitable treatment standard is closely aligned with, and overlaps, certain fundamental principles of international law — including transparency, procedural fairness, and the duty of good faith — from which other, more specific legal rules emanate' (Price 2000b).
16 *United Mexican States v. Metalclad Corporation*, 2001.
17 See also *S.D. Myers, Inc. v. Canada*, 2000.
18 Carol Rose (2000, 1) identifies regulatory disruptions of property as the most contentious area in which the underlying problem is that of 'transitions' — redefinitions of property

interests and rights: 'Taken together, these considerations create what I call the Utilitarian Dilemma, a dilemma that underlies many of the claims that property has been unconstitutionally taken. The dilemma is that the essential goal of securing property expectations clashes with the equally essential goal of managing congested resources.'

References

Abbott, Frederick M. (2000). 'The Political Economy of NAFTA Chapter Eleven: Equality before the Law and the Boundaries of North American Integration.' *Hastings International and Comparative Law Review* vol. 23, nos. 3-4, pp. 303–309.

Alvarez, Henri C. (2000). 'Arbitration under the North American Free Trade Agreement'. *Arbitration International* vol. 16, p. 393.

American Law Institute (1987). *Restatement of the Law Third: Foreign Relations Law of the United States*. Vol. 2. American Law Institute, St. Paul, MN.

'Basel Convention on the Control of Transboundary Movements of Hazardous Wastes and Their Disposal'(1999). <www.basel.int/text/con-e.htm> (December 2001).

Brower, Charles N. and Lee A. Steven (2001). 'Who Then Should Judge?: Developing the International Rule of Law under NAFTA Chapter 11'. *Chicago Journal of International Law* vol. 2, p. 193.

California Lawyer (2000). 'At 25 (Quoting Daniel Seligman, Director of the Sierra Club's Responsible Trade Program)'.

DePalma, Anthony (2001). 'Nafta's Powerful Little Secret'. *New York Times*, 11 March, s. 3. p. 1.

Enriquez, Raymundo E. (2000). 'No "Double-Dipping" Allowed: An Analysis of Waste Management, Inc. v. United Mexican States and the Article 1121 Waiver Requirement for Arbitration under Chapter 11 of NAFTA.' *Fordham Law Review* vol. 69, pp. 2655, 2662–2663.

Fracassi, Fulvio (2001). 'Confidentiality and NAFTA Chapter 11 Arbitrations'. *Chicago Journal of International Law* vol. 2, no. 1, pp. 213–222.

Free Trade Commission (2001). 'Clarifications Related to NAFTA Chapter 11'. 31 July.

Gallaird, Emmanuel (2000). 'NAFTA Dispute Arbitration under Auspices of the International Center'. *New York Law Journal* vol. 224, no. 23, p. 3.

Gantz, David A. (2001). 'Reconciling Environmental Protection and Investor Rights under Chapter 11 of NAFTA'. *Environmental Law Reporter* vol. 31, no. 7, pp. 10 646–610 668.

Gudofsky, Jason L. (2000). 'Shedding Light on Article 1110 of the North American Free Trade Agreement (NAFTA) Concerning Expropriations: An Environmental Case Study'. *Northwestern Journal of International Law and Business* vol. 21, p. 243.

Laird, Ian A. (2001). 'NAFTA Chapter 11 Meets Chicken Little'. *Chicago Journal of International Law* vol. 2, no. 1, pp. 223–229.

Lee, Jacob S. (2001). 'Expropriation under Mexican Law and Its Insertion into a Global Context under NAFTA.' *Hastings International and Comparative Law Review* vol. 23, p. 385.

Mann, Howard (2001). *Private Rights, Public Problems: A Guide to NAFTA's Controversial Chapter on Investors Rights*. International Institute on Sustainable Development and World Wildlife Fund, Winnipeg.

Mann, Howard and Konrad von Moltke (1999). *NAFTA's Chapter 11 and the Environment: Addressing the Impacts of the Investor-State Process on the Environment*. International Institute for Environment and Development, Washington DC.

Pearce, Clyde C. and Jack Coe, Jr. (2000). 'Arbitration under NAFTA Chapter Eleven: Some Pragmatic Reflections Upon the First Case Filed against Mexico'. *Hastings International and Comparative Law Review* vol. 23, p. 311.

Price, Daniel M. (2000a). 'Chapter 11: Private Party vs. Government, Investor-State Dispute Settlement: Frankenstein or Safety Valve?' *Canada-United States Law Journal* vol. 26, pp. 107–114.

Price, Daniel M. (2000b). 'Some Observations on Chapter Eleven of NAFTA'. *Hastings International and Comparative Law Review* vol. 23, nos. 3–4, pp. 421–429.

Public Citizen (1998). *School of Real-Life Results: NAFTA Report Card.* Public Citizen, Washington DC.

Rose, Carol M. (2000). 'Property and Expropriation: Themes and Variations in American Law'. *Utah Law Review* vol. 2000, no. 1, pp. 1–38.

Soloway, Julie A. (1999). 'Environmental Trade Barriers under NAFTA: The MMT Fuel Additives Controversy'. *Minnesota Journal of Global Trade* vol. 8, no. 1, p. 55.

Trakman, Leon E. (2001). 'Arbitrating Investment Disputes under NAFTA'. *Journal of International Arbitration* vol. 18, no. 4, p. 385.

Van Duzer, J. Anthony (1997). 'Investor-State Dispute Settlement under NAFTA Chapter 11: The Shape of Things to Come?' *Canadian Yearbook of International Law* vol. 35, p. 263.

Wagner, J. Martin (1999). 'International Investment, Expropriation, and Environmental Protection'. *Golden Gate University Law Review* vol. 29, nos. 1–3, pp. 465–538.

Wallace, Don (2000). 'State Responsibility for Denial of Substantive and Procedural Justice under NAFTA Chapter Eleven'. *Hastings International and Comparative Law Review* vol. 23, p. 393.

Chapter 7

Environmental Expropriation under NAFTA Chapter 11: The Phantom Menace

Julie Soloway[1]

It is not news that the dispute settlement provisions under NAFTA Chapter 11 are one of the most highly criticised aspects of the North American Free Trade Agreement (NAFTA) and, indeed, international investment regulation.[2] The expropriation provisions found in NAFTA's Article 1110 give foreign investors the right to compensation in the event that a NAFTA government has expropriated their property or adopted a measure 'tantamount to expropriation'. These three words — tantamount to expropriation — have been the subject of intense debate, because at least six of the NAFTA Chapter 11 cases initiated to date alleged that an environmental regulation or policy constituted a measure tantamount to expropriation.[3] There is, however, a lack of determinacy in defining precisely what constitutes a measure tantamount to expropriation (or a 'regulatory taking') under international law. This lack of determinacy, coupled with a lack of transparency throughout the Chapter 11 process, has fuelled broad-based concern about Chapter 11.[4]

How NAFTA's regulatory takings provisions will be interpreted has thus become a critical issue with much at stake. If the definition is too expansive, the argument goes, it could impose potentially huge financial obligations on governments, create disincentives to enact health and safety regulations, and introduce multiple distortions and social inefficiencies. On the other hand, a definition that is too restrictive would obliterate a key investment guarantee that protects foreign investors and would undermine the significant domestic and global welfare gains made possible by the creation of a North American liberalised investment regime.

The expropriation provisions of Chapter 11 have formed a major component of the anti-globalisation critique — a debate by no means confined to the desirability of trade and investment liberalisation regimes (Mann and von Moltke 1999; Kobrin 1998). Rather, these specific provisions seem to have invoked anxiety across a range of issues fundamental to liberalised economic markets and institutions, namely a questioning of the normative value of a capitalist economy, capital mobility in financial markets, deregulation of state enterprise, labour rights, and so on.[5] This anxiety has been accompanied by corresponding demands to re-evaluate the globalisation paradigm and its effects on social cohesion and integration. How NAFTA's expropriation provisions operate in practice, therefore, carries significant importance, as they will affect the tenor of this debate and possibly the future of international economic institutions, on which the health of the Canadian economy depends, such as NAFTA and the World Trade Organization (WTO).[6]

More specifically, nongovernmental organisations (NGOs) are concerned that national sovereignty is eroded as the capacity of governments to regulate in sensitive areas such as the environment is thwarted by private-party challenges. Opponents to Chapter 11 believe that the expropriation provisions will affect any 'law or regulation that impedes or will impede an investor's right to make a profit, [arguing that any] environmental, health or workers' rights legislation that could threaten profits would be interpreted as "expropriation"' (Kobrin 1998). Otherwise stated, NGOs believe that the Chapter 11 process *de facto* allows multinationals to set policy and law in ways hitherto unknown in North America.

This chapter examines the case that the expropriation provisions of NAFTA have been harmful to environmental regulation. It concludes that, based on the three tribunals that have ruled on the issue of expropriation to date, the expropriation provisions of NAFTA have not undermined environmental regulation in North America. In fact, there has so far been only one finding of expropriation (*Metalclad*). Two of the three panels (*Pope & Talbot* and *S.D. Myers*) have adopted a relatively conservative approach to the interpretation of Article 1110, thereby giving the NAFTA parties significant latitude within which to regulate economic activity within their borders. In *Metalclad*, however, the tribunal adopted a more expansive definition of expropriation beyond the traditional understanding of regulatory takings in international law.

The first section of this chapter reviews the international law of expropriation in order to provide a context for the NAFTA jurisprudence and evaluate the claim that the Chapter 11 tribunals have moved beyond the international norm. The second section examines the three NAFTA cases that have ruled on expropriation, and makes conclusions about the actual and potential threat that these tribunals pose for environmental regulation.

Expropriation

Direct Expropriation

Expropriation occurs when a host state takes property owned by a foreign investor located in the host state, ostensibly for a public purpose. The state may effect such a taking 'by declaring that the investor is no longer the owner of the property being expropriated' and may resort to force if necessary (Comeaux and Kinsella 1997, 3).

For an expropriation to occur, the state need not have acquired an interest; it is sufficient that there has been a deprivation of wealth attributable to the state. This point has been contentious — some believe that the state need acquire an interest itself as a necessary element of an expropriation (Wortley 1959). However, in more recent years, particularly within the jurisprudence of the Iran-United States Claims Tribunal, an expropriation (or a taking or a deprivation) can take place 'whenever acts attributable to a state have deprived an alien owner of property rights of value to him, regardless of whether the state has thereby obtained anything of value to it' (Aldrich 1994).

Expropriation conducted under specific circumstances is legal under international law. A state has the right to expropriate property of foreign investors within its borders. An expropriation will be considered legal if it does not discriminate against the investor, is done for a public purpose, and is accompanied by full compensation, which must be prompt, adequate, and effective.[7] An expropriation that does not meet these requirements is illegal under international law.[8] An expropriation that is either discriminatory or not for a public purpose, even though compensated, will still be illegal.[9]

There is no authoritative codification concerning the legality of expropriations under public international law. The *Restatement of the Law Third: Foreign Relations Law of the United States* (American Law Institute 1987), which purports to be a codification of current customary international law, defines state of the law as follows:

A state is responsible under international law for injury resulting from:
1) a taking by the state of the property of a national of another state that:
    a) is not for a public purpose, or
    b) is discriminatory, or
    c) is not accompanied by provision for just compensation; ...
3) other arbitrary or discriminatory acts or omissions by the state that impair property or other economic interests of a national of another state.

But, according to third *Restatement* (American Law Institute 1987, 712(g)), a state is not responsible for loss of property or other economic disadvantage resulting from *bona fide* general taxation, regulation, forfeiture from crime, or other action of the kind that is commonly considered as within the police powers of states.

Indirect Expropriation

Indirect expropriation refers to actions, omissions, or measures attributable to a government that are the functional equivalent of an expropriation. There exists no precise definition or analytic framework that can define exactly what will constitute an indirect expropriation. Where a direct expropriation entails an actual divestment of title from owner to the expropriator, an indirect expropriation does not involve such a transfer of title. Rather, an indirect expropriation can take an infinite number of forms; it can be essentially any action, omission, or measure attributable to a government that interferes with the rights flowing from the foreign-owned property to an extent that the property has been functionally expropriated. Yet defining a test that would automatically judge at what point regulation becomes expropriation is fraught with difficulty, as there will always be a fact situation that proves the theory wrong. Rupert Dolzer (1988) states that it 'is too early to speak of a comprehensive doctrine of indirect expropriation at this moment. More specifically, a good number of the solutions and answers which have so far been offered remain at the level of plausible assertions without a foundation in broader premises apt to lend firm support from a doctrinal basis'.

There is a general reluctance to define precisely what constitutes an indirect expropriation because there is a multitude of measures that can constitute expropriation. Several terms have been used interchangeably with the phrase 'indirect expropriation': creeping expropriation, *de facto* expropriation, surreptitious expropriation, constructive expropriation, measures tantamount to expropriation, disguised expropriation. There is a significant variation in how commentators and judges use these terms. At the outset, therefore, it is important to be cautious about prescribing any real significance to the various terms. There are no defined rules or classifications that explain the use of the various terminologies. As Ian Brownlie (1998, 534) states, 'the terminology of the subject is by no means settled, and in any case form should not take precedence over substance'. There is no hard and fast set of rules to apply in order to classify a measure as, for example, creeping expropriation rather than *de facto* expropriation, and no special set of analyses necessarily flows from such a classification.

Based on *Restatement of the Law Second: Foreign Relations Law of the United States*, Detlev Vagts (1978) defines 'creeping expropriation' as occurring when a government harasses a foreign investor in such a way as to make the enterprise unprofitable which results in the investor abandoning the property. The third *Restatement* (American Law Institute 1987, 7) states that a creeping expropriation will occur when a state seeks to achieve the same goal as expropriation through 'taxation and regulatory measures designed to make continued operation of a project uneconomical so that it is abandoned. In some cases the owner, faced with the prospect of continuing losses, sells to the government, accepting a modest price, but later asserts that the transaction was not in fact a sale but a taking'. Another author has defined creeping expropriation as 'measures whereby the government increasingly imposes restrictions and controls, such as excessive and repetitive tax regulatory measures, on the foreign investment enterprises so as to make it difficult to continue in business at a profit [that] leads to the sale or abandonment of the project to the government or local private investors. It is the cumulative effect of the measures which then has a *de facto* confiscatory effect and that their combined effect results in depriving the investor of ownership, control or substantial benefits over his enterprise, even when each such measure taken separately does not have this effect' (Sandrino 1994, n. 276).

Temporal considerations often are integral to the definition of a constructive taking or a creeping expropriation. Such situations will ripen or mature into explicit takeovers as events take their course (Weston 1975). The challenge is thus to define the precise time at which government measures or actions cross the line into a compensable taking. This will often be cumulative in nature, rather than pinpointing one specific event.

The term 'measures having the same effect as expropriations' has been used widely in the context of bilateral investment treaties (BITs). Yet this phrase too fails to give any special insight into the issue at hand. Dolzer (1988, 44) notes that while such terms are 'certainly not objectionable from a strictly legal point of view', it is also true 'that the legal evaluation of the measures in question is so difficult precisely because the legal and economic status of the owner concerned is not identical with that of the one whose title was taken', that is, in comparison to a direct expropriation. Therefore, BITs use the terminologies that provide no special insight on their own as to the legality of a specific government measure.

The term 'indirect expropriation' is generally used as an umbrella categorisation of the various forms of expropriation. There is no limit on what measures can constitute indirect expropriation; indeed, it 'is a matter of degree rather than of kind' (Comeaux and Kinsella 1997, 10). One author has produced a list that is by no means exhaustive but nonetheless provides an overview of the wide array of measures that can become an indirect expropriation. They include unreasonable taxation; discriminatory legislation and administrative decrees; certain cases of zoning; the granting, in certain cases, of a monopoly by a government; unreasonable price ceilings that are not allowed to keep pace with inflationary trends; and any other means of such unreasonable interference with the property rights of the alien owner that he or she is effectively deprived of the use and beneficial enjoyment of any holdings.[10]

Allahyar Mouri (1994) claims that the proposition that indirect expropriations are to be treated as direct expropriations to be a rule of international law, accepted by the Iran-U.S. Claims Tribunal. George Aldrich's (1994, 609) view of the decisions of the same tribunal is consistent with that: 'liability does not require the transfer of title of property'. The third *Restatement* declares that the rules requiring compensation for expropriation apply 'not only to avowed expropriations in which the government formally takes title to the property, but also to other actions of the government that have the effect of "taking" the property, in whole or in large part, outright or in stages ("creeping expropriation")' (American Law Institute 1987).

It is a truism that modern governments are more than ever heavily involved in broad economic and social regulation that can impose costs and benefits on individuals and firms regardless of nationality. It is also a truism that all governments impose taxation schemes and other measures that may restrict the right of owners to use and dispose of their property, namely, zoning, licensing, and so on. However, 'before such actions will be considered to amount to expropriation it must be apparent that the governmental actions have so completely deprived the owners of their property rights that the rights are rendered nugatory. Such findings are readily made where the government has the avowed intention of socializing the economy and thereby depriving private owners of their property rights' (Mapp 1992, 152).

The Scope of the Police Power Exception

Police power is defined as 'the power of the state to place restraints on the personal freedom and property rights of persons for the protection of the public safety, health and morals, or the promotion of the public convenience and general prosperity ... The police power is the exercise of the sovereign right of a government to promote order, safety, security, health, morals and general welfare within the constitutional limits and is an essential attribute of government'(*Black's Law Dictionary* 1990). Generally, states will not be liable to compensate for economic loss flowing from measures that are an exercise of a state's police power, as long as those measures are not arbitrary or discriminatory. Under international law, 'jurists supporting the compensation rule recognize the existence of exceptions, the most widely accepted of which include: a legitimate exercise of police power [which includes] loss caused indirectly by health and planning legislation and the concomitant restrictions on the use of property' (Wortley 1959, 40–57; see also Sohn and Baxter 1961, 561–562). Consistent with this, the comments in third *Restatement* read:

> A state is not responsible for loss of property or for other economic disadvantage resulting from bona fide general taxation, regulation, forfeiture for crime or other action of the kind that is commonly accepted as within the police power of states, if it is not discriminatory ... and is not designed to cause the alien to abandon the property to the state or sell it at a distress price (American Law Institute 1987, section 712(g)).

The concept of police power — a sphere in which a government may regulate without liability — is generally accepted among international law commentators. However, it is the scope of that sphere that is the subject of contention and how it will be applied in various fact situations, rather than its existence itself. Brownlie views this sphere as expansive, stating that

> state measures, *prima facie* a lawful exercise of powers of government, may affect foreign interests considerably without amounting to expropriation. Thus foreign assets and their use may be subjected to taxation, trade restrictions involving licensing or quotas, or measures of devaluation. While special facts may alter cases, in principle such measures are not unlawful and do not constitute expropriation. If the state gives a public enterprise special advantages, for example, by direction that it charge nominal rates of freight, the resulting *de facto* or quasi-monopoly is not an expropriation of the competitors driven out of business: it might be otherwise if this were the primary or sole object of a monopoly regime. Taxation which has the precise object and effect of confiscation is probably unlawful (Brownlie 1998, 565).

Mouri's view of the police power exception is similarly large, especially in the case of emergency or distress situations,

Under the rules of international law, measures taken by States or attributable to them are not considered to be wrongful or to depart from international standards of justice which may entail liability for compensation of damages inflicted, if they were taken in a distress or emergency situation reasonably necessary to conserve life and property, or if they were taken to maintain the public order or to regulate the internal affairs of the country, such as to enforce revenue or customs laws, impose exchange control regulations, *or preserve or protect the environment, health and safety of the nation* [emphasis added] (Mouri 1994, 248).

George Christie, too, enunciates an expansive definition of the police power. He sets a very low hurdle for determining whether a measure is the exercise of a *bona fide* objective, finding it unnecessary to address whether the state had ulterior motives that would not be within a state's police power. He writes:

A State's declaration that a particular interference with an alien's enjoyment of his property is justified by the so-called 'police power' does not preclude an international tribunal from making an independent determination of this issue. But, if the reasons given are valid and bear some plausible relationship to the action taken, no attempt may be made to search deeper to see whether the State was activated by some illicit motive (Christie 1988, 338).

In any event, challenging a state on the basis that it has acted for improper motives is difficult. Burns Weston (1975) argues that it 'is serious business to dispute a State's claim to "regulation". International law traditionally has granted States broad competence in the definition and management of their economies'. However, despite the writings of the many commentators, it is by no means easy to distinguish measures that fall within the police power from measures that do not.

Moreover, the concept of police power does not figure prominently in the international law jurisprudence and there are few cases that have dealt with its definition, scope, and application. It has been invoked in some cases to support the contention that a given measure by a government is in accordance with an investor's reasonable expectations and thus not expropriatory. For example, in *Parsons*, the incidental harm to property caused by a government's security measures was not compensable and was held to be within the police power of the government: in finding the destruction of the claimant's liquor stock during the handling of an 'insurrection' in Manila not to be an expropriation, the tribunal stated that 'we are satisfied that the destruction was a matter of police entirely within the powers of the military government and quite justified by the circumstances'.[11] Similarly, in *Kügele v. Polish State*, the tribunal dismissed the argument that licensing fees imposed by Poland had forced the claimant to close his brewery and were thus expropriatory.[12]

In *Gallagher v. Lynn*, it was held that 'expropriation does not normally occur through the incidental effect of legislation'.[13] The impugned regulation was designed to safeguard the health of the inhabitants of Northern Ireland by permitting the sale only of inspected milk. The law was not intended to affect trade with Southern Ireland or damage the 'goodwill' attaching to Southern Irish business, despite the fact that it had such an effect. Rather, the intent of the Northern Irish law was to 'secure the health of the inhabitants of Northern Ireland by protecting them from the dangers of an unregulated supply of milk'.[14] This reasoning was followed by the Privy Council in *Shannon v. Lower Mainland Dairy Products Board.*

Sea-Land Services, Inc. involved a situation where restrictions were imposed on the types of goods that could be unloaded at a port. Due to civil unrest, only food and medicine were permitted to be unloaded. This measure was challenged, and the Iran-U.S. Claims Tribunal found that the restrictions were 'a reasonable and legitimate measure during a time of civil unrest'.[15] Therefore, the state was not liable for the consequent damages. In *Sedco, Inc. v. National Iranian Oil Co.*, the majority wrote that 'a State is not liable for economic injury which is a consequence of *bona fide* 'regulation' within the accepted police power of states'.[16] Yet in this case, the tribunal found that there had been an expropriation for which the tribunal awarded compensation because there had been 'an outright transfer of title rather than incidental economic injury'.

In *Too v. United States*, an Iranian national was denied his claim against the United States for compensation for the seizure of a restaurant liquor licence by U.S. authorities, which had been done pursuant to the claimants' failure to submit substantial sums in employee withholding taxes.[17] Here the tribunal reaffirmed the general principle in Section 712 of the third *Restatement* that a state is not responsible for loss of property or any other economic disadvantage resulting from *bona fide*, nondiscriminatory general taxation, regulation, forfeiture from crime, or other action of the kind that is commonly considered as within the police powers of states (American Law Institute 1987, section 712(g)).

There does not seem to be a limit on the type of measure that is an exercise of the police power. Rather, its illegality will be defined by its effect, its arbitrariness, the way it discriminates, rather than the type of measure *per se*. The general principle is that *bona fide* reform is within the scope of a government's police power even if it causes loss to foreign owners. General limitations on property will not give rise to expropriation 'if those changes do not in fact dispossess them but merely lessen the value of their holdings or expectations, in the general interest, then *bona fide* changes in the public interest will not be confiscations, since the owners are left in possession of their property' (Wortley 1959, 50). This can be contrasted with the withdrawal of the full attributes of ownership, which would of course constitute expropriation.

NAFTA Chapter 11 Rulings on Article 1110

This section evaluates the three NAFTA decisions to date that have ruled on the issue of expropriation. This section, does not, however, provide an exhaustive review of the facts of each case, but rather focusses specifically on how Article 1110 was interpreted in each case.

Pope & Talbot v. Canada

The tribunal denied *Pope & Talbot's* claim for compensation against the Canadian government for expropriation. In this case, the tribunal adopted a relatively conservative approach to the interpretation of expropriation. There are a number of significant aspects to the ruling.

First, *Pope & Talbot* had claimed that certain export restrictions on lumber imposed by Canada amounted to a measure tantamount to expropriation since they had 'deprived the investment of its ordinary ability to alienate its product to its traditional and natural market'.[18] Canada contested the classification of the right to export lumber as a property right. Interestingly, the tribunal ruled that the 'investment's access to the U.S. market is a property interest subject to protection under Article 1110'.[19] This seems to imply that a measure that affected the value of property could be subject to challenge under Article 1110.

Second, the tribunal affirmed that, for a measure to be considered expropriatory, it need not be discriminatory. In other words, the tribunal contemplated that, in certain circumstances, government measures could be applied in a nondiscriminatory manner yet still be tantamount to expropriation. To interpret otherwise, the tribunal ruled would leave a 'gaping loophole' in international protections against expropriation.[20]

Third, the tribunal seemed to be open to a wide notion of what a taking could encompass for the purposes of expropriation. While stating that there was no expropriation in this case in the 'ordinary meaning' of the term, the tribunal also stated that a taking could include interference with the carrying on of business. It reasoned that while the interference in this case 'has, according to the Investor, resulted in reduced profits for the Investment, it continues to export substantial quantities of softwood lumber to the U.S. and to earn substantial profits on those sales'. The tribunal added that 'while it may sometimes be uncertain whether a particular interference with business activities amounts to an expropriation, *the test is whether that interference is sufficiently restrictive to support a conclusion that the property has been taken from the owner'* [emphasis added] and that a finding of expropriation would require a 'substantial deprivation'.[21]

Finally, the tribunal narrowed the scope of the expropriation provisions by rejecting the investor's claim that the use of the term 'tantamount to expropriation' means something more than an outright taking or creeping expropriation. The tribunal stated that 'tantamount means nothing more than equivalent' and that 'something equivalent cannot logically encompass more'.[22]

This decision, therefore, would seem to curtail the risk that the expropriation provisions could be applied to something less than a substantial loss of property rights on the part of a foreign investor. While the measures that could fall within the scope of expropriatory activity is wide, the fact that the tribunal articulated a test of substantial deprivation and limited the meaning of 'tantamount to expropriation' to nothing more than what would otherwise be a direct expropriation indicates a conservative approach consistent with the international jurisprudence reviewed above.

S.D. Myers v. Canada

The tribunal in *S.D. Myers* adopted a narrow view of expropriation. In this case, the issue involved a temporary ban by the Canadian government on the export of PCB wastes to the United States. As with *Pope & Talbot,* the tribunal found that no expropriation had taken place.

The tribunal recognised that compensating for a regulatory taking is the exception, and not the rule, as follows:

> The general body of precedent usually does not treat regulatory action as amounting to expropriation. Regulatory conduct by public authorities is unlikely to be subject to legitimate complaints under Article 1110 of the NAFTA, although the Tribunal does not rule out that possibility.[23]

The tribunal further acknowledged that although an expropriation usually amounts to a lasting removal of the ability of an owner to make use of its economic rights, in some circumstances even a temporary removal of such rights might qualify as expropriation. However, in this case, the tribunal noted that the closure of the border resulting from the regulation, during which the complainant said it lost its competitive advantage, was only temporary and thus could not be an expropriation. Such reasoning appears to leave the door open to a future finding of an expropriation for a measure that is only temporary. Had the border closing been permanent, or even simply for a longer duration, it is possible that the tribunal would have found there to have been an expropriation. This reasoning is consistent with the notion of creeping expropriation in international law — that is, at some point a measure can ripen into a full expropriation.

The tribunal agreed with the decision in *Pope & Talbot* that the term 'tantamount to expropriation' in Article 1110 merely meant equivalent to expropriation and that the use of the word 'tantamount' was meant only to include the concept of creeping expropriation.[24] However, the tribunal then added that the term 'tantamount' meant that a tribunal should look at the substance of what has occurred and not just form. In other words, a tribunal 'must look at the real interests involved and the purpose and effect of the government measure'.[25] Thus the tribunal effectively stated that for there to be a regulatory expropriation, it must result in as substantive a deprivation as a direct vexpropriation. This would seem to shut the door on the allegation that NAFTA provides a cause of action for something less, in substantive terms, than a direct expropriation. This does, however, open the door to future factual analyses for events that are not deemed to be expropriation in form may be found to be expropriation in substance.

Metalclad v. United Mexican States

Metalclad is the only one of the three cases in which the tribunal found that expropriation had taken place.[26] In this case, the refusal of local government authorities to issue a permit for the operation of a hazardous waste facility that had already been constructed was found to be an expropriation on the part of the Mexican government. The tribunal adopted a relatively expansive interpretation of expropriation, stating that

> expropriation under NAFTA includes not only open, deliberate and acknowledged takings of property, such as outright seizure or formal or obligatory transfer of title in favour of the host State, but also *incidental interference* with the use of property which has the effect of depriving the owner, in whole or in significant part, of the use or *reasonably-to-be-expected economic benefit* of property *even if not necessarily to the obvious benefit of the host State* [emphasis added].[27]

The facts in this case made for an easy determination that an expropriation had taken place (Dumberry 2001). The tribunal held that the inequitable treatment of Metalclad by local Mexican authorities, with the tolerance of the federal government, as well as the violation of representations made and the lack of basis in refusing a permit that would bar the use of the landfill permanently, amounted to indirect expropriation. Nevertheless, the tribunal adopted a more expansive interpretation of expropriation, as the paragraph above implies that future tribunals could find an expropriation even where an incidental interference occurred that deprived the owner of a 'reasonably-to-be-expected' benefit.

In contrast with *S.D. Myers*, the tribunal ruled that the government need not acquire a benefit for an expropriation to occur. This is consistent with the evolution of international law norms discussed above, namely, the Iran-U.S. Claims Tribunal rulings on this issue. Moreover, the tribunal ruled that the fact that a government did not intend to effect an expropriation was not relevant to the determination of whether an expropriation took place. These factors, taken together, seem to somewhat lower the hurdle of what constitutes an expropriation.

At the same time, however, the tribunal narrowed the substantive scope of an indirect expropriation, as it viewed as functionally equivalent the concepts of 'indirect expropriation' and acts or measures 'tantamount to expropriation'. Weiler (2001) notes that 'this finding should help to put to rest claims that NAFTA Chapter 11 somehow expanded the customary international law definition of expropriation'.

Conclusion

The international law of expropriation does not, as it currently stands, pose a threat to valid environmental regulation. Notably, there has been only one ruling where a regulatory taking was found to have taken place. To date, the NAFTA tribunals that have ruled on the issue of expropriation have been quite conservative in their approach in defining the scope of NAFTA's expropriation provisions. At the same time, however, these tribunals have not rejected the possibility of future findings of regulatory takings, including environmental regulation, and have rather articulated circumstances where such findings may be made. In this way, the NAFTA Chapter 11 tribunals to date have protected international investment without any corresponding reduction in environmental protection.

Notes

1   The author is grateful for the research assistance provided by Andrey Anishchenko, Student-at-law, Davies Ward Phillips & Vineberg LLP.
2   The specifics of the broad-based concern will be developed throughout this chapter. For a populist overview of the point of view of a nongovernmental organisation, see Tony Clarke and Maude Barlow (1998; 1997), Stephen Kobrin (1998), and Michelle Sforza-Roderick, Scott Nova, and Mark Weisbrot (1999).
3   These cases are *Ethyl Corporation v. Canada, S.D. Myers, Inc. v. Canada, Pope & Talbot v. Canada, Sunbelt, Inc. v. Canada, Metalclad Corporation v. United Mexican States,* and *Methanex v. United States.*
4   For an eloquent elaboration of these ideas see Dani Rodrik (1997). For an insightful perspective on globalisation and risk regulation, see Robert Howse (1999). For a critique of the NGO attack on the Multilateral Agreement on Investment, see Alan Rugman (1999).
5   See the entire issue entitled 'It's the Global Economy, Stupid: The Corporatization of the World' (1996) and 'Inside Globalization' (1998/99).
6   Forty-two percent of Canada's gross domestic product (GDP) is derived from exports. See John Kirton (1998).
7   The standard of what is considered legal compensation varies, a point not addressed in this chapter (see Comeaux and Kinsella 1997, 78).
8   See Ian Brownlie quoted in Paul Comeaux (1997, 441, 537–539).
9   Paul Comeaux cites Ian Brownlie, who states that expropriations will also be illegal if they include 'seizures which are part of crimes against humanity or genocide, involve breaches of international agreements, are measures of unlawful retaliation or reprisal against another state ... or concern property owned by a foreign state and dedicated to official state purposes' (Comeaux and Kinsella 1997, 538).
10 See Cynthia Wallace (1982, 277). For another wide definition of indirect expropriation, see the 1967 OECD Draft Convention on the Protection of Foreign Property and Resolution of the Council of the OECD on the Draft Convention.
11 *Parsons* (Great Britain v. United States) 6 R.I.A.A. 165 (1925).
12 *Kügele v. Polish State* 6 Ann.Dlg. 69 (1931–32) (Upper Selesian Arbitral Tribunal, 1930).
13 *Gallagher v. Lynn* [1937] A.C. 863.

14 *Shannon v. Lower Mainland Dairy Products Board* [1938] A.C. 708.
15 *Sea-Land Services, Inc.* 6 Iran-U.S. C.T.R. 149, p. 238.
16 *Sedco, Inc. v. National Iranian Oil Co.* 15 Iran-U.S. C.T.R. 23.
17 *Too v. United States* 23 Iran-U.S. C.T.R. 378.
18 *Pope & Talbot v. Canada*, Statement of Claim, para. 93.
19 *Pope & Talbot v. Canada*, Final Merits Award, para. 96.
20 *Pope & Talbot v. Canada*, Interim Award, paras. 81–86.
21 *Pope & Talbot v. Canada*, Final Merits Award, paras. 101–102.
22 *Pope & Talbot v. Canada*, Interim Award, para. 104.
23 *S.D. Myers v. Canada*, Final Award on Merits, para. 69.
24 *S.D. Myers v. Canada*, Final Award on Merits, paras. 285–286.
25 *S.D. Myers v. Canada*, Final Award on Merits, para. 285.
26 For a general view, see Todd Weiler (2001).
27 *Metalclad v. United Mexican States*, para. 103.

References

Aldrich, George H. (1994). 'What Constitutes a Compensable Taking of Property? The Decisions of the Iran-United States Claims Tribunal'. *American Journal of International Law* vol. 88, no. 4, pp. 585–610.

American Law Institute (1987). *Restatement of the Law Third: Foreign Relations Law of the United States*. Vol. 2. American Law Institute, St. Paul, MN.

Black's Law Dictionary (1990). 6th ed. West Publishing, St. Paul, MN.

Brownlie, Ian (1998). *Principles of Public International Law*. 5th ed. Oxford University Press, Oxford.

Christie, G. C. (1988). 'What Constitutes a Taking of Property under International Law'. *British Yearbook of International Law* vol. 33, no. 307.

Clarke, Tony and Maude Barlow (1997). *MAI: The Multilateral Agreement on Investment and the Threat to Canadian Sovereignty*. Stoddart Publishing, Toronto.

Clarke, Tony and Maude Barlow (1998). *MAI Round 2: New Global and Internal Threats to Canadian Sovereignty*. Stoddart Publishing, Toronto.

Comeaux, P.E. and N.S. Kinsella (1997). *Protecting Foreign Investment under International Law: Legal Aspects of Political Risk*. Oceana, Dobbs Ferry, NY.

Dolzer, Rupert (1988). 'Indirect Expropriation of Alien Property'. *ISCID Review* vol. 1, no. 41, p. 43.

Dumberry, P. (2001). 'Expropriation under NAFTA Chapter 11 Investment Dispute Settlement Mechanism: Some Comments on the Latest Case Law'. *International Arbitration Law Review* vol. 4, no. 3.

Howse, Robert (1999). 'Democracy, Science, and Free Trade: Risk Regulation on Trial at the World Trade Organization'. Paper presented at Harvard Law School, Spring Term. Boston.

'Inside Globalization' (1998/99). *Monetary Reform*. Special Section. Fall/Winter.

'It's the Global Economy Stupid: The Corporatization of the World' (1996). *The Nation* vol. 263, no. 3.

Kirton, John J. (1998). 'NAFTA, Foreign Direct Investment, and Economic Integration: A Canadian Approach'. In Organisation for Economic Co-operation and Development, *Migration, Free Trade, and Regional Integration in North America*, pp. 181–194. Organisation for Economic Co-operation and Development, Paris.

Kobrin, Stephen J. (1998). 'The MAI and the Clash of Globalizations'. *Foreign Policy*, Fall.

Mann, Howard and Konrad von Moltke (1999). *NAFTA's Chapter 11 and the Environment: Addressing the Impacts of the Investor-State Process on the Environment*. International Institute for Environment and Development, Washington DC.

Mapp, W. (1992). *The Iran-United States Claims Tribunal: The First Ten Years*. Manchester University Press, Manchester.

Mouri, Allahyar (1994). *The International Law of Expropriation as Reflected in the Work of the Iran-U.S. Claims Tribunal*. Nijhoff, Dordrecht, Netherlands.

Rodrik, Dani (1997). *Has Globalization Gone Too Far?* Institute for International Economics, Washington DC.

Rugman, Alan M. (1999). 'Negotiating Multilateral Rules to Promote Investment'. In M. R. Hodges, J. J. Kirton and J. P. Daniels, eds., *The G8's Role in the New Millennium*, pp. 143–157. Ashgate, Aldershot.

Sandrino, G. L. (1994). 'The NAFTA Investment Chapter and Foreign Direct Investment in Mexico: A Third World Perspective'. *Vanderbilt Journal of Transnational Law* vol. 27, no. 259, p. 276.

Sforza-Roderick, Michelle, Scott Nova, and Mark Weisbrot (1999). 'Writing the Constitution of a Single Global Economy: A Concise Guide to the Multilateral Agreement on Investment'. <www.globalpolicy.org/globaliz/econ/oneecon.htm> (December 2001).

Sohn, L. B. and R. R. Baxter (1961). 'Responsibility of States for Injuries to the Economic Interests of Aliens'. *American Journal of International Law* vol. 55, no. 545, pp. 553–554.

Vagts, D.F. (1978). 'Coercion and Foreign Investment Rearrangements'. *American Journal of International Law* vol. 72, no. 17.

Wallace, Cynthia D. (1982). *Legal Controls of Multinational Enterprise*. Nijhoff, The Hague.

Weiler, Todd J. (2001). 'Metalclad v. Mexico: A Play in Three Parts'. *Journal of World Investment* vol. 2, no. 4.

Weston, B.H. (1975). '"Constructive Takings" under International Law: A Modest Foray into the Problem of Creeping Expropriation'. *Virginia Journal of International Law* vol. 16, no. 103, p. 107.

Wortley, Ben Atkinson (1959). *Expropriation in Public International Law*. Cambridge University Press, Cambridge, UK.

Chapter 8

Investment and the Environment: Multilateral and North American Perspectives

Konrad von Moltke

It is increasingly important to think creatively about investment and its role in sustainable development. The opposition to the proposed Multilateral Agreement on Investment (MAI) was one of the seminal events of the 1990s in the process of attempting to develop an approach to globalisation that is sensitive to a range of considerations, in addition to those of a purely economic nature. The opposition to the MAI has, however, led to a widespread attitude, certainly in the environmental community, that an investment agreement is a bad thing. That is a fundamental mistake. It reflects inadequate research and discussion of the issues that are really at stake regarding investment.

Put as concisely as possible, environmental regulation creates a framework that is designed to promote structural economic change. Environmental policy does not seek to stop economic activity or to decrease it but to ensure that it occurs in a direction that is less harmful to the environment. Structural economic change occurs through investment, and virtually only through investment. Thus investment is in many ways the bottom line when one is talking about environmental issues from an economic perspective. For example, it is possible to view the United Nations Framework Convention on Climate Change (UNFCCC) as essentially an investment agreement. It seeks to persuade people to invest in projects that decrease greenhouse gas emissions and dissuade them from investing in projects that have the opposite effect. That is not the kind of investment agreement that the MAI was designed to be, but it certainly identifies the environmental stakes in an investment agreement differently from how they were identified in the debate about the MAI. It also constitutes a powerful argument that an international investment is really a critical concern to the community whose interest is in sustainable development.

The history of international negotiations on investment is fraught with failure. In addition to the MAI, the only major economic negotiation to have been abandoned, there was an effort spearheaded by the United Nations Centre on Transnational Corporations (UNCTC) in the 1970s to negotiate a code of conduct for multinational corporations. UNCTC was shut down for its pains, one of the extremely rare instances of any international body to have been terminated. Proposals to include investment in negotiations of the General Agreement on Tariffs and Trade (GATT) and the World Trade Organization (WTO) have been contentious ever since they first surfaced in the

Uruguay Round. The investment provisions of the North American Free Trade Agreement (NAFTA) have recently become the focus of significant controversy concerning their ability to interfere with legitimate regulatory activities of public authorities. Nevertheless there is a very large number of bilateral investment agreements and several regional ones. Presumably, it has been possible to negotiate these because their reach was more modest and they had less potential to change the delicate balance between foreign investors and host country governments.

It is not possible to view an international investment agreement in isolation, whether or not it is designed to promote sustainable development. Such an agreement would become part of international law and a good portion of its environmental dimension would need to derive from its interaction with international environmental agreements. However, the effectiveness of these agreements is a matter of concern if they are to contribute to sustainable development in conjunction with an investment agreement.

It is easy to produce reasons why international environmental agreements should not be effective. The real puzzle is why they *are* effective. Although many questions remain about the effectiveness of international environmental agreements, there is little doubt that many of them do indeed have significant positive effects. One of the dominant explanatory factors of the effectiveness of international environmental agreements is the role of civil society. There is no such agreement that is effective without a significant civil society component, taking 'civil society' to comprise scientists, industry, and commerce, environmental organisations, and the media. In other words, international civil society is not synonymous with environmental organisations (Newell 2000).

There is another, more promising approach to the issue of the effectiveness of international agreements, both generally and in the environmental domain. This approach examines these agreements and asks what is the structure of the problem. That is, what does the problem really imply that one needs to do? And it asks this question with no preconceptions about the appropriate organisational and institutional response at the international level. Indeed, the previously largely determined, normative notion of what an international organisation is and what it can do has been replaced by a much more dynamic concept of international regimes (von Moltke 1997; Young 1994, 1998).

The extent to which international environmental agreements begin with the problem and not with the organisational response is remarkable. This is presumably one of the reasons for the degree of effectiveness that they achieve. Once the definition of the problem has been addressed, the next question follows almost automatically: What are the institutions needed to deal with this problem? This question considers institutions as 'rules of the game', rather than organisations, so that, for example, transparency is an institution and research is an institution, but the United Nations Environment Programme (UNEP) is an organisation. Following identification of which institutions are needed, it is possible to ask what the fit is between these institutions and the problem. This leads finally to an organisational question, namely where to locate the needed institutions in order to address the problem that has been identified.

In a way, this is a very rational approach. Yet, it requires one fundamental assumption — that one can freely make the necessary institutional choices in international society. Not so long ago the answer to that particular question was resoundingly negative. The options available for international action on any issue, ranging from environment to economic policy, and from security to human rights, were completely limited by the operation of the principle of sovereignty and the relations between sovereign states. In all cases, the only proper approach involved mobilising international agreements through intergovernmental organisations. All the participants in this process were defined exclusively and completely by their national allegiance.

There are a number of very powerful assumptions that lie behind an analytical approach to international environmental issues based on assessing problem structure, required institutions, and organisational fit. An example of institutional choice is the decision of the Appellate Body of the WTO dispute settlement process to admit *amicus* briefs in case of asbestos, setting out a number of criteria. This was a major institutional innovation (International Centre for Trade and Sustainable Development 2001). It turns out that the criteria of the Appellate Body were taken from the criteria listed in a petition to the Methanex panel under NAFTA to justify the admittance of the International Institute for Sustainable Development as an *amicus curiae* (Mann 2001). One can see how a new institutional pattern emerges. Such innovations will be controversial and may take some time to become accepted practice. But this describes the increasing dynamism of the international system and justifies thinking about international (environmental) problems in this way.

A recent book on an international investment regime from the perspective of sustainable development took the approach just outlined for international environmental issues and applied it to the issue of investment (von Moltke 2000). It argues that the MAI negotiators did not put sufficient effort into identifying the actual problem and did not properly frame the issues being negotiated. They assumed that there was a continuity of government action on investment with a long history in the Organisation for Economic Co-operation and Development (OECD) and the GATT/WTO. This led them to a set of responses that did not properly address the underlying problem.

The historical approach to investment — embodied in bilateral investment agreements (BITs) and in the Agreement on Trade-Related Investment Measures (TRIMs) — was flawed. It was based on the assumption that nondiscrimination is a universal principle and that consequently the same institutions will be needed to achieve nondiscrimination, no matter what issue was being addressed. It turns out that this assumption is false. For trade in goods, it has proven sufficient to use the institutions of most-favoured-nation treatment, national treatment, some transparency, and dispute settlement to promote nondiscrimination. When it comes to liberalisation of foreign direct investment (FDI), however, the underlying problem structure turns out to be quite different than in the case of trade in goods.

What is really at issue in shaping an international investment agreement? It is, clearly, not the freedom of capital movements. It is not the same as what is required with trade in goods. One of the dramatic indicators of this difference is the fact that problems that arise with investment in the international domain do not typically arise when one makes the initial investment. Rather, they happen later, as circumstances change, as governments change, and as investments change. The relationships change and the question that arises concerns the nature of these relationships. They are thus different from the relations between states with respect to trade in goods that are at the core of the GATT. They are different from the relations between states with respect to trade in services that are at the core of the General Agreement on Trade in Services (GATS). The dominant concern of the GATS was to facilitate international trade in services and the creation of the necessary infrastructure for international markets. This required the availability of key services in a comparable format at the international level. To achieve that goal, it was appropriate to include provisions on investment because it was a necessary part of that particular goal and problem.

Two aspects of investment determine any international investment regime: productive investment is a long-term activity, and the investor acquires numerous rights in the host country as an individual. Problems associated with productive investments can occur five, ten, or fifteen years later. The NAFTA disputes that have arisen under Chapter 11 are emblematic. These are not disputes about the initial setting up of investment. They are disputes about the use of an investment once it is made and about changing rules that hinder the use of that investment. So the long-term relationship is a very important factor. Equally important is the fact that the investor acquires rights in the country in which the investment occurs. This can be thought of as a form of economic citizenship. The acquisition of these rights is critical. These are rights to buy and sell, to hire and fire, to use and dispose of resources, and so on.

It is instructive to look at the way in which nondiscrimination is achieved in domestic jurisdictions. This turns out to be a central challenge of governance, requiring extensive institutional resources. Typically, countries have administrative rules of procedure to ensure equitable treatment of investors under like circumstances. They have rights of public information and participation to ensure that anybody affected by an investment has an opportunity to be heard. And they use the judicial system to settle disputes that may arise, typically providing for several layers of appeal to ensure that fairness prevails. It is this institutional structure — different from one country to the next but nearly always highly evolved and complex — that an international investment regime seeks to guide. It is a daunting task, and the institutional means deployed thus far in multilateral investment agreements are clearly inadequate to the task, with the single exception of the European Union and its institutions (von Moltke 2001). The common theme among all these domestic regimes aiming for nondiscrimination in investment is that they are designed to balance private (investor) interests and public goods (typically represented by the action of public authorities). Any international investment regime must be capable of undertaking such a balancing act.

One question remains: What is the most appropriate framework for promoting the liberalisation of international investment? Thus far, there are many bilateral investment agreements — indeed, there are thousands. There are a few regional trade agreements that include investment provisions, notably the European Union, NAFTA, and Mercosur. There are also a number of sectoral agreements that contain investment provisions, for example, the GATS, the Energy Charter Treaty (among the countries of Europe),[1] or even the United Nations Convention on the Law of the Sea, which includes provisions governing the rights (and obligations) of those who invest in deep seabed mining. No universal investment regime has emerged thus far.

Another question that must be answered is thus: What is the public interest to be served by the creation of a regime that addresses this particular activity in international society? If one examines the current distribution of FDI, there is no question that there is an overwhelming public interest in ensuring a more equitable distribution and in promoting investment in places where it is most needed, from the point of view of public policy. For example, this can involve investment in poor developing countries, or investment in new technologies that reduce environmental impacts. These are the issues that should be addressed.

It may turn out that it is more sensible to pursue the pathway of sectoral agreements rather than to attempt to negotiate a universal investment regime. Thus it might be appropriate to add an investment protocol to the UNFCCC, much like the investment provisions that are already contained in the Energy Charter. It might be appropriate to develop investment rules for those who engage in sustainable forestry investments, since it should be obvious that it is not in the public interest to provide foreign investors who despoil forests of any additional rights when governments attempt to rein them in.

Conclusion

These observations set up a challenging, interesting, and promising agenda for further consideration. They strongly suggest that responsibility for governing global investment should not be entrusted to the WTO. There is a serious problem with cross-retaliation between an investment regime and the other WTO agreements. An investment agreement would put extraordinary pressures on the dispute settlement process, which is central to the success of the WTO. In general, including an investment agreement in the WTO would overburden an organisation that is currently showing signs of strain. For that reason, it is time to think creatively about the organisational framework for an international investment agreement.

Two proposals may be worth considering in more detail. First, there are lessons for an investment agreement to be drawn from the experience with international environmental agreements. One should start with a framework convention that recognises an issue exists on which the international community wishes to act but does not know where or how. As consensus emerges within that particular regime, protocols can follow.

Another option is to take a page out of the GATS book. Promotion of trade in services is a public policy that requires rules governing investment as an essential component of that policy goal. The investment provisions of the GATS provide security of investment as a way of improving the long-term relationship in that particular activity. The same can be done with the climate regime. It is reasonable to consider adding a protocol on investment to a climate regime and, paradoxically, it would look not unlike the MAI. Putting it into the climate regime would link it to the overarching public good of managing climate change and generate the kind of balance between private rights and public goods that is otherwise very difficult to achieve.

The rights accorded by an agreement like the MAI (which was based on NAFTA) as a free-standing agreement are deeply problematic. These same rights linked to the public good and dealing with climate change are an essential part of dealing with the problem as it has been identified. They are an integral part of the institutional pattern that is required to address the problem structure of climate change at the international level.

Note

1   Details about the Energy Charter Treaty can be found at <www.encharter.org>.

References

International Centre for Trade and Sustainable Development (2001). 'Asbestos Ruling Breaks New Ground in "Like Product" Determination'. *Bridges* vol. 5, no. 1–3, pp. 1–2. <www.ictsd.org/English/BRIDGES5-1-3.pdf> (December 2001).
Mann, Howard (2001). *Private Rights, Public Problems: A Guide to NAFTA's Controversial Chapter on Investors Rights*. International Institute on Sustainable Development and World Wildlife Fund, Winnipeg.
Newell, Peter (2000). *Climate for Change: Non-State Actors and the Global Politics of the Greenhouse*. Cambridge University Press, Cambridge, UK.
von Moltke, Konrad (1997). 'Institutional Interactions: The Structure of Regimes for Trade and Environment'. In O. R. Young, ed., *Global Governance: Drawing Insights from the Environmental Experience*, pp. 247–272. MIT Press, Cambridge, MA.
von Moltke, Konrad (2000). *An International Investment Regime? Issues for Sustainability*. International Institute for Sustainable Development, Winnipeg.
von Moltke, Konrad (2001). 'Misappropriation of Institutions: Some Lessons from the Environmental Dimension of the NAFTA Investor-State Dispute Settlement Process'. *International Environmental Agreements* vol. 1, no. 1, pp. 103–123.
Young, Oran R. (1994). *International Governance: Protecting the Environment in a Stateless Society*. Cornell University Press, Ithaca.
Young, Oran R. (1998). 'The Effectiveness of International Environmental Regimes: A Mid-Term Report'. *International Environmental Affairs* vol. 10, no. 4, pp. 267–289.

PART III
ENVIRONMENTAL PROTECTION: EVALUATING THE NAFTA COMMISSION FOR ENVIRONMENTAL COOPERATION MODEL

Chapter 9

Stormy Weather:
The Recent History of
the Citizen Submission Process of the
North American Agreement on
Environmental Cooperation

Christopher Tollefson

Considerable recent discussion has focussed on the emerging role of nongovernmental organisations (NGOs) in the development, implementation, and enforcement of international environmental law (Barratt-Brown 1991; Wirth 1994; Charnovitz 1997; Raustiala 1997; Knox, J. H. 2001). A key theme of this literature has been the potential of 'global civil society'[1] to lend support to new international regulatory initiatives aimed at protecting the global commons.[2] Much less attention has been paid to a related, yet critically distinct, question: Can and should global civil society be entrusted with the responsibility for helping to ensure, under the auspices of international law, that states abide by legal commitments that they have made to protect the environment and public health in the domestic realm?

The history of the citizen submission procedure under the North American Agreement on Environmental Cooperation (NAAEC) provides an illuminating case study of the challenges associated with vesting civil society organisations with this novel role. The NAAEC came into being in 1994 as the accompanying environmental side agreement to the North American Free Trade Agreement (NAFTA).[3] Under Articles 14 and 15 of the NAAEC, citizens and NGOs gained the right to bring a complaint directly to the NAAEC Secretariat alleging that a NAFTA party had failed 'to effectively enforce' its environmental laws.[4]

The citizen submission procedure was and remains a unique experiment in citizen empowerment at the international level. Of late, however, it has been weathering a storm of uncertainty. This uncertainty has been created by the perception that the NAFTA signatories — Canada, the United States, and Mexico, referred to as parties — have been wavering in their support of the existing procedure, and have been contemplating changes that would impose significant new restrictions on the autonomy and authority of the Secretariat. It would appear that, for now, this storm has passed. At a landmark meeting in June 2000, under pressure from a continental coalition of civil society groups, the three parties committed to a more transparent process for discussing the future 'elaboration and implementation' of the submission procedure

(Joint Public Advisory Committee of the North American Commission for Environmental Cooperation [JPAC] 2000). Nonetheless, important and vexing interpretive questions and institutional tensions surrounding the procedure remain. It will undoubtedly be the subject of increasing scrutiny and debate as negotiations aimed at concluding an American hemispheric trade agreement that builds on the NAFTA regime proceed.

This chapter explores, from a legal perspective, the history, operation, and potential of the Article 14-15 process. It first provides an introduction to, and short history of, the citizen submission process. It then considers the key legal and institutional issues that have emerged in the interpretation and administration of the submission process by the Secretariat. Particular attention is devoted to the uncertainties associated with defining the legal rights and responsibilities contemplated by the NAAEC, and to the institutional tensions that the process has created. The chapter concludes with some observations on how the legal uncertainties and institutional tensions relate to the broader rationale of the submission process and the purposes it serves.

The analysis that follows demonstrates that civil society organisations remain strongly committed to the citizen submission process. It also suggests that while the recent history of the process has been troubled at times, there are encouraging signs that Canada, the United States, and Mexico are coming to a common appreciation of the unique and important role that the process can and does play within the NAFTA regime. Perhaps more important, it would appear that they are also committed to taking proactive steps to ensure that the process is able to realise its full potential.

The Citizen Submissions under Articles 14 and 15

The NAAEC, the CEC, and Their Citizen Submission Process

The citizen submission procedure came into being as part of the NAAEC, the environmental side agreement to NAFTA brokered in 1992–1993 by President Bill Clinton to consolidate support for NAFTA in Congress. The NAAEC created a new institution, the Commission for Environmental Cooperation (CEC). The CEC is governed by a council composed of Cabinet level–appointees, one from each of the three member countries, who have domestic responsibility for environmental protection. The affairs of the CEC are administered by a full-time secretariat located in Montreal, under the direction of an executive director. The CEC also receives ongoing advice and information from the Joint Public Advisory Committee (JPAC), composed of 15 citizens, five from each of the three NAFTA countries (Article 16). The NAAEC also contemplates that each of the three parties may convene a national advisory committee made up of members of the public to provide ongoing advice on the implementation and further elaboration of the Agreement (Article 17).

The CEC has two key functions. The first is to foster co-operation and co-ordination among the parties on hemispheric environmental issues, and trade and environment linkages through joint research and regional initiatives. The second function is to be an environmental watchdog, mandated to oversee, under the direction of the Council of Ministers, the enforcement of environmental laws by all three parties.

The vehicle through which it performs this latter role is the citizen submission process, as elaborated in Articles 14 and 15 of the NAAEC. Any resident of the three member countries may file a submission with the Secretariat claiming that a party 'is failing to effectively enforce its environmental laws'. Providing the submission satisfies certain procedural requirements set out in Article 14(1),[5] the Secretariat then considers whether the submission merits requesting a response from that party based on criteria set out in Article 14(2). These criteria include whether the submission raises matters that deserve further study and whether 'private remedies' available under domestic law have been pursued.

Once the Secretariat has considered the response of a party, it may then recommend to the Council that a factual record be prepared. Approval to prepare a factual record requires a two-thirds vote by Council. When completed, the factual record is delivered to the Council, which, again by a two-thirds vote, may decide to release some or all of its contents to JPAC or to the public, or to both.

In preparing the factual record, the Secretariat may consider information provided by third parties including governments, NGOs, and experts. The term 'factual record' is significant. This record contains a summary of submissions received in relation to the complaint, a summary of other relevant factual information, and the facts as found by the Secretariat relating to the matters raised in the complaint (NAAEC Article 15 and Section 2.1 of the Guidelines for Submissions). Most observers agree, however, that 'given its name,' the factual record 'probably cannot include an evaluation or judgement by the Secretariat' (Johnson and Beaulieu 1996, 158), or any recommendations for remedial action. Nor is it necessarily contemplated that the Council will take any specified action or make recommendations following receipt, or release of the factual record.

The NAAEC was a product of political forces and perceptions, particularly those prevailing within the United States. NAFTA had been negotiated under the Bush administration, and was opposed by many traditional supporters of then governor Clinton in the labour and environmental communities. In his presidential campaign, Clinton promised to 'fix' NAFTA to address these concerns. One of the key environmental concerns related to the prospect that it would override domestic environmental protection law, a prospect highlighted by the 1991 decision of the General Agreement on Tariffs and Trade (GATT) that held that a U.S. law protecting dolphins by banning tuna imports constituted an invalid trade restriction. A second concern was that NAFTA would create strong incentives, particularly for Mexico, to lower environment standards and relax enforcement of environmental laws to attract trade and investment.

To a limited degree, the NAFTA text that had been negotiated addressed these concerns. Language in the investment chapter exhorted, without requiring, parties not to lower, waive, or derogate from their environmental standards to attract investment. Other provisions recognised the right of the three parties to adopt their own nondiscriminatory level of environmental protection. NAFTA was also made subordinate to certain international environmental treaties.

These provisions did not mollify U.S. environmental groups.[6] These groups lobbied the newly elected Clinton administration for an international commission to oversee the enforcement of environmental laws in the NAFTA region, with the power to impose sanctions for noncompliance. The clear preference of the NAFTA member countries, including the United States, was to achieve environmental objectives via suasion and co-operation. Relinquishing adjudicative authority over assessing domestic environment performance to a supranational body was strongly opposed.

In the result, Clinton secured support of the NAFTA partners to a compromise that left state sovereignty largely intact with respect to the determination of environmental standards, and environmental enforcement. The NAAEC imposed a new obligation on each country to enforce its environmental laws and regulations effectively, an obligation that would be subject to a citizen complaint process supervised by a fact-finding body (the Secretariat) that received instructions from a tripartite council. Ultimately, however, the 'effective enforcement' obligation was left 'effectively unenforceable' (Audley 1997, 149). Under this compromise, the only way a party could be sanctioned for breaching this obligation was in the unlikely event that the Council voted to pursue a complaint against a party to an arbitral panel. For this to occur, a party would be required to initiate proceedings in its own name, independently of citizen submission process, under Part V of the NAAEC.

Use of the Article 14-15 Procedure

From its 1994 inception through to the summer of 2000, 31 citizen submissions were filed with the CEC Secretariat. Each of the NAFTA parties has been the subject of a roughly comparable number of complaints: eight have targeted the United States, thirteen have been filed against Mexico, and ten have been brought against Canada. The volume of submissions brought each year has been relatively constant (see Appendix 9-A).

Twenty files have been closed. Of these, twelve were dismissed or terminated by the Secretariat under Article 14, four were terminated by the Secretariat under Article 15(1), in one case the Council turned down a recommendation that a factual record be prepared pursuant to Article 15(2), one case was withdrawn, and two cases had factual records prepared and made public.

There are eleven active files. In five cases, the Secretariat has recommended preparation of a factual record and is awaiting a decision from Council; included in this category is a case in which Council has indicated it wishes to defer its factual record decision. The Secretariat is currently preparing a factual record is one case; in the remaining four cases, the Secretariat has yet to decide on a disposition.

The Secretariat's first factual record involved an allegation that the Government of Mexico failed to comply with environmental assessment requirements in authorising construction of a pier at Cozumel. The other factual record that has been released involved allegations that the Government of Canada failed to enforce the *Fisheries Act* against BC Hydro, a provincial Crown power utility. In the spring of 2000, the Council rejected a recommendation to prepare a factual record in one case (Centre québécois du droit de l'environnement) and deferred its decision in another (The Friends of Oldman River). The Secretariat is currently preparing a factual record in only one case (Environmental Health Coalition), and is awaiting Council's permission to proceed with a factual record in another (Grupo Ecológico Manglar AC).

The subject matter of the complaints brought in these first seven years ranges broadly. It includes allegations of non-enforcement of air, land, and water pollution laws, species protection laws, and environmental assessment regulations.

Who May File a Submission?

Any 'NGO or person established or residing in the territory of a Party' may file a submission (Section 2.1, Submission Guidelines). The definition of NGO is broad and includes any profit or nonprofit group that is not affiliated with or directed by government (Article 45.1).

Environmental or public health organisations have virtually all of the submissions received to date. However, in three cases private corporations have also sought to invoke the complaint process (Alliance for the Wild Rockies, Neste Canada, and Mercerizados y Teñidos de Guadalajara, SA). The best-known illustration to date was a submission filed by Methanex, a Canadian-based fuel additive company with American operations that produces methyl tertiary butyl ether, or MTBE, which was scheduled to be banned by the State of California. In addition to seeking damages in connection with this ban under the investor-state claim provisions contained in Chapter 11 of NAFTA, Methanex filed a complaint that the State of California was failing to enforce its groundwater protection laws against various point-source polluters.[7]

Most submissions have been filed by environmental NGOs (ENGOs) against their home governments. In several cases, however, where the non-enforcement allegation presents transboundary implications, ENGOs from both sides of the border have collaborated in bringing the complaint.[8] In two cases, ENGOs from all three countries have filed the submission jointly.[9]

Oversight of the Submission Process by the Secretariat

In overseeing the submission process, the Secretariat performs two distinct functions: interpreting and applying the legal language of the NAAEC, and administering the process to ensure that submissions are dealt with in a timely and efficient manner. The Secretariat has received high marks on the former front. As one close observer has put it, the 'Secretariat's decisions appear to be grounded on carefully reasoned legal interpretations of the Agreement rather than on fear of adverse reactions by, or the desire to curry favour with, either the Parties or the Submitters' (Knox, J. H. 2000; also DiMento and Doughman 1998).

In terms of the timely and effective administration of the submission process, the assessment is more mixed. A common complaint is that the process is too slow, and concerns have been raised that a very serious backlog of work with respect to the preparation of factual records is imminent (Knox, J. H. 2001). Some of the key reasons for these delays are institutional tensions. If these tensions can be reduced, the timeliness of the process is likely to improve. Before considering the sources of, and prospects for minimising these tensions, it is important to consider the legal interpretive issues with which the CEC has been, or will soon be, grappling.

Interpretive Issues

Defining Environmental Law

Before processing a complaint, the Secretariat must conclude that the complaint alleges that a 'Party is failing to effectively enforce its environmental law' (Article 14.1). A key threshold issue for the Secretariat, therefore, is what constitutes an environmental law.

The NAAEC defines environmental law as laws that have as their primary purpose the protection of the environment or human life or health (Article 45.2(a)). Explicitly excluded from this definition are worker health and safety laws and laws that have as their primary purpose the harvesting of natural resources whether for commercial, subsistence, or aboriginal uses (45.2(b)). This does not mean, however, that all natural resource management laws secure immunity from review under NAAEC. As John Knox correctly points out, the primary purpose of a specific provision must be assessed on an individual basis, not by reference to the primary purpose of the statute of which it forms a part, in order to determine whether its primary purpose is to protect the environment or human health (Knox, J. H. 2001, note 342). Laws that are specifically contemplated as falling within the definition include those pertaining to pollution prevention, abatement, or control; control of hazardous substances and wastes; and protection of flora, fauna, and natural areas (Article 45.2(a)).

Intriguingly, there is no requirement that a complaint must relate to an environmental amenity that is traded among the NAFTA parties, nor that the complaint must claim that the alleged pattern of non-enforcement has trade implications or consequences.[10] To date, only a few complaints have explicitly tried to address this latter connection (specifically BC Hydro and the Sierra Club of British Columbia).

The parties deliberately exempted from the citizen submission process complaints pertaining to a government's decision to rewrite its environmental laws or standards in a manner that might detract from their effectiveness. Instead, it was decided that the concern about the downward pressure of trade on environmental laws, and interjurisdictional 'pollution haven' competition, would be dealt with by way of a non-enforceable exhortation.[11]

The obligation to defer to legislative action is recognised in several decisions of the Secretariat. In two early cases (Biodiversity Legal Foundation and Sierra Club), it declined to proceed with complaints that were based on allegations that legislative riders, passed by the U.S. Congress, nullified the ability of federal regulators to effectively enforce laws protecting endangered species. In a similar vein, the Secretariat held that it could not investigate a complaint that Canada had failed to enforce the United Nations Convention on Biodiversity. Although Canada had signed and ratified the Convention, the Secretariat concluded that it was not part of the Canadian domestic law, since the federal government had not formally implemented it by way of statute or regulation.

Defining Failure to Enforce Effectively

If the Secretariat concludes that a complaint relates to the enforcement of an environmental law, it must then consider whether there is evidence that a party is failing to enforce the law effectively.

It is notable that, for the purposes of a citizen complaint, there is no need to allege or establish that a pattern of non-enforcement has occurred. In this regard, the citizen submission provisions differ from the party-to-party dispute resolution provisions of the NAAEC, which are triggered by an allegation there is a 'persistent pattern of failure' by a party to enforce its environmental laws effectively (Article 22.1).

Deemed exemptions to the obligation to enforce effectively The NAAEC specifically provides that a party shall be deemed not to have failed in this obligation in two situations. The first is where the alleged failure 'reflects a reasonable exercise of their discretion in respect of investigatory, prosecutorial, regulatory or compliance matters'. The second arises where the alleged failure 'results from *bona fide* decisions to allocate resources to enforcement in respect of other environmental matters determined to have higher priorities' (Articles 45.1(a) and (b)).

As yet, it remains unsettled whether a party is entitled to invoke these exemptions upon being asked by the Secretariat to respond to a particular citizen submission. If this course of action were open to a party, the Secretariat would be obliged to entertain evidence and reach conclusions about whether either of these exemptions apply prior to deciding to recommend the preparation of a factual record. To make such a determination would impose on the Secretariat onerous information gathering responsibilities. To assess whether there were grounds to justify invocation of the first exemption, the Secretariat would require a comprehensive familiarity with the party's record of enforcement in similar instances; to assess whether the latter exemption applied would require familiarity with a party's environmental budgeting and priority identification processes.

Moreover, adopting such an approach would impose on the Secretariat the duty to grapple with vexing and sensitive legal questions. In relation to the first exemption, the Secretariat would be required to decide whether a party has exercised its discretion reasonably and as such would be called on to consider of a variety of factors, including whether the party fettered its discretion, acted or failed to act for improper reasons, or took into account irrelevant considerations. Presumably, the Secretariat would also have to consider whether the submitter had presented evidence that negated a party's reliance on this exemption.[12] The Secretariat would face similar interpretive difficulties were it called upon, as a threshold issue, to decide if a party should be allowed to escape the obligation to enforce its environmental laws effectively due to internal budgetary priorities. To meet the test prescribed by this exemption, it would not be enough for a party to claim that its budgetary resources limit its enforcement capabilities. Rather, a party would need to satisfy the Secretariat that it had deliberately chosen to allocate funds to other environmental priorities that would otherwise be available for enforcement.

The complexity and political sensitivity surrounding resolution of these issues would strongly suggest that they should not be dealt with by the Secretariat as threshold matters. Instead, if a party were inclined to rely on these exemptions, the better approach would be for it to so stipulate (and provide relevant documentation) during the process of preparing the factual record. This stipulation and accompanying documentation would then form part of the factual record without the necessity of a determination as to the merits or applicability of the grounds upon which the exemption was claimed.

What constitutes a failure to enforce effectively? The above exemptions deem specified government conduct not to constitute failures to enforce effectively. This leaves unsettled the broader question of what does constitute such a failure. This is a vexing and controversial issue. The Secretariat has offered its tentative views on this subject in the case of Biodiversity Legal Foundation et al. In this decision, the Secretariat suggests that failure to effectively enforce 'primarily envisage[s] administrative breakdowns (failures) resulting from acts or omissions of an agency or official charged with implementing environmental laws' (CEC 1995).

The term 'breakdown' has problematic connotations. It appears to narrow the Secretariat's jurisdiction to situations where enforcement fails due to government inadvertence: for instance, poor internal communication, lack of agency co-ordination, or regulatory negligence. This would seemingly exclude, therefore, instances where the failure to enforce is attributable to deliberate government action (that is, allocating inadequate resources, adopting policies that are inconsistent with the requirements of an environmental law, or pursuing a practice of non-adversarial, 'sympathetic' regulation). There is no reason, in principle, that enforcement failures attributable to government choice should be treated any differently than those explicable by inadvertence. This is particularly so with regard to the obligation undertaken by parties under NAAEC Article 5(1) 'to effectively enforce [their] laws and regulations through appropriate government action'.

What constitutes effective enforcement? A closely related issue of considerable contention, which has arisen in the context of the BC Hydro case, concerns how to define effective enforcement. An interpretation apparently favoured by some parties[13] is to measure the effectiveness of enforcement exclusively in terms of whether the efforts undertaken have actually protected the environment from harm.[14] Under this approach, the factual record could neither address the level of compliance with the law in question nor address the effectiveness of the law in meeting its environmental purpose (Environment Canada 1999).

Canada's National Advisory Committee (NAC) is on record as strongly opposing this proposal to narrow the Secretariat's interpretive mandate.[15] It contends that environmental harm is but one indication of effective enforcement, just as is the question of whether the law has met its environmental purpose. In its view, the ultimate issue to be addressed by a factual record is whether government has secured compliance with the law in question.

Several considerations strongly support the more liberal interpretation urged by Canada's NAC. First of all, the NAAEC does not require parties to protect the environment from harm. Parties are allowed to freely choose their own preferred level of environmental protection. The NAAEC does, however, require that parties 'effectively enforce' environmental laws they enact, which are presumably designed to achieve their chosen level of environmental protection. In short, the citizen submission process is not about preventing environmental harm *per se,* but rather about holding governments responsible for enforcing environmental laws. Focussing on environmental harm also presents substantial informational challenges. Environmental harm is not always easy to document or assess; typically, documenting and assessing compliance are much more straightforward. Finally, preventing environmental harm is not the only goal of environmental regulation. To focus narrowly on whether environmental harm has occurred means ignoring the broader question of whether and to what extent the environment has been put at risk by noncompliance.

Institutional Issues and Tensions

The Institutional History

Almost from its inception, the citizen submission process has provoked questions about the role of the Secretariat and the nature of its relationship to the parties and with the Council. In addition to administering the submissions process, the Secretariat is vested with more traditional responsibilities of providing technical, administrative, and operational support and advice to the Council. This has led some to question whether it is desirable or even possible to house within the CEC both a watchdog role and these more traditional, co-operative functions that form the bulk of its work program (Independent Review Committee [IRC] 1998, 22). In particular, some parties have raised the concern that, in carrying out this former function, the Secretariat has acted in a manner that is adversarial to the party being investigated.

On the fourth anniversary of the NAAEC, the Council commissioned the Independent Review Committee (IRC) to report on and advise with respect to these and other issues. Its report was a strong endorsement of the basic concept and design of the citizen complaint process. According to the IRC, 'any adversarial aspects of the process are outside the role or control of the Secretariat, but arise from the empowerment of individual citizens or groups to initiate a submission "against" a Party' (IRC 1998, 6). In its words, the process reflected a laudable 'trend toward increased citizen involvement in international mechanisms to address environmental issues'. The report characterised the process as 'belonging' to the 350 million citizens of North America 'who are empowered to initiate it, and for whose benefit it was developed'.

The IRC concluded its review by expressing the hope that the 'current tension' over the citizen complaint process could be reduced. This could be achieved, in its view, if the parties, rather than seeking to amend the process, worked hard to 'scrupulously apply the NAAEC' and 'respected the discretion provided to the respective decision-makers at different points in the process' (IRC 1998, 54–55). Subsequent experience has proven this hope to be somewhat wishful thinking. If anything, in the years following the IRC review institutional tensions surrounding the submissions procedure have escalated.

In the lead-up to the summer meeting of the Council and the JPAC in 1999, the Council sought public input on a package of amendments to the submission guidelines aimed at clarifying and in many respects circumscribing the powers of the Secretariat. Ultimately, under pressure from the NGOs, JPAC, and the NACs, major changes to the guidelines were postponed. However, virtually as soon as this decision was made, the parties engaged in a second 'confidential' round of discussions with respect to a proposed new set of guideline amendments (Knox, P. and McKenna 2000). The proposed changes in this round were more far-reaching than those advanced in the preceding one, and included the creation of a Council-appointed working group with responsibility to oversee the Secretariat's preparation of factual records.

When these discussions came to light a few months before the Council/JPAC meeting to be held in Dallas in June 2000, civil society groups organised a continental coalition to lobby against the contemplated changes. This coalition emerged from the Dallas meeting claiming victory. At the meeting, the Council not only deferred amending the guidelines but also passed a resolution that has the potential for making future discussions about the design and implementation of the submissions process considerably more transparent and inclusive. This resolution tasks JPAC with the ongoing role of providing advice to the Council on issues relating to the 'implementation and elaboration' of the submissions process. Under the resolution, any party, the Secretariat, or any member of the public may raise issues 'concerning the implementation or elaboration' of the submissions process with the Council, which may then refer the matter to JPAC for its consideration. It also requires the Council to provide written reasons with respect to any decision made 'following advice received from JPAC' (JPAC 2000, 2). Finally, the resolution mandates JPAC to conduct a public review of the history of the submissions process, with a view to submitting a report to the Parties on the 'lessons learned' (p. 1).

The decision to enhance the role of JPAC is a positive development. However, the issues and uncertainties that precipitated the showdown in Dallas linger and seem likely to resurface.

Institutional Tensions

The ability of the Secretariat to access information One area of continuing tension concerns the ability of the Secretariat to carry out its fact-finding function. The NAAEC imposes a general obligation on the three parties to provide the Secretariat with such information as is necessary to administer the submissions process. In reality, however, the Secretariat must rely on the co-operation of the party whose actions are being investigated to disclose this information voluntarily. As Pierre Marc Johnson and André Beaulieu (1996, 156) wryly observe, 'depending on the circumstances, there might ... be a temptation for the party complained against to procrastinate or to be lax in collecting damning evidence'. Moreover, if a party deems a request for information to be 'excessive or unduly burdensome', it may notify the Council, which, by a majority vote, can impose restrictions on scope of the request (Article 21(2)).

In a significant gesture of deference to state sovereignty, a party is also entitled to decline to disclose information if it would not be required to disclose such information under its own laws pertaining to business or proprietary information, personal privacy, or confidentiality in government decision making. If a party chooses to provide such information to the Secretariat, it may require the Secretariat to keep the information confidential (Articles 39(1) and (2)).

Governments have not been timid to invoke the benefits of these provisions. In two 1998 cases, still at the initial screening stage, the Government of Mexico has designated as confidential material it has provided the Secretariat in response to the complaint (Academia Sonorense de Derechos Humanos and Environmental Health Coalition et al.). In one of these cases, Mexico has asserted confidentiality over its entire response. Pursuant to Section 17.3 of the newly enacted Submission Guidelines, the Secretariat has requested, in these instances, that Mexico provide a summary of the information designated confidential and an explanation of its confidentiality claim. Without this information, the Secretariat will find itself in the unenviable position of having to provide reasons for dismissing the complaint or, alternatively, ordering production of a factual record, without being able to make reference to the contents of the government's response. Accordingly, it is hoped in the interests of transparency that parties will normally see fit to provide summaries of this kind to the Secretariat when requested.

Confidentiality has also become a concern during the factual record preparation process. In preparing a factual record in the BC Hydro case, the Secretariat convened an expert panel to assist it in its investigation. The panel established a procedure under which it solicited submissions from the complainants, BC Hydro, and, finally, the Government of Canada in three successive meetings. Parties were invited to attend as observers at the meetings when their counterparts where scheduled to make submissions.

While the complainants and BC Hydro co-operated fully in this arrangement, Canada refused to meet with the panel either alone, or in the presence of the other parties (Knox, P. and McKenna 2000; Scoffield 1999). It eventually agreed to answer questions in writing, due to the vague and incomplete nature of the answers provided; however, a protracted process of 'follow-up questions' ensued (CEC 2000b; Christensen 1999). One of the apparent reasons for Canada's objection to this procedure was a concern about disclosing sensitive information (Christensen 2000). Consequently, Canada has proposed that the submission guidelines be amended to require that information submitted to the Secretariat (or its independent experts) in connection with preparation of a factual record be kept secret until the Council has made a decision on whether to make the factual record public (Environment Canada 1999).

To sequester all information — confidential, sensitive, or otherwise — tendered by parties as part of the factual record process would be a significant and troubling departure from the NAAEC and current submission guidelines. The current regime is one that emphasises transparency. Subject only to confidentiality claims allowed under the NAAEC or Guidelines for Submission, the Secretariat is required to place all information it considers in preparing a factual record (including submissions from the complainant and party) in an open public file.[16] Under this regime, the touchstone for nondisclosure is confidentiality: that a party might deem disclosure of the information embarrassing or sensitive is not a justification for secrecy.

A further difficulty with the approach proposed by Canada is that, if adopted, and if the Council subsequently exercised its discretion not to make a factual record public, all the information considered by the Secretariat in preparing the record would be permanently sequestered.

Whether or not the Council will ultimately adopt Canada's suggestion is not certain, particularly since the outcome of the Dallas meeting. However, there are grounds to worry that it might well choose secrecy over transparency. Notable in this regard is its decision in June 1999 to amend the submission guidelines to impose a new requirement that the Secretariat keep secret the fact that it has recommended to the Council that a factual record be prepared until 30 days after it has so notified the Council (Section 10.2). This amendment serves to shield the parties from potentially embarrassing public scrutiny and pressure, on the question of whether they will support or reject the recommendation, until after they have decided the question (Knox, J. H. 2001, 7).

The Secretariat's discretion over preparation of factual records The BC Hydro process has also prompted Canada to raise concerns about the Secretariat's authority to determine the process by which the factual record is prepared. In particular, it suggests that the Secretariat and independent experts working on its behalf are not, and should not be, empowered to 'engage in an interactive public meeting process to gather information during the factual record process'.[17]

This suggestion is motivated in part by its apparent desire to avoid being forced to publicly disclose sensitive or embarrassing information.

It also appears to be motivated by the potential that a public process of preparing a factual record will shine an unwanted spotlight on the allegations being investigated. Canada claims that this is an undesirable result that undermines the 'integrity of the Council's decision on whether or not to make the final factual record public' (Environment Canada 1999). This is because, according to Canada, such a process encourages 'the public, submitters, governments and other stakeholders to draw conclusions on, or debate the merits of, the assertions that are the subject of the factual record' before the Council decides whether to make the record public. In the run-up to the Dallas meeting, this concern had crystallised into a proposal that the Council appoint a working group to oversee the manner in which the Secretariat carried out its factual record preparation duties.

Canada's apparent aversion to the spotlight is somewhat paradoxical in that it is precisely this spotlighting attribute that many observers suggest is among the CEC's most useful and important functions.[18] It would also appear to be inconsistent with Article 1(h) of the NAAEC, which underscores that an objective of the agreement is to 'promote transparency and public participation in the development of environmental laws, regulations and policies'.

This paradox aside, of arguably even greater concern is a proposition implicit in Canada's position, namely that the Secretariat lacks the discretion to determine its own procedure. The NAAEC neither explicitly authorises nor prevents the Secretariat from embarking on the quasi-public investigative process adopted in BC Hydro. Under Canadian and American domestic law, in matters of procedure tribunals are entitled to establish their own rules and practices as long as they do not conflict with the objectives of the general authority they have been granted. This approach is also consistent with the IRC's admonition that those involved in the complaint process respect the 'discretion provided to decision-makers at different points in the process' (IRC 1998, 22).

The positive developments in Dallas notwithstanding, it is fair to say that the parties have not heeded this admonition particularly well in the past. There is reason for concern that this pattern may be difficult to break. As one long-time NAAEC observer has put it, as the caseload of the Secretariat increases, there will be an increasing incentive 'for the Parties to take control of the procedure away from the Secretariat by micromanaging the Secretariat's discretion in considering submissions and preparing factual records' (Knox, J. H. 2000, 9).

The Secretariat's authority to apply the NAAEC and submission guidelines A final area of controversy has concerned the scope of the Secretariat's authority to interpret the NAAEC and the submission guidelines. Neither the agreement nor the guidelines specifically elaborate the Secretariat's authority in this regard, particularly in a situation where a party disagrees with the interpretation adopted by the Secretariat, as occurred in BC Hydro.

Two principles provide a starting point for considering this question. First of all, under the tripartite relationship contemplated by the NAAEC, the Secretariat answers to the Council, not to the parties. Thus, for example, if a party is concerned about a request for information made by the Secretariat during preparation of a factual record, it is instructed to raise the issue with the Council. If Council decides the concern is well founded, by a two-thirds vote the Council may issue a binding directive to the Secretariat. Second, it is the job of the Council to resolve 'questions or differences that arise *between the Parties* regarding the interpretation or application of the Agreement' [emphasis added] (Article 10(1)(d)). The NAAEC, in Article 11(4), specifically forbids the parties from seeking to influence or direct the actions of the Secretariat (Canadian National Advisory Committee 1999).

In the lead-up to the Dallas meeting, it came to light that the Council was considering several proposals aimed at clarifying and fettering the authority of the Secretariat to interpret and apply the agreement. One proposal would have required the Secretariat to seek direction from Council, even if no party had raised an objection, whenever it 'encountered an issue of interpretation' (Environment Canada 1999). The Council was also asked to consider imposing a requirement that the Secretariat halt its work and seek a Council ruling whenever a disagreement arose between the Secretariat and a party in the interpretation or application of the NAAEC.

The former proposal as drafted is clearly unworkable. Dealing with issues of interpretation is a central and inescapable feature of the Secretariat's current mandate. It is responsible for making interpretive judgements on a broad range of questions.[19] With more than a dozen complaints on its docket at any one time, imposing on the Secretariat an obligation to seek the advice of the Council routinely whenever it encounters an interpretive issue presents obvious logistical difficulties. Logistics aside, such a proposal would have a seriously detrimental impact on the Secretariat's independence and perceived legitimacy. The obvious danger with the second proposal is that it could be used by a party as a delaying tactic, seriously impairing the ability of the Secretariat to process submissions promptly and efficiently.

At the Dallas meeting, the Council decided against issuing specific guidelines that would govern when a disagreement arose between a party and the Secretariat. Instead, it opted to create a formal troubleshooting role for the JPAC in such situations. As a result, the Dallas resolution invites 'any Party, the Secretariat, members of the public through the JPAC, or the JPAC itself' to bring issues of implementation and elaboration relating to the submission process to the Council. On receipt, the Council may refer the matter to JPAC that, in turn, is empowered to 'conduct a public review with a view to provide advice to the Council as to how those issues might be addressed' (CEC 2000a). Significantly, the resolution provides that pending the completion of such a process, the Secretariat is mandated to continue processing any pending submissions.

Why Does the Citizen Submission Procedure Exist Anyway?

In the run-up to the Dallas meeting, as the storm clouds over the citizen submission process were darkening, a lead editorial in one of Canada's national newspapers posed the question 'Why exactly does this NAFTA commission exist?' ('Why Exactly Does This NAFTA Commission Exist?' 2000).

In terms of realpolitik, the answer to this question is relatively straightforward and increasingly only of historical interest. The genesis of the citizen submission procedure lies in a political compromise between what U.S.-based environmental groups wanted (a supranational body vested with powers to adjudicate complaints about domestic environmental law enforcement) and what the parties were prepared to offer (Articles 14 and 15) as a *quid pro quo* for environmentalist support (or acquiescence to) the NAFTA package in Congress.

But the question of why a citizen submission process was originally conceived can be separated from the question of what purposes and functions it may serve now and in the future. Assistance in this regard may be gleaned from the statement about objectives contained in *Article 1* of the NAAEC. It identifies a fundamental objective 'to enhance ... enforcement of environmental laws and regulations' within the territories of the three parties. Presumably, however, this objective is not intended to be an end in itself but rather a means to the broader end of promoting compliance with environmental laws, thereby protecting and improving the environment in the territories of the parties.[20] The link between effective enforcement and the goals of enhancing compliance and environmental protection is explicitly articulated in Article 5, which states that 'each Party shall effectively enforce its laws and regulations [with] the aim of achieving high levels of environmental protection and compliance with its environmental laws and regulations'.[21]

Several authors would add a third objective to this list: to better inform and involve citizens in the process by which environmental laws and regulations are developed, implemented and enforced.[22] In the words of David Markell (2000, 569), the recently departed head of the CEC's citizen submission unit, this purpose could be conceived of as being 'to promote the emergence of "civil society" in North America through creation of a new mechanism that facilitates citizens' interactions with their governments and others on the continent'.

Just how well has the citizen submission process been achieving these three objectives? Although these are still early days, this research challenge is beginning to attract interest. Clearly, there are some threshold methodological issues. One set of issues concerns defining and measuring effective enforcement, an issue with which the CEC will be grappling for the foreseeable future. Already, the CEC has initiated a project that tries to provide some of the groundwork on this front by developing indicators for evaluating the performance of the parties in implementing effective environmental enforcement.[23]

Next there is the empirical task of determining whether and to what extent the parties' enforcement practices and environmental protection records have been influenced by the existence of the citizen submission process. This, once again, is an area in which little work has been done.[24]

Finally, there is the question of how effectively the process has managed to empower civil society. How well has it served the 350 million citizens of North America to whom, as the IRC review contends, the process belongs? This, perhaps, is a more straightforward matter to address.

It can be safely surmised that for the many groups and individuals who have participated in the process of filing submissions, the ongoing consultations about the guidelines amendments, and the work of the JPAC, the process has some utility and benefit. In particular, for many within the civil society sector, the submission process will continue to have real value — even though it does not yield binding recommendations or results, let alone entail the imposition of sanctions — as long as the process offers the prospect of spotlighting deficient domestic enforcement practices. But the corollary of this is also worth bearing in mind. Were the process to lose its ability to perform this spotlighting function credibly and neutrally, civil society support for the submissions process would dissipate rapidly. In all likelihood, a co-ordinated strategy of retracting all pending complaints and boycotting the institution would ensue.

In summary, with respect to two of the key objectives of the citizen submission process — its contribution to effective enforcement of environmental laws and its longer term impact on environmental protection and enhancement — the evidence needed to evaluate how effectively the process is working is not readily available. However, in terms of the objective of providing civil society with the means to participate more effectively in government environmental decision making, one can tentatively conclude that the process is working and enjoys a conditional legitimacy within the sector it is intended to benefit.

The resolution passed by the Council in Dallas should help to restore the faith of civil society organisations in the parties' continued commitment to making the submissions process work. At the same time, the resolution reposes in the hands of the JPAC a challenging and significant new role. It is likely, for instance, that the JPAC will be called upon to make recommendations with respect to the process by which the Secretariat prepares factual records, an area that is not elaborated in the NAAEC or the guidelines and that remains unsettled in the wake of the BC Hydro controversy. Another area of continuing concern is the effective ability of the parties to thwart the process by frustrating the Secretariat's fact-finding efforts through delay, selective disclosure, or nondisclosure. Here, too, there would appear to be a need to elaborate the existing provisions of the Agreement further, with a view to vesting the Secretariat with more effective means to ensure that relevant, nonconfidential documents are produced in a timely and complete fashion.

Perhaps most significant, the JPAC may be able to use its new role to provide leadership in responding to the key question of why this submissions process exists. Over the last few years, considerable energy has been expended in battles over proposed changes to the submission guidelines. This has had at least two important implications. The first is that these battles have tended to divert attention and resources away from reflecting on larger, longer term questions of institutional purpose and outcome measurement. Second, it has contributed to a generalised feeling of battle fatigue. This sense of weariness is especially evident within the civil society sector, a sector that perceives that it has been forced to spend most of the last three years defending the submissions process instead of working to enhance it. One hopes that the JPAC will succeed in building on the lessons learned from these battles, and in reviving interest in and support for the citizen submission process and the broader mission of the CEC.

Postscript

Following a public consultation process, the JPAC submitted a report entitled 'Lessons Learned: Citizen Submissions under Articles 14 and 15 of the NAAEC' to the Council for consideration in connection with its eighth annual session held in Guadalajara, Mexico, on 28–29 June 2001 (JPAC 2001). The report affirmed that the citizen submissions process performed 'an essential role in achieving the goals of the NAAEC' and that the proper functioning of the process required an independent and properly resourced Secretariat.

In substantive terms the report emphasised the need to expedite the process and, to this end, suggested that file processing timelines should be adopted. It also made various suggestions aimed at enhancing the transparency of the process. One such suggestion was to require the Secretariat and Council to provide, as a matter of course, reasons for their decisions. Other suggestions were to abolish the controversial 30-day blackout period (which prevents the Secretariat from informing a submitter that it has recommended preparation of a factual record to the Council) and to eliminate the requirement that the Secretariat refrain from disclosing the reasons for such a recommendation until the Council has acted.

Finally, the report recommended that a party that has been the subject of a factual record should be required to report on what actions, if any, it has taken in response to the record within a reasonable time.

The response of the Council to the report builds upon, in a modest yet encouraging fashion, the progress made at Council session in Dallas meeting one year earlier. Stating that it appreciated 'the valuable role that the JPAC has played since the last Council Session' and indicating it was 'pleased with JPAC's "lessons learned" report', it committed to implementing two key recommendations contained in the report: reducing the blackout period to five days and permitting at that juncture the Secretariat to publish the reasons for its recommendation (CEC 2001). The report's other recommendations would, in its words, 'require further consideration'.

There was also encouraging evidence that Mexico may be moving toward a more liberal approach to the disclosure of government information relevant to the submission process. At the meeting, Mexico announced that it was revoking its confidentiality claim with respect to its reply to the citizen submission regarding Metales y Derivados. The Council also agreed to request the Secretariat to provide a summary of confidentiality regulations in Canada, the United States, and other countries, with a view to providing Mexico with examples in this area.

But while tentative progress is seemingly being made toward consolidating and enhancing the citizen submission process within NAFTA, there are strong indications that new battles loom on the horizon. It now appears likely that the U.S. Congress will grant fast-track authority for negotiation of the Free Trade of the Americas Agreement (FTAA). Whether, and to what extent, FTAA negotiators intend to address environmental concerns within the body of that agreement is not apparent from the draft text that was made public in the summer of 2001. Meanwhile, a broad coalition of U.S. environmental and civil society groups have gone on the offensive. In a report entitled 'Trade and Environment Principles' released in May 2001, the coalition has taken the position that an FTAA without enforceable environmental protections obligations, going far beyond those contained in the NAAEC, would be unacceptable (Kibel 2001).[25]

Notes

1 Most definitions of civil society derive from Hegel's model, which conceives of civil society as the 'autonomous realm of social interaction' existing between the family and state (Köhler 1998). The term 'global civil society' came into currency in the early 1990s (Shaw 1994; Lipschutz 1992; Walzer 1995; Charnovitz 1997; Archibugi, Held, and Köhler 1998, especially Rosenau's chapter therein; Edwards and Hulme 1996).

2 See, for example, Christopher Stone (1994) and David Wirth (1994). See also John Knox (2001), who discusses in depth one specific form of nonstate international regulation, 'supranational adjudication', whereby a tribunal is empowered to exercise jurisdiction in international disputes between nonstate parties and states or other nonstate parties. Knox uses the 'Helfer-Slaughter' evaluative model (Helfer and Slaughter 1997) for supranational adjudication to assess the specific mechanism discussed here, the North American Agreement on Environmental Cooperation (NAAEC).

3 Also negotiated at this time, in 1993, was the North American Agreement on Labor Cooperation.

4 Usually complaints filed under Articles 14 and 15 are referred to as submissions, although for the purposes of this chapter these terms are used interchangeably.

5 This chapter does not focus on the specifics of these requirements, which are well canvassed in Pierre Marc Johnson and André Beaulieu (1996) and David Markell (2000).

6 For a comprehensive discussion of the role of environmental nongovernmental organisations (ENGOs) in the NAFTA negotiations see John Audley (1997).

7 Both the Methanex and Neste submissions were dismissed by the Secretariat on 30 June 2000, under Article 14(3)(a) as the matter was 'the subject of a pending ... proceeding' namely Methanex's claim under damages under Chapter 11 of NAFTA.

8 For example, Biodiversity Legal Foundation et al. (U.S. failure to enforce endangered species legislation due to rider on military readiness act), BC Aboriginal Fisheries Commission et al. (non-enforcement of the *Fisheries Act* against BC Hydro), and Department of the Planet Earth et al. (non-enforcement of the Great Lakes Water Quality Agreement by the U.S. government).

9 For example, Sierra Club et al. (U.S. failure to enforce federal environmental due to disaster relief rider) and Alliance for the Wild Rockies (U.S. failure to enforce the *Migratory Birds Treaty Act*).

10 In an editorial, *The Globe and Mail* described the NAAEC as one of the 'strangest' international treaties and advocated that the CEC charter be rewritten to require that complainants establish that the alleged lack of effective environmental law enforcement was an attempt to secure a trade advantage ('Why Exactly Does This NAFTA Commission Exist?' 2000).

11 'There was no reason to restrict NGO submissions ... to enforcement matters. NGOs should have been allowed to present evidence establishing that a NAFTA party is lowering environmental norms in an attempt to attract investments. The possibility of preparing a factual record based on such evidence would have been a useful addition to the NAAEC' (Johnson and Beaulieu 1996, 165). See also the pollution haven exhortation contained in Article 3.

12 This might include evidence that the party had engaged in a persistent pattern of non-enforcement and that therefore the failure could not be considered as the product of a reasoned, case-specific exercise of discretion. The BC Hydro complaint illustrates this strategy; it identified 37 instances where Canada's fisheries law was violated without prosecutorial action being taken, noting that, since 1990, only two prosecutions have been

pursued. Similar evidence was put forward in Sierra Club of British Columbia et al. and Centre québécois du droit de l'environnement.

13 Following the Council's meeting in Banff in July 1999 (which led to some relatively minor amendments to the submission guidelines that were promulgated), the parties engaged in an ongoing series of confidential communications with respect to a wide range of interpretive and administrative issues (see Knox, P. and McKenna 2000). According to their report, environmentalists claimed that this secretive process was instigated by Canada with Mexican support. This proposed change was one of a series of amendments to the submission guidelines that Canada apparently proposed during these negotiations. See John Knox (2001, 70), who states that during these party discussions, 'Canada raised many of the issues, and many observers of the CEC believed that Canada's concerns resulted at least in part from disagreements between it and the Secretariat over how the Secretariat was preparing the BC Hydro factual record'.

14 See Canadian National Advisory Committee (1999). This was also the position advanced by Mexico and rejected by the Secretariat in its decision to accept the submission, in Comité para la Protección de los Recursos Naturales AC et al. (the Cozumel Pier case). See the discussion in John Knox (2001, notes 383–386).

15 See Canadian National Advisory Committee (1999). The position of Canada's NAC is consistent with the position taken by the U.S. government (see United States 2000).

16 Guidelines for Submission Section 16(1)(d): 'The Secretariat will maintain a file on each submission at its headquarters in a manner suitable for public access, inspection and photocopying ... Subject to confidentiality provisions in this Agreement and of the guidelines, the file will contain ... any other information considered by the Secretariat under Article 15(4) of the Agreement.'

17 The quoted passage is taken from a letter written by Norine Smith, Assistant Deputy Minister, Environment Canada, and sent to the Chair of NAC Canada (11 May 1999) and referred to in a subsequent letter of advice from NAC Canada (June 18, 1999). Along the same lines, John Knox (2001, 94–95), reports that 'Canada had opposed Secretariat requests to have joint meetings with a panel of experts, the submitters, and officials from the governments of Canada and British Columbia, and had disagreed with the Secretariat over what types of information could be made public.'

18 Pierre Marc Johnson and André Beaulieu (1996, 166) note that 'one of the CEC's most useful functions will be to cast the spotlight on public authorities that fail to fulfill their obligations — in particular, their obligations to effectively enforce their domestic environmental laws. These NAAEC provisions constitute a formal and permanent instrument enabling NGOs to direct the spotlight themselves.' See also the IRC (1998, 5), noting that the complaint process serves as 'some 350 million pairs of eyes to alert the Council to any "race to the bottom"'. See also David Markell's (2000, 571–572) discussion of the increasing popularity of 'spotlighting' strategies.

19 These include whether the complaint relates to an environmental law, whether it alleges a 'failure to effectively enforce' such a law, whether a complaint meets the six listed threshold criteria under Article 14(1), whether the complaint merits a response from a party having regard to the four criteria listed in Article 14(2), and whether complaint justifies a recommendation that a factual record be prepared.

20 See Article 1(g), noting the reference to compliance, and Article 1(a), which states the objective to 'foster the protection and improvement of the environment in the territories of the Parties for the well-being of present and future generations'.

21 This link is pointed out by David Markell (2000). It is also present in the language of Article 3.

22 Article 1(h): 'to promote transparency and public participation in the development of environmental laws, regulations and policies': other provisions that are relevant in this regard are Articles 2(1), 4, 5, 7(1)(b), 7(2), and 10(5). See also David Markell (2000, 569), and also Raymond MacCallum (1997, 395–400), who suggests that the 'apparent purpose of Articles 14 and 15 is to enlist the participation of the North American public to help ensure that the Parties abide by their obligation to enforce their respective environmental laws'.

23 See CEC (1999); see reference to the work on this front of the North American Working Group on Environmental Enforcement and Compliance Cooperation (EWG) described in the BC Hydro factual record.

24 To date, the principal academic contribution to this literature has offered a highly sceptical view of the benefit, in terms of environmental outcomes, of the citizen submission process (Raustiala 1995, 50–54).

25 The coalition consists of the American Lands Alliance, the Center for International Environmental Law, the Consumer's Choice Council, Defenders of Wildlife, the Earthjustice Legal Defense Fund, Friends of the Earth, the Institute for Agriculture and Trade Policy, the National Wildlife Federation, the Natural Resources Defense Council, Pacific Environment, the Sierra Club, and the World Wildlife Fund.

References

Archibugi, Daniele, David Held, and Martin Köhler (1998). *Re-Imagining Political Community: Studies in Cosmopolitan Democracy*. Polity Press, Cambridge, UK.

Audley, John J. (1997). *Green Politics and Global Trade: NAFTA and the Future of Environmental Politics*. Georgetown University Press, Washington DC.

Barratt-Brown, Elizabeth P. (1991). 'Building a Monitoring and Compliance Regime under the Montreal Protocol'. *Yale Journal of International Law* vol. 16, no. 2, pp. 519–570.

Canadian National Advisory Committee (1999). 'Letter of Advice'. 18 June. <www.naaec.gc.ca/english/nac/advice/adv991.htm> (December 2001).

Charnovitz, Steve (1997). 'Two Centuries of Participation: NGOs and International Governance'. *Michigan Journal of International Law* vol. 18, no. 2, pp. 183–286.

Christensen, Randy (1999). 'The CEC Citizen Submission Process: Citizen Empowerment or Failed Experiment?' Unpublished, on file with author.

Christensen, Randy (2000). Interview with author. 10 March.

Commission for Environmental Cooperation (1995). 'Secretariat's Determination under Article 14(2)'. Biodiversity Legal Foundation et al., 21 September. <www.cec.org/citizen/guides_registry/registrytext.cfm?&varlan=english&documentid=4> (December 2001).

Commission for Environmental Cooperation (1999). 'Indicators of Effective Environmental Enforcement: Proceedings of a North American Dialogue'. Montreal. <www.cec.org/citizen/guides_registry/index.cfm?varlan=english> (December 2001).

Commission for Environmental Cooperation (2000a). 'Council Resolution 00-09: Matters Related to Articles 14 and 15 of the Agreement'. 13 June, Dallas. <www.cec.org/who_we_are/jpac/Art14-15/index.cfm> (December 2001).

Commission for Environmental Cooperation (2000b). 'Factual Record for Submission 97-001 (BC Aboriginal Fisheries Commission et al.)'. 30 May. <www.cec.org/citizen/guides_registry/registryview.cfm?&varlan=english&submissionID=9> (December 2001).

Commission for Environmental Cooperation (2001). 'CEC Council Communiqué'. 29 June, Guadalajara. <www.cec.org/news/details/index.cfm?varlan=english&ID=2409> (December 2001).

DiMento, Joseph F. and Pamela M. Doughman (1998). 'Soft Teeth in the Back of the Mouth: The NAFTA Environmental Side Agreement Implemented'. *Georgetown International Environmental Law Review* vol. 10, no. 3, pp. 651–752.

Edwards, Michael and David Hulme (1996). *Beyond the Magic Bullet: NGO Performance and Accountability in the Post–Cold War World*. Kumarian Press Books on International Development. Kumarian Press, West Hartford, CT.

Environment Canada (1999). 'Discussion Paper'. Unpublished, on file with author.

Helfer, Laurence R. and Anne-Marie Slaughter (1997). 'Toward a Theory of Effective Supranational Adjucation'. *Yale Law Journal* vol. 107, no. 2, pp. 273–391.

Independent Review Committee (1998). 'Four-Year Review of the NAAEC'. <www.cec.org> (December 2001).

Johnson, Pierre Marc and André Beaulieu (1996). *The Environment and NAFTA: Understanding and Implementing the New Continental Law*. Island Press, Washington DC.

Joint Public Advisory Committee of the North American Commission for Environmental Cooperation (2000). 'Draft JPAC Review of Issues Concerning the Implementation and Further Elaboration of Articles 14 and 15'. October. <www.cec.org/who_we_are/jpac/pdfs/proc-e.pdf> (December 2001).

Joint Public Advisory Committee of the North American Commission for Environmental Cooperation (2001). 'Lessons Learned: Citizen Submissions under Articles 14 and 15 of the NAAEC'. 6 June. <www.cec.org/pubs_docs/documents/index.cfm?ID=121&varlan=english> (December 2001).

Kibel, Paul Stanton (2001). 'Critique of NAFTA's Environmental Side Agreement'. 6 October, on file with author.

Knox, John H. (2000). 'Comments on Lessons Learned from the History of the 14/15 Procedure'. Unpublished document submitted to the Joint Public Advisory Committee of the North American Commission on Environmental Cooperation, 22 September.

Knox, John H. (2001). 'A New Approach to Compliance with International Environmental Law: The Submissions Procedure of the NAFTA Environmental Commission'. *Ecology Law Quarterly* vol. 28, no. 1, p. 1.

Knox, Paul and Barry McKenna (2000). 'NAFTA Partners' Environmental Deal at Risk, Groups Say'. *The Globe and Mail*, 27 April. p. A8.

Köhler, Martin (1998). 'From the National to the Cosmopolitan Public Sphere'. In D. Archibugi, D. Held and M. Köhler, eds., *Re-Imagining Political Community: Studies in Cosmopolitan Democracy*. Polity Pressar, Cambridge, UK.

Lipschutz, R. D. (1992). 'Reconstructuring World Politics: The Emergency of Global Civil Society'. *Millennium* vol. 21, p. 389.

MacCallum, Raymond (1997). 'Evaluating the Citizen Submission Procedure under the North American Agreement on Environmental Cooperation'. *Colorado Journal of International Environmental Law and Policy* vol. 8, no. 2, pp. 395–422.

Markell, David L. (2000). 'The Commission for Environmental Cooperation's Citizen Submission Process'. *Georgetown International Environmental Law Review* vol. 12, no. 3, pp. 565–574.

Raustiala, Kal (1995). 'The Political Implications of the Enforcement Provisions of the NAFTA Environmental Agreement: The CEC as a Role Model for Future Accords'. *Environmental Law* vol. 25, no. 1, pp. 31–56.

Raustiala, Kal (1997). 'The "Participatory Revolution" in International Environmental Law'. *Harvard Environmental Law Review* vol. 21, no. 2, pp. 537–586.

Scoffield, Heather (1999). 'Ottawa Stifling Hearings, Groups Say: Environmentalists Claim NAFTA Side Agreement Undermined by Secrecy in BC Hydro Case'. *The Globe and Mail*, 8 March.

Shaw, Martin (1994). *Global Society and International Relations: Sociological Concepts and Political Perspectives*. Polity Press, Cambridge, UK.

Stone, Christopher D. (1994). 'Defending the Global Commons'. In P. Sands, ed., *Greening International Law*. New Press, New York.

United States (2000). 'Position of the Government of the United States of America on Legal Issues Relating to Submissions on Enforcement Matters and Preparation of Factual Records under Articles 14 and 15 of the NAAEC'. 27 March. Unpublished, on file with author.

Walzer, Michael (1995). *Toward a Global Civil Society*. Berghahn Books, Providence, RI.

'Why Exactly Does This NAFTA Commission Exist?' (2000). *The Globe and Mail*, 23 May.

Wirth, David A. (1994). 'Reexamining Decision-Making Processes in International Environmental Law'. *Iowa Law Review* vol. 79, no. 4, pp. 769–802.

Appendix 9-A: Submissions under NAAEC Articles 14 and 15

Submitter/ Registry number	Party	Subject matter	Date of filing	Outcome
1. Biodiversity Legal Foundation et al. (SEM-95-001)	U.S.	Non-enforcement of *Endangered Species Act* with respect to spotted owl protection due to a military readiness rider	30 June 1995	Terminated under Art. 14(2) on 11 Dec. 1995
2. Sierra Club et al. (SEM-95-002)	U.S.	Non-enforcement of environmental laws due to disaster relief rider	30 Aug. 1995	Terminated under Art. 14(2) on 8 Dec. 1995
3. Comité para la Protección de los Recursos Naturales, AC et al. (Cozumel Pier case) (SEM-96-001)	Mexico	Failure to comply with environmental assessment requirements in authorising pier construction at Cozumel	17 Jan. 1996	Factual record released on 24 Oct. 1997
4. Aage Tottrup (SEM-96-002)	Canada	Non-enforcement of environmental laws resulting in pollution of wetlands in fish and bird habitat	20 Mar. 1996	Terminated under Art. 14(2) on 28 May 1996
5. The Friends of the Oldman River I (SEM-96-003)	Canada	Failure to apply, comply with, and enforce habitat protection sections of fisheries and environmental assessment acts	9 Sep. 1996	Terminated under Art. 15(1) on 2 Apr. 1997

6. The Southwest Center for Biological Diversity et al. (SEM-96-004)	U.S.	Non-enforcement of *National Environmental Policy Act* in relation to U.S. Army operations	14 Nov. 1996	Withdrawn on 5 June 1997
7. Comité Pro Limpieza del Rìo Magdalena (SEM-97-002)	Mexico	Discharge of wastewater into Magdalena River in violation of environmental legislation	15 Mar. 1997	Secretariat awaiting, under Art. 21(1)(b), additional information from party
8. BC Aboriginal Fisheries Commission et al. (SEM-97-001)	Canada	Non-enforcement of *Fisheries Act* against BC Hydro	2 Apr. 1997	Factual record released on 11 June 2000
9. Centre québécois du droit de l'environnement (SEM-97-003)	Canada	Non-enforcement of several environmental standards relating to hog production	4 Apr. 1997	Council turned down Secretariat's recommendation to prepare factual record on 16 May 2000
10. Canadian Environmental Defence Fund (SEM-97-004)	Canada	Non-enforcement of laws requiring environmental assessment of federal policies and programs	26 May 1997	Terminated under Art. 14(1) on 25 Aug. 1997
11. Animal Alliance of Canada et al. (SEM-97-005)	Canada	Non-enforcement of regulation ratifying Rio Convention on Biological Diversity	21 July 1997	Terminated under Art. 14(1) on 26 May 1998

12. The Friends of the Oldman River II (SEM-97-006)	Canada	Failure to apply, comply with, and enforce habitat protection sections of fisheries and environmental assessment acts	4 Oct. 1997	On 16 May 2000, Council deferred decision on Secretariat's recommendation to prepare factual record
13. Instituto de Derecho Ambiental (SEM-97-007)	Mexico	Non-enforcement of environment law in connection with citizen complaint of degradation of river-lake basin	10 Oct. 1997	Terminated under Art. 15(1) on 14 July 2000
14. Instituto de Derecho Ambiental AC et al. (SEM-98-002)	Mexico	Failure to enforce General Law on Ecological Balance and Environmental Protection in relation to explosions	9 Jan. 1998	Terminated under Art. 14(1) on 11 Jan. 2000
15. Hector Gregorio Ortiz Martìnez (SEM-98-002)	Mexico	Improper administrative processing and persistent failure to enforce environment law in connection with a citizen complaint	10 Oct. 1997	Terminated under Art. 14(1) on 18 Mar. 1999
16. Department of the Planet Earth (SEM-98-003)	U.S.	Non-enforcement of Great Lakes Water Quality Agreement	5 May 1998	Terminated under Art. 15(1) on 5 Oct. 2001

17. Sierra Club of British Columbia et al. (SEM-98-004)	Canada	Systematic failure to enforce *Fisheries Act* provision against mining industry	29 June 1998	Secretariat recommended preparation of factual record on 11 May 2001; decision pending
18. Academia Sonorense de Derechos Humanos et al. (Cytrar I) (SEM-98-005)	Mexico	Improper authorisation of a hazardous waste landfill (Cytrar)	11 Aug. 1998	Terminated under Art. 15(1) on 26 Oct. 2000
19. Grupo Ecológico Manglar AC (SEM-98-006)	Mexico	Non-enforcement of environmental laws with respect to a shrimp farm (Aquanova)	20 Oct. 1998	Secretariat recommended preparing factual record on 4 Aug. 2000; decision pending
20. Environmental Health Coalition et al. (SEM-98-007)	Mexico	Failure to enforce laws regarding lead smelter posing serious threats to human health and environment	23 Oct. 1998	Factual record in process following Council's decision on 16 May 2000
21. Methanex Corporation (SEM-99-001)	U.S.	Failure to enforce California laws related to water resource protection and regulation of underground storage tanks	18 Oct. 1999	Terminated under Art. 14(3) on 30 June 2000 (see No. 23, Neste)

22. Alliance for the Wild Rockies (SEM-99-002)	U.S.	Non-enforcement of *Migratory Bird Treaty Act* prohibition against killing birds without a permit	19 Nov. 1999	Secretariat recommended preparing factual record on 15 Dec. 2000; decision pending
23. Neste Canada (SEM-00-002)	U.S.	Failure to enforce California laws related to underground storage tanks resulting in contamination of soil, water, and air	21 Jan. 2000	Terminated under Art. 14(3) on 30 June 2000 (see No. 21, Methanex)
24. Rosa Marìa Escalante de Fernández (Molymex I) (SEM-00-001)	Mexico	Molymex plant pollution violating air quality and environmental health standards	27 Jan. 2000	Terminated under Art. 14(1) on 25 Apr. 2000
25. Hudson River Audubon Society of Westchester (SEM-00-003)	U.S.	Non-enforcement of *Migratory Bird Treaty Act* and *Endangered Species Act*	2 Mar. 2000	Terminated under Art. 14(1) on 12 Apr. 2000
26. David Suzuki Foundation et al. (SEM-00-004)	Canada	Breach of commitments under NAAEC to effectively enforce laws necessary to protect forest resources	15 Mar. 2000	Secretariat recommended preparation of factual record on 27 July 2001; decision pending

27. Academia Sonorense de Derechos Humanos, Domingo Gutièrrez Mendìvil (Molymex II) (SEM-00-005)	Mexico	Non-enforcement of General Law of Ecological Equilibrium and Environmental Protection against Molymex	6 Apr. 2000	Secretariat considering under Art. 15 whether to recommend preparation of factual record
28. Comisión de Solidaridad y Defensa de los Derechos Humanos AC (SEM-00-006)	Mexico	Denying access to environmental justice to indigenous communities in Sierra Tarahumara (Chihuahua)	9 Sep. 2000	Secretariat considering whether application satisfies requirements of Art. 14
29. Academia Sonorense de Derechos Humanos (Cytrar II) (SEM-01-001)	Mexico	Failure to enforce environmental laws effectively in relation to Cytrar hazardous waste landfill	14 Feb. 2001	Secretariat considering under Art. 15 whether to recommend preparation of factual record
30. Names withheld under by Secretariat under Article 11(8) (SEM-01-002)	Canada	Failure to prevent AAA Packaging from exporting banned pesticide	12 Apr. 2001	Dismissed under Art. 14(1) on 25 May 2001
31. Mercerizados y Teñidos de Guadalajara, SA (SEM-01-003)	Mexico	Mexican company alleges that courts failed to account for evidence of groundwater pollution caused by another company (Dermet) in civil action	14 June 2001	Under review by the Secretariat to determine conformity with Art. 14

Source: North American Commission for Environmental Cooperation, Citizen Submissions on Enforcement Matters: Status <www.cec.org/citizen/status/index.cfm?varlan=english>. The decisions are available under Citizen Submissions on Enforcement Matters: Registry and Public Files of Submissions.

Chapter 10

Public Participation within NAFTA's Environmental Agreement: The Mexican Experience

Gustavo Alanís Ortega

The first case before the North American Commission on Environmental Cooperation (CEC), created by the environmental side agreement to the North American Free Trade Agreement (NAFTA), was the Cozumel case against the Mexican government. Brought by several civil society organisations, it was the first ever to go through the entire Article 14-15 process. It concluded with the first factual record, which was published by the CEC in October 1997. It is thus important to consider in some detail the process that was followed, the impact that the process and decisions had, and the lessons that were learned from this pioneering case.

The Cozumel Process

In considering the process followed in the Cozumel case, it is significant to recognise that everyone involved was using a new and unique instrument. It was thus an experiment, with no one knowing how the process would work or able to predict its outcome. One question that arose at the very start was why this mechanism should be used. Were there not legal tools within Mexico itself to resolve this matter?

On 22 June 1995, three local environmental nongovernmental organisations (ENGOs) from Cozumel — El Grupo de los Cien Internacional AC, El Centro Mexicano de Derecho Ambiantel AC, and Comité para la Protección de los Recursos Naturales AC — took the case before the Mexican government's Procuraduría Federal de Protección al Ambiente (PROFEPA). The groups argued that the construction of a pier in Cozumel was illegal, because, among other things, the environmental impact assessment done by the authorities was incorrect. They claimed that these authorities had evaluated only the environmental impacts of the construction in the water, but not those on the land. They also argued that other projects associated with the pier, such as a golf course, a hotel, and a shopping mall, were not environmentally evaluated, as was called for in Mexico's environmental regulations.

On 15 September 1995, PROFEPA gave a response to the three groups in Cozumel, declaring that the project was legal. After this response, the group had only three options. The first was to submit a legal recourse before PROFEPA arguing that it was wrong in its decision and asking it to reconsider the environmentalists' arguments and issue a new resolution. However, this route was not taken because although such legal recourse is contemplated in Mexico's environmental law, in practice the authority tends to confirm its previous resolution in the same general direction as before.

The groups also had the option of using the Amparo, a legal recourse written into Mexico's constitution to enable citizens to challenge the decisions made by the authorities. However, this route would have likely led to the judge ruling against the groups because of their lack of standing (the environmental groups were unable to prove that personal harm would result from the construction at Cozumel, and the right to a healthy environment was not yet enshrined in the constitution).

The third, and only promising, option was to use Articles 14 and 15 to argue before the CEC that the Government of Mexico was not enforcing its environmental laws and regulations effectively in this particular case. On 18 January 1996, the Cozumel pier case was thus formally submitted to the CEC Secretariat. Then on 6 February, the Secretariat informed the submitters that the case complied with Article 14(1). On 8 February, the Secretariat notified them that the case would go beyond Article 14(2).

On 12 February, the CEC asked for a response from the Mexican government, which made no public statement. On 22 March, the government responded to the CEC: it argued that the groups had not proven harm, that they had not exhausted local legal remedies, and that they had not submitted their bylaws and articles of incorporation to the CEC. Article 14, however, does not make such demands from petitioning groups. Yet, the Mexican government asked the CEC Secretariat to close the case without recommending that a factual record be compiled. Nonetheless, on 6 June 1996, the CEC Secretariat recommended to its Council of Ministers that one be written.

In Mexico, the reaction of the environmental authorities was very negative. They asserted that the three ENGOs were mostly concerned with protecting commercial interests. They claimed the groups were anti-Mexicans acting against the interests of the Republic. The media reported that this petition would result in economic sanctions imposed upon Mexico. Moreover, they were very critical of the CEC, which they saw as intervening in Mexico's domestic affairs, in a violation of the country's sovereignty; the CEC, they said, wanted to intervene in Mexico's internal enforcement of environmental laws and regulations.

Finally in Toronto, on 1 August 1996, the Council voted to require a factual record. It was published on 24 October 1997.

The Impact of Cozumel

The Cozumel case had several environmentally beneficial effects, in a wide variety of ways. Nine can be identified as most important. They are as follows:
- President Ernesto Zedillo declared the Cozumel reefs to be a natural protected area.

- A collaboration agreement was signed between the Mexico's Instituto Nacional de Ecología (INE) and the petitioners in order to work together in elaborating a plan to manage the natural protected area, and also to plan the ecological zoning for Cozumel.
- The Cozumel case influenced the reform of Mexico's environmental law in 1996, particularly with respect to environmental impact assessments, and a new regulation that was published in the year 2000.
- The case also contributed to creating more environmental awareness among Cozumel's population and in the whole State of Quintana Roo, where Cozumel is located.
- The experience opened the gate for other cases to reach the factual record stage.
- Much pressure was put on PROFEPA to require this agency of the Mexican government enforce environmental laws and regulations effectively.
- A trust (Fideicomiso) was created for the natural protected area, in order for it to be well preserved. Another Fideicomiso was created among the three levels of government to develop the ecological zoning of Cozumel.
- The project was not carried out as the investors had planned. Only a terminal port was built, which operates to this day. But the requests to construct a hotel, restaurants, bars, shopping mall, golf course, and so on, were denied by Mexico's environmental authorities.
- Because of all the publicity that this case received nationally as well as internationally, a moral sanction was felt by Mexico's environmental authorities.

The Lessons from Cozumel

There are many lessons that can be drawn from the process that unfolded in the Cozumel case. Several in particular warrant the greatest attention, in the ongoing effort to develop a better Article 14-15 process.

The CEC Secretariat has no time limit for proceeding from Article 14(1) to Article 14(2) and its demand for a response from one of the member countries, or parties. This step can thus go on indefinitely.

There is also uncertainty with respect to how much time the member countries have to respond to the CEC. The North American Agreement on Environmental Cooperation (NAAEC) identifies about 30 days as the time allowed, but does not say if these are working days or calendar days. Nor does it say anything about what happens if the party does not respond in 30 days. Furthermore, also unclear is the provision for the parties to respond to the CEC within 60 days under exceptional circumstances. The NAAEC never describes when a party may be under such circumstances, or even what one should understand by the term 'exceptional circumstances'.

A petitioner need not prove harm to one's own person or organisation, nor does a petitioner have to exhaust local legal remedies. These are only two considerations that the Secretariat must take into account when deciding whether to require a response from the party. This situation does not mean that a petitioner must comply with these requirements in order for the case to be reviewed.

There is a conflict of interest for the parties to the agreement: On the one hand, the parties are accused of a lack of effective enforcement of environmental laws. On the other hand, as members of the CEC's Council, they vote for or against being investigated through a factual record. This same conflict arises again with the decision to publish the factual record.

The Council has an opportunity to comment on the draft of the factual record. However, the petitioners do not.

If the Council approves the elaboration of a factual record, there is no time limit for the CEC Secretariat to conclude this investigation.

The NAAEC allows for possibility that the factual record may not be made public if the Council so decides. This shows the extent of the discretion enjoyed by the Council. It also shows that the accused party may see the content of the factual record but the petitioner may not, if the Council decides not to make the factual record public.

The factual record gives only facts. It has no conclusion and makes no recommendations. It is not legally binding on the parties. There is no sanction imposed on the party involved. It does not determine if the party did not effectively enforce its own environmental laws.

There is no provision in the NAAEC for stopping or delaying the activity cited in the petition while the case is being heard.

Once the Secretariat recommends to the Council that a factual record be compiled. there is no time limit for the Council to vote on this matter.

There is no opportunity for the petitioners to act if the Secretariat decides not to require a response from the party involved or if the Council decides to order the Secretariat not to require a factual record or not to publish a factual record. There is no provision for appeal.

Now that factual records are starting to appear, it is clear that the governments, especially those of Canada and Mexico, do not welcome the process. Thus, they are pushing very hard to restrict the ability of the Secretariat to take up petitions. They also want the process to be less accessible to the public.

Finally, it is important to remember that the guidelines for submitting petitions were intended to advise the public on how to submit a petition. They were not created to impose requirements on them or the Secretariat.

Chapter 11

Article 14-15 of the North American Agreement on Environmental Cooperation: Intent of the Founders

Serena Wilson

Canada, the United States, and the United Mexican States entered into the North American Free Trade Agreement (NAFTA) in December 1992. During the negotiation of the Agreement, there was much public debate about labour market disruptions and the implications of NAFTA on the environment. The level of controversy was unparalleled for a trade negotiation. It led the three governments to include unprecedented provisions in the trade agreement in order to address environmental concerns and to sign two supplemental agreements in September 1993: the North American Agreement on Environmental Cooperation (NAAEC) and the North American Agreement on Labor Cooperation (NAALC) (Commission for Environmental Cooperation [CEC] 1993). NAFTA and its two supplemental agreements all entered into force on 1 January 1994.

The NAAEC's Articles 14 and 15 citizen submission process was intended to give the public a voice in the enforcement of domestic environmental laws in each of the three countries. Under this process, any resident of North America can assert that any one of the parties has failed to enforce its domestic environmental laws effectively. In developing the citizen submission process, the three parties were challenged to create a mechanism that is independent of the governments, accountable to the public, accessible to the common individual, and reasonably efficient. A great burden for fulfilling this promise fell on the Commission for Environmental Cooperation (CEC) Secretariat, with which citizens file these submissions asserting ineffective enforcement of environmental laws. It is the CEC Secretariat in Montreal that must review the submissions pursuant to the criteria outlined in Articles 14 and 15 and present the CEC's Council of Ministers with a decision on whether a factual record is warranted.

During its first eight years, the citizen submission process has invited much criticism (CEC 1998). These criticisms focussed on the slow pace of producing factual records, the lack of transparency at key decision points, and the questionable benefit of a factual record that does not require government action to resolve the problem of non-enforcement. The governments have sought to revise the citizen submission process in order to clarify equivocal language in the Agreement and to guide the Secretariat in its review. Co-operative efforts among the parties and the public users of the citizen submission process to knead out the kinks in the implementation of Article 14 could result in a valuable tool for citizen participation in environmental protection.

The Negotiations

A strong impetus for the public debate was the fear that a free trade agreement between a developed economy such as the United States and a developing one such as Mexico would result in a proliferation of pollution havens along the U.S.-Mexico border. This phenomenon would occur if North American companies moved into Mexico in an attempt to benefit from the cheap labour in manufacturing exports for the markets in the North. There was also a concern that any effort to harmonise environmental standards among the three countries would lead to a 'race to the bottom' in which the weakest standards would prevail due to resource restraints in the developing country. Mexico had strong environmental laws; however, due to a lack of resources, it had a poor enforcement regime. The Mexican environmental law enforcement agency, Procuraduría Federal de Protección al Ambiente (PROFEPA), was not created until 1994. Americans feared that non-enforcement of Mexico's environmental laws in the context of increased trade under NAFTA would magnify the impact across the border of any ensuing environmental degradation.

Public oversight was rare in Mexico in the early 1990s when the NAAEC was negotiated. It was therefore difficult for three signatories to agree on the provisions that created the citizen submissions mechanism. At one extreme, the United States argued for an independent secretariat to add credibility to a process for reviewing government action. At the other extreme, Mexico argued for a process with accountability intended to assure fairness in the review of government action. The result was the NAAEC, with equivocal language that all parties could find acceptable according to their own interpretations. At the implementation stage, the same arguments resurfaced as the parties attempted to interpret the ambiguous text of the agreement.

The difficulties in implementing the citizen submission process led the three parties to draft guidelines in 1995 at the insistence of Mexico, although the guidelines are not required by the NAAEC. They were initially intended to assist both the public and the Secretariat as they tried to use this unique mechanism. The drafting of the guidelines also enabled the parties to work through some of the tough problems left unresolved by the negotiation of Articles 14 and 15. Today, as they strive to create a credible citizen submission process, the parties still seek to balance the level of Secretariat independence in the review process with accountability to the public and to the parties in its decision making. The governments needed to achieve these goals without creating such a complex process that it would be inaccessible to the common citizen, who would need to hire scholars and lawyers in order to participate. Ultimately, the citizen submission process had to provide an avenue for public oversight to achieve greater enforcement of environmental laws in a free-trade zone.

The Article 14-15 Record

During its first eight years in operation, the citizen submission process was useful, both in identifying matters in each of the three countries concerning ineffective environmental enforcement and in providing a spotlight for complaints of concern to the public. The complaints were closely balanced among the three countries. From January 1994 to February 2001, nine submissions were filed against Canada, eight against the United States, and twelve against Mexico. There was a time a few years earlier when the complaints were heavily weighted against Canada. As governments change and new environmental policies emerge, the party carrying the greatest caseload will likely continue to change as well.

Of the 29 submissions filed in those initial eight years, only two resulted in a factual record. In contrast, 18 were terminated by the Secretariat for various reasons. Unfortunately, the process is slow. The time it takes for a submission to move from the filing stage to a public factual record has run up to 38 months. This time lapse is a huge disincentive to use the mechanism for a person who is seeking resolution to a complaint. The Secretariat has made efforts to expedite the process, for example by hiring additional staff dedicated solely to the implementation of Articles 14 and 15. More needs to be done, however, if the citizen submission process is to remain a viable option for addressing citizen complaints about matters of ineffective enforcement of an environmental law having serious negative impacts.

Some of those who have attempted to use the citizen submission process protest that there is a lack of transparency on the parts of the Secretariat and the Council in their respective decision making (see Joint Public Advisory Committee [JPAC] 2001d). Many also believe that the Secretariat should have the authority to draft legal conclusions or recommendations to the Council in a factual record in order to provoke action by the offending party to reconcile the matter. The NAAEC does not preclude the Secretariat from making legal conclusions or recommendations in a factual record; however, the parties are convinced that such action by the Secretariat is inappropriate. Finally, submitters have complained about the efficiency of the process due to delayed decisions on the part of the Council or slow processing on the part of the Secretariat.

Revising the Guidelines

In discussions leading up to the 1999 meeting of the Council of Ministers in Banff, Alberta, the three parties wrestled with additional revisions to the already revised guidelines for Articles 14 and 15. At this point, Canada and Mexico each had a factual record developed on issues pertaining to enforcement of their domestic laws. The governments disputed among themselves the ongoing concerns of Mexico and Canada about the process. They proposed changes to the guidelines without public knowledge. This undertaking eventually leaked to the public and was perceived to be a government effort to sabotage the citizen submission process. When the 'secret' government discussions came to light several months before the June session of the Council, the public demanded accountability for the proposed changes and input on any future changes to the guidelines for Articles 14 and 15 (CEC 1999a, 1999b).

In response to this public uproar, at its June 2000 meeting, the Council drafted a resolution that created a mechanism to provide for public comment on any proposed changes to the guidelines (CEC 2000a, 2000b). The resolution also preserved the Council's right to interpret the NAAEC and make the final decisions on how the guidelines would operate. The public comment mechanism created under the resolution was implemented through the Joint Public Advisory Committee (JPAC). The JPAC is the public arm of the CEC and it is within its purview under Article 16 to advise the Council on any matter within the scope of the NAAEC.

Under the resolution, the JPAC had two assignments. The first was to write rules for how it will transmit public comments to the Council for consideration in future guideline revisions and to conduct this process on an ongoing basis. The second was to research lessons learned over the previous eight years of implementing the only international citizen submission process in existence.

After conducting public hearings and inviting written public comments on the benefits and flaws of the submissions process, the JPAC presented both the rules and the 'Lessons Learned' Report to the Council at the 2001 meeting of the Council of Ministers in Guadalajara, Mexico (JPAC 2001b, 2001c, 2001d). In the report, the JPAC addressed the public concerns with respect to transparency, efficiency, and the desire for legal conclusions. The Council reviewed the document and agreed to make some of the changes to the guidelines immediately and will continue to consider other issues raised (JPAC 2001a; CEC 2001). The JPAC mechanism for transmitting new comments to the Council should open the door to ongoing public input into improving the process. If the public is patient with the growing pains and does not abandon the process out of frustration, the Articles 14 and 15 process can grow into a critical tool in combating government neglect in environmental enforcement.

References

Commission for Environmental Cooperation (1993). 'North American Agreement on Environmental Cooperation between the Government of Canada, the Government of the United Mexican States, and the Government of the United States'. <www.cec.org/ pubs_info_resources/law_treat_agree/naaec/> (December 2001).

Commission for Environmental Cooperation (1998). 'Four-Year Review of the North American Agreement on Environmental Cooperation'. Report of the Independent Review Committee, June. <www.cec.org/pubs_info_resources/law_treat_agree/cfp3.cfm?varlan=english> (December 2001).

Commission for Environmental Cooperation (1999a). '6th Regular Session of the Council of the Commission for Environmental Cooperation'. Summary of interventions made during the public portion, 28 June, Banff. <www.cec.org/who_we_are/council/sessions/disp_sess.cfm?varlan=english&documentID=83> (December 2001).

Commission for Environmental Cooperation (1999b). '1999 Regular Session of the Council'. 27–28 June, Banff. <www.cec.org/who_we_are/council/sessions/disp_sess.cfm?varlan=english&documentID=82> (December 2001).

Commission for Environmental Cooperation (2000a). '2000 Regular Session of the Council'. 12–13 June, Dallas. <www.cec.org/who_we_are/council/sessions/disp_sess.cfm?varlan=english&documentID=96> (December 2001).

Commission for Environmental Cooperation (2000b). 'North American Agenda for Action: A Three-Year Program for the Commission for Environmental Cooperation'. Commission for Environmental Cooperation, Montreal.

Commission for Environmental Cooperation (2001). 'Response to the Joint Public Advisory Committee (JPAC) Report on Lessons Learned Regarding Articles 14 and 15 Process'. 29 June. Commission for Environmental Cooperation, Guadalajara.

Joint Public Advisory Committee of the North American Commission for Environmental Cooperation (2001a). 'Commission for Environmental Cooperation: Joint Public Advisory Committee Session No. 01-02'. Summary Record, 30 June. Commission for Environmental Cooperation, Guadalajara.

Joint Public Advisory Committee of the North American Commission for Environmental Cooperation (2001b). 'Joint Public Advisory Committee Round Tables on Opportunities for Enhancing North American Cooperation'. Executive Summary, 28 June. Commission for Environmental Cooperation, Guadalajara.

Joint Public Advisory Committee of the North American Commission for Environmental Cooperation (2001c). 'JPAC Public Review of Issues Concerning the Implementation and Further Elaboration of Articles 14 and 15'. Commission for Environmental Cooperation, Montreal.

Joint Public Advisory Committee of the North American Commission for Environmental Cooperation (2001d). 'Lessons Learned: Citizen Submissions under Articles 14 and 15 of the NAAEC'. 6 June. <www.cec.org/pubs_docs/documents/index.cfm?ID=121&varlan=english> (December 2001).

PART IV
WORKER PROTECTION:
EVALUATING THE
NAFTA COMMISSION FOR
LABOR COOPERATION MODEL

Chapter 12

Civil Society and the North American Agreement on Labor Cooperation

Kevin Banks[1]

What is the relationship among civil society, national governments, and international organisations under the North American Agreement on Labor Cooperation (NAALC)? This chapter can provide only a preliminary sketch of an answer to this question. It first outlines the structure of the agreement and its public participation mechanisms, and then discusses the direction that public participation has taken. It argues that civil society engagement has been skewed toward a fairly legalistic use of complaint procedures, and that this form of civil society engagement has some important limitations that should be considered by governments and civil society representatives.

The NAALC Structure and Public Participation Mechanisms

Structure

The NAALC, which took effect on 1 January 1994, has a very broad set of objectives. These are set out in Part I of the Agreement. They include improving working conditions and living standards, and promoting eleven specific labour principles.[2] The Agreement focusses on compliance with, transparency in, and effective enforcement of labour laws relating to those principles.

Part II sets out the obligations of the Agreement. Article 2 requires member states to ensure that labour laws and regulations provide for high labour standards. Articles 3 through 7 then go on to provide a reasonably specific set of obligations with respect to enforcement of the laws, providing parties with private rights of action for remedy of breaches of domestic labour law, ensuring due process in enforcement proceedings, and ensuring public awareness of labour law and proposed changes to it.

Part III establishes the institutions of the Agreement. The Commission for Labor Cooperation (CLC) comprises the Council of Ministers of Labour from the three countries and the Secretariat, now located in Washington DC. The Council has obligations to promote co-operative activities on a wide range of labour-related subjects, and to encourage the collection and publication of comparable data on the enforcement of labour law and on labour market conditions. The Secretariat has specific obligations to produce periodic reports on labour markets, labour laws and their administration, trends and administrative strategies related to the implementation and enforcement of labour laws, and human resources development.

Public Participation Mechanisms

In addition to establishing the CLC, the NAALC requires each government to set up a national administrative office (NAO). The NAO provides a point of contact between government and the public and also among each of the governments. NAOs are empowered to receive public communications on labour law matters arising within the territory and another party. Each country has established its own procedures for responding to these communications.

Each country has also established a national advisory committee (NAC) composed of employer, labour, and government representatives. The NACs have a broad mandate to advise governments on the implementation and further elaboration of the Agreement. NAC members are appointed and serve under terms established by each government.

While the NAALC has explicit channels for public participation, it is essentially an intergovernmental agreement. It specifically states that private parties do not have rights of private action to sue governments directly to enforce its obligations. Compliance mechanisms remain in the hands of the member governments. Thus a private party that wishes to spur action under the Agreement must solicit the help of a government to do so.

Parts IV and V of the Agreement establish its mechanism for international discussion and dispute resolution. Part IV provides for three mechanisms. First, any member country may initiate consultations between NAOs on any matter dealing with labour law, the administration of labour law, or labour market conditions within the territory of another country. Second, a country may seek ministerial consultations directly between ministers of labour on request in writing in order to address any matter within the scope of the Agreement. Third, the Agreement provides for a formal and independent procedure referred to as the Evaluation Committee of Experts (ECE). This is a neutral body of experts, which must, at the request of one of the consulting member countries, be established following ministerial consultations. The ECE can deal only with occupational safety and health and other 'technical labour standards' (that is, protection against employment discrimination, minimum labour standards, and child labour). Matters must also relate to trade, and be covered by mutually recognised labour laws. The ECE is empowered to analyse, in a non-adversarial manner, patterns of practice by each party in the enforcement of the relevant labour laws. The report of an ECE is published unless there is a consensus among all three countries not to do so.

Finally, Part V of the Agreement provides for dispute resolution. Following a series of meetings to attempt a settlement, an arbitral panel may be established by a majority vote of the Council. At this stage, the scope of issues that can be addressed narrows again. Dispute resolution can only address a persistent pattern of failure to enforce occupational health and safety, child labour, and minimum wage laws. The dispute resolution process can eventually lead to the formulation of an action plan to remedy systematic problems in the enforcement of the relevant laws. If the plan is not implemented effectively, trade sanctions or fines can be imposed.

There are thus two defined ongoing channels of public access in the NAALC. First, members of the public may present a public communication to their national administrative office with respect to any labour law matter arising in another member country. Public communications may then serve as a basis for consultations between NAOs and ministers of labour. Following such consultations, a more limited range of matters may be taken up in ECE or dispute resolution processes. Second, working through national advisory committees, members of the public can seek to advise the government on any matter relating to the implementation or further elaboration of the Agreement. Other more *ad hoc* channels are also available. In 1998, the three parties undertook a four-year review of the NAALC and sought the view of members of the public. A similar four-year review is planned for 2002. Of course, members of the public are also free to lobby the ministers of labour directly in order to seek an agreement to work internationally on any matter within the scope of the Agreement.

The Public Communications Procedure in Operation

The bulk of public participation under the Agreement appears thus far to have been almost exclusively driven by complaints, through public communications processes. In some respects, this is a natural development because many participants in NAALC proceedings are involved mainly in domestic labour and employment relations. Labour lawyers and union representatives work within a legal culture in which trying to get a good contract and to enforce it provides key ways of bringing about constructive change. In that environment, one often acts most effectively simply by filing a complaint and seeking legal redress.

Moreover, in some cases (notably Canada), NACs have been relatively inactive in recent years. The emphasis on the public communications process has tended to give public participation a legalistic character, so that a case of the Agreement being violated is presented and governments asked to take action to remedy the problem, with relatively little attention given to political processes supporting policy changes.

Between the inception of the NAALC and the autumn of 2000, there were 22 public communications filed under it. Fourteen of those were filed with the U.S. NAO, five with the Mexican NAO, and three with the Canadian NAO. Of those submissions, 13 dealt with issues arising in Mexico, two with issues in Canada, and the remaining seven with matters arising in the U.S. The submissions have been filed mainly by trade unions and human rights nongovernmental organisations (NGOs). Unions are among the lead parties, submitting complaints in at least 14 different cases. Human rights NGOs are among the lead parties in at least ten of them. A union–human rights

NGO partnership was formed in at least seven. Two submissions were filed by employer NGOs. In at least 11 cases there were cross-border partnerships formed — either unions from two or three of the countries working together, or unions working with NGOs in other countries. The Agreement has thus, in a limited way, acted as a catalyst to bring groups together.

The submissions have dealt with a wide range of issues. Some have dealt with fairly technical aspects of labour law enforcement, which can be addressed without extensive political debate.

For example, a complaint filed by the Yale Law School's Workers Rights Project (in conjunction with a number of other organisations) with the Canadian and Mexican NAOs alleged that a memorandum of understanding (MOU) between the U.S. Immigration and Naturalization Service and the U.S. Department of Labor effectively deprived immigrant workers of access to enforcement of the U.S. *Fair Labour Standards Act*, which deals with matters including hours of work and overtime. The MOU provided that when U.S. Department of Labor inspectors went into a workplace to investigate a complaint, they would be obliged to check the immigration records of all the workers at the same time. It was argued that this procedure gave workers reason to fear Department of Labor procedures if their immigration papers were not in order, or if those of a fellow worker were not. Following the investigation of the submission, there was a change in the MOU. Automatic immigration status checks by Department of Labor inspectors were ended.

Most other complaints have not been so amenable to technocratic or bureaucratic resolution. For example, a case filed by a number of unions and farm worker advocacy groups has raised a wide range of issues and allegations concerning the application of labour laws in the apple industry of Washington State. These include the enforcement of occupational health and safety laws and deficiencies in protections of the right to organise a union. It questions the budget allocation for government agencies responsible for enforcement. It advocates systematic change in the way that labour law is administered in the apple industry and perhaps, by extension, in many other industries as well. It is thus a pitch for a major structural reform.

Interestingly, the complainants in this case used the first public forum held in response to the complaint to mobilise agricultural workers, hold demonstrations to raise public awareness of agricultural workers' issues, and seek a dialogue with the government of Washington State. They have treated the NAALC complaint procedures as the beginning of a political process rather than as legal proceedings expected to deliver a relatively immediate remedy.[3] This more political approach has not, however, been the norm. Civil society groups have often evaluated the NAALC as though its purpose was to establish a tribunal and to provide legal remedies.

Complaint-Driven Strategies Reconsidered

It is difficult to evaluate the effectiveness of an agreement like the NAALC in part because it is difficult to attribute causation in diplomatic processes. The timing of events may suggest that changes shortly following a public complaint were not merely coincidental. But, publicly at least, governments may prefer to present them as an extension of existing policy rather than a concession to international pressure. Moreover, factors other than the complaint itself may have proven decisive behind the scenes.

Critics of the NAALC have argued that most complaints have resulted in few concrete changes in policy or administration (see, for example, Canadian Labour Congress 2001). They question the effectiveness of complaint-driven processes operating through diplomatic channels and relying primarily on moral suasion and publicity. During the first four-year review of the NAALC, many of the public submissions received from members of the Canadian and U.S. public argued for stronger enforcement mechanisms. Some specifically called for the amendment of the NAALC or its replacement in order to make the use of trade sanctions available to enforce international labour obligations (NAALC 1998).

However, even if trade sanctions were available, there would be important limits to an approach driven by complaints. Many labour policy issues raised in NAALC complaints point to alleged systemic problems. In addition to this, there is the complexity of dealing with such issues across national borders. In each country, labour policies are very politically charged, particularly in the U.S. and Mexico, but increasingly in Canada as well.

Two relatively recent works help to bring the limits of a complaint-driven approach into sharper focus. The first, entitled *The Hollow Hope,* by Gerald Rosenberg (1991), is a historical study of the use of adjudication to attempt to bring about social change in the United States. It examines whether U.S. Supreme Court decisions supporting equality rights played a significant part in driving reforms eventually won by the U.S. civil rights movement between the 1940s and 1970s. It also considers the effectiveness of litigation to promote environmental and prison reforms. Rosenberg's conclusion is that the courts were not big players in the major changes that took place. Rather, changes took place in response to the political pressures brought by social movements that gathered force after World War Two. The courts reflected changes in attitudes rather than leading them. When court decisions clashed with the attitudes of most voters, their implementation was tentative, piecemeal, and certainly not responsible for wide-scale social or political change. If a powerful domestic legal institution such as the U.S. Supreme Court is unable to bring about such change on its own using the legal remedies available to it, it is hard to see how any form of international adjudication could bring about major labour policy reforms in the absence of domestic and international political mobilisation in favour of such action.

The second, *Global Business Regulation* by John Braithwaite and Peter Drahos (2000), is an exhaustive survey of different international regimes that have been established to regulate business on a global scale. The authors conclude, among other things, that a form of international regime-building politics has developed with regard to advocacy of sets of principles and related international programs and reforms. These politics have been most decisively influenced by international networks of business lobby groups. However, some NGO groups have been quite effective as well. Where they have been most effective, NGOs have used the opportunities provided by high-profile cases not simply to point to violations of principles, but also to build international networks themselves and to advocate models of reform. In that type of politics, complaint submissions would only play a part in a larger strategy.

These reflections raise the question of whether or not there are opportunities under the NAALC for a more expanded form of civil society participation and a more expanded form of transnational politics. This would require, at a minimum, more active engagement of NACS. It probably also requires that transnational networks of advocates develop and build political support for a common agenda, seeing NAALC processes as opportunities to further this longer term project. Complaint processes alone will probably never be able to carry the weight of bringing about the changes that civil society advocates seek, whether or not the NAALC is reformed or replaced with a regime based on trade sanctions.

Notes

1   The views expressed in this chapter are those of the author as an individual and do not necessarily reflect those of the Commission for Labor Cooperation or any of its member governments.
2   Those principles cover a broad range of labour policy. They include respect for freedom of association, the right to organise, the right to bargain collectively, and the right to strike; they also include providing minimum employment standards and protecting against child labour, discrimination in the workplace, occupational injury and disease, as well as ensuring compensation for occupational injury and illness and equality of treatment for migrant workers.
3   In response to the public communication, governments agreed to an action plan that included holding a public forum on 8 August 2001 in Yakima, Washington, which is in the heart of the state's apple-growing region. The groups initiating the communication organised a number of actions designed to raise public awareness of agricultural workers' situations, including a march by several thousand workers through downtown Yakima. At the forum, governments, business, and civil society representatives discussed the case for reforms to the administration of labour laws in the Washington State agricultural industry. Officials from the Office of the Governor of the State of Washington undertook to continue a dialogue with business and worker representatives.

References

Braithwaite, John and Peter Drahos (2000). *Global Business Regulation*. Cambridge University Press, Cambridge.

Canadian Labour Congress (2001). 'Statement by the Canadian Labour Congress to the House of Commons Sub-Committee on Trade and Trade Disputes of the Standing Committee on Foreign Affairs and International Trade Regarding the Free Trade Area of the Americas'. 29 March. Canadian Labour Congress, Ottawa.

North American Agreement on Labor Cooperation (1998). 'Review of the North American Agreement on Labor Cooperation'. <www.naalc.org/english/publications/review.htm> (December 2001).

Rosenberg, Gerald (1991). *The Hollow Hope: Can Courts Bring About Social Change?* University of Chicago Press, Chicago.

Chapter 13

Giving Teeth to NAFTA's Labour Side Agreement

Jonathan Graubart

In 1993, newly elected 'New Democrat' U.S. president Bill Clinton negotiated an institutional compromise on the North American Free Trade Agreement (NAFTA) that reached out to his party's base of labour unions and environmentalists, while placating the sovereignty sensitivities of the presidents of Mexico and Canada and the wishes of his Wall Street supporters for prioritising liberalised investment in North America. Through the mechanism of side agreements, Clinton maintained the complex trade-investment agreement in the core NAFTA, while enticing enough swing Democrats in the U.S. Congress to secure passage of the NAFTA-implementing legislation. Once it took effect in 1994, the North American Agreement on Labor Cooperation (NAALC) committed each country to enforcing its own labour laws and providing adequate legal recourse for all aggrieved workers. Its primary means of implementation is a complaint-review process whereby a specially created agency within each government reviews complaints from any interested party concerning failure by another government to enforce its labour protections. These agencies gather evidence, make findings, and recommend intergovernmental consultations. They cannot order sanctions or demand compliance.

Because of its nonbinding nature, the NAALC was roundly denounced upon introduction by most independent labour movements and labour activists in the region as an empty, toothless institution. The head of the American Federation of Labor-Congress of Industrial Organizations (AFL-CIO), Lane Kirkland, expressed the common sentiment of labour activists in dismissing NAALC as a 'bad joke' (Torres 1996, 46). All NAALC does, argued critics, is set up a powerless bureaucracy in each country that issues meaningless findings (Anderson, Cavanagh, and Ranney 1996).

Despite such low expectations, the NAALC's submission process has proven noteworthy in practice. During its first eight years in operation, 24 submissions have been filed: 14 before the United States against labour practices in Mexico and two against Canadian practices; five before Mexico against U.S. labour practices; one before Canada against Mexican practices, and two against the United States. All but two of these submissions have been filed by labour movements, labour advocates, or human rights groups. These submissions have often shown considerable political and legal sophistication, with a few involving as many as 40 co-submitters from all three countries, including the major labour federations. Submitters have creatively boosted the political punch of these channels through careful legal argumentation, targeting specific companies, proposing systematic remedies, and incorporating the submissions into a multipronged effort to advance a broader cause. Many of the complaints have pressured governmental authorities to justify their actions publicly, and have provided additional momentum to specific labour organising and labour rights campaigns and helped sustain activists' resolve. Most notably, submissions have opened up public debate in Mexico on the government's historical practice of discriminating against independent unions — those unaffiliated with Mexico's long-ruling party, the Partido Revolucionario Institucional (PRI).[1] A few complaints have even prompted changes in behaviour by the government or private company in question. These include:

- the Mexican government pressuring a state labour board to reverse its denial of registration to an independent labour union, which became only the second plant in the *maquiladora* zone[2] to be represented by a nongovernmental-allied union; the Mexican government further committed itself to holding secret ballot elections routinely for union certification;
- the Quebec government agreeing to set up a commission that would discuss enacting a new law prohibiting the use of plant closings to avoid union certification; and
- Stemilt, a large apple warehouse packing company in Washington State, agreeing to card signing in place of elections to determine union certification. The Teamsters union subsequently succeeded in winning representation.

To be sure, most labour activists involved in these submissions continue to stress the many deficiencies of the NAALC's review process. The submissions, they note, have failed to reinstate more than a few jobs of wrongfully dismissed workers, and they have not produced any systematic improvements in practice in the region's labour practices. Moreover, even the most favourable results arose from a combination of factors, as discussed below. The results do, however, indicate the need for a more nuanced analysis. Rather than evaluating the review process as a stand-alone tool, a more-to-the-point standard looks to the value of these complaints as an added tool for improving labour rights, to be used in conjunction with other domestic and transnational tactics (such as union organising or picketing of company headquarters).

Examining activists' use of the NAALC submission process offers insights not only for the North American region but more broadly on the uses that social activists can make of soft law social mechanisms, generally. Soft law is a concept dating back 30 years to characterise the growing practice among state leaders to enter into codified agreements that carefully avoid provisions demanding firm, binding obligations. (Wellens and Borchardt 1989; Dupuy 1988) Soft law agreements have proliferated in the areas of the environment, human rights, and labour rights (Leary 1997; Weiss 1999, 1567). Their central appeal lies in allowing state leaders plenty of wiggle room to address pressing international issues without formally surrendering their authority to act outside the terms of the agreement. Soft law agreements, like NAALC, are likely to prove appealing for other trade agreements as well because they accommodate the growing public support for protecting labour standards while respecting the sensitivities of state leaders about outside interference in delicate domestic matters (Szasz 1999, 33; Abbott and Snidal 2000).

One obvious issue facing scholars of political science and law is determining whether and how soft law agreements on social norms matter in shaping the behaviour of states and other actors. Are they empty rhetorical gestures for international consumption or do they actually prompt signatories to adjust their behaviour to conform with the codified norms? Studies have found that soft law agreements, under certain conditions such as being accompanied by transparent and accessible implementing institutions, instil an attitude among state policy makers that is more conducive to advancing labour causes (Victor 1997; Young 1998). Such research, however, is still at an early phase. Examining the NAALC process provides a means for building on this research through focussing on the role of social activists in giving meaning to soft law. Their role, after all, is especially important in mobilising agreements from mere words into action.

The remainder of this chapter follows up on this agenda by analysing in detail the submissions filed under NAALC. It adopts a bottom-up perspective by focussing on the efforts of cross-border coalitions of labour movements and labour rights activists to give the complaint channel substance.

The NAALC Review Process

The NAALC does not establish substantive supranational standards but sets forth eleven guiding labour principles that each country is 'committed to promote':
- freedom of association and the right to organise;
- the right to bargain collectively;
- the right to strike;
- prohibition of forced labour;
- labour protections for children;
- minimum employment standards (minimum wage, maximum hours);
- elimination of employment discrimination;
- equal pay for women and men;
- prevention of occupational injuries and illnesses;
- compensation for occupational injuries and illnesses; and
- protection of migrant workers.

These reflect shared principles that each country already honours through its domestic laws. Guided by these principles, NAALC contains three general obligations: to enforce the state's domestic laws on labour rights (Article 3); to provide any aggrieved individual with 'appropriate access to administrative ... judicial or labor tribunals' for vindicating one's rights (Article 4); and to ensure 'fair, equitable, and transparent' adjudicatory proceedings (Article 5).

The complaint-review process has gained the most prominence. Housed in each country's labour department, national administrative offices (NAOs) review complaints from any interested party about the failure of another country to enforce its labour laws or meet the NAALC's procedural requirements. Each NAO consists of a politically appointed secretary and a small staff. In principle, the review process is informational rather than adversarial. NAOs commission legal studies, receive information from any interested party, exchange information with the NAO of the government in question, and issue findings and recommendations. Their formal remedies consist of requesting intergovernmental ministerial consultations. These lead to further studies and investigations including public meetings of government officials, companies, labour unions, and other interested parties.

This process is remarkably comprehensive and accessible. It imposes no standing requirements (anyone from any country can file a complaint) and allows complaints on a broad range of issues, including freedom of association and collective bargaining, long regarded as central to any regime for protecting worker rights (Charnovitz 1997). An added innovative twist is its effective encouragement of cross-border collaboration, given the logistical dynamics of complaining about one country's labour violations before another country's NAO. Petitioners typically need co-operation and assistance from cross-border allies to learn the laws and actual practices of the other country and produce direct evidence and testimony.

The NAOs have no authority to impose sanctions or demand compliance. Although the NAALC contains limited sanctions for a small subset of persistent violations dealing with child labour, minimum standards, and health and safety, they are only possible after a series of lengthy procedures have been followed that go well beyond the NAO review stage. To date no complaint has reached this phase.

Examining the Submissions

The findings set forth below come from a process-tracing of the submissions, relying on NAO documents, participants' written impressions of the process, media coverage, and interviews with submitters and NAO staff. The findings of this analysis are connected to the questions of how activists have used the complaint process, how NAOs judge, and the type of results gained by petitioners, including building a movement, getting their cause on the government agenda, or effecting actual changes in policy.

How and Why Activists Use This Process

Submitters have been filing complaints to boost ongoing advocacy campaigns, especially independent organising campaigns to challenge Mexico's historic system of privileging pro-government unions and suppressing independent labour movements (Middlebrook 1995). Submitters are overwhelmingly in agreement that the NAALC's primary value is political rather than legal, meaning they do not expect NAO findings to produce immediate, tangible changes in behaviour. Even at the first hearing, where submitters challenged suppression of a union-organising campaign in Mexico, a speaker from the United Electrical, Radio, and Machine Workers powerfully articulated the shame value to this process:

> [The NAALC] is the only forum we have for raising the issue of workers' rights in the context of NAFTA ... If you choose to do so, I believe the NAO can ... elevate the question of respect for workers' rights far beyond the level that your actual enforcement power would lead one to expect. You have the ability to create big-time headaches for corporations and government bodies that disregard labor rights, to focus the spotlight of public attention and condemnation on their behavior (United States National Administrative Office [U.S. NAO] Hearing 1994).

In the first several years, the only submitters were a handful of human rights activists, dissident Mexican labour movements, and left-leaning U.S. labour unions such as the International Labor Rights Fund, Asociación Nacional de Abogados Democráticos (ANAD), Frente Auténtico de Trabajo (FAT), and the United Electrical, Radio, and Machine Workers. Over time, the level of interest has increased. Both the AFL-CIO and the Canadian Labour Congress have reassessed their initial dismissal of the process, upon observing the political value gained from several submissions. Interest has grown to the point where the two federations have joined submissions and taken part in broad trinational strategy meetings on using NAALC (Encuentro Trinacional de Laboralistas Democráticos 1999).

Along with growing interest is increased political sophistication. The first submissions were framed as conventional legal complaints that emphasised the illegal behaviour of U.S. companies operating in Mexico rather than systematic failures by the Mexican government to enforce its laws. Moreover, the political goals of the early complaints (the first four) focussed almost exclusively on building support for a specific independent union-organising campaign at a *maquiladora* zone plant. While continuing to attack labour-organising violations at individual plants, recent complaints have thrown a spotlight on systematic abuses and pushed for broader goals, such as ending the structural bias in Mexico's system of labour boards toward pro-government unions.

Table 13.1 summarises the complaints filed and the uses that submitters have made of them. 'Plaintiff stacking' refers to including the main labour federations (especially the AFL-CIO) or numerous parties in the submissions. The term 'broader goals' means focussing on systematic problems rather than single plant violations. Both variables connote greater sophistication and increased effort on the part of the submitters.

Table 13.1 Submissions before the United States National Administrative Office[a]

Case and target	Issues	Lead submitters	Plaintiff stacking	Broader goals
United States				
940001[b], 940002: Honeywell, General Electric	Suppression of independent organising campaigns	UE, FAT, Teamsters	No	No
940003: Sony	Suppression of independent organising campaigns	ILRF, ANAD, CJM	No	No
940004: General Electric	Follow-up to 940001	UE, FAT	No	No
9601: SUTSP	Mexican federal law limiting workers in agency to one union	Human Rights Watch, ANAD, ILRF	No	Yes
9602: Maxi-Switch	Suppression of independent organising campaign	CWA, STRM	Yes	Yes
9701: Gender	Discrimination against pregnant workers and applicants	Human Rights Watch, ANAD, ILRF	No	Yes
9702: Han Young	Suppression of independent union, health and safety violations	Human Rights Watch, ILRF, ANAD, FAT, SCWM	Yes	Yes
9703: Itapsa (Echlin)	Same as above	UE, steel workers, FAT	Yes	Yes
9801: Flight Attendants	Mexican president's use of national security powers to stop a strike	AFA, ASSA	No	No
9802: Tomato/ Child Labour	Child labour in industry	Florida Tomato Exchange[c]	No	No
9901: TAESA	Free association, minimal work standards, health and safety	AFT, ASSA	No	Yes
			No	Yes
2000-01: Auto Trim/Custom Trim	Health and safety, compensation	CJM		
2000-02: Duro Bag	Free association	AFL-CIO	Yes	Yes

9803: McDonald's (Canada)	Quebec law not prohibiting union-avoidance plant closings	Teamsters, Teamsters Canada, ILRF	Yes	Yes
9804: Rural Mail Couriers	Canadian law denying rural mail carriers the right to unionise	CUPW, NALC	Yes	Yes
Mexico				
9501: Sprint ✖	Plant closing to avoid a union	CWA, STRM	No	No
9801: Solec	Health and safety, freedom of association violations	OCAW, 'October 6'[d], SCMW	No	No
9802: Apple	Violations in freedom of association, minimum employment standards, protection of migrant workers, health and safety	UNT, FAT, FDC, UFW, Teamsters	Yes	Yes
9803: Decoster Egg	Freedom of association, discrimination, protection of migrant workers, and health and safety	CTM	No	No
9804: Yale/INS	Unlawful collusion between two agencies	Workers' Rights Project	Yes	Yes
Canada				
98-1: Itapsa	Follow-up to U.S. 9703	see U.S. 9703	Yes	Yes
98-2: Yale/INS	See Mexico 9804			
99-1: LPA	U.S. NLRB prohibiting 'effective' employee involvement in non-union plants	Labor Policy Association[e]	No	Yes

a See page xxiii for a list of acronyms.
b The first two numbers reflect the year the submission was filed (e.g., 940001=1994).
c Florida Tomato Exchange is a business association.
d 'October 6' is an independent Mexican union that formed at Han Young.
e The Labor Policy Association consists of senior human resource offices from large private companies opposed to unionisation.

The strategy that has emerged incorporates the following tactics. One tactic is combining dramatic fact patterns of rights violations occurring at specific plants with allegations of systematic deficiencies in the country's substantive law and enforcement. The second tactic is generating political pressure through assembling wide, trinational coalitions of labour movements, rights groups, and community activists, and engaging in multiple parallel tactics, such as lobbying, picketing, and protesting. A third tactic is raising the stakes by including issues such as health and safety that are subject to further scrutiny beyond NAO review (including sanctions). Activists have also recognised the appeal of legal discourse and trappings by pushing the NAOs to adopt more judicial procedures such as fact finding, hearings, and cross-examinations, and having labour attorneys lead the presentations. Similarly, they have devoted careful attention to the domestic labour laws as well as international laws (according to International Labor Organization provisions) at issue.

The Itapsa submission, filed on 15 December 1997, illuminates this refined strategy. It arose out of the trinational Echlin Workers' Alliance, made up of unions organised at Echlin auto distributor plants and supporting organising drives at non-union Echlin plants. Filed to assist an organising campaign, the submission alleged that an egregious set of labour rights abuses and health and safety violations had occurred at an Echlin subsidiary in Mexico, including beatings of supporters, a biased labour board, and reckless exposure of workers to harmful chemicals. Complainants numbered more than 40, including the major labour federations. The complaint requested not only resolution of the problems at the specific plant but also broader changes in Mexican labour practices such as secret ballot union elections, a public registry of existing bargaining contracts, and an effective health and safety enforcement system. The submitters actively publicised the complaint, picketed Echlin headquarters in Connecticut, and protested at shareholder meetings. They also recruited a diverse coalition of supporters and co-submitters made up of other labour unions, rights groups, advocacy groups, and faith-based supporters (Alexander 1999).

Another sign of sophistication, concern for the legitimacy of the process, is seen in the recent effort to bring in more symmetry by filing complaints against U.S. labour practices before the Mexican NAO; four of these five have been filed since 1998. Lance Compa, a leading U.S. expert on NAALC and a labour attorney activist, spearheaded an ambitious undertaking in 1998 to address the poor U.S. record at protecting the rights of migrant workers. Focussing on the apple industry in the State of Washington, Compa helped the Teamsters, FAT, and the United Farm Workers put together the most sophisticated NAALC complaint to date in terms of alleging a wide series of systematic violations in such areas as organising, health and safety, minimum wages, and discrimination. The labour movement has, in fact, expended a great deal of effort in this case and actively publicised it in both the United States and Mexico. Compa's motivation was to deflect charges of 'Mexican bashing' with respect to use of this process. 'I wanted the Mexican government to have more of a stake in the process' (Compa 1999a).

Eliciting Aggressive Judging from the NAOs

United States National Administrative Office

The U.S. NAO has been receptive to activist-submitters' complaints (see Table 13.2). The basic pattern was established at the first review, when submitters alleged obstruction of independent union-organising efforts at two plants, General Electric and Honeywell (the two cases were consolidated). The complainants pushed for a judicial, adversarial format that included public hearings, cross-examination, and power to subpoena evidence and testimony (Compa 1999a).[3] General Electric and Honeywell opposed reviewing these complaints because they did not allege a 'pattern of non-enforcement by the government of Mexico' (U.S. NAO 1994). The U.S. Council for International Business went even further by arguing that submissions must be purely

Table 13.2 Reviews by the United States National Administrative Office*

Case	Political appeal	Focus on non-enforcement	Agree to review	Finding fault
940001, 940002: Honeywell, General Electric	Yes	No	Yes	No
940003: Sony	Yes	Yes	Yes	Yes
940004: General Electric	Yes	Yes	Withdrawn	
9601: SUTSP	No	No	Yes	No
9602: Maxi-Switch	Yes	Yes	Yes	Settled
9701: Gender	Yes	Yes	Yes	Yes
9702: Han Young	Yes	Yes	Yes	Yes
9703: Itapsa (Echlin)	Yes	Yes	Yes	Yes
9801: Flight Attendants	No	No	No	
9802: Tomato/Child Labour	Yes	No	No	
9901: TAESA	No	Yes	Yes	Yes
2000-01: Auto Trim/ Custom Trim	Yes	Yes	Yes	Yes
2000-02: Duro Bag	Yes	Yes	Pending	
9803: McDonald's (Canada)	No	Yes	Yes	Settled
9804: Rural Mail Couriers	No	No	No	

* See page xxiii for a list of acronyms.

co-operative and must avoid a review of specific company practices. It opposed holding a public hearing and requested that individual company names be omitted from NAALC submissions (Potter 1994).

Complainants won the heart of this battle. The NAO accepted the complaints for review, finding no problem with targeting specific companies so long as such actions raised issues relevant to matters of labour law enforcement. It also decided that public hearings would be a standard practice. Rather than passively receiving information, the NAO solicited it from submitters, the companies, and the Mexican government, and commissioned a report from expert consultants on Mexican labour law. The NAO did, however, refrain from demanding evidence or allowing cross-examination at hearings, arguing that 'the hearing is informational rather than adversarial' and that only the NAO Secretary is entitled to ask questions (U.S. NAO Hearing 1994).

This liberal standard of review has continued, with the NAO rarely rejecting a submission for failure to state a legitimate NAALC issue. Since the first review, the NAO has held hearings close to the border and provided simultaneous translations to ease access for Mexican witnesses. Notwithstanding NAO rejoinders of engaging in informational activity, the process has come to be viewed as adversarial and quasi-judicial in the public mind. The media commonly refer to the submissions as complaints, as do the activists and even NAO officials in informal discussions (Compa 1999b).[4]

On the substantive issue, the NAO has issued forceful criticisms on six occasions and denied review or effectively absolved the complained-of party six times (including the one filed by a business group). Three other cases were withdrawn by the submitters before the hearing phase. All the successful submissions have been carefully crafted in legal terms to meet the NAALC's mandate while appealing to the political concerns of the review body's government. Legally, they have provided careful space to allegations of systematic governmental non-enforcement. For the unsuccessful cases, the issue of non-enforcement was at the periphery, with the main charge being either company wrongdoing (General Electric and Honeywell) or a bad law on the books (Sindicato Unico de Trabajadores de la Secretaría de Pesca [Single Union of Workers of the Fishing Industry, or SUTSP]).

The most salient political appeals have been directed at labour abuses by U.S.-owned companies in the *maquiladora* zone. There is general consensus among repeat participants in the process that political factors have notably shaped the U.S. NAO's willingness to judge governments and private companies aggressively. Specifically, the Clinton administration wished to show NAALC's effectiveness in order to vindicate the NAFTA compromise and to encourage support for renewal of 'fast track' authority from Congress to negotiate future trade agreements. Thus, in cases such as Han Young and Itapsa, in which submitters managed to attract high-profile attention to labour rights abuses through such means as staging media events, lobbying politicians, and picketing outside company headquarters, the NAO strongly validated almost all of the allegations. In fact, at hearings, interviews, and in public conferences, NAO officials have repeatedly boasted of the NAO's role in furthering meaningful changes in the Mexican labour law system. At the Han Young hearing, NAO secretary Irasema Garza held a media session at which she stated, 'The agreement, I believe, has contributed to an unprecedented level of scrutiny of Mexican labour law' (U.S. NAO 1998, 69–70).

The Mexican National Administrative Office

The Mexican NAO's record has been far more ambivalent than its U.S. counterpart (see Table 13.3). On the one hand, it has strongly criticised the U.S. NAO's aggressive reviews of Mexican practices. Mexico's Secretary of Labour once even went so far as to accuse the U.S. NAO of 'supporting the demands of one side in their dispute' (Dillon 1998). Its own reviews have been short and mostly descriptive, with no findings of fault. On the other hand, political appeals of submitters have borne fruit. Each complaint before Mexico has involved abuses suffered by Mexican migrant or Latino workers. In response, the Mexican NAO has accepted all submissions for review and given them further legitimacy by deeming them worthy of further intergovernmental consultation (save one that was withdrawn), despite such complaints addressing the same types of individual legal disputes it has criticised the U.S. NAO for reviewing. This susceptibility to political appeals was most pronounced in the Washington apple pickers case, which attracted considerable publicity in both Mexico and the United States (see Velasco 1998; Moore 1998). To show its enhanced concern, the Mexican NAO took the extra step of holding an informative session with migrant workers, the closest it has come to holding a public hearing.

Table 13.3 Reviews by the Mexican National Administrative Office[a]

Case	Political appeal	Focus on non-enforcement	Agree to review	Finding fault
9501: Sprint	Yes	Yes	Yes	Partial[b]
9801: Solec	Yes	Yes	Yes	Partial
9802: Apple	Yes	Yes	Yes	Partial
9803: Decoster Egg	Yes	Yes	Yes	Partial
9804: Yale/INS	Yes	Yes	Withdrawn	

a See page xxiii for a list of acronyms.
b Partial indicates recommending further intergovernmental consultations while refraining from findings of fault.

The Canadian National Administrative Office

Fewer insights can be gathered about the Canadian NAO given the small number of submissions to date (see Table 13.4).[5] The National Labor Relations Board (NLRB) case was brought by a business lobby and made no attempt to address enforcement issues. The Immigration and Nationalization Service (INS) case concerning the practice of the U.S. Department of Labor to share information on undocumented workers with the INS was withdrawn early after the Department of Labor agreed to discontinue this practice (Human Rights Watch 2001). In the one full-blown, substantive case brought by activists, the Canadian NAO was as receptive procedurally and substantively as the U.S. NAO has been, holding a public hearing and issuing strong findings.

The Results of the Process

Success against Mexican labour practices Success in the filing of NAALC submissions has mostly taken the form of building public support for labour rights causes, increasing access of labour movements to policy circles, strengthening parallel political campaigns, and building the movement (see Table 13.5). Two cases have, however, resulted in more tangible changes in policy. In the *maquiladora* zone case concerning treatment of pregnant workers, several U.S. companies promised to discontinue pregnancy screening of job applicants while the Mexican government instituted a program to inform women of their rights (Haq 1999). In the Han Young case, the government pressured the Tijuana labour board to reverse its decision and register an independent union — only the second independent labour union registered in the *maquiladora* zone (U.S. NAO 1999). One day after the NAO public hearing, the government fined Han Young more than US$9000, the largest fine in Mexican history, for health and safety violations (Calbreath 1999; Compa 1999a; U.S. NAO 1999). Moreover, the Mexican government agreed at ministerial consultations in May 2000 to support secret-ballot elections for union certification (United States Department

Table 13.4 Reviews by the Canadian National Administrative Office*

Case	Political appeal	Focus on non-enforcement	Agree to review	Finding fault
98-1: Itapsa	Yes	Yes	Yes	Yes
98-2: Yale/INS	Yes	Yes	Withdrawn	
99-1: LPA	No	No	No	

* See page xxiii for a list of acronyms.

of Labor 2001). Five submissions appeared to have gained almost no positive results in any form from the submitters' perspectives (labelled 'minimal' in Table 13.5).

In the mixture of factors that best promote success, the political skills and resources of the submitters are of primary importance. The most effective behaviour combines the dramatic framing of the complaints and the skilful integration of the legal argument with political tactics, such as organising and mass protests. Dramatic framing involves articulating the cause as a legal right while connecting it to stories of actual labour rights abuses, such as beatings, egregious health and safety violations, and rigged union elections. Moreover, the most successful submissions are typically well organised, involving multiple parties, and are connected to networks of activists. Such cases have included the participation of the AFL-CIO, the Canadian Labour Congress,

Table 13.5 Results of Complaints against Mexican Labour Practices[a]

Case	Effort put into case	Dramatic facts	Linked to other efforts	Positive NAO finding	Results
940001, 940002: Honeywell, General Electric	Modest	Yes	Yes	No	Minimal
940003: Sony	Modest	Yes	Yes	Yes	Minimal
9601: SUTSP	Modest	No	Yes	No	Minimal
9602: Maxi-Switch	Modest	Yes	Yes	Partial[b]	Modest
9701: Gender	Modest	Yes	Yes	Yes	Strong
9702: Han Young	High	Yes	Yes	Yes	Strong
9703: Itapsa	High	Yes	Yes	Yes	Modest
Echlin/Dana (Canada)[c]	High	Yes	Yes	Yes	Modest
9801: Flight Attendants	Minimal	No	No	No	Minimal
9802: Tomato/Child Labour	Minimal	Yes	Yes	No	Minimal
9901: TAESA	Modest	No	Yes	Yes	Pending
2000-01 Auto Trim/ Custom Trim	High	Yes	Yes	Yes	Pending
2000-02: Duro Bag	Modest	No	Yes	Pending	Pending

a See page xxiii for a list of acronyms.

b The NAO's review of the complaint and scheduling of a hearing along the Mexican border prompted a settling of the case, but the NAO did not file a report.

c Echlin/Dana was an added complaint filed at the initiative of Canadian activists to gauge the attitude of the Canadian NAO.

and the recently formed Unión Nacional de Trabajadores (National Union of Workers [UNT]), an independent labour federation in Mexico. These groups (at least the first two) are very skilled at generating media attention and drawing support from prominent political figures in the legislative and executive branches of government.

Also critical to activists' success has been strong validation by the review body. Only one case (Sony) with a strong finding of fault failed to yield any meaningful results from the perspective of the submitters. By contrast, no case with a weak or negative NAO finding has achieved even modest results.

The importance of NAO validation should not obscure the significance of the efforts of activists. The Maxi-Switch case illustrates the importance of linking favourable NAO actions to sustained political activism. This case was filed by the Communication Workers of America (CWA) and the Sindicato de Telefonistas de la República Mexicana (Union of Mexican Telephone Workers [STRM]) to assist an organising campaign at a *maquiladora* plant. The campaign, which alleged suppression of union organising, was well framed and promoted. The plant was located at the site of a celebrated strike in Mexican history (Sepulveda 1999). The AFL-CIO actively publicised the case and underlying dispute. Such efforts seemed to pay off. Just before a scheduled public hearing along the border, the state governor pressed the labour board to register the STRM affiliate in exchange for submitters dropping the complaint (Nagel 1997). But the STRM leadership neglected to follow up on this victory by helping the subsequent campaign gain collective bargaining rights. As a result, the union eventually disbanded in the face of continuing resistance from Maxi-Switch and the state government (Sepulveda 1999; see also Collier 1997).

Success against U.S. and Canadian labour practices Mexican NAO validation has played a lesser role in prompting success, given that it has made no findings casting blame but has only recommended ministerial consultations. Of greater importance have been submitters' efforts in publicising complaints in the U.S. and Mexican media. Table 13.6 indicates the results of complaints about the United States and Canada, with the first two cases concerning Canada and the rest directed toward U.S. practices.

This dynamic is especially evident in the apple workers case. Complainants raised a series of systematic problems, including deficiencies with the NLRB system and the State of Washington's health and safety system as well as inadequate legal recourse for migrant workers to enforce their rights to join a union. Submitters actively promoted the case before the U.S. and Mexican media, leading to considerable publicity about the poor record of the United States in protecting the rights of migrant workers. Such efforts pushed the state to increase funding for the monitoring of farm-working conditions and influenced one company, Stemilt, to agree to card checking (gaining signatures from a majority of workers) instead of much more cumbersome elections to determine union certification.[6] The Teamsters won the card-checking campaign, the first successful union campaign in the state's apple industry (Davila 1999). All these actions occurred before the NAO issued its report. Of course, the very decision of the Mexican NAO to hold an informative session also increased the stature of the complaint and attracted prominent press attention.

Even for the less ambitious cases, the very invocation of this process has embarrassed the government agency in question to take remedial action. In the INS-Department of Labor collusion case, the filing of the complaints before both the Mexican and Canadian NAOs prompted the U.S. Department of Labor to discontinue its policy of submitting information on undocumented workers (who are complaining about labour rights violations) to the INS (Human Rights Watch 2001). In the Solec case, the allegations of collusion between Solec, a producer of solar panels, and the California Occupational Safety and Health Agency (CAL-OSHA) in not prosecuting health and safety violations prompted the federal Occupational Safety and Health Agency to investigate the CAL-OSHA system and inspect the Solec plant (Karesh 1999). This shame-through-invoking dynamic has been seen in Canada as well. The filing of the McDonald's case, concerning failure of Quebec law to prohibit anti–union-motivated plant closings, was thought to shame the Quebec government into action. In addition, an earlier threat to file a NAALC action against the Province of Alberta influenced the government to withdraw its plan to privatise the enforcement of health and safety standards ('Province's Halt of Privatization Plan Ends Looming NAFTA Complaint' 1996).

Assessing the broader cumulative results Are attitudes more conducive to advancing labour causes, consistent with the expectations raised in the theoretical literature on soft law channels (Weiss 1999; Victor 1997)? On the Mexican front, the record is encouraging,

Table 13.6 Results of Complaints against the United States and Canada*

Case	Effort put into case	Dramatic facts	Linked to other efforts	Positive NAO finding	Results
McDonald's (U.S. 9803)	Modest	Yes	Yes	Partial	Strong
Rural Mail Couriers (U.S. 9804)	High	No	Yes	No	Minimal
Sprint (Mexico 9501)	High	Yes	Yes	Partial	Minimal
Solec (Mexico 9801)	Modest	Yes	Yes	Partial	Modest
Apple (Mexico 9802)	High	Yes	Yes	Partial	Strong
Decoster Egg (Mexico 9803)	Minimal	Yes	Yes	Partial	Minimal
Yale/INS (Mexico 9804)	Strong	Yes	Yes	Withdrawn	
Yale/INS (Canada 98-2)	High	Yes	Yes	Withdrawn	Strong
LPA (Canada 99-1)	Minimal	No	No	No	Minimal

* See page xxiii for a list of acronyms.

if still limited. While frustrated with the paucity of hard results, submitters have generally credited the process with helping to open up political debate in Mexico on collusion between government and labour unions and with bolstering the voice and status of independent labour activists. The NAO findings that the Mexican government fails to enforce its legal protections have, in effect, forced it to honour its laws guaranteeing free and independent association. The result has been official and publicly held discussions with independent labour movements and rights groups. This achievement is not to be disregarded in light of Mexico's history of closed governance and preference for official groups (Hamilton 1982; Middlebrook 1995). Not only do opposition groups such as FAT and the ANAD receive more attention in the Mexican press, but they also share the stage with Mexican official unions and Mexican officials at public hearings and seminars, arranged as part of intergovernmental consultations. Maria Estela Rios (1999), of ANAD, observes that prior to the Sony case, she and other ANAD activists had never had a direct meeting with prominent governmental officials. Of more far-reaching potential is the commitment by the Mexican government to support secret-ballot union certification elections on a routine basis.

In the United States the process has been less dramatic, but it has nonetheless brought public attention to a few persistent domestic labour problems. For example, on the closing of a telemarketing facility following a union-organising drive in 1995, complainants against Sprint drew attention to companies' illegal threats to relocate plants to avoid unionization, although the complainants attained no concrete results (see, for example, Goldberg 1996). As a result of ministerial consultations, the NAALC Secretariat commissioned a study to document the rise of this practice since the passage of NAFTA (Bronfenbrenner 1997). The AFL-CIO used this study to aid its successful campaign before Congress in 1997 to defeat President Clinton's bid for fast-track renewal for negotiating trade agreements without modifications (Lee 1999). Moreover, the round of cases in 1998, especially the apple workers case, prompted added concern for migrant labour conditions. Notably, in May 2000 the U.S. government agreed to hold public fora and outreach sessions with migrant workers and community groups on the inadequacies of U.S. laws in this area. Such sessions may have long-term significance in advancing conditions for migrant workers.

Finally, NAALC's intergovernmental set-up has deepened cross-border collaboration over time, especially among U.S. and Mexican labour activists. A number of labour movements and rights groups have developed new cross-border contacts through this process. Such contacts have expanded in recent years with the onset of plaintiff stacking. In addition, the need to exchange detailed information on each country's laws and actual practices has sharpened cross-border awareness even among activists with pre-existing contacts on both sides of the borders. Indeed, participants have consistently credited the review process with greatly increasing their understanding of the conditions and obstacles facing their cross-border collaborators (Lujon 1999; Beatty 1999; Compa 1999a; Rios 1999).

Conclusion

The NAALC's complaint mechanism matters but not in the conventional legal sense of generating rulings that produce immediate changes in behaviour. Rather, the process matters through the invocation of legal process and legal argumentation by labour rights activists as an added political weapon to boost broader campaigns. NAO rulings are not the sole criteria for measuring success. The political efforts occur throughout the process, from the framing of the complaint, the mobilisation of allies and favourable publicity, and the marshalling of political and legal arguments at the hearings to post-ruling efforts to promote the ruling and exploit the public agenda-raising opportunities offered by ministerial consultation.

Without discounting the unique factual patterns of the social and political cultures in North America, it is nonetheless helpful to suggest some tentative generalisations on the impact of other trade-linked soft law agreements on labour standards. The record of the NAALC review process suggests that such channels will be primarily employed by social activists to assist ongoing political and legal campaigns at home. The factors most likely to give substance to soft law mechanisms are sustained political engagement by activists, receptive review-implementing bodies, and targets susceptible to international shame campaigns. For countries that lack a tradition of independent activism and where appeals to legal rights carry little resonance, NAALC-like channels may register little impact. Nevertheless, the willingness of a number of Mexican activists to invoke the NAALC procedure indicates that neither a highly developed civil society nor a legal rights culture is essential.[7] In fact, the Mexican record conforms to other recent studies showing a growing legal rights culture taking place among civil societies in many parts of the developing world (Ellmann 1998; Risse and Sikkink 1999). Similarly, the receptivity shown by the NAOs is likely to be demonstrated by other trade-linked review bodies as well in order to demonstrate sensitivity to growing public anxieties over the negative social ramifications of international trade-investment agreements.

Although semi-authoritarian countries, such as Mexico, seeking to trumpet their liberal democratic credentials may be most vulnerable, the NAALC experience indicates that well-focussed, sustained soft law mobilisation can succeed against established liberal democracies. Indeed, the fact that so many governments, in all continents, have made a point of ratifying core labour standards of the International Labour Organization suggests a widespread concern for international image that can be primed for political effect by committed activists through soft-law social channels (see Organisation for Economic Co-operation and Development 1996).

To be sure, NAALC-like channels may be of negligible importance in societies less receptive to legal rights appeals, less supportive of labour causes, and lacking in independent activism. NAALC, itself, has notable limitations. Although a number of activists have come to appreciate NAALC's value, they strongly desire a harder mechanism with the rulings that are regarded as binding and noncompliers that are sanctioned. As it now stands, even the biggest victories come with qualifications, such as at Han Young where the registered independent union is still struggling to gain actual bargaining rights. George Becker, president of the United Steelworkers, summarises the mixed attitude of submitters: 'This is our strongest weapon to expose the horrors facing workers who try to organize in Mexico, and we vigorously pursue such cases. But at the end of the day, dozens of workers have still lost their jobs' ('NAFTA Report Cites Dana Corp. In Small Step for Justice in Mexico' 1999).

But harder labour linkages are probably not in the cards for the near-term future. Moreover, many of the NAALC's inadequacies arise less from its nonbinding nature and more from the broader structural disadvantages of labour movements in a world of increasingly mobile investors. Independent Mexican labour advocates observe that their biggest obstacle is confronting the Mexican government's overarching desire to attract foreign investment through offering a cheap and relatively pliant labour force (regardless of the party in power). The NAALC will never serve as a primary vehicle for altering this imbalance. It can, however, serve as a useful complement to a broader political strategy. At the very least, as remarked by one repeat submitter, NAALC can serve as 'a small finger in a big hole in a large dike' (Haq 1999). Given the incremental nature of politics, such a function is not to be discounted. Labour and other activists will likely continue to pursue a dual-track strategy of condemning the softness of NAALC-like channels while filing politically potent complaints to boost ongoing campaigns.

Notes

1 It is still too early to determine what effect the election of a president from the Partido Acción Nacional (PAN) will have on Mexico's labour union system. Independent labour activists have, however, found the PAN state government in Chihuahua to be as discriminatory as the PRI, nationally, against independent unions (Alexander 1999, 143).
2 The *maquiladora* zone is the area in Mexico along the U.S. border where mostly U.S.-based companies operate *maquilas* (plants) that produce tariff-free goods for export to the United States.
3 The U.S. NAO formally adopted its procedures on 1 April 1994 (U.S. NAO 1994).
4 Lance Lewis Karesh (1999), Deputy Secretary of the U.S. NAO (at the time of writing, Acting Secretary), compared these submissions to complaints.
5 Canada only became a full party to NAALC, entitled to conduct reviews, in 1997.
6 Although a number of factors provoked Stemilt's decision, in the course of negotiations the company did ask whether the NAO case 'would go away' (Compa 1999a).
7 Historically, Mexico has had a weak civil society due to the efforts of the long ruling party, the PRI, to co-opt labour movements, farmers, indigenous groups, and other civil actors (Hamilton 1982; Middlebrook 1995). Recently, however, an independent civil society has grown and is likely to receive a further boost with the first loss ever by the PRI of the presidency.

References

Abbott, Kenneth W. and Duncan Snidal (2000). 'Hard and Soft Law in International Governance'. *International Organization* vol. 54, no. 3, pp. 421–456.

Alexander, Robin (1999). 'Experience and Reflections on the Use of the NAALC'. In Encuentro Trinacional de Laboralistas Democráticos, ed., *Memorias: Encuentro Trinacional de Laboralistas Democráticos*. Universidad Nacional Autonoma de México, Mexico City.

Anderson, Sarah, John Cavanagh, and David Ranney (1996). 'NAFTA: Trinational Fiasco'. *The Nation* vol. 263, no. 3, pp. 26–29.

Beatty, Tim (1999). Interview with author. 9 August.

Bronfenbrenner, Katie (1997). 'We'll Close! Plant Closing Threats, Union Organizing and NAFTA'. *Multinational Monitor* vol. 18, pp. 8–13.

Calbreath, Dean (1999). 'Mexico Fines Han Young as Hyundai Is Drawn into Fight'. *San Diego Union Tribune*, 28 April.

Charnovitz, Steve (1997). 'Two Centuries of Participation: NGOs and International Governance'. *Michigan Journal of International Law* vol. 18, no. 2, pp. 183–286.

Collier, Robert (1997). 'NAFTA Labor Problems Haunt New Trade Debate'. *San Francisco Chronicle*, 10 September. p. A1.

Compa, Lance (1999a). Interview with author, Washington DC. 7 June.

Compa, Lance (1999b). 'The North American Agreement on Labor Cooperation and International Labor Solidarity'. In Encuentro Trinacional de Laboralistas Democráticos, ed., *Memorias: Encuentro Trinacional de Laboralistas Democráticos*. Universidad Nacional Autonoma de México, Mexico City.

Davila, Florangela (1999). 'Judge Confirms Teamsters' Victory'. *Seattle Times*, 20 October. p. B4.

Dillon, Sam (1998). 'Bias Said to Hurt Independent Mexican Unions'. *New York Times*, 30 April. p. A8.

Dupuy, Pierre-Marie (1988). 'Remarks, a Hard Look at Soft Law (Panel Discussion)'. *American Society of International Law Proceedings* vol. 82, pp. 381–386.

Ellmann, Stephen (1998). 'Cause Lawyering in the Third World'. In A. Sarat and S. Scheingold, eds., *Cause Lawyering: Political Commitments and Professional Responsibilities*. Oxford University Press, New York.

Encuentro Trinacional de Laboralistas Democráticos (1999). *Memorias: Encuentro Trinacional de Laboralistas Democráticos*. Universidad Nacional Autonoma de México, Mexico City.

Goldberg, Carey (1996). 'U.S. Labor Making Use of Trade Accord It Fiercely Opposed'. *New York Times*, 28 February. p. A11.

Hamilton, Nora (1982). *The Limits of State Autonomy: Post-Revolutionary Mexico*. Princeton University Press, Princeton.

Haq, Farhan (1999). 'Labour: NAFTA Body Gets Mixed Reviews'. *Inter Press Service*. 10 March.

Human Rights Watch (2001). 'Trading Away Rights: The Unfulfilled Promise of Nafta's Labour Side Agreement'. *Canada/Mexico/United States* vol. 13 (April), p. 2B. <www.hrw.org/reports/2001/nafta> (December 2001).

Karesh, Lewis (1999). Interview with author. 9 June, Washington DC.

Leary, Virginia (1997). 'Nonbinding Accords in the Field of Labor'. In E. B. Weiss, ed., *International Compliance with Nonbinding Accords*. American Society of International Law, Washington DC.

Lee, Thea (1999). Interview with author, Washington DC. 10 June.

Lujon, Bertha (1999). Interview with author, Mexico City. 16 March.

Middlebrook, Kevin (1995). *The Paradox of Revolution: Labor, the State and Authoritarianism in Mexico*. Johns Hopkins University Press, Baltimore.

Moore, Molly (1998). 'Mexican Farmhands Accuse U.S. Firms'. *Washington Post*, 3 December. p. A36.

'NAFTA Report Cites Dana Corp. in Small Step for Justice in Mexico' (1999). *PR Newswire*, 22 March.

Nagel, John (1997). 'NAFTA: Mexican Labor Group Calls for Action Following Victory in Maxi-Switch Campaign'. *Daily Labor Report*, 28 April. p. d12.

Organisation for Economic Co-operation and Development (1996). *Trade, Employment, and Labour Standards: A Study of Core Workers' Rights and International Trade*. Organisation for Economic Co-operation and Development, Paris.

Potter, Edward (1994). Letter to U.S. National Administrative Office. U.S. Council for International Business. 31 August, on file with U.S. National Administrative Office.

'Province's Halt of Privatization Plan Ends Looming NAFTA Complaint' (1996). *Inside NAFTA*. 25 December, p. 14.

Rios, Maria Estela (1999). Interview with author, Mexico City. 12 August.

Risse, Thomas and Kathryn Sikkink (1999). 'The Socialization of Human Rights Norms and Domestic Practices: Introduction'. In T. Risse, S. Ropp and K. Sikkink, eds., *The Power of Principles: International Human Rights Norms and Domestic Change*. Cambridge University Press, Cambridge, UK.

Sepulveda, Alicia (1999). Interview with author, Mexico City. 16 August.

Szasz, Paul C. (1999). 'General Law-Making Processes'. In C. C. Joyner, ed., *The United Nations and International Law*. American Society of International Law and Cambridge University Press, Cambridge, MA.

Torres, Blanca (1996). 'Redes y Coaliciones en el Proceso de Negociacion y Aprobacion del Tratado de Libre Comercio de America del Norte'. In A. Borja, G. Gonzalez and B. J. R. Stevenson, eds., *Regionalismo y Poder en America: Los Limites del Neorrealismo*. CIDE, Mexico City.

United States Department of Labor (2001). 'Status of Submissions'. 19 September. <www.dol.gov/dol/ilab/public/programs/nao/status.htm> (December 2001).

United States National Administrative Office (1994). *Public Report of Review*. 12 October.

United States National Administrative Office (1998). Public Hearing on Submission 9702. 18 February.

United States National Administrative Office (1999). 'Report'. 28 April.

United States National Administrative Office Hearing (1994). 12 September.

Velasco, Elizabeth (1998). 'Trabajadores Agricolas Denuncian Explotación en E.U.' *La Jornada*, 3 December. p. 41.

Victor, David G. (1997). The Use and Effectiveness of Nonbinding Instruments in the Management of Complex International Environmental Problems. Proceedings of the Annual Meeting-American Society of International Law.

Weiss, Edith Brown (1999). 'Understanding Compliance with International Environmental Agreements: The Baker's Dozen Myths'. *University of Richmond Law Review* vol. 32, no. 5, pp. 1555–1589.

Wellens, K. C. and G. M. Borchardt (1989). 'Soft Law in European Community Law'. *European Law Review* vol. 14, no. 5, pp. 267–321.

Young, Oran R. (1998). *Creating Regimes: Arctic Accords and International Governance*. Cornell University Press, Ithaca.

PART V
ASSESSING
ENVIRONMENTAL EFFECTS:
LOCAL, NORTH AMERICAN,
AND GLOBAL PERSPECTIVES

Chapter 14

Understanding the Environmental Effects of Trade: Some Lessons from NAFTA

Scott Vaughan[1]

When the Berlin Wall tumbled, its fall came to symbolise the twin triumph of democracy and free markets. A decade later, as the wall went up in Quebec City during the April 2001 Summit of the Americas meeting, that wall came to symbolise the widening divide between the voice of popular democracy and the architects of free markets.

The growing wedge between economic policies and democracy challenges a fairly entrenched view that economic prosperity and democratic freedom are inseparable. Work by Seymour Lipset (1959) and others shows that economic growth and prosperity stimulate democracy in several ways, through higher levels of education, an enlarged middle class, the fostering of public institutions and tools to curb corruption, to name but a few. Subsequent empirical work also demonstrates a strong correlation between increased gross domestic product (GDP) per capita and the strengthening of democracy (Barro 1999).

Given this link, many policy analysts remain mystified about the breadth of public grievance about the durability of democracy to withstand economic globalisation. Indeed, politicians point to increased rates of economic growth — on average — that have been fuelled by trade liberalisation, increased foreign investment, and other forms of globalisation. This chapter will first examine some of the general concerns found in the debates over globalisation and trade liberalisation and then focus on the specific environmental concerns related to the North American Free Trade Agreement (NAFTA). The final part of the chapter will review some of the most recent empirical evidence on the environmental effects of NAFTA and attempt to determine whether NAFTA has been 'good' or 'bad' for the environment.

Globalisation Concerns

One reason for mounting public concern about globalisation is the increasingly uneven distribution of prosperity. While income growth and prosperity have occurred in most countries that have enacted liberalisation policies, a different picture emerges when one looks beyond average or aggregate levels of economic performance. For example, in all three NAFTA countries — Canada, Mexico, and the United States — a widening gap in income levels continues between the rich and the poor. Integration in the global economy, propelled by free trade and other policies, is not yielding the kind of conditional economic convergence upon which comparative advantage assumptions are grounded. (Under that theory of convergence, it is assumed that as countries become more open to trade and other kinds of economic exchange and market integration, differences in GDP per capita narrow and income levels eventually converge.)

Recent economic evidence points to a divergence — rather than convergence — in per capita income within North America. For example, earnings inequality between higher wage and lower wage groups in Canada and the United States has remained wide over the past two decades, although that gap widened marginally faster in the U.S. than in Canada during this period. Recent work suggests that the poorest three fifths of households in Canada made less at the end of the 1990s than they did a decade before, when the Canada-United States Free Trade Agreement (FTA) was signed. In terms of wealth accumulation, the wealthiest one fifth of Canadian households saw their assets grow by almost 40 percent from 1984 to 1999, while the poorest one fifth of Canadian households saw asset values actually contract. A similar pattern is taking place in the United States, in which the income of the poorest one fifth of households has contracted by 2.4 percent in the past decade.

Similarly, evidence points to a growing gap in earning levels within Mexico, with the most pronounced divergence occurring between the northern and southern states of Mexico. What is most disturbing about the Mexican situation is that this gap is taking place both in relative terms — the rich are growing at a faster pace than the poor — and also, more importantly, at the absolute level — the poor appear to have undergone an absolute loss in income in certain southern regions of Mexico since NAFTA.

The widening gap in wage earnings in North America tends to mirror a trend underway (albeit in a somewhat less pointed way). On a global level, the income gap between rich and poor countries has widened rather than narrowed in the past two decades. Today, that gap is described even in a recent report of the World Trade Organization (WTO) (2000) as 'huge'. Richer countries grow much faster than poorer ones, and income disparities between developed and developing countries on average are widening.[2]

At first blush, the gap between rich and poor — which provides insight into part of the public's misgivings about globalisation — does not seem to have much to do with the debate about free trade and the environment. However, the income question is directly relevant for two broad reasons. First, it has been recognised since before the 1972 United Nations Stockholm Conference that poverty is a leading cause and effect of environmental degradation. An argument for free trade is not only that it contributes to an overall increase in wealth, but also that wealth expansion directly alleviates poverty. Poverty alleviation, in turn, can help reduce environmental degradation. To illustrate this link, in making the case for a new trade round under the WTO, the *Financial Times* recently noted that 'a successful liberalisation drive could increase growth by Dollars 600bn and a particularly welcome boost to poor countries' ('Vital Trade Round' 2001).

The environmental argument that more precisely aligns greater prosperity to environmental improvements is widely referred to as the environmental Kuznets curve hypothesis. Following initial work by economists Gene Grossman and Alan Krueger (1995) in forwarding the hypothesis that some rates of pollution emission reverse course — from an increase at lower per capita GDP levels to a flattening and decrease at higher income levels — a very lively debate has continued about what these observations actually mean. Analyses based on the Grossman-Krueger work suggest that for some environmental indicators, such as sulphur dioxide, oxides of nitrogen, or suspended particulate matter, a downward trajectory (or improvement) can be identified as per capita income increase. At the same time, analysis suggests that as GDP moves from lower to middle income levels, pollution emissions proceed toward a second turning point, at which emissions tend to stabilise or move toward a slight ascent (Grossman and Krueger 1995; Hettige, Mani, and Wheeler 2000). Other studies (Kaufmann et al. 1998) have noted that at higher levels, certain indicators, such as sulphur dioxide, undergo an absolute increase, moving from the assumed inverted U-shaped curve to an N-shaped curve. Further studies have then shown that for other kinds of environmental indicators — notably carbon dioxide emissions and rates of loss of biodiversity — there appears to a continuous increase in emissions or degradation with growth in GDP per capita, thereby refuting the Kuznets curve hypothesis (Galeotti and Lanza 1999).

The hypothesis has proven to be a useful way to think about the relationship between economic prosperity and the environment. Empirical analysis shows that measuring environmental effects related to the economy reveals non-uniform changes in indicators of environmental quality. Put simply, some environmental indicators improve as income rises, while others — notably carbon dioxide (the principal greenhouse gas) or biodiversity — provide little or no evidence that a uniform decoupling of rates of economic growth and environmental change always occurs. Put another way, the notion that a country can always grow out of its environmental problems is not backed by evidence.

The environmental Kuznets curve hypothesis, when placed against recent economic data, drives home a simple point: economic growth — if it does occur — brings with it both environmental gains and environmental costs. Like other kinds of economic policy reforms, free trade brings mixed outcomes. There are winners and losers in the global economy, measured both at the firm and sector-specific level, as well as when measuring changes in environmental indicators. This issue of winners and losers becomes even more mixed and complex in light of environmental quality issues, where evidence points to very uneven income distribution between and within countries.

The second very general aspect of the debate about globalisation that has provided insight the trade-environment debate (and vice versa) relates to public policy safety nets. There is growing concern that globalisation is not simply about the integration of markets. It also raises questions about the integration of public policies, whereby public policy intervention is increasingly constrained in addressing such issues as income gaps, social dislocation, or environmental degradation that occur during the transitional periods of liberalisation. Although market integration may accelerate rates of economic growth at the aggregate level, it makes it simultaneously more difficult for domestic policy to implement equity-based social policies, including those related to education, health care, pension security, minimum wage levels, and the environment and conservation — the very processes that are supposed to arise from economic prosperity and that Lipset noted support democracy.

Among the reasons national governments feel constrained to implement equity-based policies is the concern that in so doing, they will either distort or undermine their competitiveness in tightening global markets or will run afoul of a new set of international economic rules being devised to accelerate economic growth. Increased capital mobility, one of the key attributes of globalisation, makes it more difficult for governments to tax capital, and in response many countries have shifted tax policies to labour.[3]

The paradox facing public policy is perhaps most starkly revealed when one turns away from aggregate levels of increased prosperity — tailed by the International Monetary Fund (IMF) on a regular basis by way of per capita GDP — and the reality of a permanent underclass of people within many industrialised countries, unable to find their place in the new economy. Average rates of economic growth mean very little for families and communities, regions, and sectors.

Polarisation of the Debate over NAFTA

The task of disentangling observations about average or aggregate levels of either environmental or economic change from particular areas of change — although hardly new to either environmental or economic policy — has been unfamiliar to the trade-environment debate. Indeed, a great deal of the rhetoric about trade-environment issues is based on a highly polarised debate waged between the environment 'versus' free trade, or vice versa. Although the debate has become more informed and nuanced on both sides in recent years, the initial friction explains some of the more strident opposition of environmental groups to NAFTA, the WTO, and, more recently, the Free Trade Area of the Americas (FTAA).

This polarisation related to NAFTA began in the early 1990s. Supporters of the free trade agreement — essentially from government and business — promised that NAFTA would be uniformly good for the economy, and in turn good (or at least neutral) for the environment. Advocates of NAFTA promised that free trade would deliver higher levels of economic prosperity in all three countries, leading in a linear manner to higher rates of per capita GDP, more jobs, better jobs, and other kinds of prosperity.

Environmentalists responded in kind, asserting that NAFTA would be bad for the environment. The divisive debate about the assumed environmental effects of NAFTA generally broke out into four categories.

First, as free trade expands total economic activity, increased pressures are placed on the natural environment, both through increased requirements for resource inputs such as the energy, or timber or freshwater resources needed to fuel expanded production, as well as increased hazardous wastes or toxic releases generated from production. Although scale effects can be partially mitigated by technological fixes, they cannot be offset entirely. Moreover, as trade liberalisation prompts the reallocation of productive resources through specialisation, as well as through scale economies, the concentration of economic activities places even more pressure on the environment.

Second, as free trade sharpens the competitiveness of domestic markets now exposed to world competition, pressure increases at the company level to minimise environmental expenditures, in exactly the same way that all sunk costs are avoided. This concern of domestic industries is transmitted to governments, which move to relax the monitoring and enforcement of environmental regulations in order to keep companies at home. This argument bears a striking resemblance to the jobs-versus-environment debates of the 1970s, with the playing field expanded by trade liberalisation. The shorthand terms for these assertions are 'the race to the bottom' and 'regulatory chill'.

Third, if domestic governments maintain strict environmental regulations in the face of increased market competition, companies — responding to capital mobility opportunities — will leave countries with high environmental regulations (or enforcement) and move to countries with either no regulations or no enforcement of those regulations. The shorthand for this hypothesis is the 'pollution haven effect'.

Finally, even if governments reject competitiveness concerns and maintain environmental regulations, those regulations are likely to run afoul of trade law. Hard-fought protection for the environment, human health, food safety, and wildlife and the conservation of renewable resources such as fresh water and forests are predicted to collide with trade rules. The aftermath of that collision almost always involves the trumping of trade law. Areas of particular concern include the effects of NAFTA Agreements on Technical Barriers to Trade (TBT) and Sanitary and Phytosanitary Measures (SPS) on domestic environmental provisions.

If the trade community was guilty of overselling the economic gains of NAFTA, the environmental community was equally guilty of overstating its environmental costs. Unfortunately, the good versus bad NAFTA debate — in displaying an astonishing disregard about the basic functioning of trade and environmental policy — undercut the prospects of the informed dialogue upon which policy co-ordination of any kind must be built.

Free traders promised that NAFTA would lead to uniformly higher rates of economic growth across the board, but they failed to point out that free trade brings with it economic costs as well. The effects of trade liberalisation on any economy are largely indirect, and entail mainly the reorganisation of capital and labour into areas that yield higher rates of return at international prices. In this reorganisation, some sectors expand as they take advantage of new export opportunities. Other sectors contract as they buckle in the face of international competition. On balance, trade liberalisation is supposed to deliver more economic winners than losers, leading to general welfare gains evenly (and thinly) spread across the economy. However, to say that NAFTA (or any trade accord) would ensure only economic benefits has more to do with marketing than with economic reality.

In hindsight, among the most notable assertion fielded to sell NAFTA was that it would lead directly and uniformly to economic growth, in the same way that free trade always leads to economic growth. For example, in supporting U.S. fast-track authority, the Emergency Committee for American Trade — a coalition of U.S. business groups — recently argued that 'trade liberalization agreements globally, bilaterally, and regionally is essential to promoting our economic growth and to building a higher standard of living for American workers and their families' (Emergency Committee for American Trade 2001). In pointing to a strong causal link between trade liberalisation and economic growth, many environmentalists, worried about past trends in which economic growth led to depleted resource stocks, displaced rural communities, or pollution, in turn identified free trade as the catalyst for all kinds of environmental woes. And hence the causality debate began, with a great deal of work on attempting to clarify a direct relationship between free trade and environmental change — and with free traders arguing that no causal link could be established.

The free traders were right to a point. It is hard, although certainly far from impossible, to delineate specific environmental effects from specific trade accords like NAFTA. But then free traders already knew this going into the NAFTA marketing campaign, because any direct causal link between free trade itself and economic growth is weak. True, an extensive body of literature shows an indirect, dynamic, and complex relationship between trade liberalisation and economic growth. There is also a strong body of literature that reveals that countries that adopt more open sorts of economic policies tend to grow faster than countries that maintain closed economic policies.[4]

However, a statistically robust linear relationship between trade and economic growth is mixed or weak. This contrasts with other strongly established causal links explaining growth, notably foreign direct or other investment, increases in physical and human capital, technological progress, and the structure of institutions and incentives under which investment and technological innovation accelerate rates of productivity growth.

While debates about the determinants of economic growth are divided between neoclassical and endogenous growth models, more recent rates and patterns of economic growth that occurred in particular in the past decade challenge assumptions about the drivers, cycles, and trajectory of economic performance over the long term.

For example, the cautious Bank for International Settlements (BIS) recently wondered if the productive capacity of the U.S. economy — which in the 1990s surpassed records set in the 1970s and 1980s — was experiencing some kind of new and permanent level of increase (Bank for International Settlements 2000). Among the new drivers of economic growth is the current revolution in information technologies. E-commerce represented US$127 billion in transactions in 1998, with forecasts suggesting they would surpass US$1.4 trillion by 2003. The effects of technological innovation on productivity growth has led (according to Alan Greenspan [2000] of the U.S. Federal Reserve Bank) to a period of rapid innovation, in which 'something profoundly different from the typical postwar business cycle' appears to be underway.

The point is that in pinpointing key determinants of economic growth, trade liberalisation is not the dominant factor by almost any measure. However, efforts to sell the benefits of NAFTA and free trade led to exaggerated claims about the contribution trade always makes in support of long-term economic growth. In addition, from a policy debate perspective, they also provided the focus for environmentalists who were worried about the accelerating pace of environmental degradation, and were searching for underlying economic causes.

On the environmental side, assertions that overall environmental impacts (by any measure) would be 'bad' ignored a fact that environmental indicators remain incapable of stating: whether on average, environmental quality — like per capita GDP — is getting better or worse. Environmental indicators continue to be aggregated, so that one can get an approximate insight into whether air quality (composed, for example, of emissions of oxides of nitrogen, oxides of sulphur, carbon monoxide, particulate matter, carbon dioxide, smog, or toxic chemicals) is improving or worsening. Despite efforts by various groups and organisations to bring forward composite environmental indicators, assertions that overall environmental quality is 'good' or 'bad' in its own right remain faint at best, while assertions that NAFTA was primarily responsible for environmental problems seemed divorced from what is actually known about environmental change.[5]

A decade into the trade-environment debate, the polarisation that marked its early stages has been tempered. A more informed debate is emerging, both because the methods to assess trade-environment links have improved and because case studies are providing an expanding empirical base on which to learn. These studies include work by the World Wildlife Fund International (1998), the series of extremely useful country-case studies sponsored by United Nations Environmental Programme (UNEP) (1999a, 1999b, 1999c, 1999d, 1999e), and case studies supported by the Commission for Environmental Cooperation (CEC) (1999), as well as growing body of academic research in this area.

Application of an Analytical Framework

A recent contribution to the work on assessing the environmental effects of trade in general, and the NAFTA in particular, was the North American Symposium on Assessing the Environmental Effects of Trade. The symposium, organised by the CEC — the environmental side accord to the NAFTA established by the governments of Canada, Mexico, and the United States in 1994 — was held in October 2000 at the World Bank in Washington DC. The two-day meeting brought together more than 300 environmental and trade experts, development analysts, private sector representatives, and government representatives from environment, trade, industry, and other departments from Canada, Mexico and the United States, as well as representatives of several international organisations involved in the ongoing trade and environment debate (for example, the Secretariat of the WTO, UNEP, the Organisation for Economic Co-operation and Development, and others). The purpose was to disseminate leading research on the application of the CEC's recently completed analytical framework for assessing the environmental effects of NAFTA (CEC 1999).

The steps for applying this analytical framework start with a definition of the issue or sector under consideration, followed by a description of applicable NAFTA rules and institutions and their trade and transborder investment effects. Next, the framework examines four critical areas through which these effects can have an impact on the natural environment: processes of production, physical infrastructure, social organisation, and government policy. The final element of the framework is the identification and measurement of the resulting environmental pressures, supports, and changes to air, water, land, and living things.

The 14 research papers presented at the symposium represent the work of individuals and nongovernmental organisations (NGOs) from Canada, Mexico, and the United States. Papers were solicited by means of a public call for papers and authors were given complete editorial independence and modest financial support to conduct research. Among the welcome outcomes of this process was the creation or support of networks of NGOs and research institutes stretching across national borders. Some key lessons that emerged from the papers are noted below.

Building Transparency and Ensuring the Participation of Civil Society

Transparency and effective public consultation processes are essential to democratic governance. A useful barometer of the degree of public trust in a public policy is the extent to which that policy is developed in the context of full transparency and meaningful public participation, whereby civil society is consulted early and consulted often on key policy issues.

Nowhere is this more true than in the very public debate concerning the environmental effects of free trade and economic globalisation more generally.

A recurring theme of recent public concern about the trade and globalisation agendas is the opaque manner in which important economic policies — policies that profoundly affect not only economic issues but also social, human health, cultural, regional development, and environmental policies — are negotiated. Misgivings about the agendas of NAFTA, the WTO, and the FTAA have focussed to a large extent on the lack of transparency and public accountability of these accords and institutions.

Perhaps the single most important lesson learned at the symposium relates to *who* ought to be involved in environmental reviews of free trade. The clear message is that assessments are measurably stronger when civil society is included at the centre of this work. Environmental reviews of trade can bridge the divide between two distinct approaches to public policy formulation. Indeed, the environmental agenda finds its deepest roots in the commitment of civil society — of NGOs, community groups, and advocacy organisations — to pushing environmental values forward. The symposium confirmed that civil society is fully capable of engaging in an informed debate on a range of trade-environment issues, and has the technical expertise to undertake rigorous environmental reviews of trade.

If one turns to *what* has been learned about the environmental effects of trade thus far, the symposium provided several important insights. It is important to note that for those who looked to it to provide a final word as to whether the NAFTA has been 'all good' or 'all bad' for the environment, the results were disappointing, in that they are mixed.

Some indicators of environmental quality — for example, air pollution emissions linked to growth in road freight transport — have worsened in specific geographic areas since NAFTA. The cause of these changes can be traced back to the trade agreement. Other environmental indicators, such as changes in fish stocks or forest quality or quantity, continue to undergo increasing stress and deterioration, although a weak link has been found between NAFTA and changes in environmental quality. Still other indicators, such as the pollution per unit of industrial output for some Mexican export sectors, have shown a marginal improvement since NAFTA.

These mixed environmental results hardly lend themselves to banners for those arguing either 'against' or 'for' NAFTA and, more generally, free trade. Part of the reason why no single environmental outcome emerged from the symposium is that no single environmental indicator exists that supports general or aggregate observations that North America's environment is better or worse, let alone that links the cause of this improvement or deterioration to a trade accord. Certainly, considerable progress has been made in developing aggregate environmental indicators — ones that broadly parallel key economic indicators such as GDP. However, the day is still a long way off when one indicator, or even a composite set of indicators, is capable of telling us that overall environmental quality is better, worse, or the same.

Instead, environmental assessments are based on a number of relatively disaggregated indicators that provide insights into different kinds of environmental quality issues. Indicators include different air and water pollution indicators — including changes in oxides of sulphur, oxides of nitrogen, carbon monoxide, carbon dioxide, air-borne toxic releases, smog, ground-layer ozone, particulate matter, and other indicators. They also include other indicators that tend to be more qualitative, as well as changes in forest cover and forest quality, changes in biodiversity, changes in risks associated with toxic emissions, and so on.

A second reason for mixed outcomes from the symposium papers is that the methods and approaches of trade reviews remain distinct from the project-specific work of environmental impact assessments (EIAs). Certainly, several tools used in trade assessments have emerged over 30 years of experience in EIAs. At the same time, trade policy reform agreements such as the NAFTA, the Uruguay Round of the WTO, or the proposed FTAA present altogether different methodological problems from assessments that are specific to a project or activity. To understand these differences, it is useful to understand the broad process of trade liberalisation itself.

By contrast, indicators that suggest trade-related economic growth tend to be highly aggregated, suggesting changes at both the economy-wide and sector-specific levels. Economic changes linked to multisectoral trade accords such as NAFTA or the WTO happen simultaneously. These economic changes generally involve marginal shifts in relative prices, whereby the price wedge between domestic and world prices tends to narrow as trade liberalisation proceeds. Under trade liberalisation, some sectors expand as trade restrictions and distortions applied at the border come down, and other sectors contract once exposed to international competition. In other words, there are winners and losers within countries undergoing liberalisation. However, on balance — according to trade theory and empirical evidence — trade liberalisation leads to a marginal net gain in general welfare.

Understanding the economic effects of trade liberalisation is complicated, partly because of the asymmetrical relationship between the expansion and contraction in sector-specific economic activity. For example, a 10 percent contraction in the textiles sector may be accompanied by a 20 percent increase in certain parts of the agriculture sector, coupled with a 2 percent contraction in the steel sector. Since trade negotiations tend to emphasise multisectoral liberalisation — as opposed to sector-specific accords (there are exceptions, notably the post–Uruguay Round WTO accords on telecommunications or financial services) — many areas of economic activity change at the same time, and to differing degrees. While it is difficult to predict with precision economic outcomes among sectors, an extensive body of empirical economic research shows that on average, a country that opens up its economy will grow faster than a country that maintains a closed economy. At the same time, perhaps the most important environmental *quality* effect related to trade liberalisation relates to changes in the allocation of resources both within and between economic sectors.

As noted, the outcomes at the symposium found that the environmental effects of NAFTA have been mixed, and that changes mostly have occurred at the margins.

However, the real challenge is not to understate the consequences of environmental change at the margins, but rather to burrow below aggregate measures and pinpoint specific areas of environmental change.

Among the main observations from the CEC symposium were the following:

• Confirmation of trade-environment links: The symposium confirmed that trade liberalisation can and does affect both environmental quality and environmental policies. Effects on environmental quality tend to be indirect, and involve the complex and dynamic process by which trade liberalisation affects changes in relative prices. Effects on environmental policies tend to be more direct, and involve the threat or actual collision of trade and environmental rules. The symposium did not allay doubts about the robustness of causal links between trade liberalisation and the environment.

• Environmental effects of NAFTA-related freight transport expansion: Environmental effects at the sector-specific level are mixed. For example, a robust and direct link between free trade and changes in environmental quality exists in the area of international road freight transport. Research shows an absolute increase in air pollution concentrations at Mexico-U.S. and U.S.-Canada border crossing points due to the scale effects of increased road fright transport since NAFTA. Improvements in infrastructure in border areas have not kept pace with this expansion in freight transport, so that border traffic congestion and related engine idling have exacerbated air pollution. Specific areas of concern include El Paso and the Windsor-Detroit border areas. Most affected by these increases are communities adjacent to border crossing areas. In addition to an increase in various kinds of air pollution, border communities have been adversely affected by increased noise pollution and other kinds of environmental pressures (Sierra Club and Holbrook-White 2000).

• Changes in industrial pollution: The effects of NAFTA on industrial pollution are mixed. Economic modelling work suggests that changes in industrial air pollution resulting from NAFTA are concentrated in three sectors: petroleum, base metals, and transportation equipment. The main increases in air pollution resulting from NAFTA are carbon monoxide and sulphur dioxide in the United States and sulphur dioxide in Mexico. Modelling work suggests significant reduction may occur in air pollution in the Canadian and Mexican paper sectors and in the Canadian chemicals sector. For particulate matter, carbon monoxide, sulphur dioxide, and nitrogen dioxide, the greatest increases occur in the U.S. base metals sector and in the Mexican petroleum sector. The transport equipment sectors of Canada and the U.S. are large sources of volatile organic compounds (Reinert and Roland-Holst 2000).

• Testing the pollution-haven hypothesis: Since the onset of the trade-environment debate, a repeated concern is that differences in domestic environmental regulations between countries could create a shift in pollution-intensive manufacturing from countries with high standards to those with lower standards. Results from the symposium suggest that, on average, little empirical evidence supports this concern. For example, a quantitative economic model presented at the symposium, which examined changes in the location of pollution intensive industries in relation to levels of environmental standards, found no evidence for the pollution haven effect (Fredrikkson and Milliment 2000).

At the same time, different results were found when examining specific sectors.

• Textiles: A study that examined environmental regulations related to the textiles sector (specifically denim) found that differences in the enforcement of environmental regulations between the U.S. and Mexico have played a contributing role in the locational shift in textiles production from the U.S. to Mexico since NAFTA. However, factors other than environmental regulations — notably differences in labour costs — played a far greater role (Abel and Phillips 2000).

• Hazardous wastes: One study examined changes in the transborder flow of hazardous wastes since NAFTA and found that an approximately five-fold increase in hazardous waste imports to Canada from the U.S. has occurred. This sharp increase in waste imports has originated mainly from U.S. steel and chemical industries. However, the increase in trade should be seen against an absolute decline in waste generation: since NAFTA, hazardous waste generation has declined in the U.S. After examining several explanations for the increase, the authors point to the comparatively less stringent environmental standards in Canada compared to the U.S. In addition, the authors note that during the time of NAFTA implementation, spending in several Canadian jurisdictions on environmental protection decreased dramatically, by as much as 40 percent (Jacott, Reed, and Winfield 2000).

NAFTA and Environmental Policies

Concern persists about NAFTA rules and environmental regulations, in particular about the extent to which trade law can 'trump' environmental law. Trade rules intended to secure market access and ensure fairness in competition can undermine — and appear already to have done so — some specific regulations governing the environment, human health, and food safety. One paper presented at the symposium pointed in particular to new burdens in trade relating to risk assessment, contained in sanitary and phytosanitary agreements and technical barriers to trade agreements (in NAFTA and the WTO); this situation raises the threat of a collision between commercial law and the objectives of environmental protection. The recent debate between trade and environmental experts over the operational implications of precaution was cited as a case in point of the difference between trade and environmental objectives (Mann 2000).

Of more immediate concern was the effect of NAFTA's investment liberalisation rules on environmental regulations. Among the most important Chapter 11 cases are those involving investor-state disputes over domestic environmental regulations. The reach of Chapter 11 is apparently wide, arbitrary, or capricious in challenging environmental regulations under expropriation provisions and it appears to be able to challenge such diverse areas as the management of hazardous wastes, and the sustainable use and conservation of renewable resources. In particular, it was noted that Canada's prohibition of bulk freshwater transfers, including export, could be undermined by Chapter 11 disputes. A recurring and clear observation made by participants at the symposium was the need to clarify and exclude environmental NAFTA Chapter 11 cases (Elwell 2000).

NAFTA and Renewable Natural Resources

The effects of NAFTA on the sustainable management of renewable resources also appear mixed, and depend on the resource examined. NAFTA has had little impact on the sustainability of North American fisheries at the aggregate level. Most trade in fish and fish products was duty free prior to NAFTA, and therefore tariff-related liberalisation has been negligible. NAFTA may have relieved pressure on fisheries in Mexico, by increasing the substitution of imported fish for domestic catches. Non-NAFTA fish trade, in particular trade between North America and Asian countries, remains substantial, and international trade may be linked to the chronic over-fishing that plagues much of the world's fish stocks (Chomo and Ferrantino 2000).

The effects of NAFTA on the forestry sector have been marginal, particularly given very low pre-NAFTA tariff rates. Case studies suggest that with NAFTA, foreign direct investment (FDI) in Mexico's forestry sector has increased competition within the country, placing pressures on the remaining Mexican-owned paper and forest product companies to lower production costs in order to remain competitive in world markets. Although empirical evidence is scarce, evidence suggests that increased exposure to international competition may increase pressures on wood-processing companies to circumvent environmental controls, thereby making sustainable forestry management practices difficult (Guerrero et al. 2000).

Trade liberalisation may also indirectly compound environmental and human-health stresses associated with intensive farming. Among the causes of the crisis in Ontario involving contaminated drinking water was the increase in intensive animal farming coupled with a retreat of regulatory authorities and transfer of various responsibilities to the municipal level, the privatisation of water management, the disruption to the chain of reporting and responsibilities among appropriate authorities, and significant reductions in environmental budgets (Elwell 2000).

The absence of comprehensive and comparable environmental data continues to hamper analysis of links between the economy and the environment. Many researchers at the symposium called for the CEC to improve its gathering of comprehensive environmental data at the North American level. It was noted that while progress has been made in the use of quantitative economic models to help show trade-environment links, these models had several limitations, including their static nature, and revealed the need to weigh qualitative variables that do not easily fit into such models. Although the CEC analytical framework had limitations, it provided a useful tool in finding ways to combine quantitative and qualitative information.

Policy Implications

While work on assessing the environmental effects of trade agreements has increased in recent years, the policy implications of these effects remain unclear. Clearly, policies must be shaped that mitigate negative environmental effects — such as the 400 percent increase of hazardous waste imports to Canada since NAFTA — and maximise positive environmental outcomes. However, a long-standing debate is where policy interventions should occur. That debate still tends to break out into either the incorporation of tougher environmental exceptions in trade law (for example, Article XX of the General Agreement on Tariffs and Trade [GATT], or Chapter 11 in NAFTA) or tougher environmental laws capable of keeping pace with the quickly changing contours of economic integration. To date, there have been no formal trade-rule amendments to include environmental provisions in either NAFTA or WTO.

Notes

1   The author thanks several reviewers for their comments and editorial advice, including Greg Block, Douglas Kirk, and Charles Dickson, although any errors are the sole responsibility of the author. The views expressed in this chapter do not represent the views of the Commission for Environmental Cooperation or of its parties.
2   From the specific perspective of international trade policy, the question is whether trade liberalisation narrows or widens income gaps. Evidence suggests that export and import relations may lead to the convergence of income at roughly equal rates.
3   The most visible tool for addressing equity issues is the use of income redistribution schemes. That is, since the capacity of governments to undertake income redistribution policies in the face of globalisation is seen to be small, it is assumed that addressing equity goals through redistributed revenue is seen as more effective than adjusted tax rates.
4   No single, unambiguous definition of 'openness to trade' exists. Definitions include measuring the overall ratio of exports to GDP, the ratio of imports to GDP (which may say more about the extent of trade-distorting measures), or the combined trade density to GDP. However, the trade-to-GDP ratio may say little about trade policies *per se*, and more about other factors, such as the size of the internal market (as in the case of the United States).

5 In the past decade, much progress has been made in developing such aggregated indicators, intended to gather diverse measurements of environmental quality, in the same way as GDP or other economic indicators compile data. Work by the Scientific Committee on Problems of the Environment (SCOPE), the United Nations Environmental Programme (UNEP), the World Resources Institute, the Organisation for Economic Co-operation and Development (OECD), the Global Environment Fund, the Center for International Earth Science Information Network (CIESIN), and the Yale Center for Environmental Law and Policy points to progress in developing aggregated, quantitative indicators capable of showing changes in air or water quality, based on changes in total pollution. However, progress in honing nonpollution indicators — capable of showing changes in biodiversity, forest cover, habitats, and ecosystems — remains less developed and certainly less quantitative than pollution-related indicators. One example of very highly effective environmental indicators is the release of the World Wildlife Fund's (2000) Living Planet Index, which shows changes in the natural wealth of the Earth's forests, freshwater ecosystems, oceans, and coasts.

References

Abel, Andrea and Travis Phillips (2000). 'The Relocation of El Paso's Stonewashing Industry and Its Implications for Trade and the Environment'. Paper presented at the First North American Symposium on Understanding the Linkages between Trade and Environment, 11–12 October. Washington DC. <www.cec.org/programs_projects/trade_environ_econ/pdfs/ Abel.pdf> (December 2001).

Bank for International Settlements (2000). '70th Annual Report'. 5 June. Basel.

Barro, R. J. (1999). 'Determinants of Democracy'. *Journal of Political Economy* vol. 107, no. 6, pt. 2, suppl., pp. S158–S183.

Chomo, G. and M. Ferrantino (2000). 'NAFTA Environmental Impacts on North American Fisheries'. Paper presented at the First North American Symposium on Understanding the Linkages between Trade and Environment, 11–12 October. <www.cec.org/programs_projects /trade_environ_econ/pdfs/Chomo.pdf> (December 2001).

Commission for Environmental Cooperation (1999). 'Indicators of Effective Environmental Enforcement: Proceedings of a North American Dialogue'. Montreal. <www.cec.org/citizen/ guides_registry/index.cfm?varlan=english> (December 2001).

Elwell, Christine (2000). 'NAFTA Effects on Water: Testing for NAFTA Effects in the Great Lakes Basin'. Paper presented at the First North American Symposium on Understanding the Linkages between Trade and Environment, 11–12 October. Washington DC. <www.cec.org/programs_projects/trade_environ_econ/pdfs/Elwell.pdf> (December 2001).

Emergency Committee for American Trade (2001). 'ECAT Joins in Formation of Broad Alliance to Support Passage of Trade Promotion Authority This Year'. 19 June. <ecat.policy.net/ proactive/newsroom/release.vtml?id=22846> (December 2001).

Fredrikkson, P. and D. Milliment (2000). 'Is There a Race to the Bottom in Environmental Policies? The Effects of NAFTA'. Paper presented at the First North American Symposium on Understanding the Linkages between Trade and Environment, 11–12 October. Washington, DC. <www.cec.org/programs_projects/trade_environ_econ/pdfs/Fredrik.pdf> (December 2001).

Galeotti, M. and A. Lanza (1999). 'Richer and Cleaner? A Study on Carbon Dioxide Emissions in Developing Countries'. *Energy Policy* vol. 27, no. 10, pp. 565–573.

Greenspan, Alan (2000). 'Technology and the Economy: Monetary and Fiscal Policies'. *Vital Speeches of the Day* vol. 66, no. 8, pp. 226–230.

Grossman, Gene M. and Alan B. Krueger (1995). 'Economic Growth and the Environment'. *Quarterly Journal of Economics* vol. 110, no. 2, pp. 353–377.

Guerrero, M. T., F. de Villa, M. Kelly, et al. (2000). 'The Forestry Industry in the State of Chihuahua: Economic, Ecological, and Social Impacts, Post-NAFTA'. Paper presented at the First North American Symposium on Understanding the Linkages between Trade and Environment, 11–12 October. Washington DC. <www.cec.org/programs_projects/ trade_environ_econ/pdfs/Guerrero.pdf> (December 2001).

Hettige, H., M. Mani, and D. Wheeler (2000). 'Industrial Pollution in Economic Development: The Environmental Kuznets Curve Revisited'. *Journal of Developmental Economics* vol. 62, no. 2, pp. 445–476.

Jacott, M., C. Reed, and M. Winfield (2000). 'The Generation and Management of Hazardous Wastes and Transboundary Hazardous Waste Shipments between Mexico, Canada, and the United States, 1990–2000'. Paper presented at the First North American Symposium on Understanding the Linkages between Trade and Environment, 11–12 October. Washington DC. </www.cec.org/programs_projects/trade_environ_econ/pdfs/Cielp.pdf> (December 2001).

Kaufmann, R. K., B. Davidsdottir, S. Garnham, et al. (1998). 'The Determinants of Atmospheric SO2 Concentrations: Reconsidering the Environmental Kuznets Curve'. *Ecological Economics* vol. 25, no. 2, pp. 209–220.

Lipset, Seymour Martin (1959). *Social Mobility in Industrial Society*. University of California Press, Berkeley.

Mann, Howard (2000). 'Assessing the Impact of NAFTA on Environmental Law and Management Processes'. Paper presented at the First North American Symposium on Understanding the Linkages between Trade and Environment, 11–12 October. Washington DC. <www.cec.org/ programs_projects/trade_environ_econ/pdfs/mann.pdf> (December 2001).

Reinert, K. A and D. W. Roland-Holst (2000). 'The Industrial Pollution Impacts of NAFTA: Some Preliminary Results'. Paper presented at the First North American Symposium on Understanding the Linkages between Trade and Environment, 11–12 October. Washington DC. <www.cec.org/ programs_projects/trade_environ_econ/pdfs/Reinert.pdf> (December 2001).

Sierra Club and S. Holbrook-White (2000). 'NAFTA Transportation Corridors: Approaches to Assessing Environmental Impacts and Alternatives'. Paper presented at the First North American Symposium on Understanding the Linkages between Trade and Environment, 11–12 October. Washington DC. <www.cec.org/programs_projects/trade_environ_econ/pdfs/ sierra.pdf> (December 2001).

United Nations Environmental Programme (1999a). *Environmental Impacts of Trade Liberalization and Policies for the Sustainable Management of Natural Resources: A Case Study of Bangladesh's Shrimp Farming Industry*. United Nations Environmental Programme, Economics and Trade Unit, Nairobi.

United Nations Environmental Programme (1999b). *Environmental Impacts of Trade Liberalization and Policies for the Sustainable Management of Natural Resources: A Case Study of Chile's Mining Sector*. United Nations Environmental Programme, Economics and Trade Unit, Nairobi.

United Nations Environmental Programme (1999c). *Environmental Impacts of Trade Liberalization and Policies for the Sustainable Management of Natural Resources: A Case Study of India's Automobile Sector*. United Nations Environmental Programme, Economics and Trade Unit, Nairobi.

United Nations Environmental Programme (1999d). *Environmental Impacts of Trade Liberalization and Policies for the Sustainable Management of Natural Resources: A Case Study of Romania's Water Sector*. United Nations Environmental Programme, Economics and Trade Unit, Nairobi.

United Nations Environmental Programme (1999e). *Environmental Impacts of Trade Liberalization and Policies for the Sustainable Management of Natural Resources: A Case Study of the Philippines' Forestry Sector*. United Nations Environmental Programme, Economics and Trade Unit, Nairobi.

'Vital Trade Round' (2001). *Financial Times*, 2 August. p. 20.

World Trade Organization (2000). *Special Study: Trade, Income Disparity, and Poverty*. World Trade Organization, Geneva.

World Wildlife Fund (1998). *Developing a Methodology for the Environmental Assessment of Trade Agreements*. World Wildlife Fund International, Gland, Switzerland.

World Wildlife Fund (2000). 'Living Planet Report 2000'. <www.panda.org/livingplanet/lpr00/> (December 2001).

Chapter 15

Sustainability Assessments of Trade Agreements: Global Approaches

Sarah Richardson

Sustainable development can be defined, most broadly, as development that meets the economic, environmental, and social needs of the present while protecting the ability of future generations to meet their own needs (World Commission on Environment and Development 1987). It demands that policy makers consider the consequences of their actions in an integrated fashion over the long term, so that current economic development does not come about at the expense of environmental and social capital that will be expensive, difficult, or impossible to replace. A sustainability assessment of trade liberalisation is one way for governments and other interested parties to develop policies that operationalise the concept of sustainable development while ensuring economic benefits brought about by liberalisation. This chapter examines various national and global approaches to assessment of trade liberalisation to support policy making that promotes sustainable development.

Environmental or sustainability assessment of trade liberalisation is on the agenda of a number of international organisations as well as of a number of national governments. This work, combined with the myriad of studies produced in the nongovernmental sector has generated a wealth of information over the past decade. There now exists a body of literature that provides guidance on how to undertake sustainability assessments. Together with sectoral or economy-wide case studies, the literature provides a better understanding of the relationships between trade and sustainable development and a solid basis for further work. In addition, data related to agreements signed in the early 1990s, such as the North American Free Trade Agreement (NAFTA), are now available, allowing for relatively robust after the fact (*ex post*) analysis from which important lessons can be drawn for future (*ex ante*) assessments. It remains a relatively dynamic time for assessment, and the body of literature on sustainability assessment of trade liberalisation continues to grow.

There is also more information available from key governmental and nongovernmental organisations (NGOs) than there was ten, or even five, years ago. In part this is because more and more information is posted on the World Wide Web and is thus accessible to large numbers of people at a low cost. In addition, organisations such as the World Trade Organization (WTO) are making available position statements and background notes with a frequency that would have been unthinkable a decade ago. The World Wildlife Fund (WWF) has developed a Web site that acts as a clearinghouse for all available information on sustainability assessment in order to promote transparency and help build capacity in this realm.[1] Transparency on trade-related issues and policies is by no means complete, but it has dramatically increased in the past decade, largely as a result of the continued demands of nongovernmental actors for improved access to information.

Improved access to information and adherence, in some organisations, to principles of public participation over the past decade have brought about increased understanding between those in the trade community and those in the environmental or social communities. That is not to say that there is necessarily agreement or even real trust, but the trade community is learning the language of, and the concepts behind, sustainable development, and vice versa. A lexicon for the issue of sustainability assessment itself is growing, and includes terms such as 'flanking' policies or 'mitigation and enhancement' measures, terms that did not exist five years ago. This evolution is partly as a result of increased participation by the nontrade community in processes related to trade — and relationships can only improve as both sides of the policy debate increasingly understand and learn to trust each other.

Despite such progress, there remains much to be done not only to promote the broad synergies between trade and sustainable development but also to ensure that any negative consequences are mitigated though trade-related or other policy initiatives. There is general agreement among international organisations and national governments involved in these processes, as well as among nongovernmental actors undertaking assessments and participating in the development of assessments at the national and international levels, that environmental or sustainability assessments of trade agreements carried out by national governments can serve as a tool for sound domestic policy making. Governments considering such undertakings are quick to point out that the work focusses on the impacts of trade liberalisation on sustainability at home. However, this only captures half the story. A country committed to sustainable development, with the resources to undertake an assessment of trade liberalisation, is missing an opportunity to identify potentially significant impacts for its trading partners or those that are important from a transboundary or global perspective. The policies that flow from trade liberalisation have major implications for the economic, environmental, and social well-being of citizens within and beyond the countries that implement those policies. Given these regional and global implications of environmental or social policies (such as global warming, migration, or poverty), a narrow domestically oriented approach appears limited in today's era of globalisation, in which economic, environmental, and social interrelationships exist between and among countries and national or international policy packages can be designed. At the very least, countries should encourage their trading partners to conduct sustainability assessments of their own, and acknowledge that there is no 'one size fits all' approach to assessment.

Limitations in some approaches exist with regard to the scope of issues considered to be the subject for assessment. There is some degree of consensus that changing tariff structures and even nontariff barriers are appropriate for examination. However, there is no such emerging consensus that issues of investment, or even trade-related policies such as privatisation — let alone changes in the way explicit and implicit property rights are defined and protected — are appropriate to include in an assessment. Again, given the breadth of some current liberalisation initiatives or the efforts of some countries to prepare for trade liberalisation through the pursuit of market-oriented reform, it would be prudent to re-examine the scope of the exercise and enhance the comprehensiveness of all assessments to capture relevant impacts of trade-related policies that might not be traditionally associated with classic trade liberalisation.

There is a good deal of agreement that assessments should be undertaken in an interdisciplinary way to involve the views of a range of stakeholders. None the less, procedures for undertaking assessments by national governments do not yet reflect a process that is based on the principles of sustainable development — that is, with equal weight accorded to the economy, the environment, and social well-being. First, a number of assessments are limited to a consideration of environmental issues and therefore do not purport to address the third pillar of sustainable development, namely social well-being. Second, processes for undertaking assessments tend to reside with trade ministries, even when there is a stated need for consultation and interagency participation. A more balanced approach would see trade ministries sharing a leadership role with environment ministries and those in the government responsible for social and development issues. And, third, although a number of approaches to assessment suggest that the exercise should be undertaken early in the negotiation process, it is not clear how, if at all, the results of an assessment can be integrated substantively into the trade policy process beyond sensitising or informing negotiators. Given the lack of direction in existing approaches, the practical application of assessments by governments should shed more light on how the process of policy integration will occur.

This chapter will first examine some of the definitions and objectives of sustainability assessments. It will then review major national and international efforts to undertake assessments of trade agreements in an effort to promote more integrated policy making. Not all these efforts are sustainability assessments. Indeed, most governments or government-led bodies have yet to make the jump from environmental assessment to sustainability assessment. This could be a result of calls from their membership, which might not be in a position to implement a full sustainability assessment, a response to specific mandate, or simply a choice to develop an approach that reflects immediate priorities in a time of limited resources. To the extent that environmental reviews or assessments of trade liberalisation do not consider social impacts, they do not claim to be sustainability assessments. Nevertheless, to the extent that they explore the links between environment and trade, and encourage governments and others to undertake such assessments, they are useful building blocks for those developing sustainability assessments now and for the development and application of sustainability assessments by governments and others in the future. This chapter will not consider the approach of the Commission for Environmental Cooperation (CEC), which is dealt with elsewhere in this volume. Neither will it consider methodologies developed by NGOs, notably that of the WWF-International (see WWF-International 1999).

What Is a Sustainability Assessment?

A number of terms exist in the policy world to refer to assessments of trade agreements as distinct from standard environmental impact assessment (EIA), which has been long employed by governments and others to determine the environmental impacts of major projects such as dams. The language coined for the various approaches generally offers a clue to the breadth of their general scope. For example, in recent years, EIAs that have been extended to include policies or programs (including trade policies) have been referred to by some governments, such as that of the United States, as 'environmental reviews'. The Canadian government refers to this extension of EIA as a 'strategic environmental assessment', although the term 'environmental review' is also used. Both approaches consider only the environmental impacts of policies or programs as opposed to their impacts on sustainable development.

At the international level, the Organisation for Economic Co-operation and Development (OECD) also refers to an environmental review of trade in its own methodology; again, this approach is limited to environmental impacts. Other organisations extend the concept of environmental assessment to include impacts of trade on social well-being and development. The European Commission calls its approach a 'sustainability impact assessment' (SIA); the United Nations Environment Programme (UNEP) puts forward an 'integrated approach' (integrating economy, environment, and social well-being), and WWF-International uses the term 'sustainability assessment'. In all cases, these approaches recommend the inclusion in the assessment of variables such as employment, the mobility and quality of the labour force, migratory flows, living standards including income level and distribution, and cultural and gender issues, in addition to environmental issues.

Approaches that reflect the multiple components of sustainability are to be applauded for their comprehensiveness in their recognition that sustainable development includes economic, environmental, and social elements, which are important in their own right as well as in the way they interact with one other. However, sustainability assessments present challenges associated in particular with a lack of experience in using indicators for social well-being, combined with data limitations and additional complexity in the analysis.

For the purposes of this chapter, the term 'sustainability assessment' will be used except when in reference to a specific approach that may be narrower — such as an environmental review — or an approach that might simply be known by a different name, such as a sustainability impact assessment or integrated assessment. This reflects the direction in which the assessment of trade and trade-related policies should move in order to capture fully the interrelationships between policy areas that will ultimately determine the sustainability of future economic development.

Sustainability Assessment as a Tool for Policy Making

Sustainability assessments that consider the economic, environmental, and social impacts of trade liberalisation can promote sustainable development and can help secure policy decisions that are based on the integration of the values of the economy, the environment, and society and the equal relevance accorded to those values. An effective sustainability assessment should be viewed as a strategic opportunity and an innovative tool for trade and other policy makers to use in meeting their responsibilities to promote sustainable development.

There are a number of ways that changing trade policies and rules can affect economies, environments, and development. Changes in rules governing trade can affect specific sectors, traded products, or the ways goods are produced to promote or deter trade in more or less environmentally beneficial goods or methods of production. Trade liberalisation can reinforce patterns of comparative advantage or lead to specialisation and concentrated production. Areas of concentration might be those best suited and equipped (with environmental and socially supporting infrastructure and transportation networks) to absorb the concentration. On the other hand, liberalisation may concentrate economic activity in sectors, firms, or geographic areas unsupported by adequate technology, management, or physical infrastructure, or without the institutional capacity to handle growth, or where ecological stress is already acute. The impact of these changes on the environment and social well-being will be magnified by their scale, namely the levels of economic activity and growth that might be induced by trade liberalisation.

In addition to the physical impacts of products and their production patterns, as barriers to trade are lowered at the border, trade liberalisation increasingly affects domestic regulations. This might make it more difficult for countries to regulate for environmental protection, or to protect culture or other social imperatives. Alternatively, a government-led or voluntary effort might encourage an upward movement of environmental standards toward a common higher norm that supports modern production methods.

Despite considerable progress, few governments have given full and timely attention to the broad economic, social, and ecological impacts of past or prospective trade-related policies or trade liberalisation agreements. There are important, policy-relevant reasons for governments to improve their analytical capacity to conduct integrated assessments at the national level; three are presented below (see United Nations Environmental Programme 2001).

Analytical Awareness in an Era of Globalisation

Assessing the environmental and social impacts of trade as well as economic impacts has become an analytic necessity in a globalising world in which trade has an ever broader and deeper impact on national policy and daily life. Not only is trade growing in magnitude, but it is also growing in scope, with liberalising policies covering a wider range of sectors than ever before and penetrating more deeply into areas of national policy. There is emerging, therefore, a much broader range of policies for those policy makers concerned with trade-related policies and liberalisation, and also for those concerned with environment, natural resources, agriculture, and all responsible for social policy and development. This creates the need for an approach to assessment that can trace the complex and often subtle impacts and identify corresponding opportunities that trade can bring — not just economic ones, but environmental and social opportunities as well. An effective sustainability assessment can suggest ways to meet economic, environmental, and social goals simultaneously.

National Policy Development That Supports Sustainability

A sustainability assessment can assist national policy makers develop policies to support sustainable development. It can become an operational tool for making policy recommendations to help identify win-win-win opportunities across trade, environmental, and social domains or to ensure the accompaniment of changes in economic activity with appropriate environmental and social policies. Results generated can help governments focus resources on key sectors of long-term national advantage as part of an overall economic development strategy. A sustainability assessment can thereby be a powerful tool for ensuring overall coherence and interministerial co-ordination and consistency in national policy, mobilising other government actors and policies by identifying how trade liberalisation can help accomplish desired policy change in related fields.

International Competitive and Negotiating Advantage

The results of a sustainability assessment can guide efforts to shape the agenda and process of trade negotiations, helping national policy makers prepare for and pursue future trade liberalisation by identifying national positions that offer the most significant benefits. In addition, assessments of one kind or another are on their way to becoming a global normal practice and should thus be approached as a competitive instrument. Some countries recognise these advantages and conduct assessments in the quest, *inter alia*, to shape trade liberalisation agreements in a particular way. It is prudent for countries to pursue their own assessments rather than leave the field open to others that may have different policy objectives or be faced with different contexts and constraints. Moreover, an effective sustainability assessment with meaningful policy recommendations will demonstrate that trade policy makers can address a broader set of values than merely economic ones, and are actively engaged in constructing a sound trade policy that makes use of this more complete set of information. When undertaken using an inclusive process, a sustainability assessment can contribute to enhanced civil society participation in the trade governance process, remove the veil of secrecy, and clarify any lack of understanding that leads to fear and mistrust between various constituencies with an interest in the process. This could help secure public support for existing and future trade policies.

Ultimately, sustainability assessments that consider how trade liberalisation affects both the environment and social development promise to promote sustainable development. It is no surprise then, that in the post-Seattle climate of trade liberalisation, assessments are receiving a good deal of attention at the national, regional, and international levels as concern rises about the pace and nature of globalisation and governments struggle to pursue liberalisation of trade and investment in all regions of the world.

In order to address the above policy imperatives, there is considerable agreement that the immediate purpose of an assessment exercise should be stated at the outset. The *Reference Manual for the Integrated Assessment of Trade-Related Policies*, published by UNEP (2001), presents potential (but not exclusive) purposes for integrated assessment under the following five topics:
- clarifying the links among trade, environment, and development;
- informing policy makers throughout government;
- informing negotiatiors;
- developing policy packages; and
- increasing transparency in decision making.

These are equally valid for sustainability assessments and environmental reviews.

Clarifying the links among trade, environment, and development Sustainability assessments can clarify the links among trade, environment, and development. In the long term, a better understanding of these relationships can encourage policy makers to develop — and stakeholders to support — sustainable development strategies and policies.

Informing policy makers throughout government Sustainability assessments can inform policy makers throughout government of the implications of proposed trade policies and contribute to intragovernmental co-operation and consensus building. They can allow for a comprehensive set of policy priorities to be identified prior to the start of negotiations, and for the development of an integrated negotiating position or integrated trade-related policies. The results of a sustainability assessment might also direct the pace or scope of trade liberalisation, which includes the proper sequencing of liberalisation to ensure that effective national environmental policies exist in vulnerable sectors. If undertaken comprehensively, the results of a sustainability assessment can help countries develop trade policies in a co-ordinated way that reflects the interdependence of economic, environmental, and social goals. A sustainability assessment that includes all relevant government departments should also help build capacity and consensus within government.

Informing negotiators A sustainability assessment can inform negotiators of some of the tradeoffs that might be associated with certain economic initiatives. It can ensure that trade, environment, and development issues are addressed during such negotiations in ways that promote sustainable development. It can identify environmental and development effects of different trade-related policies or trade agreements at an early point in the negotiations, allowing time for the appropriate complementary flanking mechanisms to be put into place to prevent any damage or promote positive synergies. At this early stage, this could include modification of the trade-related policy or agreement under negotiation.

Developing policy packages A sustainability assessment can help policy makers develop appropriate domestic policy packages to implement in conjunction with trade liberalisation of complementary economic, environmental, and social policies at the national level to accompany the trade-related policy or agreement, as well perhaps at the international level. These policies, which are commonly referred to as flanking policies, can promote any beneficial impacts of the trade liberalisation or mitigate any negative impacts. Flanking policies might include more stringent environmental oversight in a sector in which liberalisation could have immediate and important effect. At the international level, a policy package could include an initiative as broad as that taken in conjunction with the implementation of NAFTA, where the three signatories established a parallel environmental regime designed to promote co-operation on issues of mutual concern and encourage the effective enforcement of environmental laws in order to allay concerns related to potential negative impacts of trade and investment liberalisation in North America. Additional policies could be implemented as necessary as a result of any monitoring or review processes. The implementation of appropriate flanking policies can support sustainability. In some cases, such policies might also be useful to build public support for liberalisation domestically. Likewise, at the international level they can help build confidence and trust in trade liberalisation process.[2]

Increasing transparency in decision making A sustainability assessment, undertaken with a high degree of public participation, can increase transparency in government policy and decision making with regard to trade liberalisation. The involvement of nongovernmental actors in the assessment process can help strengthen national capacity and encourage the incorporation of multiple points of view in making decisions. In addition, an integrated assessment that puts economic, social, and environmental issues forward for consideration in an integrated fashion, undertaken with the assistance of stakeholders, can enhance public support for the policy-making process. At a time when national governments and international institutions are receiving calls to reform the policies that govern openness and transparency in trade-related matters, such an approach might help allay fears based on lack of information.

Environmental Assessment at the National Level

Significant attempts to examine the links between trade and the environment have been undertaken at the government level. In particular, the governments of Canada and the United States stand out in this regard. Both governments have undertaken environmental reviews of trade agreements extending back almost a decade when NAFTA was being negotiated. And, significantly, both governments have recently developed methodologies to be applied systematically in future assessments.

Canada: Framework for Conducting Environmental Assessments of Trade Negotiations

In 1993, the Government of Canada undertook an environmental review of NAFTA (Department of Foreign Affairs and International Trade (DFAIT) 1992). The following year, Canada was one of the few nations to conduct an environmental review of the WTO's Uruguay Round (DFAIT 1994). Its principal purpose was to identify the extent to which the results of the Uruguay Round would affect Canada's ability to regulate for environmental protection. Canada has signed agreements on environmental co-operation with both the United States and Mexico in a parallel agreement to NAFTA. Under the auspices of the CEC, the governments of Canada, Mexico, and the United States are obliged to examine on an ongoing basis the environmental impacts of NAFTA (CEC 1993, art. 10(d)). A parallel agreement on the environment was negotiated between Canada and Chile in conjunction with its trade agreement with that country ('Canada-Chile Agreement on Environmental Cooperation' 1997). Neither the bilateral agreement with Chile nor a more recent agreement with Costa Rica appear to have been the subject of an environmental review.

Over the past two years, however, the Government of Canada developed the Framework for Conducting Environmental Assessments of Trade Negotiations. This process began in early 1999 in the lead-up to the WTO meeting in Seattle. As a first step, Canada undertook a retrospective analysis of the 1994 Canadian environmental review of the Uruguay Round of multilateral trade negotiations, which was released in November 1999 (DFAIT 1999). The Framework for Conducting Environmental Assessments of Trade Negotiations was finalised in February 2001 (DFAIT 2001).

The approach put forward in the framework is also known as a 'strategic environmental assessment' (SEA) — a process for evaluating the environmental consequences of policies, plans, or program proposals. Its stated goal is to integrate environmental considerations into the negotiation of trade agreements at the earliest stage and it is therefore considered an *ex ante* framework, undertaken prior to the negotiations. The framework is to apply on an agreement-by-agreement basis. The level and scope of analysis are determined according to the issue within the potential agreement, conforming to the significance of the likely environmental impacts. The primary focus of the environmental assessments will be the most likely and significant environmental impacts of trade negotiations in relation to Canada. Transboundary, regional, and global environmental impacts will be considered only if they have a direct impact on the Canadian environment.

The methodology is applied in the first instance to the new round of negotiations at the WTO. It will be carried out by an environmental assessment committee composed of representatives from all relevant government departments and co-ordinated by Canada's Department of Foreign Affairs and International Trade (DFAIT). The identification of potential policy and regulatory effects was guided by looking at the range of environmental concerns that had been raised by governmental organisations and NGOs over the course of the negotiations. These views were gathered through either direct contact with NGOs or by an examination of published sources and letters received from members of the public.

A process in four stages is suggested in conducting the analysis. In the first stage, the coverage of the potential agreement and its overall economic relevance in the Canadian context would be determined. This can include identifying sectors likely to be affected, changes in consumption of specific products, exports of natural resources, or effects on standards and on subsidy disciplines.

In the second stage, different forms of environmental impacts of such economic changes are considered; economic changes could, for example, have an impact on Canada's commitments under multilateral environmental agreements (MEAs), on the transfer of environmentally sound technologies, or on environmental goods and services sectors. In stage three, the significance of likely environmental impacts are assessed, inquiring, for example, into the frequency and duration of impact, the geographical scope or an established high level of risk, or the potential irreversibility of the impact. Attention is also paid to cumulative impacts. Finally, mitigation and enhancement measures are devised. These might include new policy programmes or modifications to existing ones or co-operative efforts with other countries or organisations. In addition, it might be recommended that negotiation positions be modified.

While it is significant that the Government of Canada has undertaken an SEA of any new round of multilateral trade negotiations, there are some limitations in its approach (WWF Canada 2000; International Institute on Sustainable Development 2000). First, it only includes environmental impacts and ignores social issues, despite the fact that there is a state commitment to sustainable development. Second, the framework does not consider regional and global environmental impacts unless they directly affect the Canadian environment. Depending upon the nature of environmental issues in a potential trading partner, this could ignore a myriad of important impacts that, while not relevant to Canada, are critical at a local, regional, or global scale.

Third, as presented, the SEA appears not to be part of the trade policy process and there is no indication of how the two policy spheres might be integrated. While the framework states that it seeks to inform negotiators, it is unclear how the results of an assessment will be taken into account in a way that accommodates environmental considerations in trade negotiations in any substantive way. The process is led by DFAIT, with other relevant government departments as members of an assessment committee. It draws on input from members of civil society invited to provide comments as the process unfolds. All this occurs outside of the trade policy arena and it is up to DFAIT to integrate the results. The results and the impact of the current SEA approach will go a long way to informing those watching the process as to how it will assist the Government of Canada develop policy and positions on trade agreements that respect environmental imperatives.

It is unclear whether this framework will apply only to the multilateral trade talks at the WTO or whether it is an attempt to institutionalise the concept of assessment as a key component of trade negotiations at the multilateral, regional, and bilateral levels. The latter approach would suggest a higher level of commitment to pursuing trade liberalisation across the board that seeks promote the positive synergies between trade and environment and mitigate any negative impacts. An approach that included social variables would indicate the strongest commitment to sustainable development.

United States: Environmental Reviews of Trade Agreements

The office of the United States Trade Representative (USTR) has considerable experience conducting environmental reviews of trade agreements. The United States prepared the first written environmental review of a major trade agreement in 1993 when it released 'The NAFTA: Report on Environmental Issues' (USTR 1993). It has also conducted reviews of the Uruguay Round agreements of 1994, the accelerated tariff liberalisation initiative in forest products in 1999 by Asia-Pacific Economic Cooperation (APEC) (USTR 1999), and the U.S.-Jordan Free Trade Agreement (USTR 2000). In February 2001, the USTR began an interagency process to analyse the environmental effects of the Free Trade Agreement of the Americas (FTAA). As part of the review policy, the USTR also announced that it would proceed with an environmental review of the negotiations on agriculture and services currently underway in the WTO. Environmental reviews of free trade agreements with Singapore and Chile are also in progress.

Environmental reviews of trade agreements were institutionalised in the United States by Executive Order 13141—Environmental Review of Trade Agreements in November 1999 (United States White House 1999). *Guidelines for Implementation of Executive Order 13141, Environmental Review of Trade Agreements* were published in December 2000 (Council on Environmental Quality and USTR 2000). The executive order identifies certain types of agreements for which an environmental review is mandatory: comprehensive multilateral trade rounds, bilateral or plurilateral free trade agreements, and major new trade liberalisation agreements in natural resource sectors. For other types of agreements, the executive order and guidelines direct the USTR to determine whether a review is warranted based on such factors as the potential significance of reasonably foreseeable positive and negative environmental impacts. Under the guidelines reviews should begin early enough to be a productive part of the negotiations.

The guidelines call for the reviews to be conducted *ex ante* — initiated early enough in the trade policy process to inform negotiating positions although they shall not be a condition for the timely tabling of a particular negotiating proposal. There is an important component for public participation that is included in the guidelines, which call for public comment and information on the scope of the review. The USTR is designated as the lead agency in the process within the basic interagency decision-making mechanism on trade policy.

Each review is likely to incorporate uniquely tailored qualitative and quantitative analytical approaches. Limitations in the analysis due to certain assumptions and uncertainty in the data and methodologies are to be documented. Despite variations in approaches, consistency is to be achieved in the review process through a consistent documentation format and content. Environmental reviews are to include both an analysis of the regulatory environmental impacts and the environmental impacts that might flow from direct economic changes estimated to result from the trade agreement. For the latter endeavour, modelling and other similar techniques are deemed important, albeit not sufficient in and by themselves. The problem of aggregate analysis of broad economic trends and more localised analysis of environmental impacts is recognised. Baseline scenarios for comparisons of the likely environmental impacts with and without the trade agreement are to take into account changes that might occur in the economy and the environment even in the absence of the proposed trade agreement. The result of the reviews can lead to instructions to negotiators on specific issues relevant to a given trade agreement. And where significant positive or negative environmental impacts are identified, response options could include changes to negotiating positions and measures taken outside the agreement.

Despite the fact that it is an important and meaningful step forward, the approach put forward in the executive order and guidelines also contains limitations (American Lands Alliance et al. 2001; WWF-International 1999). Again, first and foremost, it considers only environmental implications and therefore will not capture the interrelationships among economic, environmental, and social issues by not considering the latter. Second, the approach purports to focus on environmental impacts within the United States despite the reality that many environmental problems are global in their scope. Third, the approach is heavily weighted toward the environmental impacts of tariff-related changes in U.S. imports, and does not adequately prioritise issues including investment, subsidies, or government procurement. The approach also stresses the desirability of a quantitative approach. While economic modelling is useful, the guidelines should consider as equally valid a more qualitative approach that does not require the same complexity, level of resources, reliance on assumptions and hypotheses upon which there might be little agreement, and is, in the long run, more accessible to a wider audience.

Nevertheless, unlike the Canadian approach, the U.S. executive order considers the review of a number of different types of trade agreement to be mandatory, as opposed to deciding whether to conduct one on a case-by-case basis. This goes further toward institutionalising the process of assessment and is important insofar as the process of conducting the environmental review appears to guarantee a certain amount of public participation in the formulation of U.S. trade policy.

Environmental Assessments at the Regional (Plurilateral) and Multilateral Levels

Despite the fact that a number of international organisations are looking at issues of sustainability assessment, there is some degree of consensus particularly among governments that assessments are a national responsibility and should be carried out by national governments (WWF and Fundación Futuro Latinoamericano 2000). The OECD effort is designed to be applied by national governments, and the multilateral effort underway at UNEP is also aimed at national governments, in both developed and developing countries.

OECD: Methodologies for Environmental and Trade Reviews

The OECD has been working on issues of assessment since June 1993 when it developed procedural guidelines for integrating trade and environment policies intended to help governments in the development and implementation of policies where trade and environment meet (OECD 1993). Following endorsement of the procedural guidelines by OECD ministers, in 1994 the OECD's Joint Session of Trade and Environment Experts developed a general methodology for conducting environmental reviews of trade policies and agreements and trade reviews of environmental policies and agreements (OECD 1994b).

In general, the OECD methodology suggests that environmental reviews of trade measures are meant to identify the potential positive and negative implications of trade policy on the environment. It also highlights policy approaches for enhancing the contribution of trade policies and agreements to the goal of sustainable development. This should take into account the wider economic, environment, and development needs as well as the policies and objectives of each country. The goal is to achieve improved adherence to trade rules, disciplines, and commitments or to reveal the need for an adjustment of this regulatory framework.

In its approach, the OECD divides economic effects of trade measures into the categories of scale effects, structural effects, product effects, and technology effects. Scale effects are those that relate to the overall level of economic activity created by trade policies or agreements. For example, increases in scale can translate into higher rates of use of natural and environmental resources or services or into increased levels of pollution. Structural effects are those brought about by changes in the composition of goods and services in a country as it specialises and trades those goods that have provided a comparative advantage as a result of liberalisation; depending upon whether the changes favour industries that are relatively less or more polluting, a range of environmental effects could occur. Product effects are those that relate to the flow of products or services between trading countries. Some of these products or services may be environmentally friendly, while some may be hazardous to the environment; the effects, therefore, can be positive or negative, depending on the nature of the products traded as well as their volume. Technology effects are those that relate to the nature of the technology used in production activities associated with trade and those related to the trade itself in technologies. Trade policies or agreements can trigger the transfer of technologies that can be harmful or friendly to the environment.

The OECD approach also considers regulatory effects by examining the impacts of trade policies and agreements on environmental laws and regulations. Positive regulatory effects could also occur when the trade measures do not impinge upon the ability of governments to implement effective environmental policies. However, there can be negative regulatory effects if provisions in a trade agreement undermine the ability of governments to set standards for environmental protection.

The OECD has applied its methodology in a number of case studies and has gained considerable experience and expertise in this realm (OECD 1994a). In October 1999, the OECD held a workshop to take stock of past work and to identify gaps in existing methodologies for environmental assessments of trade liberalisation agreements. The proceedings and a final report were brought together in *Assessing the Environmental Effects of Trade Liberalisation Agreements: Methodologies* (OECD 2000). The workshop yielded a number of important conclusions about existing work and gaps that might be addressed in the future. The OECD notes that environmental assessments are best carried out by national governments and that, to be successful, the process necessitates political commitment. It adds that the process must be politically independent in order to be credible. It also notes that there is a need to invest in capacity building for assessment in developing countries. Furthermore, despite major advances in analysing trade-environment linkages, the causal link is not sufficiently robust. Another conclusion that is important from a policy perspective is that more attention should be paid to how recommendations that emerge from assessments are carried out. Such increased attention would add credibility to the studies and assist policy makers.

As part of its ongoing work in this area, the OECD is currently undertaking analysis examining the application of its methodology to trade in services.

European Commission: The World Trade Organization New Round and Sustainability Impact Assessments

The European Union was early off the mark on assessment. In 1992, it conducted an assessment of sorts of the creation of a single market. In 1999, the European Commission undertook an SIA of the new round of WTO negotiations, undertaken, in its first two phases, by a team of researchers from the University of Manchester in the United Kingdom. During Phase One, from mid July to mid September 1999, case studies and literature reviews were conducted in order to develop a methodology for use in Phase Two (Kirkpatrick, Lee, and Morrissey 1999). Phase Two lasted from mid September to mid November 1999 and involved a preliminary assessment of the sustainability impacts of the proposed new round of trade negotiations, applying the methodology developed in Phase One (Kirkpatrick and Lee 1999). The main objective of this work was to develop a methodology that would encompass all aspects of sustainable development — the economy, the environment, and social well-being. The purposes of this *ex ante* assessment was to make some preliminary and broad qualitative assessments of likely impacts on sustainable development and to identify possible measures to mitigate any negative impacts and enhance any positive ones.

The SIA methodology is broad and qualitative. It looks at direct economic effects of changes in trade flows. Liberalisation scenarios were developed with varying degrees regarding changes to trade measures. The first stage of the assessment methodology is a screening exercise to determine what measures require an SIA because they are likely to have significant impacts. The next stage is to establish the appropriate coverage of each SIA, taking each of the measures identified in the screening exercise and identifying the components of those measures that are likely to have an impact. The economic effects are then analysed and linked to a set of sustainability indicators to measure the impact of further liberalisation and changes in rule making. The indicators are balanced between economic, environmental, and social indicators. This preliminary SIA was intended to identify potential significant effects, positive and negative, on sustainable development. The core sustainability indicators were combined with significance criteria (for example, the extent of existing stress, nature or order of magnitude, and spatial characteristics) to determine a level of significance of the impacts. Finally, the SIA suggested mitigation and enhancement measures to promote beneficial impacts and mitigate negative impacts.

Work on Phase Three, which will include more detailed sectoral assessments as well as a refinement of the assessment methodology, is being prepared at the time of writing. In September 2001, the European Commission issued public tenders for continued work on the SIA of the WTO and to begin work on an SIA of the EU-Mercosur trade negotiation process.

This approach should be applauded for its comprehensiveness and, in particular, for its treatment in the analysis of equal importance to economic, environmental, and social issues. Nevertheless, its limitations as a tool for policy making at the end of Phase Two are linked closely to its highly ambitions scope (see also Richardson 2000). First, the study is built on an assumption that implicitly limits the scope of its analysis so as to make it appear unbalanced. It focusses on a new round of multilateral trade negotiations and the terms of reference for the study state: 'For this exercise, it is taken as a basic working assumption that non-inflationary growth world-side will be boosted by multilateral trade liberalisation and rule making, and that this is desirable'. Instead, the SIA process should be informing political decisions on whether and when a new WTO round should start and how it should unfold, and how comprehensive it should be.

Phase Two of the study is weak in its ability to identify trade-induced effects in a broader economic context and thereby trace causality or even correlation to any identified impacts. Although it identifies economic impacts of trade liberalisation, it does not include a set of variables and relationships that show how economic effects of trade liberalisation are transmitted into environmental and social effects, such as those offered by the OECD in its environmental review methodology: scale, structure, product, technology, or regulatory effects.

A further feature that might be difficult to translate into policy is the metric for assigning significant impacts — a scale of +/– 1 and +/– 2 — selected to capture their economic, environmental, and social impacts. Such a five-point scale (including a zero value) has the advantage of being appropriate to the level of uncertainty about impacts at this stage and to the assumption that impacts can be equally good or bad. But the seemingly arbitrary compression of possible impacts into a limited five-point range may mean that more finely graded variation may be missed, and that the possibility of step-level, exponential gains or losses may be ignored.

The study notes the wide range of indicators available to study sustainability impacts. It chooses to focus on three for each of the three key areas of sustainable development: economic impacts, environmental impacts, and social impacts. While the task of selecting indicators for use in such a broad exercise is admittedly very difficult, by focussing on three indicators in each impact area, one is left with a relatively limited concept of economic, social, and environmental impacts, with varying degrees of relevance to the measures under consideration in the study. There is also little reference to the selected indicators as being determinants for the significance, or lack thereof, of potential impacts. Finally, from a policy perspective, the mitigatory measures included are at a level of generality that, without further analysis, provide little guidance for their implementation at either the national or international levels.

Further development and practical application of this approach in Phase Three may well remedy the limitations that exist in the current approach with regard to its immediate relevance for policy makers.

United Nations Environment Programme: Integrated Assessment of Trade-Related Policies

In June 2001, the Economics and Trade Unit of UNEP's Division of Technology, Industry, and Economics released the *Reference Manual for the Integrated Assessment of Trade-Related Policies* (UNEP 2001). The manual is part of the unit's ongoing work to improve countries' understanding of the links between trade and environment and to enhance their capacities to develop mutually supportive trade and environment policies. The manual seeks to help policy makers and practitioners in both developed and developing countries to conduct integrated assessments of the economic, environmental, and social impacts of trade policy and trade liberalisation. It defines an integrated assessment as one that considers the economic, environmental, and social effects of trade measures and identifies ways to avoid or mitigate negative consequences and ways to enhance positive effects.

The manual does not prescribe the use of a specific methodology for conducting integrated assessments. Rather, it develops a general approach based on core components of an assessment and suggests a range of options and approaches that can be adopted or adapted by the user, depending on priorities, resources, and other contextual circumstances. The core components of an integrated assessment are classified into the following categories: setting the stage, designing an integrated assessment, integrating approaches and techniques, and integrating policy responses.

The manual was developed with advice from an international group of experts that included representatives from a number of national institutions from developing countries conducting case studies in co-operation with the Economics and Trade Unit. UNEP is working on the manual in parallel with a project designed to catalyse and encourage work in developing countries on assessment. Since 1997, UNEP has been working closely with groups in Bangladesh, Chile, India, the Philippines, Romania, and Uganda on projects to identify t he impacts of trade and trade liberalisation on specific sectors and to propose the use of economic instruments to manage negative impacts. It has recently extended a new round of funding to projects in Argentina, China, Ecuador, Nigeria, Senegal, and Tanzania. The manual is intended to be a 'living document' that incorporates lessons from case studies and guides the development of those studies. The UNEP process has already had a major impact by encouraging institutions in developing countries to undertake their own assessments.

The manual is comprehensive, recognising that there is no common approach to assessment that can apply broadly to a range of countries with different priorities, different levels of resources, and varying levels of development. Nevertheless, it identifies key elements that should be considered in undertaking assessments (such as robust public participation) and presents a range of options, based on existing literature, for countries to build an approach that suits their needs. The manual also presents a range of issues that might be appropriate for consideration, including elements contained in structural adjustment programmes that might be outside the ambit of a more traditional assessment but are nevertheless highly relevant in a number of developing countries. Therefore, although it is not prescriptive, the manual provides the raw materials to those who wish to undertake their own assessment. This promises to be its greatest strength insofar as it encourages countries to conduct meaningful assessments of the economic, environmental, and social implications of trade-related policies and trade liberalisation agreements. It is still too early to tell whether governments and others will use the manual to put forward robust approaches to assessment that include the many elements outlined by UNEP in its menu of items for developing integrated assessments.

Conclusion

Sustainability assessments hold out great promise for sound domestic policy making and international action that are integrated, transparent, and participatory, and support sustainable development. Given the complexity and controversy surrounding issues that link trade, the environment, and social well-being, it is not surprising that progress has been slow. Nevertheless, the level of activity in this field — by governments, international organisations, and nongovernmental actors — during the past decade is encouraging and paves the way for continued development of theoretical underpinnings and the practical application of meaningful sustainability assessments.

In order to ensure that future efforts promote sustainability, attention should be paid to a number of key elements associated with sustainability assessment. First, countries should strive to include social variables in their assessments in order to capture fully the impacts of liberalisation on sustainability. Second, assessments should be broad in their outlook and consider domestic issues as well as important impacts related to their trading partners and elsewhere at the regional and global levels. Third, the traditional notions of trade as tariff- and nontariff-related issues needs to be re-examined so as to capture the many facets of modern efforts to liberalise. This includes not only areas such as services, investment, and government procurement that might be included in broadly based future agreements on liberalisation, but also a range of trade-related policies such as privatisation, financial reform, and balance-of-payments issues that might be necessary conditions to pave the way for liberalisation in some countries. Fourth, work should continue to focus on increasing transparency and implementing robust processes of public participation in order to enrich further efforts to develop or apply sustainability assessments by drawing on the experience and expertise of those in the nongovernmental community. To this end, approaches to assessment should be accessible to a broad range of stakeholders using both qualitative and quantitative approaches that allows for the inclusion of a variety of evidence, including, as necessary, interviews and even anecdotal evidence to capture observed impacts in the field. Finally, governments undertaking sustainability assessments should approach these exercises in a balanced way according equal weight to trade, environment, and social issues to develop integrated policies that truly support sustainable development.

Notes

1 This clearinghouse was developed by the World Wide Fund for Nature (WWF-International) and World Wildlife Fund U.S. (WWF-U.S.) as part of an ongoing project on Sustainability Assessment of Trade Agreements. See <www.panda.org/balancedtrade>.
2 The OECD's 1994 methodology suggests that the range of policy responses to environmental reviews might include modification of some aspects of the trade measure or agreement, inclusion of environmental safeguards in the trade measure or agreement, or implementation of a complementary environmental mechanism to accompany the trade measure or agreement (OECD 1994b).

References

American Lands Alliance, Center for International Environmental Law, Consumer's Choice Council, et al. (2001). 'Comments on Guidelines for Implementation of Executive Order 13141'. <www.ciel.org/Publications/EO13141Comments.pdf> (December 2001).
'Canada-Chile Agreement on Environmental Cooperation' (1997). <can-chil.gc.ca/English/Resource/Agreements/AECCC/AECCC_1.cfm> (December 2001).
Commission for Environmental Cooperation (1993). 'North American Agreement on Environmental Cooperation between the Government of Canada, the Government of the United Mexican States, and the Government of the United States'. <www.cec.org/pubs_info_resources/law_treat_agree/naaec/> (December 2001).
Council on Environmental Quality and United States Trade Representative (2000). 'Guidelines for Implementation of Executive Order 13141'. <www.ustr.gov/releases/2000/12/guides.html> (December 2001).
Department of Foreign Affairs and International Trade (Canada) (1992). 'North American Free Trade Agreement Canadian Environmental Review'. <www.dfait-maeci.gc.ca/sustain/environa/strategic/MenuNaftaCom-e.asp> (December 2001).
Department of Foreign Affairs and International Trade (Canada) (1994). 'Uruguay Round of Multilateral Trade Negotiations: Canadian Environmental Review (Complete)'. <www.dfait-maeci.gc.ca/sustain/environa/strategic/sea0299-e.asp> (December 2001).

Department of Foreign Affairs and International Trade (Canada) (1999). 'Retrospective Analysis of the 1994 Canadian Environmental Review of the Uruguay Round of Multilateral Trade Negotiations'. Ottawa. <www.dfait-maeci.gc.ca/tna-nac/retrospective-e.pdf> (December 2001).

Department of Foreign Affairs and International Trade (Canada) (2001). 'Framework for Conducting Environmental Assessments of Trade Negotiations'. <www.dfait-maeci.gc.ca/tna-nac/Environment-e.asp> (December 2001).

International Institute on Sustainable Development (2000). 'Comments on Canada's Draft Environmental Assessment Framework for Trade Negotiations'. <www.iisd.org/pdf/trade_dfait_eaf_final.pdf> (December 2001).

Kirkpatrick, Colin and Norman Lee (1999). *WTO New Round: Sustainability Impact Assessment Study. Phase Two, Main Report*. 18 November. Institute for Development Policy and Management and Environmental Impact Assessment Centre, University of Manchester, <europa.eu.int/comm/trade/pdf/sia_ent.pdf> (December 2001).

Kirkpatrick, Colin, Norman Lee, and Oliver Morrissey (1999). *WTO New Round: Sustainability Impact Assessment Study. Phase One Report*. 1 October. Institute for Development Policy and Management and Environmental Impact Assessment Centre, University of Manchester; Centre for Research on Economic Development and International Trade, University of Nottingham, <europa.eu.int/comm/trade/pdf/repwto.pdf> (December 2001).

Organisation for Economic Co-operation and Development (1993). 'Trade and Environment'. <www.olis.oecd.org/olis/1993doc.nsf/linkto/ocde-gd(93)99> (December 2001).

Organisation for Economic Co-operation and Development (1994a). *The Environmental Effects of Trade*. Organisation for Economic Co-operation and Development, Paris.

Organisation for Economic Co-operation and Development (1994b). 'Methodologies for Environmental and Trade Reviews'. <www.olis.oecd.org/olis/1994doc.nsf/linkto/ocde-gd(94)103> (December 2001).

Organisation for Economic Co-operation and Development (2000). 'Joint Working Party on Trade and Environment: Methodologies for Environmental Assessment of Trade Liberalisation Agreements'. Report of the OECD Workshop, 26–27 October 1999. <www.olis.oecd.org/olis/1999doc.nsf/linkto/com-td-env(99)92-final> (December 2001).

Richardson, Sarah (2000). 'A 'Critique' of the EC's WTO Sustainability Impact Assessment Study and Recommendations for Phase III'. Commissioned by Oxfam GB, World Wildlife Fund-European Policy Office, Save the Children, and ActionAid. <www.oxfam.org.uk/policy/papers/wto/wto6.htm> (December 2001).

United Nations Environmental Programme (2001). *Reference Manual for the Integrated Assessment of Trade-Related Policies*. United Nations, New York and Geneva. <www.unep.ch/etu/etp/acts/manpols/rmia.htm> (December 2001).

United States Trade Representative (1993). 'The NAFTA: Report on Environmental Issues'. <www.ustr.gov/environment/nafta93report.pdf> (December 2001).

United States Trade Representative (1999). 'Accelerated Trade Liberalization in the Forest Products Sector: A Study of the Economic and Environmental Effects'. <www.ustr.gov/releases/1999/11/forest.html> (December 2001).

United States Trade Representative (2000). 'Draft Environmental Review of the Proposed Agreement on the Establishment of a Free Trade Area between the Government of the United States and the Government of the Hashemite Kingdom of Jordan'. <www.ustr.gov/environment/nafta93report.html> (December 2001).

United States White House (1999). 'Executive Order: Environmental Review of Trade Agreements'. <www.ustr.gov/environment/execo.htm> (December 2001).

World Commission on Environment and Development (1987). *Our Common Future*. Oxford University Press, Oxford; New York.

World Wildlife Foundation Canada (2000). 'Canada's Draft Environmental Assessment Framework for Trade Negotiations: Comments by WWF Canada'. 6 October.

World Wildlife Fund and Fundación Futuro Latinoamericano (2000). 'International Experts Meeting on Sustainability Assessment of Trade Liberalisation'. <www.panda.org/resources/publications/sustainability/iem/> (December 2001).

World Wildlife Fund International (1999). 'Initiating an Environmental Assessment of Trade Liberalisation in the WTO'. Vol. II. <www.panda.org/resources/publications/sustainability/wto-papers/initiate.html> (December 2001).

Chapter 16

Concern for the Environmental Effects of Trade in Canadian Communities: Evidence from Local Indicator Reports

Virginia W. Maclaren

In the debate about the environmental effects of free trade, the existence and impact of such effects in urban areas and local communities seem to have been neglected. Empirical research has focussed on the country-wide impacts of the North American Free Trade Agreement (NAFTA) (Reinert and Roland-Holst 2000) and broad sectoral impacts, such as found in electricity production (Moscarella et al. 1999; Plagiannakos 2000), the automotive industry (Kirton 1998), hazardous waste management (Jacott, Reed, and Winfield 2001), and cattle feedlotting (Runge 1999). There have also been studies on the impacts of trade agreements on individual provinces in Canada (Chambers et al. 1999; Plagiannakos 2000), but nothing on the environmental impact of trade on urban areas. One potentially useful source for tracking these impacts and community concern about them may be the local or community indicator report.

Local indicator reports are becoming a widespread phenomenon in North America. A survey in 1998 identified more than 200 communities in Canada and the United States with indicator reports (Redefining Progress 2001). Anecdotal evidence on indicator listserves[1] suggests that the number is still growing. These reports can take a wide variety of forms. As yet, there is no general agreement about what a local indicator report should contain, other than indicators on a variety of local conditions. The reports place varying emphasis on environmental, social, and economic conditions in a community. They often provide an analysis of the factors that influence the current state of these conditions and past trends. The geographical scope of the report can range from a neighbourhood to a local municipality to an urban region or even to a watershed. The authors of such reports have included community groups, local governments, nongovernmental organisations (NGOs), and partnerships among these groups. Although the primary goal of the reports may vary by author, almost all emphasise the need to raise public awareness about issues of local concern. Some go further and seek to mobilise the community around these issues.

This chapter will search local indicator reports for evidence of community concern over the environmental effects of trade in local communities. While examining the goals of local community reporting, it will also touch on the contribution of such reports toward building social cohesion. Finally, it will assess the extent to which the environmental information and analysis found in these reports can contribute to a better understanding of the environmental effects of trade at the local level. Nowhere else can one find such a comprehensive assembly of local environmental data than one finds in these indicator reports. The chapter will begin by comparing the different types of local indicator reports and their goals before investigating their environmental content.

The research for this chapter is based on a review of 66 local indicator reports in Canada, spanning the period 1993 to 2001. The reports were collected between 1998 and 1999 by means of a telephone survey of 154 of Canada's largest municipalities. Follow-up work in 2001 identified a handful of additional reports. The sample of reports therefore represents a fairly comprehensive inventory of such reports in the country.

Types of Local Indicator Reports

Although there is much overlap among the different types of local indicator reports, making it difficult to define them precisely, some of the more widely recognized types are state-of-the-environment (SOE) reports, quality-of-life (QOL) reports, sustainability reports, state-of-the-city (SOC) reports, and state-of-the-watershed (SOW) reports.

SOE reports focus on indicators of the state of the biophysical environment. They may also include indicators of human activity stressors on the environment, such as the amount of automobile traffic, or indicators of human health effects from poor environmental quality, such as the number of hospital admissions for asthma treatment. In Canada, local government staff wrote most local SOE reports with little to moderate amounts of input from members of the public and stakeholder groups.

QOL reports have a broader perspective than SOE reports in that they include indicators not only of the biophysical environment, but also of the economy and of social conditions in a community. QOL reports tend to place more emphasis on social and health indicators than SOE reports. The authors of most Canadian QOL reports to date have been local governments or NGOs. Like SOE reports, there has been some general public input in their development, but not a great deal of it.

SOC reports also have a broad perspective and are very similar to QOL reports, except that they are more balanced in their coverage and often focus solely on indicators that can be influenced by local government policy or that measure the performance of local government policies and programs.

Sustainability reports are similar to SOC reports in their coverage of issues, but their stated intention is to describe a community's progress toward sustainability. To this end, they often attempt to include indicators that represent the basic principles of sustainability, namely intergenerational equity, intragenerational equity, and geographical equity. Recognition of the importance of intergenerational equity gives sustainability reports a more forward-looking perspective than QOL and SOC reports have, as they tend to focus on current conditions and, sometimes, on past trends. Most sustainability reports adopt the well-known definition of intergenerational equity popularised by the World Commission on Environment and Development (1987, 8), which states that equitable development across generations is development that 'meets the need of the present without compromising the ability of future generations to meet their own needs'. Examples of environmental problems that have significant implications for future generations because of their long-term nature include global warming and ozone depletion.

Indicators of intragenerational equity might address problems of environmental justice for different income, racial, or ethnic groups. Indicators of geographical equity measure how local activities influence the degradation of distant areas and the transfer of uncompensated environmental costs to other communities (Haughton 1998). Pollution trade, such as the transfer of air pollution generated in one community to the airspace of a downwind community, is a form of geographical inequity.

Sustainability reports also attempt to illustrate how actions or conditions in one sphere of the community, such as the environment, can affect conditions in another sphere, such as the economy. Since sustainability is such a value-laden concept, a fundamental characteristic of sustainability reports is that they incorporate a broad level of public input.

A final type of local indicator report is the watershed report. Typically, these reports are similar to SOE or SOC reports except that natural boundaries rather than political ones determine the geographical scope of the report. There are only a few examples of watershed reports in Canada, all prepared with considerable input from community groups or prepared by the community groups themselves. The main reason for the trend toward strong community involvement in report preparation is that most of these groups have been active in community-driven watershed rehabilitation projects and watershed planning.

Among the different reporting types, SOE reports tend to be the most technical and have the greatest number of indicators, about 50 on average. QOL, sustainability, and SOC reports have a smaller number of indicators, including about five or six dealing with environmental issues. In choosing indicators, these latter types of reports place great importance on finding those that can be readily understood by the general public.

The Goals of Indicator Reporting

Developing a local indicator report can be both time consuming and expensive. Why do local communities and governments spend tens of thousands of dollars and thousands of hours of time on preparing local indicator reports? What are those reports supposed to accomplish? The goals of indicator reports vary considerably. The primary goals of SOE reports have a slightly different emphasis than those found in other types of indicator reports. Figure 16.1 shows that SOE reports are mostly concerned with developing baselines against which to compare future conditions in the community. The two most important goals in other types of local indicator reports are creating a framework for action or change in the community and raising public awareness. In other words, they tend to be more proactive in their intent than SOE reports.

None of the reports examined for this chapter specified that its goal was to assess the environmental effects of trade. However, some communities might choose to develop indicators of these effects in order to achieve other goals, such as establishing a baseline or measuring progress toward improved environmental quality in a community. Whether communities actual developing such indicators will be established in the next section.

To what extent do indicator reports contribute to increases in the social cohesion of communities? It is difficult to say. Not only is it difficult to measure social cohesion and but it is also difficult to link improvements in social cohesion with the results of indicator reporting. Although none of the reports surveyed had improving social cohesion as a stated goal, 43 indicator reports identified raising public awareness of community problems and achievements as a goal. This can be a first step toward developing community cohesion for a particular issue. There have been no studies to date that have examined the success of indicator reports in raising public awareness. Clearly, this would be a difficult task.

Another closely related aspect of social cohesion is community mobilisation. Twenty-six reports, mostly SOC and sustainability reports, cite creation of a framework for community action as a goal of the reporting exercise. The following quote from the coordinator of a SOC report gives one example of this action-oriented emphasis:

Figure 16.1   Goals of Local Indicator Reports

SOE reports   Other local reports

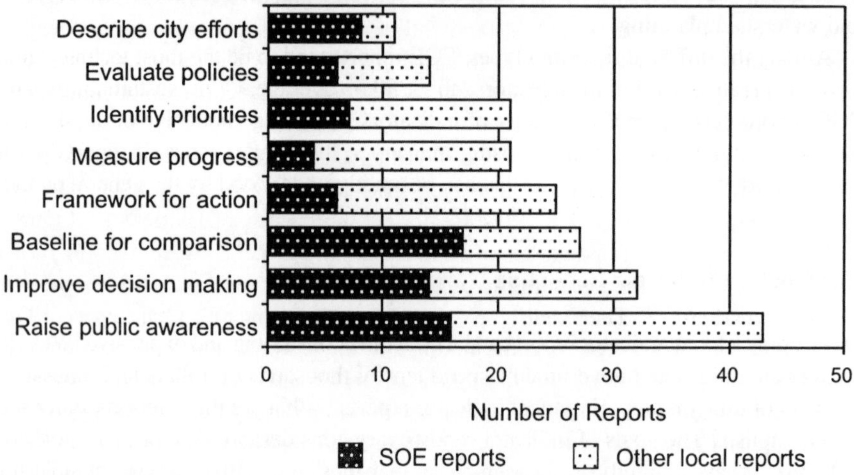

The goals [for the report] were based on an analysis of some of the key problems facing our community. The key concerns that we were addressing were the declining local economy and rising poverty in the community, a community that is in transition and increasingly divided. Therefore, leadership was a key problem in this community. The goal of the project was to strengthen the community to be better able to respond to all these issues. Our goal was to mobilize the community.

One feature of successful mobilisation is the number of people who are willing to volunteer their time toward the preparation of indicator reports. As noted by Noel Keough in Chapter 17, more than 2000 people volunteered more than 10 000 hours to the preparation of the Sustainable Calgary report over a period of four years (Sustainable Calgary 2001). This high level of community involvement provides support for Tim O'Riordan's (1998, 2) claim that the process of developing sustainability indicators offers an exciting opportunity for 'exploring a new democracy and a fresh approach to individual self-confidence and communal partnership'. Although the level of volunteer effort and community consultation is usually much lower in SOE, QOL, and SOC reports, there is at least some amount of community input in all types of reports. To varying degrees, therefore, the process of report preparation contributes to social cohesion by forging new relationships among disparate groups, including NGOs, industry, government, the education sector, health services, and the general public.

Tracking the Environmental Effects of Trade on Local Communities

This section will examine the information and indicators found in local indicator reports that may be useful for tracking the environmental effects of trade at the local level. There is no question that local indicator reports contain a great deal of environmental information, but how much of this information is relevant to assessing the impacts of specific trade agreements, such as NAFTA, or of trade in general?

If one turns first to specific trade agreements, one finds that only three local indicator reports in Canada make mention of NAFTA or NAFTA organisations. The State of the Fraser Basin report (Fraser Basin Management Program 1995) refers to the potential for water exports under NAFTA. The Regional Municipality of Halton's QOL report (1997) talks about the implications of NAFTA and the General Agreement on Tariffs and Trade (GATT) for agricultural production. Neither report discusses specific environmental effects. The Ontario Social Development Council's QOL report (1998) for 12 cities in Ontario refers to the findings of the Commission for Environmental Cooperation's (1998) 'Taking Stock' publication on pollution reporting in North America but it does not attempt to link these findings with the environmental effects of NAFTA.

Despite the lack of interest in NAFTA and other specific agreements, some local indicator reports nonetheless address pollution trade problems. Twenty-nine of the 66 local indicator reports surveyed include trade-related environmental indicators or discuss environmental problems that can be linked to trade (see Table 16.1). SOE reports tend to mention trade-related environmental issues and indicators more than other types of indicator reports because they have a stronger emphasis on environmental indicators.

For the most part, the reports do not attempt to make a link between pollution trade and liberalised trade regimes. They are not so much concerned with the causes of international pollution as with the effects. It is helpful here to distinguish between indicators of pollution trade and indicators of pollution from trade. The former term — pollution trade — refers to the movement of pollutants across local, regional, and national boundaries. Local indicator reports were found to contain several indicators of global and regional transboundary pollution, as shown in Table 16.2. 'Pollution from trade' refers to pollution generated as result of trade-related economic production activities.

Transboundary pollution may have its origin in pollution from trade. Alternatively, it may come from pollution generated by increased activity in economic production that is tied to increases in local rather than trade-related demand. Strictly speaking, only the former type of transboundary pollution is of interest to those concerned about the environmental impacts of trade agreements, but determining whether the origin of pollution trade is a response to locally derived demand or international demand can be extraordinarily difficult. Therefore, it is not surprising that pollution trade indicators found in local indicator reports do not specify whether the pollution trade can be linked to trade-related economic production.

Global Pollution Trade

Global warming and the contribution made by local communities to global warming were the most frequently mentioned types of global pollution trade in indicator reports. One report addressed the issue of trade in toxic contaminants, noting that certain contaminants, such as dichlorodiphenyltrichloroethane (DDT), are still present in the food chain of the Great Lakes Basin because they originate from countries where there is no legislation banning their use (Regional Municipality of Hamilton-Wentworth 1994).

Regional Pollution Trade

Ground level ozone from coal-burning power plants in the United States Midwest was the most frequently mentioned pollution trade issue in Ontario indicator reports (Regional Municipality of Hamilton-Wentworth 1994; City of Hamilton 2001; Metropolitan Toronto 1995; Regional Municipality of York 2000; Regional Municipality of Peel 1995). Scarborough's SOC report notes that the opening of U.S. borders to polychlorinated biphenyl (PCB) waste imports from Canada has implications for management of the growing accumulation of PCBs stored on site in the city (City

Table 16.1 Local Indicator Reports Mentioning Pollution Trade or Pollution from Trade, by Type of Report and by Province

Type of report	Province	Mentions indicators or issues related to pollution trade	Mentions indicators or issues related from pollution trade
State of the City	Ontario	Scarborough (1997) City of Hamilton (1999) City of Toronto (1993)	
Sustainability	Alberta	Calgary (1998, 2001)	Calgary (1998, 2001)
	Ontario	Reg. Mun. of Hamilton-Wentworth (1994) Ottawa (2000)	
Quality of Life	Ontario	Quality of Life for Ontario Municipalities (1998) Reg. Mun. of Halton (1997)	
State of the Watershed	B.C.	Fraser River Basin (1996)	
	Ontario	Humber River (2000)	Humber River (2000)
State of the Environment	B.C.	Vancouver (1993) Victoria (1997) Kamloops (1994) Kelowna (1998) Burnaby (1993)	
	Alberta	Calgary (1998)	
	Sask.	Regina (1994, 1997)	Regina (1997)
	Ontario	Metro Toronto (1995) Reg. Mun. of Halton (1997) Reg. Mun. of Hamilton-Wentworth (1994) Reg. Mun. of Peel (1995) Woolwich (1998) Kingston-Frontenac (1998) Region of York (2000) Burlington (1998) Sudbury (1994)	
	N.B.	Saint John (1996)	

of Scarborough 1997). Referring to another waste-related topic, the Regional Municipality of Hamilton-Wentworth's SOE report (1994) identifies the export of solid waste by private haulers to less expensive landfill sites in the United States as a reason for a decline in deliveries to its own landfill.

A trade-related indicator that is receiving growing attention in the community indicator movement is the ecological footprint. It is the only example found in the indicator reports that is close to being an explicit indicator of pollution from trade. This indicator measures the amount of land consumed by populations within a given area, such as a city. Land consumption occurs not primarily from physical occupation of the land by people, but mainly as a result of the imported food, energy, and manufactured products consumed in cities and from exports of wastes. Both imports and exports consume land in their production or their disposal and the total amount of land consumed by the population of a community is that community's footprint. Typically, a community's footprint is much greater than its physical area. For example, Mathis Wackernagel and William Rees (1996) estimated the ecological footprint of Vancouver to be 22 times greater in size than its political boundaries. A smaller footprint is seen as being more desirable and geographically equitable because it implies that a community has greater self-sufficiency and has less impact on the ecological carrying capacity of other regions. It also implies limited trading activity with other regions. In this sense, the ecological footprint is a type of anti-trade indicator.

Among the community indicator reports examined, two mention the need to develop an indicator of the community's ecological footprint in the future (Humber Watershed Alliance 2000; Regina Urban Environmental Advisory Council 1997). Although not referring specifically to the ecological footprint concept, the first sustainability report for Calgary includes an indicator of the amount of food grown locally (Sustainable Calgary 1998). The report advocates locally grown food because it reduces fossil fuel use for transporting imported food from elsewhere in North America or from overseas. In its second report, Calgary became the first community in Canada to include an ecological footprint indicator in a local indicator report (see Chapter 17). The results

**Table 16.2 Types of Pollution Trade and Number of Mentions in Local
Indicator Reports (number of reports)**

	Regional pollution trade	Global pollution trade
Air	Ground level ozone (14)	Stratospheric ozone depletion (3)
	Acid rain (4)	Global warming (11)
Water	Toxics in water (2)	
Land	Solid and hazardous waste exports (4)	
	Toxics in food (1)	Ecological footprint (3)
	Food imports (3)	
Biota	Bioaccumulation of toxics (1)	—

show that the footprint for Calgary residents is 9.2 hectares per person, drawing on a total area of 80 000 square kilometres. This area is approximately 111 times greater than the size of Calgary itself and about 4.5 times greater in size than the footprint was in 1950. Referring to world-wide estimates of 1.5 hectares of available productive land per person, the report's authors conclude that Calgarians use more than six times their share of the world's productive land and they challenge Calgarians to

> examine our lifestyle in relation to what the earth can provide. Our actions and our lifestyle have impacts on people around the globe. If we are using more than our share of the earth's productive land, then necessarily, other communities must make do with less than their share. Clearly there is a need to move toward a less consumptive lifestyle that provides a good quality of life for all Calgarians (Sustainable Calgary 2001, 45).

Conclusion

Most local indicator reports in Canada contain indicators of pollution trade or discuss the implications of pollution trade. Many local communities are taking the axiom to 'think globally, act locally' to heart in the sense that they are concerned about global environmental pollution arising from economic activity within their own community. Regional pollution trade is also a concern, particularly in central Canadian communities that are exposed to downwind ozone pollution from the U.S. Midwest.

Local indicator reports developed to date provide very little evidence of community concern with the environmental effects of pollution from trade. With few exceptions, none of the indicator reports attempts to link backward to the economic origins of the pollution being generated, whether the activity is related to trade or not. This is not surprising because to make such a link is a challenging task requiring research expertise and time commitments that may not be available to local community groups or local governments. There is some evidence in the more recent reports that a trade-related community concern is emerging, but the difficulty of developing complex trade-related indicators such as the ecological footprint is proving daunting (Sustainable Calgary 1998, 2001; Humber Watershed Alliance 2000; Regina Urban Environmental Advisory Council 1997).

It would also appear that the process of preparing local indicator reports contributes to social cohesion. Although this contribution varies by type of report, experience illustrates the importance of involving a wide range of community interests in the development of indicators and local assessments of environmental effects.

In conclusion, although local indicator reports contain a plethora of environmental information, the link made between such information and the environmental effects of trade on local communities is not strong. More research is needed to develop methodologies and indicators that can effectively capture such relationships at the local level. This research can help to fill an important gap in our understanding of the spatial distribution of the environmental effects of trade.

Note

1   See, for example, the listserv hosted by Redefining Progress at <www.rprogress.org/ resources/cip/cinet/cinet_listserve.html>.

References

Chambers, Edward J., Rolf Mirus, Barry Scholnick, et al. (1999). 'Alberta: Evaluating a Decade's Experience with the Canada-U.S. Free Trade Agreement (FTA)'. Western Centre for Economic Research, Faculty of Business, University of Alberta. <www.bus.ualberta.ca/ CIBS-WCER/WCER/pdf/54.pdf> (December 2001).
City of Hamilton (2001). 'The City of Hamilton's Sustainability Indicators: 1999 Background Report'. City of Hamilton Planning and Development Department, Hamilton, ON.
City of Scarborough (1997). 'Scarborough 1997 State of the City Report'. City of Scarborough, Scarborough, ON.
Commission for Environmental Cooperation (1998). 'Taking Stock: North American Pollutant Releases and Transfers'. Montreal. <www.cec.org/pubs_docs/documents/index.cfm?varlan= english&ID=141> (December 2001).
Fraser Basin Management Program (1995). 'State of the Fraser Basin: Assessing Progress Towards Sustainability'. Fraser Basin Management Board, Vancouver.
Haughton, G. (1998). 'Geographical Equity and Regional Resource Management: Water Management in Southern California'. *Environment and Planning B — Planning & Design* vol. 25, no. 2, pp. 279–298.
Humber Watershed Alliance (2000). 'A Report Card on the Health of the Humber River Watershed'. Toronto and Regional Conservation Authority, Toronto.
Jacott, M., C. Reed, and M. Winfield (2001). 'The Generation and Management of Hazardous Wastes and Transboundary Hazardous Waste Shipments between Mexico, Canada, and the United States, 1990–2000'. Texas Center for Policy Studies, Austin. <www.texascenter.org/ publications/haznafta.pdf> (December 2001).
Kirton, John J. (1998). 'The Impact of Environmental Regulation on the North American Automotive Industry in the NAFTA Era'. In S. Weintraub and C. Sands, eds., *The North American Auto Industry under NAFTA*. Center for Strategic and International Studies Press, Washington DC.
Metropolitan Toronto (1995). 'State of the Environment Report: Metropolitan Toronto'. Metropolitan Toronto Planning Department, Toronto.
Moscarella, J. P., E. Hoyt, R. Cavanaugh, et al. (1999). 'Electricity in North America: Some Environmental Implications of the North American Free Trade Agreement'. In Commission for Environmental Cooperation, *Assessing Environmental Effects of North American Free Trade Agreement (NAFTA): An Analytic Framework (Phase II) and Issue Studies*, pp. 259–384. Commission for Economic Cooperation, Montreal.
Ontario Social Development Council and Social Planning Network of Ontario (1998). 'The Quality of Life in Ontario, Fall 1998'. Ontario Social Development Council, Toronto.

O'Riordan, Tim. (1998). 'Sustainability Indicators and the New Democracy'. *Environment* vol. 40, no. 9, p. 2.

Plagiannakos, T. (2000). 'Will Free Trade in Electricity between Ontario, Canada, and the U.S. Improve Environmental Quality?' Paper presented at the First North American Symposium on Understanding the Linkages between Trade and Environment, 11–12 October. Washington DC.

Redefining Progress (2001). 'Community Indicators'. <www.rprogress.org/projects/indicators> (December 2001).

Regina Urban Environmental Advisory Council (1997). 'State of the Environment 1997: Sustainability and Waste Management'. Regina Urban Environmental Advisory Council, Regina.

Regional Municipality of Halton (1997). 'Halton Quality of Life: First State of the Environment Report for Halton Region'. Regional Municipality of Halton, Oakville, ON.

Regional Municipality of Hamilton-Wentworth (1994). 'State of the Environment 1994 Update'. Regional Municipality of Hamilton-Wentworth, Planning and Development Department, Hamilton, ON.

Regional Municipality of Peel (1995). 'State of the Environment: Atmosphere Report'. Regional Municipality of Peel, Brampton, ON.

Regional Municipality of York (2000). 'Our Environment, Our Home: York Region State of the Environment Summary Report 2000'. Regional Municipality of York, Newmarket, ON.

Reinert, K. A and D. W. Roland-Holst (2000). 'The Industrial Pollution Impacts of NAFTA: Some Preliminary Results'. Paper presented at the First North American Symposium on Understanding the Linkages between Trade and Environment, 11–12 October. Washington DC. <www.cec.org/programs_projects/trade_environ_econ/pdfs/Reinert.pdf> (December 2001).

Runge, Ford (1999). 'Feedlot Production of Cattle in the United States and Canada'. In Commission for Environmental Cooperation, ed., *Assessing Environmental Effects of North American Free Trade Agreement (NAFTA): An Analytic Framework (Phase II) and Issue Studies*. Commission for Economic Cooperation, Montreal.

Sustainable Calgary (1998). 'State of Our City Report 1998'. Sustainable Calgary, Calgary.

Sustainable Calgary (2001). 'State of Our City Report 2001'. Sustainable Calgary, Calgary.

Wackernagel, Mathis and William E. Rees (1996). *Our Ecological Footprint: Reducing Human Impact on the Earth*. New Society Publishers, Gabriola Island, BC.

World Commission on Environment and Development (1987). *Our Common Future*. Oxford University Press, Oxford; New York.

Chapter 17

Using Indicators to Engage the Community in Sustainability Debates

Noel Keough

What do healthy birthweights, Christmas bird counts, water quality, food bank usage, energy consumption, and a sense of community have in common? They are all indicators of Calgary's sustainability documented in Sustainable Calgary's 2001 State of Our City Report (Sustainable Calgary 2001). The report documents 36 social, ecological, and economic sustainability indicators — indicators of the long-term health and vitality of Calgary.

Citizens around the globe are coming together to develop tools to help move their communities toward a sustainable future. Sustainability indicator reporting is one such tool that has been implemented in more than 200 communities in North America alone. The motivation for sustainability indicator reporting is, in part, the perceived negative effects of globalisation — the intuition that economic globalisation has come at the expense of local communities, social cohesion, and the environment. Globalisation has been built upon the narrow economic perspective that assumes that unfettered market forces, privatisation, and stimulation of economic growth constitute the magic formula for progress and improved quality of life for all (Keough 1995; Korten 1995, 1999; Daly, Cobb, and Cobb 1989).

The movement toward local sustainability indicators is consistent with a growing realisation that cities, regions, nations, and the global community all rely upon a solid foundation of sustainable local communities. Many communities are learning that the conventional ways of measuring progress, which rely on a narrow set of economic indicators, are not adequate (GPI Atlantic 2001). This chapter discusses the process, outcomes, and future directions for Sustainable Calgary's indicators project. It also responds to the question of what insights these local experiences have to offer to the discussion of international trade agreement reform.

In short, viewed through the lens of local community sustainability reporting, international trade agreements are found wanting. They lack an appropriate process for engaging citizens in the discussion and the lack of appropriate tools for measuring success or failure of the agreements and the trade they promote.

Part I: The Sustainable Calgary Story

In 1996, a core group of citizens came together to form Sustainable Calgary under the banner of the Arusha Centre, a community development centre with a 30-year history in Calgary. Sustainable Calgary is a citizen-led, nonprofit society with a mission to promote, encourage, and support community-level discussion, actions, and initiatives that move Calgary toward a sustainable future. Sustainable Calgary was founded after a series of public forums was called to discuss issues of quality of life in Calgary and how citizens could become proactive in redefining how they measure the long-term health of their community. Sustainable Calgary is made up of educators, university students, engineers, planners, social workers, environmentalists, and small business owners.

Calgary, the sixth largest city in Canada, is home to more than 860 000 people within a land area of 720 square kilometres. The city is generally considered to have benefited tremendously from trade liberalisation. The oil and gas sector is experiencing a boom, with exports to the United States and optimism for growth in the information technology sector (Promoting Calgary Inc. 2001). However, the combination of unprecedented economic growth and the influx of new Calgarians is challenging the sustainability of many sectors of the community. Even Peter Lougheed (2000), the former premier of the province of Alberta and one of the champions of the Canada-U.S. Free Trade Agreement (FTA), has recently expressed doubts about the outcome of the free trade regime in terms of impacts on communities and the sovereignty of the Canadian economy.

The sustainability indicators project is an exciting opportunity to discover what constitutes a sustainable quality of life. Citizens exercise their rights and responsibilities to choose how to measure progress as a community. They wrestle with issues such as how to measure the value placed on cultural diversity, how to measure the spiritual health of the community, what makes a diverse sustainable economy, how to know that the biodiversity of life is being protected within the urban environment, and what effect urban sprawl has on the economy, citizens' health, and the environment.

While the production of the sustainability reports is an important goal, the process of developing the report is equally, if not more, valuable. Experience has shown that the way to attain a set of indicators that is truly meaningful, useful, and representative of a community is to involve a broad cross-section of citizens in the indicator selection process. This helps develop new understandings of issues and new insights into potential solutions. The small businessperson begins to understand the ecological impacts of packaging choices, while the social worker sees new links among jobs, poverty, and habitat preservation.

What can be learned from this process is that there is a need to move beyond the narrow set of economic indicators currently employed to make decisions. It is necessary to understand the links that extend across ecological, social, and economic boundaries and to develop the skills to bring a broad range of indicators into the decision-making process without having to reduce everything to dollars and cents.

Community Indicator Projects

Currently across North America, more than 150 community indicator projects are underway (International Institute on Sustainable Development 2000). Sustainable Seattle (1995) has been the inspiration for many of these projects. In Canada, there are indicator projects in Calgary, Banff, Lethbridge, and Canmore, Alberta, in Hamilton-Wentworth and Toronto, Ontario, and in Glace Bay, Nova Scotia. Many of these projects are designed, researched, and co-ordinated by local community members. Outside North America, the Cities Environment Reports on the Internet (CEROI) network promotes community indicators projects in communities as diverse as Hobarth, Australia, Arendal, Norway, Tbilisi, Georgia, and Kiev, Ukraine.[1]

The Indicators Development Process

Sustainable Calgary's first year of work was confined to researching community indicator projects and the relevant literature, networking with a diverse group of individuals and organisations throughout the city, and defining its mission, objectives, principles, and sustainability indicators. It was also spent creating a public process to help realise a first State of Our City report.

Sustainable Calgary identified five major objectives for its work:
- To create a focal point for discussing sustainability issues in general and to raise these issues to a higher level of public debate;
- To provide an educational tool for teachers, private- and public-sector decision makers, and community organisations;
- To monitor issues, actions, and policies that have an impact on Calgary's sustainability and quality of life;
- To provide a basis for action and to influence policy, planning, and community processes; and
- To highlight the links among social, economic, and ecological spheres of activity.

Participants as citizens A key element of the participatory process was a clear understanding of the role of the citizen. John Ralston Saul (1992) has written extensively on the importance of acting as citizens in what he describes as a very corporate world. The following passage was included in the materials distributed to workshop participants.

In this process we are asking people to participate as citizens of Calgary. We are not asking you to represent a particular sector or stakeholder. The issue at stake is the sustainability of our community, not a particular sector or interest. While expertise in a particular area is valuable and a necessary contribution, the process works best when you step out of your own area of expertise and contribute with the big picture in mind, with the good of the community as a whole in mind. Each sectoral think tank should ideally be made up of people with a wide variety of expertise — business people in the community sector, health care professionals in the economic sector, etc.

Each person comes to the process with particular indicators they think are important. These views need to be heard and you should be passionate about making your case as to why they are important. In the end we will all be asked, as citizens, to judge what we think are the best indicators to include in the 2001 Report. We should all bear in mind that everybody's choices may not be selected in that process, but it will be a collective decision arrived at through a fair and open process.

Following a review of current literature and practice (Campbell, Spear, and Maclaren 1996; Sustainable Seattle 1995), the project team crafted the following set of eight criteria for selecting indicators:

• Does the indicator link economic, social, and/or ecological factors?
• Will people understand and care about this indicator?
• Will this indicator trigger action?
• Is this indicator responsive to interventions?
• Is there a way to measure this indicator accurately?
• Are the data for this indicator cost effective to collect?
• Is this indicator comparable to other reference points and standards?
• Is the indicator consistent with Sustainable Calgary's sustainability principles?

A clear definition of a sustainability indicator was established: An indicator is something that helps one understand where one is, which way one is going, and how far one is from where one wants to be. A good indicator is an early warning of an emerging problem and helps make it possible to recognise what needs to be done to fix it. One distinguishing feature of a sustainability indicator is its ability to illuminate the links among indicators — a direct or indirect relationship between two or more indicators, where changes in one affect the status of another.

Two attributes have made the work of Sustainable Calgary effective, namely attention to process and the determination to involve as many people as possible. The process consisted of five phases:

1. Indicator analysis and nomination workshops For the 2001 State of Our City Report, the first phase consisted of a series of more than 50 workshops. Some of these were open workshops held at the public library. Others were hosted by particular organisations. The host organisations were a diverse group that included the Chamber of Commerce, the Rotary Club, the Developmental Disabilities Resource Centre, Calgary aldermen and staff, university classes, the Calgary Mennonite Centre for Newcomers, and neighbourhood community associations. In these workshops, the 24 indicators that had been documented in the 1998 report were presented; participants were asked to comment on the appropriateness of the current indicators and nominate new indicators for the 2001 report. Participants were aided in their deliberations by the indicator criteria and the sustainability principles.

2. Indicator think tanks The next phase was to hold a series of three 'indicator think tanks'. The think tank sessions were open to all those who had participated in the workshops. Participants self-selected into one of six think tanks, or sectoral groups, as outlined in the 2001 report. These think tanks met three times over a six-week period. Each reviewed all the new indicator nominations that had come out of the public workshops and brainstormed additional indicators. Each sectoral group nominated five indicators to be considered for inclusion in the 2001 report, resulting in 30 nominated indicators.

3. Dotmocracy in action In the third phase, the 30 indicators nominated at the think tanks were presented by teams to a plenary 'dotmocracy' session. All those present were given five stickers and asked to place them beside the indicators they thought were the most important indicators to include in the 2001 report. All the votes were tallied and the top 12 indicators were added to the original 24 from the 1998 report. Thus, a list of 36 indicators was developed for the 2001 report.

4. Task forces During the process to create the 2001 State of Our City Report, a series of task forces was established to study the indicators in progress from the first report in more detail. 'Indicators in progress' was a designation given to indicators reported in 1998 but for which no suitable measure was found. Research was commissioned with the collaboration of various funders, and workshops were held with individuals with interest, experience, or expertise in the indicators in progress. Some of this task force work remains ongoing and has resulted in original research to gather data on the indicators in progress.

5. Community-based research The fifth phase involved a youth creative writing and art contest throughout Calgary as a way to engage youth in the process. More than 50 young people submitted their visions of what a sustainable Calgary would look like in the year 2020. Prizes for poetry, creative writing, and poster were awarded in four age groups.

In August 2000, volunteers were again invited to join the process as community researchers. Their task was to clarify the precise measure for each of the selected indicators, research the data and background information, and write a draft of the indicator page for the report.

To date, almost 2000 people have volunteered more than 10 000 hours to creating Sustainable Calgary's State of Our City reports.

What Is Sustainability?

Of course, central to the indicators project is an understanding of sustainability. Sustainable development has been the concept on which much of the debate over the future of the planet, countries, cultures, and communities has focussed for the past decade. With the release of *Our Common Future* (World Commission on Environment and Development 1987), known as the Bruntland Report, 'sustainable development' has almost become a household term. Today, sustainable development has become a motherhood statement, its desirability widely accepted as a given. Almost every institution, from small nongovernmental organisations (NGOs) to the World Bank, accepts sustainable development as the path to the future. Problems arise, however, in the operational definition of the term. What does it mean?

What should be sustained? To examine this question, one must understand the ends to be achieved and the means chosen to achieve those ends. The goal of a sustainable community is to attain a good quality of life that includes love, comfort, health, education, physical sustenance, meaningful work, spiritual meaning, and a sense of belonging. In a sustainable community, one seeks to gain these qualities through the most efficient and wise use of time, effort, and resources.

For a long time now, economic growth has been the chosen means to achieve a good quality of life. Sustainability reporting helps examine whether economic growth is the appropriate means to achieve the desired ends. Perhaps a more fitting model, reflecting the natural world, would be a state of dynamic equilibrium in which change, innovation, and development are possible and desirable, but do not depend on constant growth.

The relationship between lifestyle and quality of life is key to sustainability. Most Calgarians enjoy a high quality of life. High levels of resource consumption characterise the particular lifestyle that supports their quality of life. Sustainability reporting challenges the community to examine whether this lifestyle is sustainable for the long term and, if not, what changes can be made to create a sustainable lifestyle that can deliver an equal or greater quality of life for Calgary's children, grandchildren, and future generations.

What would a sustainable community look like? A sustainable community would be resilient, self-reliant, creative, and resourceful. A sustainable community understands that there are limits in a finite world and lives within its economic, social, and ecological means. A sustainable community fosters stewardship of the natural environment and ethical behaviour, and takes seriously its rights and responsibilities. In a globalising world, all human communities are becoming more and more interconnected. A sustainable community seeks to achieve balance and fairness in its relations with all other communities, wherever they may be.

Community sustainability principles The following sustainability principles guide the work of Sustainable Calgary.

- Maintain or enhance ecological integrity. A sustainable community lives in harmony with the natural world. It protects the air, water, soil, flora, fauna, and ecosystems on which it depends for its survival. These are the life-support systems for all human communities.
- Promote social equity. In a sustainable community, each and every citizen is afforded access to the benefits and opportunities that the community has to offer without social or economic discrimination.
- Provide the opportunity for meaningful work and livelihood for all citizens. A strong, resilient, dynamic local economy is essential for community sustainability. A sustainable economy provides the opportunity for meaningful work and livelihood for each citizen.
- Encourage democratic participation of all citizens. The bedrock of a democracy is citizen participation in the functioning, planning, and decision making of society. In a sustainable community, participation is both a right and a responsibility and should be available to every citizen.

Is Calgary Sustainable?

Sustainable Calgary's analysis reveals that there are signs of wear in the fabric of Calgary's community life (see Table 17.1). Tentative steps are being taken to address resource consumption, and the city's citizens enjoy a relatively healthy natural environment. Calgary's education and health systems are still among the best in the world but are showing signs of stress. Economically, the city's prosperity still rests on a lucrative but finite resource and masks intolerable inequities. Given global trends represented by indicators such as the ecological footprint (Wackernagel and Rees 1996) and the Living Planet Index (World Wildlife Fund 2000), and, given the predominant energy- and resource-intensive lifestyle, Calgary cannot be considered sustainable.

Community The community indicators suggest a mixed message. Calgarians pride themselves on their volunteerism and attachment to the city. However, according to the City of Calgary's 2000 citizen satisfaction survey, only 43 percent of Calgarians felt that their quality of life is very good, as compared to 56 percent in 1997 (City of Calgary 2000). The prevailing mood seems to be a concern that the quality of life is a little more tenuous than it was five years earlier. While volunteerism is still strong, the city has slipped in comparison to other cities and regions. The area of most concern in this sector is how Calgarians value cultural diversity. The leadership among institutions of power and influence in Calgary does not reflect the cultural diversity of the city.

On the positive side, crime has been decreasing for several years. In addition, the survey of major public festivals in Calgary found that in the past ten years the number and diversity of festivals available to Calgarians has increased significantly.

Economy The economy is perhaps the most elusive piece of the sustainability puzzle for Calgary. Contrary to most conventional economic analyses of Calgary, the assessment of the sustainability of the economy is troubling. Despite the city experiencing a boom, housing affordability has decreased, homelessness is at a historic high, the gap between rich and poor has increased, and individuals or families who make minimum wage must work long hours to meet their basic needs.

Table 17.1 Calgary's 36 Community Sustainability Indicators

Community Indicators		*Natural Environment Indicators*	
Crime rate and rate of victimisation	☺	Air quality	☺
Leisure activity	☺	Bird population surveys	☺
Membership in		Food grown locally	☺
community associations	☺	Pesticide use	☹
Number of and attendance		Surface water quality	☺
at public festivals	☺	Water consumption	☺
Sense of community	☺		
Valuing cultural diversity	☹	*Resource use indicators*	
Volunteerism	☺	Ecological footprint	☹
		Domestic waste	☺
Economy Indicators		Energy use	☹
Housing affordability	☹	Population density	☹
Economic diversification		Transportation infrastructure	
— Oil and gas reliance	☺	spending	☺
Food bank usage	☺	Transit usage for work trips	☹
Hours required to meet basic			
needs at minimum wage	☹	*Wellness indicators*	
Income equity:		Childhood asthma	
Gap between rich and poor	☹	hospitalisation rate	☹
Unemployment rate	☺	Support for the most vulnerable	☹
		Healthy birthweight babies	☺
Education Indicators		Access to primary and	
Grade three achievement scores	☺	alternative health resources	☹
Adult literacy	☹	Self-rated health	☹
Daycare worker salaries and turnover	☹	Youth wellness	☺
Lifelong learning — Library use	☺		
Teacher/student ratios	☹		

On the positive side, food bank usage has levelled off over the past two years and employment trends are still strong. There are positive but tentative steps toward diversification. But the oil and gas sector has allowed the creation of a high-maintenance city and an affluent lifestyle that a post–oil-and-gas economy will likely not support.

Education   Results are also mixed in the education sector. Grade three achievement scores in language arts continue to improve, and the public library is still a pillar of the community and a vital resource for lifelong learning. However, budget cutbacks have contributed to slightly increased teacher-student ratios over the past five years and Calgary now has one of the highest ratios in the country. There are no new numbers for adult literacy since the 1998 report, but with the growing importance of self-directed learning literacy has become a more important issue. Too many people function at low levels of literacy. Perhaps the most urgent problem is the lack of attention given to early childhood education. Alberta lags far behind the rest of the country in terms of resources directed toward early childhood education. Workers in this sector do not earn a living wage, and as a consequence turnover rates are very high and the quality of care is in question.

Natural environment   The natural environment sector shows the most positive signs. The increased environmental awareness of the past ten years seems to be paying off in a generally healthy natural habitat. Air quality remains relatively good, although there are signs that the level of improvement over the past decade has reached a peak. Bird populations are, for the most part, healthy and water quality shows signs of improvement; the city's water consumption continues to decline. There is a small but growing trend toward Calgarians growing their own food and supporting local producers through farmers' markets. The biggest red flag in this sector is the continuing use of chemical pesticides on public land and even more so around private residences.

Resource use   This sector presents one of the biggest challenges. Most of the indicators have stabilised and there are signs that a turning point has been reached, but levels of consumption are still among the highest in the world. Energy use is still high above that even of European countries, and Calgary produces more greenhouse gases per unit of energy consumed today than it did ten years ago. However, there is a slow shift to renewable energy sources. Transit usage for getting to and from work has stalled at about 15 percent of commuters. The sprawl of the city acts a deterrent to more sustainable modes of transportation, but with new subdivision and inner-city developments in the works, there exists an opportunity to design and build more compact communities.

After several years without funding, the city has begun to reinvest in transportation infrastructure and take the opportunity to promote bicycle, pedestrian, and transit travel. The volume of domestic waste continues to decrease, and proven models in other Canadian cities such as Edmonton and Halifax point the way to even greater gains. Calgary is on the verge of turning the corner in this regard, but much creativity and resolve will be needed to put the city on a sustainable course.

Wellness The wellness sector reveals an interesting dichotomy. While Canada's access to health care is still the envy of most of the world, the trend for most of Calgary's wellness indicators is away from sustainability. The number of hospital visits related to childhood asthma has decreased over the past five years but remains very high. There has been a slight increase in the percentage of babies born below a healthy birthweight, but there are several factors related to the increase that do not necessarily reflect badly on the healthcare system. One area of concern is the lack of movement toward a preventive care model in the healthcare system. Alternative health care is growing in popularity, but it is not covered within the province's universal healthcare system. One of the most troubling new indicators is the meagre resources made available for the most vulnerable in Calgary. The youth wellness indicator reveals both positive and negative trends.

Part II: Outcomes to Date

The point of the sustainability indicator exercise is not only to report on indicators. Reporting is only the beginning. Ultimately, this tool should be a mechanism for real change in the way people live their lives and govern ourselves — change in how people relate to their neighbours, other communities and nations, and the natural world. What follows is a account of what has achieved to date.

As of February 2001, Sustainable Calgary had produced two State of Our City reports. Almost 2000 copies of the 1998 report are in circulation and another 2000 of the second report were printed. In the past six years, Sustainable Calgary has held more than 100 events, hosted by a range of organisations including Rotary Clubs, the Developmental Disabilities Resource Centre, L'arche, City of Calgary Aldermen, Promoting Calgary Inc., Calgary's Chamber of Commerce, Calgary Community Adult Learning Association, the Sierra Youth Coalition, and the Calgary Mennonite Centre for Newcomers.

The profile of Sustainable Calgary and thus of the issues of sustainability continues to grow. The release of the second report received significant media exposure in the city, with week-long coverage on television and radio and in newspapers. The organisation's presence is requested at more and more visioning, planning, and consultative forums both within the city as well as at the provincial and federal levels. In May 1999, Sustainable Calgary received the Mayor of Calgary's Achievement Award for Excellence in Environmental Communication.

These efforts have also been recognised internationally. The United Nations' Habitat Best Practices Program has added the 1998 Sustainability Indicators Report to its Best Practices Web Site. The 2001 State of Our City Report was nominated for the Provincial Emerald Award for Environmental Excellence. Most satisfyingly, the efforts that have been put into the process have been recognised: Sustainable Calgary was awarded the Developmental Disabilities Resource Centre's Award of Distinction for its inclusion of people with disabilities.

Focus on Continuing Education

One of the most important objectives of Sustainable Calgary, if not the most important in the long term, is education. One aspect of that focus is the Tools for Citizenship for the Twenty-First Century Course, an informal adult education course that began in May 2001. Sustainable Calgary also participates regularly in events such as Alberta's Global and Outdoor Education Conference and the Calgary Regional Health Authority's Quality of Life Symposium. Other projects — the Calgary Green Map and Our Ecological Footprint — also maintain an education focus.

Build a Constituency in the Region and Nationally

Sustainable Calgary has become a valuable resource for other communities embarking upon similar initiatives. Communities that have sought advice on indicators initiatives include Banff, Canmore, and Lethbridge in Alberta and Nelson in British Columbia. This work has brought the realisation that these grassroots efforts to define the quality of life must have an effect at the regional, provincial, and national levels. Most of the indicators do not respect political boundaries. Action at all levels is required to make a difference.

Nationally, Sustainable Calgary has contributed to the quality of life projects of the Canadian Policy Research Network (CPRN) and the Federation of Canadian Municipalities. It supports the work of Joe Jordan, member of Parliament, to legislate a national indicators report. Sustainable Calgary's findings have also been shared with communities in the United States, Ukraine, and Malaysia.

This outreach activity has exposed a global movement. It is not a co-ordinated movement, but it exists at the grassroots level, with a common link in the desire to understand what constitutes quality of life and how to redefine progress in this century.

Original Research

Sustainable Calgary has become a catalyst for new community research. One of the criteria originally established for indicator selection was the need for readily available data. However, the first report documented four indicators in progress for which no suitable measure was found (Sustainable Calgary 1998). As a result of the task forces created in the process of preparing the 2001 report, Sustainable Calgary has become engaged in significant original research. These research efforts have focussed on economic diversification, local food production, cultural diversity, sense of community, and arts and culture.

Economic diversification Sustainable Calgary's research demonstrated that even though economic diversification was much talked about in Calgary over the past several years, there was no real understanding of what a diversified economy would look like or of any outstanding measures of economic diversification. The second report documents a prototype indicator called a 'reliance index'. This indicator attempts to present a realistic picture of the level of reliance of the Calgary economy on the oil and gas industry. The index combines the rate of employment, the contribution to gross domestic product (GDP), and the percentage of import-export balance represented by the oil and gas sector in Calgary.

Valuing cultural diversity In August 2000, Sustainable Calgary convened a Valuing Cultural Diversity Task Force workshop of 15 individuals with an interest in cultural diversity or with expertise and experience in related issues. These included individuals who work in the immigrant-serving agency sector, for the City of Calgary, and for diversity program funders such as United Way, as well as university researchers. After examining several potential measures of how to value cultural diversity, the group came to a consensus on a measure of the diversity represented in positions of power and influence in Calgary. Sustainable Calgary volunteers gathered data on a group of 220 positions representing elected representatives, corporate boards, NGO agency boards, and media to measure the representation of women, visible minorities, and aboriginal people in this group as compared with the general population.

Sense of community Sustainable Calgary convened a working group including the City of Calgary, the Calgary Regional Health Authority, the United Way, and the Calgary Foundation to create a measurement tool for sense of community. This is the first such effort in Canada and its outcome will be relevant to communities across the country. This effort represents a model of citizen initiative in public and nonprofit sector collaboration that can be adapted to other issues and sectors.

Arts and culture activity There was a strong feeling throughout this process that arts and culture must be addressed in the indicator set. Again faced with a lack of information, volunteers completed a survey of the twelve high-profile festivals in the city to establish when they began and the current attendance numbers. This measure serves as an indicator of the growing vibrancy of arts and culture in Calgary.

Part III: What Is Next?

Success Stories

A new addition to the 2001 report is a section called Success Stories. This is an effort to begin to show the path to sustainability being laid out by individuals and organisations in Calgary. The stories include organic farmers, wind energy entrepreneurs, eco-building managers, local currency promoters, and collective kitchen organisers. Calgary was built on a pioneer spirit, but a new kind of pioneer is needed to make the transition to sustainability in the twenty-first century. Many people do not believe the status quo is sustainable. Sustainable Calgary will continue to recognise the pioneers who are showing that an alternative is being created.

A People's Agenda

Another initiative, begun since the publication of the 2001 report, is to begin translating indicators into policy and action. To this end, Sustainable Calgary has begun holding discussions on the drafting of a people's policy agenda. In this way, the indicators can be used to point the way to specific policies, programs, and projects that will move Calgary toward sustainability.

The foundation for this work is the priority actions that were identified in the 2001 report. The project team put out a call for nominations for priority actions — a short list of actions that have the most potential to act as a catalyst to move toward sustainability. This was met with a tremendous response. Four priority actions were highlighted in the report:

- Create a sense-of-community audit for assessing all major developments. There needs to be a better understanding of what contributes to a strong sense of community and what detracts from it. This knowledge can then be incorporated in every aspect of the city's economy, social, and physical infrastructure as well as in community planning and design. During the process of creating the first State of Our City Report, Calgarians said they considered a sense of community to be integral to their quality of life. Yet in researching the issue, it was revealed that the concept is difficult to understand and measure. Components of a sense-of-community audit will be identified from the current research that is being conducted with the collaboration of several city agencies and might include, for example, the effects of particular developments on pedestrian movement in a community or on local business.

- Reduce greenhouse gas emissions by 50 percent over 30 years through reduced energy consumption and a shift to renewable sources. The indicators presented in the 2001 report demonstrate that a reduction in energy consumption and a shift to nonpolluting forms of energy have the potential to improve Calgarians' health, environment, and economy. Two reports, 'Power Shift: Cool Solutions to Global Warming' published by the David Suzuki Foundation (2000) and the 'Low Impact Renewable Energy' published by the Canadian Association for Renewable Energies (1999), outline how these goals can be achieved. This will require that a shift in energy production to renewable sources, the reduction and recovery of waste materials, emphasis on human-powered and mass transit, and redesigned homes, workplaces, and communities so they are more efficient; it will also demand an examination of the resource costs of leisure and recreational activities. Such a shift will require a concerted effort by the municipal government, businesses, and citizens.

- Integrate a green tax system, an ecological footprint analysis, and the genuine progress indicator (GPI) into municipal decision making. People are trying to build a twenty-first–century society with twentieth-century economic tools. Full-cost accounting (economic, ecological, and social costing) of all developments must be integrated into economic planning models. In order to begin to understand all the costs of activities and decisions, it is necessary to track a GPI for the city. A municipal ecological footprint accounting system must be established for long-term planning. The Pembina Institute (2001) has created a model for this work with its provincial GPI and ecological footprint project. The current tax system that taxes work needs to be replaced with one that taxes resource consumption. In *Natural Capitalism* (Hawken, Lovins, and Lovins 1999), Amory Lovins outlines many of these tax options.
- Support and promote a culture of simplicity. People need to redefine their quality of life based on healthy living, a spiritual sense of purpose, voluntary simplicity (Burch 2000), and a balance of work, family, and community. One way to facilitate this balance at a household level is to make people more aware of the impact of their consumption choices by creating a method to monitor household ecological footprints. At the municipal government and community levels, policies and programs can be designed to support this shift in lifestyle, and policies that make it more difficult can be eliminated. The future quality of life need not be equated with a bigger house, two- or three-car households, expensive belongings, and throw-away lifestyles. People can prosper by creating a community where they can raise a family in a safe and nurturing environment, with time and opportunity for leisure and for healthy and active living, and where people can enjoy a diverse, cosmopolitan city and a healthy ecosystem.

A Collaborative Research Agenda

In its most recent strategic planning exercise, Sustainable Calgary focussed on collaborative research. Experience with the indicators in progress and its association with the University of Calgary and major civic social development funders such as the United Way and the Calgary Foundation led the organisation in this direction. Sustainable Calgary's work has demonstrated that there are significant gaps in knowledge about community issues that citizens have identified as important. It is hoped that this research agenda will be solidified and the collaboration with funders, NGOs, and the university will be strengthened.

Part IV: Implication for International Trade Agreements

It is obvious that the community sustainability indicators have ramifications beyond the local community. Many of the hundreds of indicator projects around the world have come about, at least in part, in response to the effects of globalisation over the past ten years (Barnet and Cavanagh 1994; Korten 1995; Douthwaite 1999; Fraser 2001). It certainly contributed to the birth of Sustainable Calgary. It is in part an attempt to reclaim local communities from the global economy when people are given the message that there is no choice but to submit to the inevitable march of globalisation (Yergin and Stanislaw 1998; Friedman 2000).

From the start, Sustainable Calgary has situated its work within a global perspective. Many of the founders of Sustainable Calgary have extensive international experience. They believe the sustainability of their own communities must be achieved within a ethical relationship to their neighbours and partners in the global village.

The Global Perspective: Calgary in the Global Village

Sustainable Calgary's 2001 report contained a detailed discussion of Calgary in the global village. This assessment of the city's sustainability is set in the context of relevant global economic, environmental, and social development indicators, including an ecological footprint, the Living Planet Index, the United Nations' Human Development Index, and the genuine progress indicator.

The ecological footprint The relationships between Calgarians and citizens around the world are very complex, especially in this period of accelerating global trade. The ecological footprint model interprets this complexity by examining the amount of resources consumed by an individual, community, or nation and determining how much land area is required to provide those resources on a sustainable basis. How much land does the average Calgarian need in order to provide the materials, the food, and the energy resources he or she consumes? An ecological footprint analysis suggests that Calgarians' lifestyle is not sustainable. If every individual on the earth consumed as many resources as the average Canadian, four more planets would be needed to provide for everyone. Each year, human society consumes 30 percent more of the Earth's natural capital than is regenerated (Wackernagel and Rees 1996).

Genuine progress indicator The GPI is an alternative to the gross national product (GNP). For more than a decade, economists from around the world have recognised the inadequacy of the GNP as a measurement (Daly, Cobb, and Cobb 1989; Redefining Progress 1995). It is simply the sum of all the monetary transactions made in a given year. Expenditures for environmental clean-ups, for the criminal and judicial system, for repair bills for automobile accidents, and for legal bills for divorce proceedings are all counted as benefits to society. In the GPI, negative costs are subtracted in the calculation of a nation's progress and other costs, such as unpaid household work, are included to give a more realistic picture of how much progress is being made. If environmental degradation and clean-up are properly accounted for, and the amount of money spent on social problems and resource depletion is included, then even Alberta is experiencing a reduction in well-being (Pembina Institute 2001). Similar work is being carried out in Nova Scotia, New Zealand, and Australia (Waring 1999). Even though Calgarians enjoy an undeniably high quality of life, the GPI suggests it is deteriorating.

Living Planet Index The World Wildlife Fund for Nature has created the Living Planet Index and has tracked its progress since 1960 (World Wildlife Fund 2000). This index assesses the health of the planet's major life support systems — oceans, shorelines, forests, and arable land. The index suggests that every major ecosystem type on the planet is in decline. In fact, since 1960 there has been a 33 percent reduction in the productivity of these ecosystems.

Human Development Index The United Nations ranks countries annually according to its Human Development Index. This index combines indicators of economic performance, health, education, poverty, and equality to give an overall picture of the comparative health of the countries of the world. For three success years, Canada was ranked as the best country in the world to live in, mainly on the strength of its social programs. However, in the 1999 and 2000 reports on the Human Development Index, the authors warned that Canada is losing ground as its social programs decline and the gap between rich and poor grows (United Nations Development Programme 1999).

Local Experience: A Contribution to International Trade Reform

Three particular themes have been identified with regard to how local community sustainability indicators projects can contribute to the discussion of environmental reform of global trade.

Participatory democratic process The experience of Sustainable Calgary highlights the need for a more democratic process in globalisation. In Canada, it appears to be an uninformed secretive process with little consultation and an apocalyptic air about it — Canadians must globalise or die, because it is futile to resist. The outcome of Sustainable Calgary's citizen-led process to create a State of Our City report demonstrates the wisdom of allowing citizens a voice in crafting the future of their communities. It is not beyond comprehension to imagine a democratic participatory process to inform discussions about global trade agreements. In fact, citizens groups have been demanding such a process for many years, culminating in Seattle in 1999 and continuing at every major international trade meeting since.

Questioning the mythology of economic growth A recent report by Alberta's Parkland Institute (2001) highlighted the fact that a decade of economic growth in the province has not resulted in improved household incomes. In fact, many households have experienced a reduced real income through this period. What, then, is the value of economic growth? Herman Daly, John Cobb, and Clifford Cobb (1989) have written about 'misplaced concreteness' in people's conception of the economy, by which they mean bestowing reality upon a concept that is a model of reality, rather than addressing the reality itself. In other words, the market is a model created by human thought in order to help explain behaviour. But it has been given a life of its own, in so far as people treat it as if it is a real thing: 'the market dictates that we cut interest rates'. In reality, the market is a creation of the human mind, an attempt to approximate reality. Experience is beginning to show that the models — the market and economic growth — are not up to the task of providing a good quality of life for the majority of people on the planet (Daly 1996; Harris 1998).

The Pembina Institute in Alberta and GPI Atlantic have recently released reports highlighting an alternative to the GDP, which has been the most quoted proxy for national well-being for the past half century. The GPI accounts are demonstrating that well-being has in fact been deteriorating for a quarter century if more indicators are included in the system of accounts. These global indicators, along with the suite of local indicators reported in Sustainable Calgary's 2001 State of Our City Report, suggest that economic growth is not increasing well-being. Indeed, a strong case can be made that economic growth is contributing to a reduction in well-being at this point in history. In this full world, economic growth is depleting both natural capital and social capital.

Redefining progress No equivalent to the sets of local indicators seen in Calgary, Seattle, and other communities has been compiled internationally. By implementing international trade agreements, the cart has been put before the horse. It is an act of faith, built upon discredited models of well-being, that these agreements will lead to better quality of life.

The indicators work provides an example of the kind of instrument that could be used to gauge the success of such agreements. Citizens have identified what is important to them, via these indicators. There is no reason why a set of indicators based upon a similarly broad analysis of the economy, social conditions, and ecology should not be used as tool to measure the success of global trade agreements. What good are trade agreements and an increased flow of resources around the planet if such activity does not contribute to a better quality of life in real terms at the local level?

These three themes lead to questioning the foundation upon which international trade agreements are founded. During the period in which these agreements were established, the work of Sustainable Calgary and others suggests the quality of life has not improved, nor has the sustainability of the local community. It seems obvious that people are without the tools to assess the appropriateness of trade.

Part V: Conclusion

Democratise the Process

Events of the past year have shown that there is a growing demand for, at least, a place at the table in trade negotiations for civil society organisations of all types and, at most, a radical restructuring or abandonment of the economic globalisation agenda. The work conducted by Sustainable Calgary suggests that participatory processes can be established to allow democratic decision making in the international arena. In truly democratic societies, is there any alternative? The process must be democratised, and the chips can fall where they may.

Re-equip the Toolbox

Calgary's journey to defining quality of life and sustainability has also revealed a lot about the real economy — that which provides well-being for families and communities — is all about. It is not just the sum of all monetary transactions. It is unpaid household and community volunteer work, and it is the work of nature in providing clean water, air, and soil and functioning ecosystems. What has been learned is that current economic models are lacking. They are a poor reflection of reality. They provide bad information on which to base decisions. It is impossible to gauge the costs and benefits of international trade without the proper tools to do so. Therefore, it is imperative to develop more appropriate tools and models that approximate reality more accurately and allow better decisions to be made.

Note

1   Full details on the CEROI network are available at www.ceroi.net.

References

Barnet, Richard J. and John Cavanagh (1994). *Global Dreams: Imperial Corporations and the New World Order*. Simon & Schuster, New York.

Burch, A. Mark (2000). *Stepping Lightly: Simplicity for People and the Planet*. Gabriola Island, BC, New Society Publishers.

Campbell, Monica, Diane Spear, and Virginia Maclaren (1996). 'Municipal State of the Environment Reporting in Canada: Current Status and Future Needs'. Occasional Paper Series No. 6. Environment Canada, Ottawa.

Canadian Association for Renewable Energies (1999). 'Low Impact Renewable Energy: Options for a Clean Environment and Health Canadian Economy'. Canadian Association for Renewable Energies, Ottawa.

City of Calgary (2000). 'The City of Calgary Corporate Customer Satisfaction Survey 2000'. <www.gov.calgary.ab.ca/custsurvey/index.htm> (December 2001).

Daly, Herman E. (1996). *Beyond Growth: The Economics of Sustainable Development*. Beacon Press, Boston.

Daly, Herman E., John B. Cobb, and Clifford W. Cobb (1989). *For the Common Good: Redirecting the Economy toward Community, the Environment, and a Sustainable Future*. Beacon Press, Boston.

David Suzuki Foundation (2000). 'Power Shift: Cool Solutions to Global Warming'. David Suzuki Foundation, Vancouver.

Douthwaite, R. J. (1999). *The Growth Illusion: How Economic Growth Has Enriched the Few, Impoverished the Many, and Endangered the Planet*. Rev. ed. New Society Publishers, Philadelphia.

Fraser, Jill Andresky (2001). *White-Collar Sweatshop: The Deterioration of Work and Its Rewards in Corporate America*. 1st ed. Norton, New York.

Friedman, Thomas L. (2000). *The Lexus and the Olive Tree*. Rev. ed. Farrar Straus Giroux, New York.

GPI Atlantic (2001). 'Nova Scotia's Ecological Footprint'. GPI Atlantic, Tantallon, NS.

Harris, Michael (1998). *Lament for an Ocean: The Collapse of the Atlantic Cod Fishery — A True Crime Story*. McClelland and Stewart, Toronto.

Hawken, Paul, L. Hunter Lovins, and Amory B. Lovins (1999). *Natural Capitalism: Creating the Next Industrial Revolution*. 1st ed. Little Brown and Co., Boston.

International Institute on Sustainable Development (2000). 'Measurement and Indicators for Sustainable Development'. <iisd1.iisd.ca/measure/> (December 2001).

Keough, Noel (1995). 'Reclaiming Our Communities from the Global Economy'. Conference Proceedings, 'Sustainable Development in the 21st Century Americas: Alternative Visions of Progress'. University of Calgary, Division of International Development, Dialogue on Development Series.

Korten, David. (1995). *When Corporations Rule the World*. Kumarian Press, West Hartford, CT.

Korten, David. (1999). *The Post-Corporate World: Life after Capitalism*. 1st ed. Berrett-Koehler, San Francisco.

Lougheed, Peter (2000). 'Major Forces Shaping a New Canada'. *Calgary Herald*, 1 December. p. A33.

Parkland Institute (2001). 'Advantage for Whom: Declining Family Income in a Growing Alberta Economy'. Parkland Institute, University of Alberta, Edmonton.

Pembina Institute (2001). 'The Alberta Geniune Progress Indicator Accounts: A Blueprint for the Way We Really Live'. Pembina Institute for Appropriate Development, Drayton Valley, AB.

Promoting Calgary Inc. (2001). 'C-Prosperity: Regional Diagnosis'. Promoting Calgary Inc., Calgary.

Redefining Progress (1995). 'The Genuine Progress Indicator: Summary of Data and Methodology'. Redefining Progress, San Francisco.

Saul, John Ralston (1992). *Voltaire's Bastards: The Dictatorship of Reason in the West*. Penguin, Toronto.

Sustainable Calgary (1998). 'State of Our City Report 1998'. Sustainable Calgary, Calgary.

Sustainable Calgary (2001). 'State of Our City Report 2001'. Sustainable Calgary, Calgary.

Sustainable Seattle (1995). 'Sustainable Seattle State of Our City Report'. Sustainable Seattle, Seattle.

United Nations Development Programme (1999). *Human Development Report 1999*. Oxford University Press, Oxford.

Wackernagel, Mathis and William E. Rees (1996). *Our Ecological Footprint: Reducing Human Impact on the Earth*. New Society Publishers, Gabriola Island, BC.

Waring, Marilyn (1999). *Counting for Nothing: What Men Value and What Women Are Worth*. 2nd ed. University of Toronto Press, Toronto.

World Commission on Environment and Development (1987). *Our Common Future*. Oxford University Press, Oxford; New York.

World Wildlife Fund (2000). 'Living Planet Report 2000'. <www.panda.org/livingplanet/lpr00> (December 2001).

Yergin, Daniel and Joseph Stanislaw (1998). *The Commanding Heights: The Battle between Government and the Marketplace That Is Remaking the Modern World*. Simon and Schuster, New York.

Chapter 18

Development and Usability of a System for Environment and Health Indicators: A Case Study

David L. Buckeridge and Carl G. Amrhein[1]

Indicators are data intended to reflect some characteristics of a population. Recent improvements in data storage and computer networking have facilitated access to data and made it easier to develop indicators. These changes create opportunities to enhance decision making through new indicators, but they also raises questions about how to develop indicators from available data. Although it is obvious, it bears noting that indicators are a means for enhancing decision making, and are not an end in their own right. Therefore, in addition to examining the development of indicators, it is also important to examine how indicators are used. The goal of this chapter is to identify and discuss issues that influence indicator development, and the use of indicators for decision making. This is approached through the use of a case study.

The case study in question is of a project that aimed to improve access to community health information. The project used an action research methodology (Boog et al. 1996) to develop and refine a geographic information system (GIS), which provided ready access to routinely collected community-level data about environment and health, via an active collaboration between the community and university. A GIS is a set of tools for collecting, storing, and analysing geographically referenced data. A GIS was chosen for this project because this technology facilitates the integration of disparate data sources and provides an intuitive means of data visualisation, namely mapping. In order to assess the GIS, the logistical, conceptual, and technical problems that were encountered during system development were studied, system users were surveyed, and a qualitative analysis was conducted of the issues that arose in the collaborative process. This chapter focusses on the development issues and user perspectives of the systems. A more complete overview of the project is available elsewhere (Buckeridge et al. 2001).

The chapter is divided into three sections. Immediately following this introduction is a description of the evolution of the community-university collaboration that supported the case study, an overview of the system development, and a brief illustration of the characteristics of the GIS. Further on, developmental issues are discussed, as is the use of the system of health and environment indicators. The chapter concludes with some recommendations for the development of future systems of indicators.

The Case Study

Background

The project behind this chapter was, in many ways, the product of two trends in community health research in Canada throughout the 1980s and 1990s: the increasing involvement of community stakeholders in the joint design, conduct, and dissemination of research concerning local health problems; and attempts to bridge narrow academic disciplinary perspectives by fostering truly transdisciplinary investigation (Rosenfield 1992; Health Canada 1997; World Health Organization 1997). Within this context, the project was fostered by a deeply held conviction, shared by both the community and the university partners participating in this project, that a better job of understanding and acting on the 'upstream causes' of ill health at the population level (McKinlay 1979) could be done through partnering and integrating the diverse perspectives and resources represented in the project.

Because events prior to the initiation of collaborative projects have the potential to shape the nature and influence the success of what subsequently develops (Altman 1995; Hodgson and Abbasi 1995; Guldan 1996), a brief project history is provided. The project represents a unique community-university partnership. The community partners in this project were all members of the Southeast Toronto (SETO) coalition, which is a group of health agencies, social services, and residents in a discrete geographical area of the city of Toronto. SETO was formed in 1989 to strengthen agency collaboration and community involvement in identifying and responding to the health needs of residents. The university partners included academics from several departments in four faculties at the University of Toronto – Arts and Science (Geography and Planning), Architecture, Medicine (Public Health Sciences), and Social Work.

The downtown Toronto community served by SETO members has, by Canadian standards, a high prevalence of low-income, unemployment, single-parent families, and teen births and elevated mortality rates from a variety of causes. In addition, certain groups face barriers to accessing healthcare information and services and to involvement in decision making. Southeast Toronto also has a long history of community mobilisation. For example, Toronto's first legal clinic was established in the area, and many other services were established as a result of the residents' commitment and ability to take action. Accessible community health information has been an interest of SETO since its inception. For example, one coalition partner, the Toronto Public Health Department, designed a series of neighbourhood profiles for use by local agencies. SETO partners had also explored the use of maps for health assessment and service planning, and were interested in further investigating the potential of this method of representing health information.

From an academic perspective, this project arose out of a deliberate effort on the part of the University of Toronto to facilitate a collaborative applied research initiative, which was to focus on the basic determinants of urban health, employ interdisciplinary teams, and involve local community organisations as active partners. This three-year initiative began in 1994 and was led by the newly appointed Provostial Advisor on Population Health. The first steps were a series of *ad hoc* meetings of academics interested in such research collaboration, together with members of SETO. The project that ultimately received funding was a direct outcome of these initial meetings.

In the years leading up to the funded project, SETO partners identified two issues of specific interest: respiratory health and the need for accessible and relevant community health information. In 1995, a team of co-investigators including SETO members and researchers from the University of Toronto, submitted an initial research proposal to a national public-sector funding agency to develop health data maps that would be accessible and useful to SETO members. This initial proposal was rejected and, in 1996, SETO and the University of Toronto Research Office provided the 'health data mapping project' team with seed funding to conduct an exploratory investigation into the nature and extent of respiratory illness in this area of the city. The results of this preliminary investigation indicated that rates of hospital admissions for respiratory illness were greater than expected. Although the limited information available did not allow for a thorough examination of the determinants and status of community respiratory health status, it did confirm that both respiratory health and access to a greater breadth and depth of health information were priorities for SETO members. At the same time as this exploratory study was being carried out, the project team continued to revise the more extensive research proposal, which was re-submitted in September 1996. This submission was successful and funding was received for a two-year project that began in September 1997.

Development Process

System development followed a collaborative, interdisciplinary action research design (Boog et al. 1996). Within this paradigm, development of the GIS involved iteration through the steps depicted in Figure 18.1. This approach drew upon theory and methods encapsulated in standard models of information system development (Checkland and Holwell 1998), with a particular focus on participatory design (Sjoberg and Timpka 1998) and GIS development methods (Becker et al. 1995). The following paragraphs offer comments on the most notable steps in a single iteration of the development cycle. Broadly summarised, the steps shown in Figure 18.1 fall into three areas: determination of community partner needs and abilities (Figure 18.1, a–d), development or refinement of the information system (Figure 18.1, e–i), and assessment of the system by community partners (Figure 18.1, j).

In the initial step (Figure 18.1, a), university and community partners developed a conceptual data model. The purpose of this model was to facilitate data integration and enable discussion of respiratory health concepts among participants from different

Figure 18.1 Overview of Iterative System Development Process

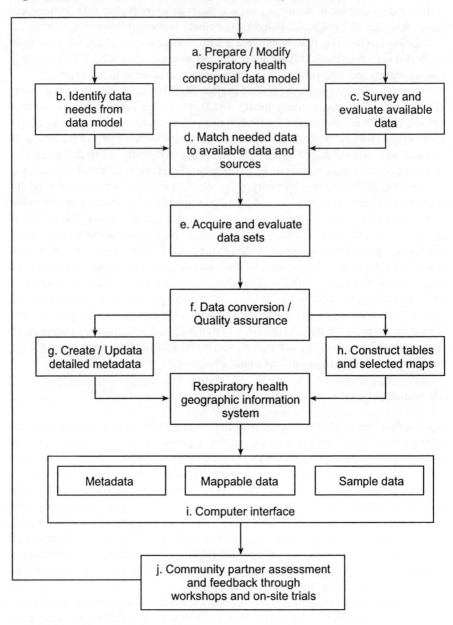

Source: Adapted from Becker et al. (1995).

backgrounds. The data model was developed through discussion and modification of a determinants of health model (Evans and Stoddart 1990; Frank 1995). That model was chosen because it explicitly acknowledges the influence of nonmedical determinants (such as income, occupation, environment) on population health status, qualitatively relates these determinants to health outcomes, and has been used successfully as the basis for other population health information systems (Roos et al. 1995). The resulting conceptual data model was consistent with theories of population health (Evans and Stoddart 1990; Frank 1995) and respiratory health (Rosen 1999; Stone 2000; Valacer 2000), while still being straightforward enough for use in a community setting.

The next steps involved identifying, evaluating, and acquiring potentially relevant data sets (Figure 18.1, b–d). For lack of other available mechanisms, investigators relied upon previously existent or informal contacts to identify relevant data for the project. Separate conditions were negotiated with each data holder to allow data set access and transfer. The conditions of access usually centred on the data set being used only for research purposes. To facilitate a standard approach to data evaluation, a metadata model was devised based on the Canadian federal standards (Inter-Agency Committee on Geomatics 1996) and U.S. federal standards (Federal Geographic Data Committee 1994) for geographic metadata. Metadata are literally data about data. In the context of large data sets, metadata generally refer to the descriptive data that accompany a data set (for example, the date of collection, variable names). The metadata model developed for this project was used as an evaluation framework for data sets prior to their inclusion in the system, and as a template to describe each data set in full after inclusion in the information system (Figure 18.1, c, e, g).

Once data were acquired, they were integrated into the GIS using the data model and the spatial unit of the enumeration area (the enumeration area [EA] was a census sampling area with a median population of 400 in Southeast Toronto) to relate data sets to one another (Figure 18.1, f). Base maps of EA boundaries were constructed in using software called MapInfo (version 5.0, MapInfo Corporation, Troy, NY) and ARC/INFO (version 7.1, Environmental Systems Research Institute, Redlands, CA) formats to provide lattices for the integration and display of data. Georeferenced data sets were translated into MapInfo tables and stored in a directory structure reflecting the conceptual data model.

When necessary, data were modified to facilitate appropriate interpretation of rates, and to ensure confidentiality of sensitive data (Figure 18.1, h). Calculating standardised or stratified rates addressed confounding effects such as age and gender. Unstable rates resulting from small numbers of events in geographic areas were smoothed using empirical Bayes estimation (Marshall 1991). Despite the lack of personal identifiers attached to the data, privacy was still a concern in some cases given the small size of the enumeration area. Consequently, some data were subjected to one or more methods to protect confidentiality (Cox 1996) either before acquisition by the project or prior to inclusion in the information system. For example, census data for small areas were subject to random rounding, dot maps were constructed by placing dots randomly within an area, and health data were only made available in aggregate form or as standardised rates. The need to protect data in this manner depends on the type of data and the level of data resolution. In general, health outcome data pose the greatest potential threat to privacy, and must be treated with considerable care. Also, since a GIS allows users to view data at various resolutions (as in, users can 'drill down'), steps must be taken to ensure that data are not viewed at a resolution that would infringe on privacy.

On the basis of user comments, the system was limited to three types of map that were most easily interpreted (shaded or choropleth maps, dot density maps, and graduated symbol maps). Map creation was limited by data type to ensure appropriate depiction for a given data type (for example, counts could be mapped as dot density or graduated symbol, but not as choropleth or shaded maps). A graphical user interface was designed to allow users with varying levels of skill to have access to metadata and to view or create maps in a manner suited to their skills (Figure 18.1, i). The iterative nature of the overall project design and the close involvement of users in system design drew upon both user-centred and rapid prototyping/iterative design methods (Patel and Kushniruk 1997).

Community partner needs and abilities continually directed the development of the information system through a series of four university-based workshops as well as on-site testing at community partner locations (Figure 18.1, j; workshops summarised in Table 18.1). At briefings held after the workshops, investigators discussed their observations and user comments, and developed action plans for making necessary modifications to the system. At the on-site trials, system users completed a questionnaire addressing data content, system interface, and system utility. Completed questionnaires were analysed by calculating summary statistics for responses to questions on a Likert scale, and by identifying themes in responses to open questions. Following the first three workshops and the on-site trial, another iteration was initiated through the system development cycle.

System Characteristics

The GIS was implemented on a personal computer platform using standard software for mapping (MapInfo Professional, MapInfo Corporation, Troy, NY), data storage (Excel 97, Microsoft Corporation, Redmond, WA), and storage of data set descriptions (Word 97, Microsoft Corporation, Redmond, WA). Only the graphical user interface required extensive customisation, through the MapBasic programming language (MapInfo Corporation, Troy, NY). Through three different levels of custom interface (Figure 18.2) users could view pre-made maps; they could also create, overlay, and analyse custom maps through series of prompts from the system (that is, use a 'wizard'), or have access to the full functionality of MapInfo for more complex map creation and analysis. Examples of sample maps created for the first level of the interface are shown in Figure 18.3. All levels of the interface allowed access to metadata as brief overview 'pop up' screens or links to detailed metadata files. Users could also store maps they had constructed, and print them. Table 18.2 lists a range of data describing the determinants and manifestations of respiratory health that were included in the GIS.

Table 18.1 Community Partner Assessment and Feedback during System Development

Event	Month of project*		Aim	Organisation
	1	2	Introduce project to potential system users at partner organisations; gather initial user input on system requirements.	Half-day session in meeting room, presentation by research team; open discussion of system requirements.
	2	10		Hands-on half-day workshops in university computer laboratory; users worked on simulated scenarios (developed with community partners); co-investigators gathered opinions on system content and interface.
Workshop	3	16	Community partner assessment of information system; feedback to research team on aspects of system to refine in next iteration of system development cycle.	
On-site testing		20		Two-week period of on-site system use by community partners at community organisations; initial training session and ongoing support; feedback gathered via questionnaire.
Workshop	4	24	Present initial results to system users; discuss future directions.	Half-day session in meeting room, presentation by research team; open discussion of future directions.

*Project duration was 24 months.

Figure 18.2   Screenshots of the Customised User Interface

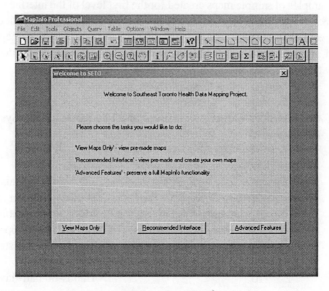

a. Initial screen following logon. Three levels of interface are suited to different levels of user skill. 'View Maps Only' accesses a selection of pre-made maps; 'Advanced Features' provides full access to MapInfo.

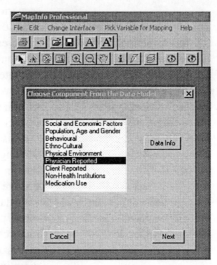

b. First screen of intermediate interface. The user selects a data model component for mapping ('Physician Reported'). The interface is now simplified, and metadata are accessible by clicking 'Data Info'.

Figure 18.2   Screenshots of the Customised User Interface, cont'd

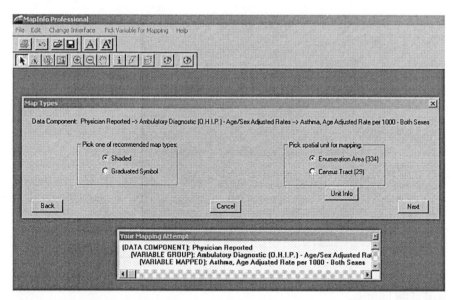

c. Intermediate interface after selecting a data model component, a variable group, and a specific variable to map. The user is now prompted for a map type and a spatial resolution. The user's path through the data model is shown at the top of the 'Map Types' window and in the 'Your Mapping Attempt' window. Available map types are constrained by the type of variable (i.e., the user is mapping a rate, so the 'dot density' map type is not available), and more information about spatial resolution can be accessed by clicking on 'Unit Info'.

Table 18.2 Data Contained in Geographic Information System

Organisation data acquired from	Data acquired
Data describing determinants of respiratory health	
Statistics Canada	Census, cartographic files
City of Toronto	Land use, traffic volume
Environment Canada	Air monitoring and emissions
Ontario Ministry of the Environment	Air monitoring
Compusearch	Consumer spending patterns
Data describing outcomes of respiratory health	
Canadian Institute for Health Information	Hospital separations
Ontario Health Insurance Plan	Ambulatory physician visits and procedures
IMS	Prescription drug sales

Figure 18.3   Sample Maps Created for the 'View Maps Only' Interface

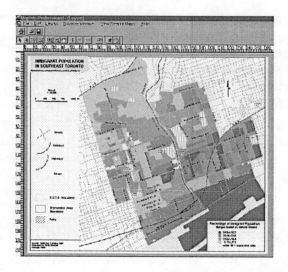

a. Example of a single data-layer shaded (choropleth) map taken from the 'View Maps Only' level of the interface.

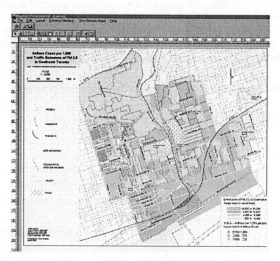

b. Example of a two data layers on a single map taken from the 'View Maps Only' level of the interface. The shaded map shows hospital admissions for asthma, and the line map shows modelled motor vehicle emissions. Compound maps are useful for exploratory analyses, but present a problem in ensuring appropriate data interpretation.

Issues Influencing Development and Usability

In the course of the project, a number of issues were encountered that influenced the development and usability of the system for environment and health indicators. These issues are summarised in Table 18.3 and discussed below under the following headings: stakeholder involvement in development, logistical problems in gathering data, and presenting data to users.

Table 18.3 Issues Influencing the Development and Usability of Indicator Systems

Aspect of development process	Examples from the case study	
	Major issue encountered	Solutions
Stakeholder involvement in development	Difficult to maintain involvement of community partners.	Used hands-on development workshops and on-site system pilots; included community partners on technical development team.
Logistical problems in gathering data	No means to systematically locate data.	Used informal research networks; approached branches of government.
	Unclear legal and administrative grounds for sharing data.	Negotiated separate conditions of use for each data set and confirmed data would be used for research.
	Limited and inconsistent descriptions of existing data (i.e., metadata).	Adopted standard metadata model to represent available descriptions in an organised manner.
Presenting data to users	Differing conceptions of respiratory health among participants.	Jointly developed data model through discussion between academic and community partners.
	Potential for data display to be misleading.	Limited available map types and constrained map types by data types; provided access to metadata during map making and display.
	Range of user skill and needs.	Developed user interface with different levels to match classes of skill level.

Stakeholder Involvement in Development

Indicators are a means to an end. It would therefore seem reasonable when developing them to start with their intended use and work backward to arrive at the appropriate indicators. In information systems development, a user-centred design approach is intended to accomplish this, and 'participatory design' goes even further by continuing to involve users throughout the design process (Lorenzi et al. 1997; Checkland and Holwell 1998; Gremy, Fessler, and Bonnin 1999). The project relied on both user-centred and participatory design methods to develop a system that would meet the needs of users. In order to determine how successful it was in this respect, a survey was administered to elicit user opinions of data content, the interface, and the relevance of the GIS.

Eight users completed the questionnaire while testing the system at five community partner sites. The four female and four male respondents were all in positions that required frequent use of computers to manipulate health data (such as health promoter, health information analyst, research manager). In addition, some (three) regularly used mapping and statistical software, and the majority (five) regularly used database software. As Table 18.4 shows, users found that the intermediate level interface was easy to use, and felt that the system in general was useful (average response of 3.3 for

Table 18.4 Questionnaire Responses for Selected Questions (n = 8)

Area	Question	Average[*]	Max.	Min.
Usability	Overall, how easy/difficult was it to use the mapping program?	3.3	4	2
Data	How relevant are the types of data in the mapping program to your work?	2.9	4	0
	How appropriate is the level of detail of the data in the mapping program to your work?	2.4	3	2
	How relevant are the types of maps produced by the mapping program to your work?	2.8	4	2
General system	Overall, if you had access to a similar mapping program in the future, how useful would it be for your work?	3.3	4	2

[*]Responses were given according to a five-point Likert scale, with a maximum value of 4, and a minimum of 0.

both questions on a scale from 4 to 0). Users also thought that the types of data and types of maps were relevant (average responses 2.9 and 2.8, respectively), but there was less satisfaction with the level of detail in the available data (average response 2.4). Users commented that it would be helpful to have more recent data, data for neighbouring areas (to support comparisons), and specific data sets not already included in the system (for example, cancer, communicable diseases). When questioned about what activities that the GIS could facilitate, nearly all users (seven) indicated it was useful for describing the community, many (six) thought it was useful for health advocacy and planning, and some (five) thought that it would useful for health services and disease aetiology research. Only half the respondents (four) indicated that the system would be useful for delivery of health services. Specific comments made about the utility of the system included: 'It is useful to see trends in the patient population within a service area', and 'The system provides a way of presenting information that is easy for an audience to understand'.

The user feedback suggests that the objective of collaboratively developing an interactive, accessible GIS was met. The system appeared to meet some needs of a select group of users for environment and health indicators relevant to the population of Southeast Toronto. The continuing involvement of users in the development process likely played an important role in the outcome. There are, however, some qualifications that should be noted. First, the evaluation results are based on a small sample of relatively proficient computer users who routinely handle health data. Users with different skill levels and tasks (such as social service agencies or community residents) will likely view the system functionality differently and have different data needs. It should also be noted that although the continuing involvement of users appeared to be instrumental, it was also difficult to maintain, and co-ordinating user involvement required considerably more resources than had been estimated at the outset of the project. These difficulties were encountered despite the strong 'official' interest of the community partner agencies in the project. Enabling factors for involving users appeared to be the iterative development process, direct involvement of users in the development team, and on-site system evaluation at community partner locations. The difficulties encountered appeared to be due to factors such as heavy workloads of community partners and limited project resources for scheduling meetings and workshops. Issues such as the ongoing restructuring of the provincial healthcare system may have also contributed. These problems did not have an impact on the system development timeline, but they did result in less user involvement in the design process than the researchers had originally hoped for. The ultimate impact on the system itself is difficult to assess. In general, participatory development of a system across a number of organisations in a community is a logistically complex undertaking. Given the problems encountered in maintaining user involvement in system development within a single organisation (Lorenzi et al. 1997; Checkland and Holwell 1998), it is not surprising that user involvement was problematic in a community setting.

Logistical Problems in Gathering Data

Development of a meaningful system of environment and health indicators requires gathering data from a number of sources. However, despite the potential benefit from combining different data sources (Office of Health and the Information Highway 1998; Stead et al. 2000), few systems exist that successfully accomplish this (van Oers 1993; Roos et al. 1995; Berndt, Hevner, and Studnicki 1998; Linger et al. 1998). This limited success is likely attributable in part to logistical problems, such as identification, description, and acquisition of data sets, and privacy concerns (Twigg 1990; Marrett et al. 1998; Mettee, Martin, and Williams 1998; O'Dwyer and Burton 1998).

Data identification, description, and acquisition In the case study, identification of data sets was difficult due to the lack of any sort of data directory. Most data were identified through public sources, as the appropriate contacts data were often more readily identifiable in the public sector (namely the appropriate level or branch of government) than in the private sector. Evaluation of data quality was found to be difficult for many routinely collected data sets. The difficulty often stemmed from the lack of available data documentation (that is, metadata) or from the lack of a human contact who could provide a verbal description of the data. It is increasingly being recognised that good metadata are important for ensuring data quality and facilitating appropriate data use. Adoption of a standard metadata model made it easier to assess different data sets in a standard manner, but it did not help to assess data for which no metadata were available. It is noteworthy that system users consistently found metadata important for meaningful interpretation of data, but brief descriptions of data quality were often felt to be sufficient.

The issues encountered in identifying and describing data sources for community health can be stated succinctly as a lack of directories for locating existing data (Ramroop and Pascoe 1999), generally poor descriptions (metadata) for existing data (O'Dwyer and Burton 1998), and nonstandard encoding of data. Web access to directories of data would greatly facilitate identifying data sources, and there are efforts underway to develop these in some countries (Office of Health and the Information Highway 1998). Considerable effort has been directed at vocabularies and data standards in clinical medicine (Cimino 1998; McDonald et al. 1998), but progress in community health has been slow (Godden, Pollack, and Pheby 2000), despite development of standard health data models by some countries (Australian Institute of Health and Welfare 1995; Partnership for Health Informatics/Telematics 1999). The importance of these issues must be acknowledged within public and community health, and concrete steps must be taken to address them.

Privacy Another issue routinely encountered in attempting to acquire data sets was a concern over privacy. Many data holders did not have an established protocol for access to their data or a clearly identified person with the authority to release data. In the absence of these, data holders were reluctant to release data, and acquisition of some data required a considerable amount of discussion and follow-up. Negotiations to obtain data centred on the research nature of the project, and it would likely be quite difficult to gain access to the necessary data in a nonresearch context. The difficulties encountered in acquiring data indicate that privacy concerns present a serious obstacle to system development. Concerns have been raised in a number of countries about the use of population level health data (Gostin 1997; Horner 1998; Privacy Commissioner of Canada 1999). In order to provide a socially acceptable and practically useful framework (McCarthy et al. 1999) for community health information system development, a legislative balance must be struck between the right to privacy and the social benefit of using data for community health (Willison 1998). Without such a clearly articulated balance, acquisition of community health data will likely continue to be an arduous process.

Presenting Data to Users

Access to information is clearly important to enable individuals and communities to address health issues (World Health Organization 1986), but once accessed, information must be presented in a comprehensible manner that enables its use. The ability to make use of assembled data is influenced by many factors, including the underlying structure of the data, how the data are depicted, and the skill and knowledge of the system user.

Data structure As information systems increase in prevalence and complexity, models of the relationships among data elements are becoming increasingly important. Data models, more correctly called 'ontologies', explicitly define how concepts (that is, variables) within data sources relate to each other. In a sense they are explicit 'mental models' or 'conceptual models' that facilitate integration of data by information systems (Davidson, Overton, and Buneman 1995) and support a common understanding of data by people (Chandrasekaran and Josephson 1999). The case study found that community partner representatives and university researchers from different disciplines tended to use different vocabularies and concepts. The conceptual data model developed by participants over a number of meetings was successful in facilitating a common dialogue about health and environmental issues, and in enabling access to data.

Data depiction Early in the project, it was apparent that a range of data depiction options (from premade maps to a full-function GIS) would be necessary to meet the variable needs of different end users. The complex nature of the data and the heterogeneity in user skill and knowledge both demanded consideration in the design of data depictions in order to facilitate appropriate interpretation. Data manipulations, limitation of map type by data characteristics, and provision of access to metadata partially addressed this issue. In addition, the workshops provided opportunities to review critical issues in data depiction. Visual depiction of complex demographic, healthcare utilisation, consumer, and environmental information is challenging (Tufte 1997). This is especially the case when combining data from disparate sources and working across disciplinary boundaries. The potential for misinterpretation of data was minimised by providing descriptions of data sets and by constraining how data types could be depicted (Byrom and Pascoe 1999). It was not an objective of this study to explore the relationships between user skill level and data depiction issues systematically. No authoritative comment is therefore offered on what types of information or interface are best suited to different skill levels. This is an important area for further research.

User skill and knowledge The range of user skill and knowledge was partially addressed by developing a graphical user interface with a number of different levels, each supporting a different level of users with different skills and knowledge. Problems with the interface design included incorporation of a variety of visualisation methods (such as tables, text, maps) into a single interface, and the need to change the interface constantly to accommodate a refined understanding of user needs and changes in the underlying data structure. Standard software engineering methods, such as design models and modular programming, helped to address these problems. Users of indicator systems will nearly always have variable skills and organisational contexts (Medyckyj-Scott 1993), and this variability influences system requirements (Bowker and Star 1999). Creation of multiple levels of user interface, as done in this study, is one possible approach to this problem of variable user characteristics. Another approach is to use artificial intelligence, as employed in decision support systems, to facilitate user control of information visualisation (Shahar and Musen 1996; Andrienko and Andrienko 1999).

Conclusion

This chapter concludes with some suggestions, based on experience, to facilitate both the development of environment and health indicator systems for communities. Geographic information systems, and information systems in general, have the potential to be powerful resources for integrating and presenting health and environment indicators. However, there are clearly several issues that hinder the development and use of these systems. Based on their findings, the researchers in this project recommend some steps for enabling system development and usability. First, system developers should employ design methodologies that facilitate user involvement, while being aware of the effort required to maintain user involvement in the design process. Second, governmental and nongovernmental data creators and holders should take steps to improve environment and health data accessibility and usability. This should include actions to improve data documentation (that is, metadata), create data directories, develop data standards, and enhance compliance with existing standards. In addition, a wide range of stakeholders in society must collectively address the issues of privacy and stewardship of data. Third, health informatics research should explore methods to optimise the use of assembled population health data. Methods to allow visualisation and analysis of data from a variety of sources across space and time must be developed and evaluated.

Note

1   The authors would like first to acknowledge the contributions of the investigators in the Health Data Mapping Group from the University of Toronto. Without their efforts, the case study described in this chapter could not have been completed. They are also grateful for the far-sighted support of Professor Adel Sedra (Office of the Provost, University of Toronto), Professor Heather Munroe-Blum (Vice-President, Research and International Relations, University of Toronto), and the members of the Southeast Toronto coalition, all of whom were instrumental to the vision and completion of this project. In addition, they gratefully acknowledge the support of the National Health Research Development Program (NHRDP), which provided funding for the research project and also the financial support of the Community Medicine Residency Program at the University of Toronto.

References

Altman, D. G. (1995). 'Sustaining Interventions in Community Systems: On the Relationship between Researchers and Communities'. *Health Psychology* vol. 14, no. 6, pp. 526–536.

Andrienko, G. and N. Andrienko (1999). 'Data Characterization Schema for Intelligent Support in Visual Data Analysis'. In C. Freksa and D. M. Mark, eds., *Spatial Information Theory: Cognitive and Computational Foundations of Geographic Information Science*, pp. 349–365. Springer-Verlag, Berlin.

Australian Institute of Health and Welfare (1995). 'National Health Information Model, Version 1'.

Becker, P., H. Calkins, C. J. Cote, et al. (1995). *GIS Development Guide*. Erie County Water Authority, National Center for Geographic Information and Analysis, State University of New York at Buffalo, GIS Resource Group Inc., Albany, NY.

Berndt, D. J., A. R. Hevner, and J. Studnicki (1998). 'Catch/It: A Data Warehouse to Support Comprehensive Assessment for Tracking Community Health'. Proceedings of the annual symposium of the American Medical Informatics Association, pp. 250–254.

Boog, B., H. Coenen, L. Keune, et al., eds. (1996). *Theory and Practice of Action Research*. Tilburg University Press, Tilburg.

Bowker, G. C. and S. L. Star (1999). 'Building Information Infrastructures for Social Worlds: The Role of Classifications and Standards'. In T. Ishida, ed., *Community Computing and Support Systems: Social Interaction in Networked Communities*, pp. 231–248. Springer-Verlag, Berlin.

Buckeridge, D. L., R. Mason, A. Robertson, et al. (forthcoming). 'Making Health Data Maps: A Case Study of a Community/University Research Collaboration'. *Social Science and Medicine*.

Byrom, G. M. and R. T. Pascoe (1999). 'Design Considerations for Minimising the Inappropriate Use of Spatial Data in a GIS'. 11th Annual Colloquium of the Spatial Information Research Centre, University of Otago, Otago, New Zealand.

Chandrasekaran, B. and J. R. Josephson (1999). 'What Are Ontologies and Why Do We Need Them?' *IEEE Intelligent Systems* vol. 14, no. 1, pp. 20–26.

Checkland, P. and S. Holwell (1998). *Information, Systems, and Information Systems*. John Wiley and Sons, Chichester.

Cimino, J. J. (1998). 'Desiderata for Controlled Medical Vocabularies in the Twenty-First Century'. *Methods of Information in Medicine* vol. 37, no. 4–5, pp. 394–403.

Cox, L. H. (1996). 'Protecting Confidentiality in Small Population Health and Environmental Statistics'. *Statistics in Medicine* vol. 15, no. 17–18, pp. 1895–1905.

Davidson, S. B., C. Overton, and P. Buneman (1995). 'Challenges in Integrating Biological Data Sources'. *Journal of Computational Biology* vol. 2, no. 4, pp. 557–572.

Evans, R. G. and G. L. Stoddart (1990). 'Producing Health, Consuming Health Care'. *Social Science and Medicine* vol. 31, no. 12, pp. 1347–1363.

Federal Geographic Data Committee (1994). *Content Standards for Digital Spatial Metadata*. Federal Geographic Data Committee, Washington DC.

Frank, J. W. (1995). 'The Determinants of Health: A New Synthesis'. *Current Issues in Public Health* vol. 1, pp. 233–240.

Godden, S., A. Pollack, and D. Pheby (2000). 'Informational on Community Health Services: More and Better Information Is Needed — Not Less'. *British Medical Journal* vol. 320, p. 265.

Gostin, L. (1997). 'Health Care Information and the Protection of Personal Privacy: Ethical and Legal Consideration'. *Annals of Internal Medicine* vol. 127, no. 8, pt. 2, pp. 683–690.

Gremy, F., J. M. Fessler, and M. Bonnin (1999). 'Information Systems Evaluation and Subjectivity'. *International Journal of Medical Informatics* vol. 56, pp. 13–23.

Guldan, G. S. (1996). 'Obstacles to Community Health Promotion'. *Social Science and Medicine* vol. 43, no. 5, pp. 689–695.

Health Canada (1997). *Health Promotion in Canada: A Case Study*. Health Canada, Ottawa.

Hodgson, R. and T. Abbasi (1995). *Effective Mental Health Promotion: Literature Review*. Health Promotion Wales.

Horner, J. S. (1998). 'Research, Ethics, and Privacy: The Limits of Knowledge'. *Public Health* vol. 112, no. 4, pp. 217–220.

Inter-Agency Committee on Geomatics (1996). 'Barriers to the Use of Geomatics Data, Data Quality, and Documentation Standards'. Working Group on Coordination and Cooperation.

Linger, H., F. Burstein, A. Zaslavsky, et al. (1998). 'Conceptual Development of an Information Systems Framework for Improving Continuity in Epidemiological Research'. *European Journal of Epidemiology* vol. 14, no. 6, pp. 587–593.

Lorenzi, N. M., R. T. Riley, A. J. Blyth, et al. (1997). 'Antecedents of the People and Organizational Aspects of Medical Informatics: Review of the Literature'. *Journal of the American Medical Informatics Association* vol. 4, no. 2, pp. 79–93.

Marrett, L. D., B. Theis, M. I. Baker, et al. (1998). 'Challenges of Developing a Cervical Screening Information System: The Ontario Pilot Project'. *Cancer Prevention and Control* vol. 2, no. 5, pp. 221–227.

Marshall, R. J. (1991). 'Mapping Disease and Mortality Rates Using Empirical Bayes Estimators'. *Applied Statistics* vol. 40, no. 2, pp. 283–294.

McCarthy, D. B., D. Shatin, C. R. Drinkard, et al. (1999). 'Medical Records and Privacy: Empirical Effects of Legislation'. *Health Services Research* vol. 34, no. 1, pt. 2, pp. 417–425.

McDonald, C. J., J. M. Overhage, P. Dexter, et al. (1998). 'What Is Done, What Is Needed, and What Is Realistic to Expect from Medical Informatics Standards'. *International Journal of Medical Informatics* vol. 48, no. 1–3, pp. 5–12.

McKinlay, J. B. (1979). 'Epidemiological and Political Determinants of Social Policies Regarding the Public Health'. *Social Science and Medicine* vol. 13A, no. 5, pp. 541–558.

Medyckyj-Scott, D. (1993). 'Designing Geographical Information Systems for Use'. In D. Medyckyj-Scott and H. M. Hearnshaw, eds., *Human Factors in Geographic Information Systems*, pp. 87–100. Belhaven Press, London.

Mettee, T. M., K. B. Martin, and R. B. Williams (1998). 'Tools for Community-Oriented Primary Care: A Process for Linking Practice and Community Data'. *Journal of the American Board of Family Practice* vol. 11, no. 1, pp. 28–33.

O'Dwyer, L. A. and D. L. Burton (1998). 'Potential Meets Reality: GIS and Public Health Research in Australia'. *Australian and New Zealand Journal of Public Health* vol. 22, no. 7, pp. 819–823.

Office of Health and the Information Highway (1998). *Virtual Integration for Better Health: From Concept to Reality*. Health Canada, Ottawa.

Partnership for Health Informatics/Telematics (1999). 'Canadian Health Data Model (Draft)'. Canadian Institute for Health Information, Toronto.

Patel, V. L. and A. W. Kushniruk (1997). 'Human-Computer Interaction in Health Care'. In J. H. van Bemmel and M. A. Musen, eds., *Handbook of Medical Informatics*, pp. 473–493. Springer-Verlag, Heidelberg.

Privacy Commissioner of Canada (1999). *Annual Report 1998–99*. Minister of Public Works and Government Services Canada, Ottawa.

Ramroop, S. and R. T. Pascoe (1999). 'Processing of Spatial Metadata Queries with Federated GISs'. 11th Annual Colloquium of the Spatial Information Research Centre, University of Otago, Otago, New Zealand.

Roos, N. P., C. D. Black, N. Frohlich, et al. (1995). 'A Population-Based Health Information Systems'. *Medical Care* vol. 33, no. 12, suppl., pp. DS13–29.

Rosen, M. J. (1999). 'Epidemiology and Risk of Pulmonary Disease'. *Seminars in Respiratory Infections* vol. 14, no. 4, pp. 301–308.

Rosenfield, P. L. (1992). 'The Potential of Transdisciplinary Research for Sustaining and Extending Linkages between the Health and Social Sciences'. *Social Science and Medicine* vol. 35, no. 11, pp. 1343–1357.

Shahar, Y. and M. A. Musen (1996). 'Knowledge-Based Temporal Abstraction in Clinical Domains'. *Artificial Intelligence in Medicine* vol. 8, no. 3, pp. 267–298.

Sjoberg, C. and T. Timpka (1998). 'Participatory Design of Information Systems in Health Care'. *Journal of the American Medical Informatics Association* vol. 5, no. 2, pp. 177–183.

Stead, W. W., R. A. Miller, M. A. Musen, et al. (2000). 'Integration and Beyond: Linking Information from Disparate Sources and into Workflow'. *Journal of the American Medical Informatics Association* vol. 7, no. 2, pp. 135–145.

Stone, V. (2000). 'Environmental Air Pollution'. *American Journal of Respiratory and Critical Care Medicine* vol. 162, no. 2, pt. 2, pp. S44–47.

Tufte, E. R. (1997). *Visual Explanations*. Graphics Press, Cheshire, CT.

Twigg, L. (1990). 'Health-Based Geographical Information Systems: Their Potential Examined in the Light of Existing Data Sources'. *Social Science and Medicine* vol. 30, no. 1, pp. 143–155.

Valacer, D. J. (2000). 'Childhood Asthma: Causes, Epidemiological Factors, and Complications'. *Drugs* vol. 49, suppl. 1, pp. 1–8, discussion pp. 43–45.

van Oers, J. A. M. (1993). *A Geographic Information System for Local Public Health Policy*. Van Gorcum, Assen, the Netherlands.

Willison, D. J. (1998). 'Health Services Research and Personal Health Information: Privacy Concerns, New Legislation, and Beyond'. *Canadian Medical Association Journal* vol. 159, no. 11, pp. 1378–1380.

World Health Organization (1986). *Ottawa Charter for Health Promotion*. World Health Organization, Geneva.

World Health Organization (1997). *The Jakarta Declaration on Leading Health Promotion into the 21st Century*. World Health Organization, Geneva.

PART VI
CONCLUDING REFLECTIONS

Chapter 19

Fix It or Nix It?
Will the NAFTA Model Survive?

Sylvia Ostry

NAFTA as a Non-Model

The North American Free Trade Agreement (NAFTA) is not a model for other regional agreements and certainly not for the World Trade Organization (WTO). NAFTA is unique in a number of ways. There is one overwhelmingly dominant power, the United States, and there is one developing country, Mexico, which was the initial *demandeur*. NAFTA originated when Mexican president Raoul Salinas wanted to lock in his economic reforms and Mexico to become a North American investment magnet. He had gone to Europe and Japan to invite investors to enter Mexico, but was not confident they would come in the absence of a strong enticement — access to the U.S. market. The U.S. Treasury Department saw Mexico as a model for Latin American reform and thus also pushed for the trade agreement. Finally, NAFTA was part of a U.S. regional domino policy, a game launched in the 1980s with the Canada-U.S. Free Trade Agreement (FTA). The ultimate objective of the domino policy was to broaden and deepen the global system. In the case of the FTA and NAFTA, this was achieved by securing agreement on issues, such as services, intellectual property, and investment, that were easier to achieve in a regional agreement first; then they could be shifted into the WTO. Canada was caught. If Canada had not joined NAFTA, its outsider status would have eroded the preferences it had achieved through the FTA. Thus, what was Canada otherwise to do — sign a bilateral free trade agreement with Mexico?

The World Trade Organization Context

If NAFTA is not a model for other regional agreements, is there one? This question must be put in a global context, especially in the context of the new political economy of the multilateral trading system housed in the WTO and of the fallout from the Uruguay Round of negotiations that established this new institution.

The Uruguay Round can be characterised as a north-south 'grand bargain'. Prior to the Uruguay Round, developing countries negotiated mainly in order to secure unreciprocated access to the markets of member countries of the Organisation for Economic Co-operation and Development (OECD) (Ostry 1997). Most of those developing countries lacked the expertise and analytical resources for trade policy making. However, that really did not matter much: the focus of negotiations was on border barriers for industrial products and the exclusion of agriculture.

The Uruguay Round, launched at Punta Del Este, Uruguay, in September 1986 and concluded at Marrakech, Morocco, in March 1994, was a watershed in the evolution of that system. For the first time, agriculture was at the centre of the negotiations, to the consternation of the European Community. Moreover, a group of developing countries (the G10) and led by Brazil and India, was adamantly opposed to the so-called 'new issues' of trade in services and intellectual property and investment. They worked with the Europeans to delay the launch of the negotiations.

However, by the onset of the 1990s, a major change in economic policy was underway. The debt crisis of the 1980s, and thus the role of the International Monetary Fund (IMF) and the World Bank, together with the fall of the Berlin Wall — a confluence of two unrelated events — ushered in a major transformation in the paradigm of economic policy. Economic reforms, including reform of key service sectors, were seen as essential elements for encouraging and sustaining growth. Consequently, well before the end of the Uruguay Round, the G10 had disappeared. Coalitions of developing countries concentrated on liberalisation of agriculture, textiles, and clothing.

Thus the grand bargain was completed. It was quite different from the old-time reciprocity of the General Agreement on Tariffs and Trade (GATT). It was essentially an implicit deal: the opening of OECD markets to agriculture and labour-intensive manufactured goods, especially textiles and clothing, in exchange for the inclusion in the trading system of trade in services (the General Agreement on Trade in Services, or GATS), intellectual property (trade-related aspects of intellectual property, or TRIPs) and — albeit to a lesser extent than originally demanded — investment (trade-related investment measures, or TRIMs). This came with the creation of a new institution, the WTO, with the strongest dispute settlement mechanism in the history of international law. Since the WTO consisted of a 'single undertaking' (in WTO legalese) the deal, which also included the Tokyo Round Codes, was pretty much a 'take it or leave it' proposition for the southern countries. So they took it. However, they did so without a full comprehension of the profoundly transformative implication of this new trading system.

The northern part of the bargain consisted of some limited progress in agriculture, with a commitment to go further in new negotiations starting in 2000, and limited progress in textiles and clothing involving a promise to end the Multifibre Arrangement on textiles in 2005, with most of the restrictions to be eliminated later rather than sooner. It also included a rather significant reduction in tariffs in goods in exchange for deeper cuts and more comprehensive bindings by developing countries (which had higher tariffs with a smaller percentage of bindings) and with significant tariff peaks remaining on manufactured exports from developing countries.

The essence of the southern side of the deal — the inclusion of the new issues and the creation of the new institution — was to transform the multilateral trading system.

The most significant feature of the transformation was the shift in policy focus from the border barriers of the GATT to domestic regulatory and legal systems.

Thus the grand bargain turned out to be a bad deal for the South. In exchange for market access that has been less than expected, especially in agriculture, many developing countries need to invest in a major upgrading in their institutional infrastructure — in effect, they must undertake investment with uncertain returns. The World Bank has estimated that implementation costs for the poorer countries would exceed several years' of those countries' development budgets. And, because of severe budgetary constraints, very little technical assistance is available from the WTO.

A wide north-south divide was one of the unintended consequences of the grand bargain. To be sure, the notion of such a divide among the members of the WTO is an oversimplification. The southern countries are hardly homogeneous and include the poorest or least developed countries (perhaps 50 to 60 members) as well as middle income countries. Yet, before Seattle there was a broad consensus among the southern countries that the Uruguay Round Agreement was asymmetric and must be 'rebalanced' before any new negotiations were launched. There was also a consensus against the inclusion of new agenda items such as investment, competition policy, and especially labour and environment standards.

What is most interesting about those pre-Seattle discussions, however, was the proactive role of the southern countries. They submitted over half of the more than 250 specific proposals for the ministerial meeting. And, of course, the Seattle meeting in 1999 ended with the walkout of virtually all the non-OECD countries, sparked by U.S. president Bill Clinton's statement about the use of sanctions to enforce labour standards (Ostry 2000).

Two reasons why the South is more active today are because of the rise of democracy and the growing awareness of trade policy issues among the general public, the political institutions, and the business community. But another reason concerns the role of a number of nongovernmental organisations (NGOs) created in developing countries during the 1990s in order to provide information ranging from technical research to policy strategy papers. Furthermore, since the mid 1990s, the internet has accelerated the links between southern NGOs and many northern partners in both Europe and the U.S. These NGOs together act, in effect, as a 'virtual secretariat', often collaborating with a newly revitalised United Nations Conference on Trade and Development (UNCTAD).

But the virtual secretariat is not the only — or, indeed, the main — exemplar of the rise of the NGOs on the world scene. Another unintended consequence of the Uruguay Round was to catalyse a growing antiglobalisation movement, mainly because of WTO dispute settlement decisions concerning social regulatory issues (food safety and environment), which are very sensitive in terms of public opinion in OECD countries. Inevitably, as is the case with all courts and legal rules, WTO panels and especially the Appellate Body have been forced to interpret the relevant WTO rules and thus in effect 'make law'. This intrusion into domestic policy has enraged and emboldened many NGOs and broadcasts a particular message, namely that the WTO is the agent of the multinational corporations (in collusion with rich country governments). In response, a message of anticorporate globalisation is crafted and managed by a group of NGOs in what could be termed 'mobilization networks', for which a major objective is to rally support for dissent at a specific event — a WTO meeting, a meeting of the World Bank and the IMF, the Summit of the Americas, the G8, and so on. Although these networks are loosely knit coalitions of very disparate groups, an analysis of a number of meetings from Seattle in 1999 to Genoa in 2001 shows that there is a core group headed by a new breed of policy entrepreneurs (Ostry 2001). This core group is heavily weighted toward northern NGOs, and one of their demands is the WTO include labour and environmental standards.

The Southern Perspective on Trade and Environment-Labour Standards

Southern countries have several reservations about including environment and labour standards in trade agreements. In India, the environment minister has claimed, at a meeting sponsored by the Confederation of Indian Industry, that India has very high standards that cannot be implemented, because Indian industries do not have the capacity to implement them. The key issue is not will but a lack of capacity. During the 1970s and the new international economic order and the creation of UNCTAD, there was much enthusiasm for a development model based on import substitution. Today, not a single developing country still holds that model.

Several factors led to its demise. One was the Mexico financial crisis in 1982, the 'decade of despair' in Latin America, and the role of the IMF and the World Bank in the transformation of the development model. Then, there was the 'Ronald-Thatcher' revolution that transformed the idea of neoliberalism. In the Uruguay Round, the final blockage by Brazil and India ended, as they realised they had no real supporters and so were willing to accept services and TRIPs. Thus from the middle of the 1970s and the first Organization of the Petroleum Exporting Countries (OPEC) crisis, there was a major transformation.

At the same time, one should consider why developing countries are so opposed to dealing with these two issues, especially as the environment is already included in the WTO. Why do developing countries oppose even discussing environmental and labour standards? In the latter case, they fear that the standards will become a protectionist tool to block labour-intensive imports. But the minutes of the WTO's Committee on Trade and the Environment show that the north-south divide remains wide — a veritable dialogue of the deaf.

What is most frightening is the paralysis of world leaders, especially because these issues are not being discussed in any rational way. On the issue of the environment, there is no forum for a real discussion of the issues involved. There are conflicts between the neoliberal utopian view and the deep ecologist utopian view, but there are other views as well. There are major areas where a rational discussion is possible. Yet there is no leadership to launch such discussions.

The Future of the World Trading System

After the debacle at Seattle, it is widely argued that another failed effort to launch a new round would strike a fatal blow to the already beleaguered WTO. At a minimum, it would be essential to make an effort to 'rebalance' the asymmetry of the Uruguay Round (for example, by improving market access for agricultural and textile and clothing exports of southern countries) and to narrow the growing divide between the European Union and the U.S. over environmental issues. After the events of September 11, 2001, and the new 'war', the role of the mobilisation networks will likely remain considerably diminished, although it might be premature to announce the death of the movement. Creatively ambiguous drafting can be very effective in securing agreement to 'do something' — especially if it is not at all clear what that 'something' is. But the launch of the new round at Doha in November 2001 will not by itself be sufficient to deal with the serious challenges facing the global economy and policy, of which the wide gap between rich and poor countries is the most glaring and most formidable to handle. This will require not only the reform of the WTO as an institution but also a significant and complex co-ordination of policies among international institutions. There are, as yet, no signs of recognition of this challenge among world leaders. The real question to confront, therefore, is not whether the NAFTA model or the WTO will survive, but whether and when the vital missing ingredient — leadership — will emerge.

References

Ostry, Sylvia (1997). *The Post-Cold War Trading System: Who's on First?* University of Chicago Press, Chicago.

Ostry, Sylvia (2000). 'Making Sense of It All: A Post-Mortem on the Meaning of Seattle'. In R. B. Porter and P. Sauvé, eds., *Seattle, the WTO, and the Future of the Multilateral Trading System*, pp. 81–94. Harvard University, Kennedy School, Cambridge, MA.

Ostry, Sylvia (2001). 'The Future of the World Trade System'. Symposium on the 50th anniversary of the Institut der deutschen Wirtschaft Köln. Berlin.

Chapter 20

Conclusions

Virginia W. Maclaren and John J. Kirton

Given the dimensions of the challenge of globalisation, the passion of the continuing debate over the North American Free Trade Agreement (NAFTA), and the wealth of disciplinary perspectives and professional experiences represented in this volume, it is hardly surprising that no single set of integrated conclusions emerges from these analyses — let alone actionable policy recommendations. Nonetheless, there is considerable agreement on the central questions to be addressed, certain key issues, the importance of the ongoing search for answers, and some of the broad directions that must be followed. This conclusion, therefore, summarises these points of agreement by discussing them in the context of the five broad tasks prescribed for this book in Chapter 1.

NAFTA: Working for People and Their Habitat

The first, and most fundamental, question examined in this book is the central issue of whether the NAFTA regime has provided a model for linking trade, environmental, and social values, in practice as well as in principle and potential, and whether it has done so in ways that work within North America and prospectively for the wider world. On the whole, the answer is mixed. Many authors are confident that NAFTA has proven to be an acceptable initial architecture for addressing environmental and social concerns within North America, that the worst fears have not been realised, and that several ecological and social, as well as economic, gains have come. Yet all are equally aware that many of the gains have been modest, that the NAFTA regime in operation has had its full share of ecological and social downsides and disappointments, and that a large act of continued construction, refinement, and reform lies ahead. In short, NAFTA works for many, but not all, and not nearly as well as it could or should. As a result, the NAFTA experience contains valuable precedents for meeting the global challenge, as well as useful lessons about what to avoid.

North America and a Globalising World: Identifying the Intersections

Is NAFTA a model for other trade liberalisation agreements? Some of the authors in this volume claim that it is, while others disagree. Perhaps the words of Pierre Marc

Johnson best summarise the middle ground: 'It is less than certain ... whether this model could be replicated in other trade regimes ... Nonetheless, many of its elements could serve as an inspiration to integrate nontrade issues in furthering trade-centred globalisation.' With the NAFTA regime's extensive array of environmental and social provisions built into the core trade agreements, with its novel side agreements and their accompanying interlinked regional organisations, with their innovative provisions for civil society participation, and with the ongoing effort to monitor, review, and adjust, NAFTA remains very different from any of the other trade liberalisation projects in the world. The growing globalisation-bred demand for foreign direct investment (FDI), civil society participation, and democratic governance, combined with the extensive ecological stresses that North America and the world share, renders the NAFTA experience increasingly relevant, and makes it an integral element in what can be accomplished abroad. NAFTA is leading the way in many areas, notably civil society participation in international governance, procedures to help governments ensure their own environmental laws are adequately enforced, and the need for sophisticated ongoing sustainability assessments of trade liberalisation.

Even here, however, the message is one of steady, incremental effort and continuous improvement, as well as vigilant civil society engagement, in response to national governments that can be reluctant to realise the value of unfamiliar ways to address pressing concerns. Clearly, there are strong political obstacles to acceptance by the world's developing countries of environmental and labour conditions in multilateral trade agreements, even in the mild and benign form that exists within NAFTA. Nevertheless, Mexico's growing enthusiasm for the full NAFTA principle of 'sustainable development', the accumulating evidence of its benefits, and the ongoing effort to defend and improve its ecological and social protections are potent talking points for the broader trade liberalisation debate.

Linking Trade, Environment, and Society: NAFTA and the Global Record

The force of these talking points and the confidence of those who use them are reinforced by the fact that, whatever its failures, NAFTA's linkage of trade, environment, and social considerations remains far in advance of anything yet constructed on any regional or multilateral plane. It is not only that the effort to include such broader values have failed, as it did at the World Trade Organization (WTO) ministerial meeting in 1999; it is also that efforts to continue the core trade and investment liberalisation efforts themselves have died or stalled, as with the Multilateral Agreement on Investment (MAI) or the Asia-Pacific Economic Cooperation (APEC) conference, or in the WTO itself. Even the prospects of concluding the Free Trade Agreement of the Americas (FTAA) by the target date of 2005 and a timely conclusion of the new WTO round launched at Doha in November 2001 remain uncertain hopes as much as assured outcomes. Perhaps most tellingly, even when the most powerful democratic countries in the world — in the form of the G8 — collectively endorse forward-looking, NAFTA-like ecological and social links, the inherited international organisational imbalances of the old system based on the United Nations (UN) have thus far inhibited the easy realisation of those linkages. Furthermore, it will not be easy for the September 2002 World Summit on Sustainable Development to produce an effective architectural solution. For North Americans and their bilateral associates, it appears to be 'NAFTA or nothing' for a long period of time.

If so, they can be confident that NAFTA is by no means insignificant in its environmental and social contributions. On the whole, NAFTA has not brought any regulatory 'race to the bottom', production has not run away to pollution havens, and competitiveness-driven pressures for regulatory chill have not increased — even during the difficult 1990s when the budgets of most North American governments were slashed and when home-grown ideological rejections of traditional statist strategies took hold. Indeed, NAFTA has contributed to the new generation of environmental regulation and the regional harmonisation that is clearly, if too slowly in the view of many, taking place. Above all, the NAFTA regime gives Canada and Mexico, and the regional environmental community, opportunities for influence and desired outcomes that they would otherwise lack. It remains to be seen whether, the NAFTA regime can continue to exert this potent sustainable development pull in a period in which the powerful United States has become a reluctant environmentalist, even as Mexico has become a more committed one, and when all three North American countries have become preoccupied with responding to the terrorist attacks of 11 September 2001 in North America.

Bringing in Civil Society: Corporations and Citizens in North American and Global Environmental Governance

If it is clear that the NAFTA regime and organisations matter, it is even more apparent that NAFTA on its own is not enough. It takes civil society — its corporations, its nongovernmental organisations (NGOs), and its citizens — to activate the new dispute settlement mechanisms made available by NAFTA. Those mechanisms deepen a culture of respect for the rule of law in North America as well as experience with it, even as they encourage their governments to respect their own laws and international obligations. Even NAFTA's much criticised Chapter 11 on investment has, in several instances, inspired governments to find better ways of devising environmental regulations, rather than relying on crude trade protectionist instruments that can so easily be corrupted by those whose ecological awareness and commitments are much in doubt. The use of the Article 14-15 process proves that governments can do a better job than they otherwise would in enforcing their own environmental regulations, even if they do much to resist this conclusion. The experience with similar procedures by the Commission for Labor Cooperation (CLC) on the labour front has been the same, although to a lesser extent. But both the CLC's experience and that of the Commission for Environmental Cooperation (CEC), with the attempt to revise the citizen submission guidelines, show that civil society actors must remain active and vigilant on a broad array of fronts if those NAFTA mechanisms are to have real force. While they may be a necessary minimum, they are not enough on their own. Indeed, embarrassing governments by using widespread publicity to expose the rights or wrongs of individual cases has often proven to be a more effective way for civil society to achieve its goals than the formal complaint process itself.

Assessing the Environmental Effects of Trade: Approaches, Indicators, and Impacts

One of the most recent and far-reaching efforts to assess the *ex post* environmental effects of trade can be found in the application of the CEC's analytical framework to several case studies in North America. A lesson drawn from the research to date is that, even after taking into account the methodological challenges of measurement and causality, it is difficult to determine whether the overall effects of NAFTA on the environment have been positive or negative. In some sectors and in some regions, environmental quality has improved slightly; in others, it has deteriorated to a similar degree. Across all regions and sectors, some pollutants have increased while others have decreased or remained stable. Even though the range of case studies is by no means comprehensive in scope, being limited in the number of sectors and the degree of spatial analysis, the implication is that it may be impossible to answer definitively whether the environmental effects of NAFTA have had a negative or positive effect overall.

Perhaps this is not the question that needs to be answered in the first place. Looking at changes in aggregate hides individual negative environmental changes that may be borne inequitably by certain regions or economic or social groups. Identifying, understanding, and mitigating these negative changes may be more important for maintaining social cohesion than demonstrating that the overall effects of a trade liberalisation regime were positive. Despite impressive progress in developing and testing the tools for measuring the *ex post* environmental effects of NAFTA, much more work remains to be done, especially in incorporating social indicators into the NAFTA effort, applying such assessments at the global level, and making them a routine rather than a periodic and peripheral part of the process of globalisation and its governance.

Those working with *ex ante* trade assessment tools are moving forward in addressing these challenges. Most importantly, a few organizations are now going beyond a narrow focus on assessing the environmental effects of trade to examine sustainability impacts of those that affect the economy, the environment, and society together. This change in focus arises partly out of the realisation that trade-related impacts on the environment often have repercussions outside the environmental sphere. Environmental change may lead to multiple additional effects on health, livelihood, and overall quality of life. The immense methodological complexity of the sustainability assessment effort has so far resulted in only one application of such a model, employing a qualitative and broad approach rather than a focussed one. Clearly, this is an exciting new methodological development that requires some time to evolve.

Another relatively new development is the growth in capacity at the community level for creating and tracking indicators of local environmental quality. The proliferation of environmental and sustainability indicator reports in North America offers a potentially rich source of data for assessing the environmental effects of trade at the local level. This spatial focus has so far been ignored by national and global trade assessment initiatives. Unfortunately, there are as yet few good examples of local trade-related indicators. More research is needed to understand how trade agreements affect the environment and sustainability in local communities, but the growing interest and expertise in developing local indicators bode well. Notwithstanding the slow pace of activity in developing local trade-related indicators, community reporting offers a valuable lesson in the way that participatory processes can benefit trade assessments. There are several examples at the local level of how the process of indictor development and reporting provides opportunities for greater public discourse about local environmental and sustainability concerns. This discourse has, in turn, led to a strengthening of social cohesion on these issues. The successful record of these participatory efforts reinforces the call for increased civil society involvement in national and international assessments.

What Is to Be Done: A Policy Research and Action Agenda

This volume offers a rich array of specific suggestions and even visionary proposals about how ecological and social values can be more strongly embedded within the process of trade and investment liberalisation. Together, those ideas suggest some central strategic directions for helping the unfolding NAFTA regime realise its sustainable ideals and respond to the pressures brought by globalising world, and by contributing to the ongoing effort to create a socially and ecologically sustainable process of trade, investment, and finance liberalisation on a global scale. It is important to build in ecological and social principles, provisions, and procedures, and to assess — from the start — trade agreements for their impact on these values. It is equally important to do so repeatedly, if only because mid-course corrections are necessary, and also because there are constantly new challenges in a region and world where so many ecosystems are under increasing stress. In this effort, institutions matter, even if they are as modest as the CEC and CLC. At the global level, their equivalents neither exist at all nor enjoy the same built-in interrelationship with the trade regime. But institutions work well only if they operate with a degree of transparency that citizens in democratic polities — as much as corporations in liberalised international markets — expect and deserve. Above all, ongoing, meaningful civil society participation is essential if these open institutions are to meet the comprehensive demands and integrated agenda they now face.

This book is by no means complete in its assessment of NAFTA or, more generally, of the links among trade liberalisation, environmental protection, and social cohesion. Significant elements are missing: assessments of NAFTA's regional impacts on environment and social cohesion in Mexico (see Morales 1999) and on the Mexico-U.S. border (see Liverman et al. 1999); the role of soft law as it complements formal trade arrangements;[1] or how the principles, rules, and organisations created at the 1992 Rio United Nations Conference on Environment and Development (UNCED) have operated, and now require reinforcement, revision, or renewal. In addition, some of the more important long-term structural effects of trade liberalisation in North America may not appear until a decade or even two from now. Consequently, this volume's conclusion about the effectiveness of the NAFTA regime and of other trade liberalisation efforts does not represent the final word on the subject, nor is it the end of the story. It can nonetheless be said that NAFTA has had many small and several large successes. Not everyone is happy with the results of the NAFTA experiment, but most support it. After almost a decide of experience, the experiment is still in progress; healthy debates over its past and future can only make it stronger.

Most broadly, NAFTA's institutional provisions show that it was deliberately devised to be a minimum platform on which to build. Its accession clause shows that it was carefully crafted so that any country anywhere could join. It was thus introduced not only to end an early 1990s political debate about trade liberalisation within North America, with its environmental provisions replicated in many of the bilateral trade agreements signed by Canada and the U.S. with countries beyond North America, but also to conduct an expanding experiment of making trade and investment liberalisation work for sustainable development in North America, all its localities, and in the world as a whole. After almost ten years of experience, the evidence shows that the NAFTA experiment is still alive, well, and, above all, worthwhile for North Americans and the world.

Note

1 Voluntary standards in particular and soft law in general will be the theme of a future EnviReform edited volume in Ashgate's Global Environmental Governance series.

References

Liverman, D. M., R. G. Varady, O. Chavez, et al. (1999). 'Environmental Issues along the United States–Mexico Border: Drivers of Change and Responses of Citizens and Institutions'. *Annual Review of Energy and the Environment* vol. 24, p. 607.

Morales, I. (1999). 'NAFTA: The Institutionalization of Economic Openness and the Configuration of Mexican Geo-Economic Spaces'. *Third World Quarterly* vol. 20, no. 5, pp. 971–993.

Bibliography

Abbott, Frederick M. (1996). 'From Theory to Practice: The Second Phase of the NAFTA Environmental Regime'. In R. Wolfrum, ed., *Enforcing Environmental Standards*, pp. 451–478. Springer-Verlag, Berlin.

Abbott, Frederick M. (2000). 'NAFTA and the Legalization of World Politics: A Case Study'. *International Organization* vol. 54, no. 3, pp. 519–548.

Abbott, Frederick M. (2000). 'The Political Economy of NAFTA Chapter Eleven: Equality before the Law and the Boundaries of North American Integration.' *Hastings International and Comparative Law Review* vol. 23, no. 3–4, pp. 303–309.

Abbott, Kenneth W. and Duncan Snidal (2000). 'Hard and Soft Law in International Governance'. *International Organization* vol. 54, no. 3, pp. 421–456.

Abbott, Kenneth, Robert Keohane, Andrew Moravcsik, et al. (2000). 'The Concept of Legalization'. *International Organization* vol. 54 (Summer), pp. 401–420.

Abel, Andrea and Travis Phillips (2000). 'The Relocation of El Paso's Stonewashing Industry and Its Implications for Trade and the Environment'. Paper presented at the First North American Symposium on Understanding the Linkages between Trade and Environment, 11–12 October. Washington DC. <www.cec.org/programs_projects/trade_environ_econ/pdfs/Abel.pdf> (December 2001).

Aldrich, George H. (1994). 'What Constitutes a Compensable Taking of Property? The Decisions of the Iran-United States Claims Tribunal'. *American Journal of International Law* vol. 88, no. 4, pp. 585–610.

Alexander, Robin (1999). 'Experience and Reflections on the Use of the NAALC'. In Encuentro Trinacional de Laboralistas Democráticos, ed., *Memorias: Encuentro Trinacional de Laboralistas Democráticos*. Universidad Nacional Autonoma de México, Mexico City.

Altman, D. G. (1995). 'Sustaining Interventions in Community Systems: On the Relationship between Researchers and Communities'. *Health Psychology* vol. 14, no. 6, pp. 526–536.

Alvarez, Henri C. (2000). 'Arbitration under the North American Free Trade Agreement'. *Arbitration International* vol. 16, p. 393.

American Lands Alliance, Center for International Environmental Law, Consumer's Choice Council, et al. (2001). 'Comments on Guidelines for Implementation of Executive Order 13141'. <www.ciel.org/Publications/EO13141Comments.pdf> (December 2001).

American Law Institute (1987). *Restatement of the Law (Third): The Foreign Relations Law of the United States*. Vol. 2. American Law Institute Publishers, St. Paul, MN.

Anderson, Sarah, John Cavanagh, and David Ranney (1996). 'NAFTA: Trinational Fiasco'. *The Nation* vol. 263, no. 3, pp. 26–29.

Andrienko, G. and N. Andrienko (1999). 'Data Characterization Schema for Intelligent Support in Visual Data Analysis'. In C. Freksa and D. M. Mark, eds., *Spatial Information Theory: Cognitive and Computational Foundations of Geographic Information Science*, pp. 349–365. Springer-Verlag, Berlin.

Audley, John J. (1997). *Green Politics and Global Trade: NAFTA and the Future of Environmental Politics*. Georgetown University Press, Washington DC.

Australian Institute of Health and Welfare (1995). 'National Health Information Model, Version 1'.

Baker, Andrew (2000). 'The G-7 as a Global "Ginger Group": Plurilateralism and Four Dimensional Diplomacy'. *Global Governance* vol. 6 (April-June), pp. 165–190.

Bank for International Settlements (2000). '70th Annual Report'. 5 June. Basel.

Barnet, Richard J. and John Cavanagh (1994). *Global Dreams: Imperial Corporations and the New World Order*. Simon & Schuster, New York.

Barratt-Brown, Elizabeth P. (1991). 'Building a Monitoring and Compliance Regime under the Montreal Protocol'. *Yale Journal of International Law* vol. 16, no. 2, pp. 519–570.

Barro, R. J. (1999). 'Determinants of Democracy'. *Journal of Political Economy* vol. 107, no. 6, pt. 2, suppl., pp. S158–S183.

'Basel Convention on the Control of Transboundary Movements of Hazardous Wastes and Their Disposal'(1999). <www.basel.int/text/con-e.htm> (December 2001).

Bayne, Nicholas (1999). 'Continuity and Leadership in an Age of Globalisation'. In M. R. Hodges, J. J. Kirton and J. P. Daniels, eds., *The G8's Role in the New Millennium*, pp. 21–44. Ashgate, Aldershot.

Bayne, Nicholas (2001). 'The G7 and Multilateral Trade Liberalisation: Past Performance, Future Challenges'. In J. J. Kirton and G. M. von Furstenberg, eds., *New Directions in Global Economic Governance: Creating International Order for the Twenty-First Century*, pp. 171–187. Ashgate, Aldershot.

Beatty, Tim (1999). Interview with Jonathan Graubart. 9 August.

Becker, P., H. Calkins, C. J. Cote, et al. (1995). *GIS Development Guide*. Erie County Water Authority, National Center for Geographic Information and Analysis, State University of New York at Buffalo, GIS Resource Group Inc., Albany, NY.

Bergsten, C. Fred and C. Randall Henning (1996). *Global Economic Leadership and the Group of Seven*. Institute for International Economics, Washington DC.

Berndt, D. J., A. R. Hevner, and J. Studnicki (1998). 'Catch/It: A Data Warehouse to Support Comprehensive Assessment for Tracking Community Health'. Proceedings of the annual symposium of the American Medical Informatics Association, pp. 250–254.

Bernstein, Steven (2000). 'Ideas, Social Structure, and the Compromise of Liberal Environmentalism'. *European Journal of International Relations* vol. 6, no. 4, pp. 464–512.

Bernstein, Steven (2001). *The Compromise of Liberal Environmentalism*. Columbia University Press, New York.

Birdsall, Nancy and Augusta de la Torre (2001). 'Washington Contentious'. *Politica Internazionale* vol. 29 (January-April), pp. 97–104.

Black's Law Dictionary (1990). 6th ed. West Publishing, St. Paul, MN.

Boog, B., H. Coenen, L. Keune, et al., eds. (1996). *Theory and Practice of Action Research*. Tilburg University Press, Tilburg.

Bowker, G. C. and S. L. Star (1999). 'Building Information Infrastructures for Social Worlds: The Role of Classifications and Standards'. In T. Ishida, ed., *Community Computing and Support Systems: Social Interaction in Networked Communities*, pp. 231–248. Springer-Verlag, Berlin.

Braithwaite, John and Peter Drahos (2000). *Global Business Regulation*. Cambridge University Press, Cambridge.

Bronfenbrenner, Katie (1997). 'We'll Close! Plant Closing Threats, Union Organizing and NAFTA'. *Multinational Monitor* vol. 18, pp. 8–13.

Brower, Charles N. and Lee A. Steven (2001). 'Who Then Should Judge?: Developing the International Rule of Law under NAFTA Chapter 11'. *Chicago Journal of International Law* vol. 2, p. 193.

Brownlie, Ian (1998). *Principles of Public International Law*. 5th ed. Oxford University Press, Oxford.

Buckeridge, D. L., R. Mason, A. Robertson, et al. (forthcoming). 'Making Health Data Maps: A Case Study of a Community/University Research Collaboration'. *Social Science and Medicine*.

Burch, A. Mark (2000). *Stepping Lightly: Simplicity for People and the Planet*. Gabriola Island, BC, New Society Publishers.

Byrom, G. M. and R. T. Pascoe (1999). 'Design Considerations for Minimising the Inappropriate Use of Spatial Data in a GIS'. 11th Annual Colloquium of the Spatial Information Research Centre, University of Otago, Otago, New Zealand.

Calbreath, Dean (1999). 'Mexico Fines Han Young as Hyundai Is Drawn into Fight'. *San Diego Union Tribune*, 28 April.

California Lawyer (2000). 'At 25 (Quoting Daniel Seligman, Director of the Sierra Club's Responsible Trade Program)'.

Cameron, Maxwell A. and Brian W. Tomlin (2000). *The Making of NAFTA: How the Deal Was Done*. Cornell University Press, Ithaca.

Campbell, Monica, Diane Spear, and Virginia Maclaren (1996). 'Municipal State of the Environment Reporting in Canada: Current Status and Future Needs'. Occasional Paper Series No. 6. Environment Canada, Ottawa.

'Canada-Chile Agreement on Environmental Cooperation' (1997). <can-chil.gc.ca/English/Resource/Agreements/AECCC/AECCC_1.cfm> (December 2001).

Canadian Association for Renewable Energies (1999). 'Low Impact Renewable Energy: Options for a Clean Environment and Health Canadian Economy'. Canadian Association for Renewable Energies, Ottawa.

Canadian Labour Congress (2001). 'Statement by the Canadian Labour Congress to the House of Commons Sub-Committee on Trade and Trade Disputes of the Standing Committee on Foreign Affairs and International Trade Regarding the Free Trade Area of the Americas'. 29 March. Canadian Labour Congress, Ottawa.

Canadian National Advisory Committee (1999). 'Letter of Advice'. 18 June. <www.naaec.gc.ca/english/nac/advice/adv991.htm> (December 2001).

Cerny, Philip G. (1995). 'Globalization and the Changing Logic of Collective Action'. *International Organization* vol. 49, no. 4, pp. 595–625.

Chambers, Edward J., Rolf Mirus, Barry Scholnick, et al. (1999). 'Alberta: Evaluating a Decade's Experience with the Canada-U.S. Free Trade Agreement (FTA)'. Western Centre for Economic Research, Faculty of Business, University of Alberta. <www.bus.ualberta.ca/CIBS-WCER/WCER/pdf/54.pdf> (December 2001).

Chandrasekaran, B. and J. R. Josephson (1999). 'What Are Ontologies and Why Do We Need Them?' *IEEE Intelligent Systems* vol. 14, no. 1, pp. 20–26.

Charnovitz, Steve (1997). 'Two Centuries of Participation: NGOs and International Governance'. *Michigan Journal of International Law* vol. 18, no. 2, pp. 183–286.

Checkland, P. and S. Holwell (1998). *Information, Systems, and Information Systems.* John Wiley and Sons, Chichester.

Chomo, G. and M. Ferrantino (2000). 'NAFTA Environmental Impacts on North American Fisheries'. Paper presented at the First North American Symposium on Understanding the Linkages between Trade and Environment, 11–12 October. <www.cec.org/programs_projects /trade_environ_econ/pdfs/Chomo.pdf> (December 2001).

Christensen, Randy (1999). 'The CEC Citizen Submission Process: Citizen Empowerment or Failed Experiment?' Unpublished, on file with Christopher Tollefson.

Christensen, Randy (2000). Interview. 10 March.

Christie, G. C. (1988). 'What Constitutes a Taking of Property under International Law'. *British Yearbook of International Law* vol. 33, no. 307.

Cimino, J. J. (1998). 'Desiderata for Controlled Medical Vocabularies in the Twenty-First Century'. *Methods of Information in Medicine* vol. 37, no. 4–5, pp. 394–403.

City of Calgary (2000). 'The City of Calgary Corporate Customer Satisfaction Survey 2000'. <www.gov.calgary.ab.ca/custsurvey/index.htm> (December 2001).

City of Hamilton (2001). 'The City of Hamilton's Sustainability Indicators: 1999 Background Report'. City of Hamiton Planning and Development Department, Hamilton, ON.

City of Scarborough (1997). 'Scarborough 1997 State of the City Report'. City of Scarborough, Scarborough, ON.

Clarke, Tony and Maude Barlow (1997). *MAI: The Multilateral Agreement on Investment and the Threat to Canadian Sovereignty.* Stoddart Publishing, Toronto.

Clarke, Tony and Maude Barlow (1998). *MAI Round 2: New Global and Internal Threats to Canadian Sovereignty.* Stoddart Publishing, Toronto.

Clarkson, Stephen (1998). 'Fearful Asymmetries: The Challenges of Analyzing Continental Systems in a Globalizing World'. *Canadian-American Public Policy* vol. 35, pp. 1–6.

Cohn, Theodore H. (2001). 'Securing Multilateral Trade Liberalisation: International Institutions in Conflict and Convergence'. In J. J. Kirton and G. M. von Furstenberg, eds., *New Directions in Global Economic Governance: Creating International Order for the Twenty-First Century*, pp. 189–218. Ashgate, Aldershot.

Cole, Elizabeth and Prescott Ensign (1997). 'An Examination of United States Foreign Direct Investment into Mexico and Its Relation to the North American Free Trade Agreement: Towards a Balanced Understanding of the Effects of Environmental Regulation and Factor Endowments That Affect Location Decisions'. Paper presented at the annual convention of the Academy of International Business, 8–12 October. Monterrey.

Collier, Robert (1997). 'NAFTA Labor Problems Haunt New Trade Debate'. *San Francisco Chronicle*, 10 September. p. A1.

Comeaux, P.E. and N.S. Kinsella (1997). *Protecting Foreign Investment under International Law: Legal Aspects of Political Risk*. Oceana, Dobbs Ferry, NY.

Commission for Environmental Cooperation (1993). 'North American Agreement on Environmental Cooperation between the Government of Canada, the Government of the United Mexican States, and the Government of the United States'. <www.cec.org/pubs_info_resources/law_treat_agree/naaec/> (December 2001).

Commission for Environmental Cooperation (1995). 'Secretariat's Determination under Article 14(2)'. Biodiversity Legal Foundation et al., 21 September. <www.cec.org/citizen/guides_registry/registrytext.cfm?&varlan*337*=english& documentid=4> (December 2001).

Commission for Environmental Cooperation (1998). 'Four-Year Review of the North American Agreement on Environmental Cooperation'. Report of the Independent Review Committee, June. <www.cec.org/pubs_info_resources/law_treat_agree/ cfp3.cfm?varlan=english> (December 2001).

Commission for Environmental Cooperation (1998). 'Taking Stock: North American Pollutant Releases and Transfers'. Montreal. <www.cec.org/pubs_docs/documents/ index.cfm?varlan= english&ID=141> (December 2001).

Commission for Environmental Cooperation (1999). '1999 Regular Session of the Council'. 27–28 June, Banff. <www.cec.org/who_we_are/council/sessions/ disp_sess.cfm?varlan= english&documentID=82> (December 2001).

Commission for Environmental Cooperation (1999). '6th Regular Session of the Council of the Commission for Environmental Cooperation'. Summary of interventions made during the public portion, 28 June, Banff. <www.cec.org/ who_we_are/council/sessions/disp_sess.cfm?varlan=english&documentID=83> (December 2001).

Commission for Environmental Cooperation (1999). 'Indicators of Effective Environmental Enforcement: Proceedings of a North American Dialogue'. Montreal. <www.cec.org/citizen/guides_registry/index.cfm?varlan=english> (December 2001).

Commission for Environmental Cooperation (2000). '2000 Regular Session of the Council'. 12–13 June, Dallas. <www.cec.org/who_we_are/council/sessions/disp_sess.cfm?varlan= english&documentID=96> (December 2001).

Commission for Environmental Cooperation (2000). 'Council Resolution 00-09: Matters Related to Articles 14 and 15 of the Agreement'. 13 June, Dallas. <www.cec.org/who_we_are/jpac/Art14-15/index.cfm> (December 2001).

Commission for Environmental Cooperation (2000). 'Factual Record for Submission 97-001 (BC Aboriginal Fisheries Commission et al.)'. 30 May. <www.cec.org/citizen/guides_registry/registryview.cfm?&varlan=english&submissionID=9> (December 2001).

Commission for Environmental Cooperation (2000). 'North American Agenda for Action: A Three-Year Program for the Commission for Environmental Cooperation'. Commission for Environmental Cooperation, Montreal.

Commission for Environmental Cooperation (2001). 'CEC Council Communiqué'. 29 June, Guadalajara. <www.cec.org/news/details/index.cfm?varlan=english&ID=2409> (December 2001).

Commission for Environmental Cooperation (2001). 'Response to the Joint Public Advisory Committee (JPAC) Report on Lessons Learned Regarding Articles 14 and 15 Process'. 29 June. Commission for Environmental Cooperation, Guadalajara.

Compa, Lance (1999). Interview with Jonathan Graubart, Washington DC. 7 June.

Compa, Lance (1999). 'The North American Agreement on Labor Cooperation and International Labor Solidarity'. In Encuentro Trinacional de Laboralistas Democráticos, ed., *Memorias: Encuentro Trinacional de Laboralistas Democráticos*. Universidad Nacional Autonoma de México, Mexico City.

Council on Environmental Quality and United States Trade Representative (2000). 'Guidelines for Implementation of Executive Order 13141'. <www.ustr.gov/releases/2000/12/guides.html> (December 2001).

Cox, L. H. (1996). 'Protecting Confidentiality in Small Population Health and Environmental Statistics'. *Statistics in Medicine* vol. 15, no. 17–18, pp. 1895–1905.

Dallaire, Sébastien (2001). 'Continuity and Change in the Global Monetary Order'. In J. J. Kirton and G. M. von Furstenberg, eds., *New Directions in Global Economic Governance: Managing Globalisation in the Twenty-First Century*, pp. 95–111. Ahsgate, Aldershot.

Daly, Herman E. (1996). *Beyond Growth: The Economics of Sustainable Development*. Beacon Press, Boston.

Daly, Herman E., John B. Cobb, and Clifford W. Cobb (1989). *For the Common Good: Redirecting the Economy toward Community, the Environment, and a Sustainable Future*. Beacon Press, Boston.

David Suzuki Foundation (2000). 'Power Shift: Cool Solutions to Global Warming'. David Suzuki Foundation, Vancouver.

Davidson, S. B., C. Overton, and P. Buneman (1995). 'Challenges in Integrating Biological Data Sources'. *Journal of Computational Biology* vol. 2, no. 4, pp. 557–572.

Davila, Florangela (1999). 'Judge Confirms Teamsters' Victory'. *Seattle Times*, 20 October. p. B4.

De Sombre, Elizabeth (1995). 'Baptists and Bootleggers for the Environment: The Origins of United States Unilateral Sanctions'. *Journal of Environment and Development* vol. 4 (Winter), pp. 53–75.

Deardorff, Alan V. and Robert Mitchell Stern (2000). *Social Dimensions of U.S. Trade Policies*. University of Michigan Press, Ann Arbor.

DePalma, Anthony (2001). 'Nafta's Powerful Little Secret'. *New York Times*, 11 March, s. 3, p. 1.

Department of Foreign Affairs and International Trade (Canada) (1992). 'North American Free Trade Agreement Canadian Environmental Review'. <www.dfait-maeci.gc.ca/sustain/environa/strategic/MenuNaftaCom-e.asp> (December 2001).

Department of Foreign Affairs and International Trade (Canada) (1994). 'Uruguay Round of Multilateral Trade Negotiations: Canadian Environmental Review (Complete)'. <www.dfait-maeci.gc.ca/sustain/environa/strategic/sea0299-e.asp> (December 2001).

Department of Foreign Affairs and International Trade (Canada) (1999). 'Retrospective Analysis of the 1994 Canadian Environmental Review of the Uruguay Round of Multilateral Trade Negotiations'. Ottawa. <www.dfait-maeci.gc.ca/tna-nac/retrospective-e.pdf> (December 2001).

Department of Foreign Affairs and International Trade (Canada) (2001). 'Framework for Conducting Environmental Assessments of Trade Negotiations'. <www.dfait-maeci.gc.ca/tna-nac/Environment-e.asp> (December 2001).

Department of Foreign Affairs and International Trade (Canada) (2001). 'Pettigrew Welcomes NAFTA Commission's Initiatives to Clarify Chapter 11 Provisions'. News release 116, 1 August. <198.103.104.118/minpub/Publication.asp?FileSpec=/Min_Pub_Docs/104441.htm> (December 2001).

Department of Foreign Affairs and International Trade (Canada) (2001). 'Trade Liberalization with European Union Could Bring Economic Gains'. News release 86, 21 June. <198.103.104.118/minpub/Publication.asp?FileSpec=/Min_Pub_Docs/104322.htm> (December 2001).

Dillon, Sam (1998). 'Bias Said to Hurt Independent Mexican Unions'. *New York Times*, 30 April. p. A8.

DiMento, Joseph F. and Pamela M. Doughman (1998). 'Soft Teeth in the Back of the Mouth: The NAFTA Environmental Side Agreement Implemented'. *Georgetown International Environmental Law Review* vol. 10, no. 3, pp. 651–752.

Dluhosch, Barbara (2001). 'The G7 and the Debt of the Poorest'. In J. J. Kirton, J. P. Daniels and A. Freytag, eds., *Guiding Global Order: G8 Governance in the Twenty-First Century*, pp. 79–92. Ashgate, Aldershot.

Dolzer, Rupert (1988). 'Indirect Expropriation of Alien Property'. *ISCID Review* vol. 1, no. 41, p. 43.

Donges, Juergen and Peter Tillman (2001). 'Challenges for the Global Financial System'. In J. J. Kirton and G. M. von Furstenberg, eds., *New Directions in Global Economic Governance: Managing Globalisation in the Twenty-First Century*, pp. 33–43. Ashgate, Aldershot.

Douthwaite, R. J. (1999). *The Growth Illusion: How Economic Growth Has Enriched the Few, Impoverished the Many, and Endangered the Planet*. Rev. ed. New Society Publishers, Philadelphia.

Dumberry, P. (2001). 'Expropriation under NAFTA Chapter 11 Investment Dispute Settlement Mechanism: Some Comments on the Latest Case Law'. *International Arbitration Law Review* vol. 4, no. 3.

Dupuy, Pierre-Marie (1988). 'Remarks, a Hard Look at Soft Law (Panel Discussion)'. *American Society of International Law Proceedings* vol. 82, pp. 381–386.

Dymond, William A. (1999). 'The MAI: A Sad and Meloncholy Tale'. In F. O. Hampson, M. Hart, and M. Rudner, eds., *A Big League Player? Canada among Nations 1999*, pp. 22–54. Oxford University Press, Toronto.

Dymond, William A. (2001). 'Core Labour Standards and the World Trade Organization: Love's Labour Lost'. *Canadian Foreign Policy* vol. 8, no. 3 (Spring), pp. 99–114.

Dymond, William A. and Michael Hart (2000). 'Post-Modern Trade Policy: Reflections on the Challenges to Multilateral Trade Negotiations after Seattle'. *Journal of World Trade* vol. 34, no. 3 (June), pp. 21–28.

Economic Policy Institute (1997). *The Failed Experiment: NAFTA at Three Years*. Economic Policy Institute, Washington DC.

Edwards, Michael and David Hulme (1996). *Beyond the Magic Bullet: NGO Performance and Accountability in the Post–Cold War World*. Kumarian Press Books on International Development. Kumarian Press, West Hartford, CT.

Ellmann, Stephen (1998). 'Cause Lawyering in the Third World'. In A. Sarat and S. Scheingold, eds., *Cause Lawyering: Political Commitments and Professional Responsibilities*. Oxford University Press, New York.

Elwell, Christine (2000). 'NAFTA Effects on Water: Testing for NAFTA Effects in the Great Lakes Basin'. Paper presented at the First North American Symposium on Understanding the Linkages between Trade and Environment, 11–12 October. Washington DC. <www.cec.org/programs_projects/trade_environ_econ/pdfs/Elwell.pdf> (December 2001).

Emergency Committee for American Trade (2001). 'ECAT Joins in Formation of Broad Alliance to Support Passage of Trade Promotion Authority This Year'. 19 June. <ecat.policy.net/proactive/newsroom/release.vtml?id=22846> (December 2001).

Encuentro Trinacional de Laboralistas Democráticos (1999). *Memorias: Encuentro Trinacional de Laboralistas Democráticos*. Universidad Nacional Autonoma de México, Mexico City.

Enriquez, Raymundo E. (2000). 'No "Double-Dipping" Allowed: An Analysis of Waste Management, Inc. v. United Mexican States and the Article 1121 Waiver Requirement for Arbitration under Chapter 11 of NAFTA.' *Fordham Law Review* vol. 69, pp. 2655, 2662–2663.

Environment Canada (1999). 'Discussion Paper'. Unpublished, on file with Christopher Tollefson.

Esty, Daniel C. and Damien Geradin (1997). 'Market Access, Competitiveness, and Harmonization: Environmental Protection in Regional Trade Agreements'. *Harvard Environmental Law Review* vol. 21, no. 2, pp. 265–336.

Esty, Daniel C. and Institute for International Economics (1994). *Greening the GATT: Trade, Environment, and the Future*. Institute for International Economics, Washington DC.

Evans, R. G. and G. L. Stoddart (1990). 'Producing Health, Consuming Health Care'. *Social Science and Medicine* vol. 31, no. 12, pp. 1347–1363.

Federal Geographic Data Committee (1994). *Content Standards for Digital Spatial Metadata*. Federal Geographic Data Committee, Washington DC.

Fracassi, Fulvio (2001). 'Confidentiality and NAFTA Chapter 11 Arbitrations'. *Chicago Journal of International Law* vol. 2, no. 1, pp. 213–222.

Frank, J. W. (1995). 'The Determinants of Health: A New Synthesis'. *Current Issues in Public Health* vol. 1, pp. 233–240.

Fraser Basin Management Program (1995). 'State of the Fraser Basin: Assessing Progress Towards Sustainability'. Fraser Basin Management Board, Vancouver.

Fraser, Jill Andresky (2001). *White-Collar Sweatshop: The Deterioration of Work and Its Rewards in Corporate America*. 1st ed. Norton, New York.

Fredrikkson, P. and D. Milliment (2000). 'Is There a Race to the Bottom in Environmental Policies? The Effects of NAFTA'. Paper presented at the First North American Symposium on Understanding the Linkages between Trade and Environment, 11–12 October. Washington, DC. <www.cec.org/programs_projects/trade_environ_econ/pdfs/Fredrik.pdf> (December 2001).

Free Trade Commission (2001). 'Clarifications Related to NAFTA Chapter 11'. 31 July.

Freytag, Andreas (2001). 'Internal Macroeconomic Policies and International Governance'. In J. J. Kirton and G. M. von Furstenberg, eds., *New Directions in Global Economic Governance: Managing Globalisation in the Twenty-First Century*, pp. 21–32. Ashgate, Aldershot.

Friedman, Thomas L. (2000). *The Lexus and the Olive Tree*. Rev. ed. Farrar Straus Giroux, New York.

G7 (1975). 'Declaration of Rambouillet'. 17 November, Rambouillet. <www.library.utoronto.ca/g7/summit/1975rambouillet/communique.html> (December 2001).

G7 (1976). 'Joint Declaration of the International Conference'. 28 June, San Juan. <www.library.utoronto.ca/g7/summit/1976sanjuan/communique.html> (December 2001).

G7 (1977). 'Declaration: Downing Street Summit Conference'. 8 May, London. <www.library.utoronto.ca/g7/summit/1977london/communique.html> (December 2001).

G7 (1978). 'Declaration'. 17 July, Bonn. <www.library.utoronto.ca/g7/summit/1978bonn/communique/index.html> (December 2001).

G7 (1979). 'Declaration'. 29 June, Tokyo. <www.library.utoronto.ca/g7/summit/1979tokyo/communique.html> (December 2001).

G7 (1980). 'Declaration'. 23 June, Venice. <www.library.utoronto.ca/g7/summit/1980venice/communique/index.html> (December 2001).

G7 (1981). 'Declaration of the Ottawa Summit'. 21 July, Ottawa. <www.library.utoronto.ca/g7/summit/1981ottawa/communique/index.html> (December 2001).

G7 (1982). 'Declaration of the Seven Heads of State and Government and Representatives of the European Communities'. 6 June, Versailles. <www.library.utoronto.ca/g7/summit/1982versailles/communique.html> (December 2001).

G7 (1983). 'Williamsburg Declaration on Economic Recovery'. 30 May, Williamsburg. <www.library.utoronto.ca/g7/summit/1983williamsburg/communique.html> (December 2001).

G7 (1984). 'London Economic Declaration'. 9 June, London. <www.library.utoronto.ca/g7/summit/1984london/communique.html> (December 2001).

G7 (1985). 'The Bonn Economic Declaration Towards Sustained Growth and Higher Employment'. 4 May, Bonn. <www.library.utoronto.ca/g7/summit/1985bonn/communique/index.html> (December 2001).

G7 (1986). 'Tokyo Economic Declaration'. 6 May, Tokyo. <www.library.utoronto.ca/g7/summit/1986tokyo/communique.html> (December 2001).

G7 (1987). 'Venezia Economic Declaration'. 10 June, Venice. <www.library.utoronto.ca/g7/summit/1987venice/communique/index.html> (December 2001).

G7 (1988). 'Toronto Economic Summit Economic Declaration'. 21 June, Toronto. <www.library.utoronto.ca/g7/summit/1988toronto/communique/index.html> (December 2001).

G7 (1989). 'Economic Declaration'. 16 July, Paris. <www.library.utoronto.ca/g7/summit/1989paris/communique/index.html> (December 2001).

G7 (1990). 'Houston Economic Declaration'. 11 July, Houston. <www.library.utoronto.ca/g7/summit/1990houston/communique/index.html> (December 2001).

G7 (1991). 'Economic Declaration of the G8 Summit'. 17 July, London. <www.library.utoronto.ca/g7/summit/1991london/communique/index.html> (December 2001).

G7 (1993). 'Economic Declaration: A Strengthened Commitment to Jobs and Growth'. 9 July, Tokyo. <www.library.utoronto.ca/g7/summit/1993tokyo/communique/index.html> (December 2001).

G7 (1994). 'G7 Communiqué'. 9 July, Naples. <www.library.utoronto.ca/g7/summit/1994naples/communique/index.html> (December 2001).

G7 (1995). 'Halifax Summit Communiqué'. 16 June, Halifax. <www.library.utoronto.ca/g7/summit/1995halifax/communique/index.html> (December 2001).

G7 (1996). 'Economic Communiqué: Making a Success of Globalization for the Benefit of All'. 28 June, Lyon. <www.library.utoronto.ca/g7/summit/1996lyon/communique/index.html> (December 2001).

G7 (1997). 'Confronting Global Economic and Financial Challenges. Denver Summit Statement by Seven.' 21 June, Denver. <www.g7.utoronto.ca/g7/summit/1997denver/confront.htm> (December 2001).

G7 (2001). 'G7 Statement'. 20 July, Genoa. <www.g7.utoronto.ca/g7/summit/2001genoa/g7statement.html> (December 2001).

G8 (1998). 'Communiqué'. 15 May, Birmingham. <www.library.utoronto.ca/g7/summit/1998birmingham/finalcom.htm> (December 2001).

G8 (1999). 'G8 Communiqué Köln 1999'. 20 June, Cologne. <www.library.utoronto.ca/g7/summit/1999koln/finalcom.htm> (December 2001).

G8 (2000). 'G8 Communiqué Okinawa 2000'. 23 July, Okinawa. <www.g7.utoronto.ca/g7/summit/2000okinawa/finalcom.htm> (December 2001).

G8 (2001). 'Communiqué'. 22 June, Genoa. <www.g7.utoronto.ca/g7/summit/2001genoa/finalcommunique.html> (December 2001).

Galeotti, M. and A. Lanza (1999). 'Richer and Cleaner? A Study on Carbon Dioxide Emissions in Developing Countries'. *Energy Policy* vol. 27, no. 10, pp. 565–573.

Gallaird, Emmanuel (2000). 'NAFTA Dispute Arbitration under Auspices of the International Center'. *New York Law Journal* vol. 224, no. 23, p. 3.

Gallup Canada (1993). '46% Oppose Free Trade Deal, Poll Suggests'. *The Globe and Mail*, 30 August. p. A11.

Gantz, David A. (2001). 'Reconciling Environmental Protection and Investor Rights under Chapter 11 of NAFTA'. *Environmental Law Reporter* vol. 31, no. 7, pp. 10 646–610 668.

Gherson, Giles (1998). 'Canadians Are Activists at Heart, New Poll Finds'. *Ottawa Citizen*, 24 April. p. A5.

Gill, Stephen (1999). 'Structural Changes in Multilateralism: The G-7 Nexus and the Global Crisis'. In M. Schecter, ed., *Innovation in Multilateralism*. St. Martin's Press, New York.

Gill, Stephen (2000). 'The Constitution of Global Capitalism'. Paper presented at the annual convention of the International Studies Association, 15 March. Los Angeles.

Gilligan, M. (1997). 'Lobbying as a Private Good with Intra-Industry Trade'. *International Studies Quarterly* vol. 41, no. 3, pp. 455–474.

Glasgow, Laurette (2001). Deputy Head of the Canadian Mission to the European Union. Interview with William Dymond, Brussels. September.

Godden, S., A. Pollack, and D. Pheby (2000). 'Informational on Community Health Services: More and Better Information Is Needed — Not Less'. *British Medical Journal* vol. 320, p. 265.

Goldberg, Carey (1996). 'U.S. Labor Making Use of Trade Accord It Fiercely Opposed'. *New York Times*, 28 February. p. A11.

Goldstein, Judith and Lisa Martin (2000). 'Legalization, Trade Liberalization, and Domestic Politics: A Cautionary Tale'. *International Organization* vol. 54, no. 3, pp. 603–632.

Goldstein, Judith, Miles Kahler, Robert Keohane, et al. (2000). 'Introduction: Legalization and World Politics'. *International Organization* vol. 54, no. 3, pp. 385–399.

Goldstein, Judith, Miles Kahler, Robert Keohane, et al. (2000). 'Legalization and World Politics'. *International Organization* vol. 54, no. 3.

Gostin, L. (1997). 'Health Care Information and the Protection of Personal Privacy: Ethical and Legal Consideration'. *Annals of Internal Medicine* vol. 127, no. 8, pt. 2, pp. 683–690.

GPI Atlantic (2001). 'Nova Scotia's Ecological Footprint'. GPI Atlantic, Tantallon, NS.

Greenspan, Alan (2000). 'Technology and the Economy: Monetary and Fiscal Policies'. *Vital Speeches of the Day* vol. 66, no. 8, pp. 226–230.

Gremy, F., J. M. Fessler, and M. Bonnin (1999). 'Information Systems Evaluation and Subjectivity'. *International Journal of Medical Informatics* vol. 56, pp. 13–23.

Groetzinger, Jon (1997). 'Nafta's Environmental Provisions: Are They Working as Intended? Are They Adequate?' *Canada-United States Law Journal* vol. 23, pp. 401–428.

Grossman, Gene M. and Alan B. Krueger (1995). 'Economic Growth and the Environment'. *Quarterly Journal of Economics* vol. 110, no. 2, pp. 353–377.

Grossman, Perry (2000). 'Globalization and the Linkage of Trade and Environmental Issues: A Comparative Analysis of the Canada-United States and North American Free Trade Agreements'. Ph.D. diss. New York University, New York.

Gudofsky, Jason L. (2000). 'Shedding Light on Article 1110 of the North American Free Trade Agreement (NAFTA) Concerning Expropriations: An Environmental Case Study'. *Northwestern Journal of International Law and Business* vol. 21, p. 243.

Guerrero, M. T., F. de Villa, M. Kelly, et al. (2000). 'The Forestry Industry in the State of Chihuahua: Economic, Ecological, and Social Impacts, Post-NAFTA'. Paper presented at the First North American Symposium on Understanding the Linkages between Trade and Environment, 11–12 October. Washington DC. <www.cec.org/programs_projects/trade_environ_econ/pdfs/Guerrero.pdf> (December 2001).

Guldan, G. S. (1996). 'Obstacles to Community Health Promotion'. *Social Science and Medicine* vol. 43, no. 5, pp. 689–695.

Hajnal, Peter (1999). *The G7/G8 System: Evolution, Role, and Documentation.* Ashgate, Aldershot.

Hamilton, Nora (1982). *The Limits of State Autonomy: Post-Revolutionary Mexico.* Princeton University Press, Princeton.

Haq, Farhan (1999). 'Labour: NAFTA Body Gets Mixed Reviews'. *Inter Press Service.* 10 March.

Harris, Michael (1998). *Lament for an Ocean: The Collapse of the Atlantic Cod Fishery — A True Crime Story.* McClelland and Stewart, Toronto.

Hart, Michael (1998). *Fifty Years of Canadian Tradecraft: Canada at the GATT 1947–1997.* Centre for Trade Policy and Law, Ottawa.

Hart, Michael (2000). 'The Role of Dispute Setlement in Managing Canada-U.S. Trade and Investment Relations'. In M. A. Molot and F. O. Hampson, eds., *Vanishing Borders: Canada among Nations 2000.* Oxford University Press, Toronto.

Haughton, G. (1998). 'Geographical Equity and Regional Resource Management: Water Management in Southern California'. *Environment and Planning B — Planning & Design* vol. 25, no. 2, pp. 279–298.

Hawken, Paul, L. Hunter Lovins, and Amory B. Lovins (1999). *Natural Capitalism: Creating the Next Industrial Revolution.* 1st ed. Little Brown and Co., Boston.

Health Canada (1997). *Health Promotion in Canada: A Case Study.* Health Canada, Ottawa.

Helfer, Laurence R. and Anne-Marie Slaughter (1997). 'Toward a Theory of Effective Supranational Adjucation'. *Yale Law Journal* vol. 107, no. 2, pp. 273–391.

Helleiner, Gerald (2001). 'Markets, Politics, and Globalization: Can the Global Economy Be Civilized?' *Global Governance* vol. 7, no. 3, pp. 243–263.

Hettige, H., M. Mani, and D. Wheeler (2000). 'Industrial Pollution in Economic Development: The Environmental Kuznets Curve Revisited'. *Journal of Developmental Economics* vol. 62, no. 2, pp. 445–476.

Hockin, Thomas A. (2001). *The American Nightmare: Trade Politics after Seattle.* Lexington Books, Lanham.

Hodges, Michael R., John J. Kirton, and Joseph P. Daniels, eds. (1999). *The G8's Role in the New Millennium.* Ashgate, Aldershot.

Hodgson, R. and T. Abbasi (1995). *Effective Mental Health Promotion: Literature Review.* Health Promotion Wales.

Horner, J. S. (1998). 'Research, Ethics, and Privacy: The Limits of Knowledge'. *Public Health* vol. 112, no. 4, pp. 217–220.

Housman, Robert (1994). 'The North American Free Trade Agreement's Lessons for Reconciling Trade and Environment'. *Stanford Journal of International Law* vol. 30, pp. 379–422.

Howse, Robert (1999). 'Democracy, Science, and Free Trade: Risk Regulation on Trial at the World Trade Organization'. Paper presented at Harvard Law School, Spring Term. Boston.

Hufbauer, Gary Clyde, Daniel C. Esty, Diana Orejas, et al. (2001). *NAFTA and the Environment: Seven Years Later*. Institute for International Economics, Washington DC. <www.iie.com/publications/publication.cfm?pub_id=322&source=none> (December 2001).

Human Rights Watch (2001). 'Trading Away Rights: The Unfulfilled Promise of Nafta's Labour Side Agreement'. *Canada/Mexico/United States* vol. 13 (April), p. 2B. <www.hrw.org/reports/2001/nafta> (December 2001).

Humber Watershed Alliance (2000). 'A Report Card on the Health of the Humber River Watershed'. Toronto and Regional Conservation Authority, Toronto.

Ikenberry, John (1998/99). 'Institutions, Strategic Restraint, and the Persistence of American Postwar Order'. *International Security* vol. 23 (Winter), pp. 43–78.

Ikenberry, John (2001). *After Victory: Institutions, Strategic Restraint, and the Rebuilding of Order after Major Wars*. Princeton University Press, Princeton.

Independent Review Committee (1998). 'Four-Year Review of the NAAEC'. <www.cec.org> (December 2001).

'Inside Globalization' (1998/99). *Monetary Reform*, Special Section. Fall/Winter.

Inter-Agency Committee on Geomatics (1996). 'Barriers to the Use of Geomatics Data, Data Quality, and Documentation Standards'. Working Group on Coordination and Cooperation.

International Centre for Trade and Sustainable Development (2001). 'Asbestos Ruling Breaks New Ground in "Like Product" Determination'. *Bridges* vol. 5, no. 1–3, pp. 1–2. <www.ictsd.org/English/BRIDGES5-1-3.pdf> (December 2001).

International Institute on Sustainable Development (2000). 'Comments on Canada's Draft Environmental Assessment Framework for Trade Negotiations'. <www.iisd.org/pdf/trade_dfait_eaf_final.pdf> (December 2001).

International Institute on Sustainable Development (2000). 'Measurement and Indicators for Sustainable Development'. <iisd1.iisd.ca/measure/> (December 2001).

International Labour Organization (2001). 'ILO Fundamental Declaration of Principles and Rights at Work'. <www.ilo.org/public/english/standards/decl/declaration/text/index.htm> (December 2001).

'It's the Global Economy Stupid: The Corporatization of the World' (1996). *The Nation* vol. 263, no. 3.

Jacott, M., C. Reed, and M. Winfield (2000). 'The Generation and Management of Hazardous Wastes and Transboundary Hazardous Waste Shipments between Mexico, Canada, and the United States, 1990–2000'. Paper presented at the First North American Symposium on Understanding the Linkages between Trade and Environment, 11–12 October. Washington DC. <www.cec.org/programs_projects/trade_environ_econ/pdfs/Cielp.pdf> (December 2001).

Jansen, Heinz (2001). 'Induced Institutional Change in the Trade and Environment Debate: A Computable General Equilibrium Application to NAFTA with Endogenous Regulation Setting'. *Environmental and Resource Economics* vol. 18, pp. 149–172.

Johnson, Pierre Marc (1999). 'Five Windows for the Future of NAFTA's Environmental Commission'. *Policy Options* vol. 20, no. 5 (June), pp. 27–32.

Johnson, Pierre Marc (2001). 'Creating Sustainable Global Governance'. In J. J. Kirton, J. P. Daniels and A. Freytag, eds., *Guiding Global Order: G8 Governance in the Twenty-First Century*, pp. 245–282. Ashgate, Aldershot.

Johnson, Pierre Marc and André Beaulieu (1996). *The Environment and NAFTA: Understanding and Implementing the New Continental Law*. Island Press, Washington DC.

Joint Public Advisory Committee of the North American Commission for Environmental Cooperation (2000). 'Draft JPAC Review of Issues Concerning the Implementation and Further Elaboration of Articles 14 and 15'. October. <www.cec.org/who_we_are/jpac/pdfs/proc-e.pdf> (December 2001).

Joint Public Advisory Committee of the North American Commission for Environmental Cooperation (2001). 'Commission for Environmental Cooperation: Joint Public Advisory Committee Session No. 01-02'. Summary Record, 30 June. Commission for Environmental Cooperation, Guadalajara.

Joint Public Advisory Committee of the North American Commission for Environmental Cooperation (2001). 'Joint Public Advisory Committee Round Tables on Opportunities for Enhancing North American Cooperation'. Executive Summary, 28 June. Commission for Environmental Cooperation, Guadalajara.

Joint Public Advisory Committee of the North American Commission for Environmental Cooperation (2001). 'JPAC Public Review of Issues Concerning the Implementation and Further Elaboration of Articles 14 and 15'. Commission for Environmental Cooperation, Montreal.

Joint Public Advisory Committee of the North American Commission for Environmental Cooperation (2001). 'Lessons Learned: Citizen Submissions under Articles 14 and 15 of the NAAEC'. 6 June. <www.cec.org/pubs_docs/documents/index.cfm?ID=121&varlan= english> (December 2001).

Jones, Laura, Laura Griggs, and Liv Fredricksen (2000). *Environmental Indicators*. 4th ed. Fraser Institute, Vancouver.

Juricevic, Diana (2000). 'Controlling for Domestic-Level Commitments: An Analysis of the Authoritative National Commitments Made in Canada and the United States from 1995 to 2000'. 7 November. <www.g7.utoronto.ca/g7/scholar/juricevic2000/juricevic.pdf> (December 2001).

Kaiser, Karl, John J. Kirton, and Joseph P. Daniels, eds. (2000). *Shaping a New International Financial System: Challenges of Governance in a Globalizing World*. Ashgate, Aldershot.

Karesh, Lewis (1999). Interview with Jonathan Graubart. 9 June, Washington DC.

Kaufmann, R. K., B. Davidsdottir, S. Garnham, et al. (1998). 'The Determinants of Atmospheric SO2 Concentrations: Reconsidering the Environmental Kuznets Curve'. *Ecological Economics* vol. 25, no. 2, pp. 209–220.

Keohane, Robert and Joseph Nye (1977). *Power and Interdependence: World Politics in Transition*. Little, Brown, Boston.

Keohane, Robert, Andrew Moravcsik, and Anne-Marie Slaughter (2000). 'Legalized Dispute Resolution: Interstate and Transnational'. *International Organization* vol. 54, no. 3, pp. 457–488.

Keough, Noel (1995). 'Reclaiming Our Communities from the Global Economy'. Conference Proceedings, 'Sustainable Development in the 21st Century Americas: Alternative Visions of Progress'. University of Calgary, Division of International Development, Dialogue on Development Series.

Kibel, Paul Stanton (2001). 'Critique of NAFTA's Environmental Side Agreement'. 6 October, on file with Christopher Tollefson.

Kirkpatrick, Colin and Norman Lee (1999). *WTO New Round: Sustainability Impact Assessment Study. Phase Two, Main Report*. 18 November. Institute for Development Policy and Management and Environmental Impact Assessment Centre, University of Manchester, <europa.eu.int/comm/trade/pdf/sia_ent.pdf> (December 2001).

Kirkpatrick, Colin, Norman Lee, and Oliver Morrissey (1999). *WTO New Round: Sustainability Impact Assessment Study. Phase One Report*. 1 October. Institute for Development Policy and Management and Environmental Impact Assessment Centre, University of Manchester; Centre for Research on Economic Development and International Trade, University of Nottingham, <europa.eu.int/comm/trade/pdf/repwto.pdf> (December 2001).

Kirton, John J. (1989). 'Contemporary Concert Diplomacy: The Seven-Power Summit and the Management of International Order'. Paper presented at the annual convention of the International Studies Association, 29 March–1 April, London.

Kirton, John J. (1990). 'Sustainable Development at the Houston Summit'. Paper prepared for the Foreign Policy Committee, National Round Table on the Environment and the Economy, 6 September.

Kirton, John J. (1996). 'Commission for Environmental Cooperation and Canada-U.S. Environmental Governance in the NAFTA Era'. *American Review of Canadian Studies* vol. 26 (Autumn), pp. 1–14.

Kirton, John J. (1997). 'The Commission for Environmental Cooperation and Canada-U.S. Environmental Governance in the NAFTA Era'. *American Review of Canadian Studies* vol. 27, no. 3, pp. 459–486.

Kirton, John J. (1998). 'NAFTA, Foreign Direct Investment, and Economic Integration: A Canadian Approach'. In Organisation for Economic Co-operation and Development, *Migration, Free Trade, and Regional Integration in North America*, pp. 181–194. Organisation for Economic Co-operation and Development, Paris.

Kirton, John J. (1998). 'NAFTA's Trade-Environment Institutions: Regional Impact, Hemispheric Potential'. Center for International Relations, University of Southern California, Columbia International Affairs Online. <www.ciaonet.org/srchfrm.html> (December 2001).

Kirton, John J. (1998). 'The Impact of Environmental Regulation on the North American Automotive Industry in the NAFTA Era'. In S. Weintraub and C. Sands, eds., *The North American Auto Industry under NAFTA*. Center for Strategic and International Studies Press, Washington DC.

Kirton, John J. (1999). 'Explaining G8 Effectiveness'. In J. J. Kirton and J. P. Daniels, eds., *The G8's Role in the New Millennium*, pp. 45–68. Ashgate, Aldershot.

Kirton, John J. (1999). 'Successful Strategies for Environmental Regulation in the North American Automotive Industry under NAFTA'. Paper prepared for the project on 'The North American Automotive Industry under NAFTA', Center for Strategic and International Studies. Washington DC.

Kirton, John J. (2000). 'Deepening Integration and Global Governance: America as a Globalized Partner'. In T. Brewer and G. Boyd, eds., *Globalizing America: The USA in World Integration*. Edward Elgar, Cheltenham.

Kirton, John J. (2001). 'The G20: Representativeness, Effectiveness, and Leadership in Global Governance'. In J. J. Kirton, J. P. Daniels and A. Freytag, eds., *Guiding Global Order: G8 Governance in the Twenty-First Century*, pp. 143–172. Ashgate, Aldershot.

Kirton, John J. and Alan M. Rugman (1999). 'Regional Environmental Impacts of NAFTA on the Automotive Sector'. *Canadian Journal of Regional Science* vol. 21 (Summer), pp. 227–254.

Kirton, John J. and et al. (1999). *Assessing the Environmental Effects of the North American Free Trade Agreement (NAFTA): Final Analytic Framework and Methodological Issues and Empirical Background*. Commission for Environmental Cooperation, Montreal.

Kirton, John J. and Joseph P. Daniels (1999). 'The Role of the G8 in the New Millennium'. In M. Hodges, J. J. Kirton and J. P. Daniels, eds., *The G8's Role in the New Millennium*, pp. 3–17. Ashgate, Aldershot.

Kirton, John J. and Rafael Fernandez de Castro (1997). *NAFTA's Institutions: The Environmental Potential and Performance of the NAFTA Free Trade Commission and Related Bodies*. Commission for Environmental Cooperation, Montreal.

Kirton, John J. and Sarah Richardson (1995). *The Halifax Summit, Sustainable Development, and International Institutional Reform*. National Round Table on the Environment and the Economy, Ottawa.

Kirton, John J., Joseph P. Daniels, and Andreas Freytag, eds. (2001). *Guiding Global Order: G8 Governance in the Twenty-First Century*. Ashgate, Aldershot.

Knox, John H. (2000). 'Comments on Lessons Learned from the History of the 14/15 Procedure'. Unpublished document submitted to the Joint Public Advisory Committee of the North American Commission on Environmental Cooperation, 22 September.

Knox, John H. (2001). 'A New Approach to Compliance with International Environmental Law: The Submissions Procedure of the NAFTA Environmental Commission'. *Ecology Law Quarterly* vol. 28, no. 1, p. 1.

Knox, Paul and Barry McKenna (2000). 'NAFTA Partners' Environmental Deal at Risk, Groups Say'. *The Globe and Mail*, 27 April. p. A8.

Kobrin, Stephen J. (1998). 'The MAI and the Clash of Globalizations'. *Foreign Policy*, Fall.

Köhler, Martin (1998). 'From the National to the Cosmopolitan Public Sphere'. In D. Archibugi, D. Held and M. Köhler, eds., *Re-Imagining Political Community: Studies in Cosmopolitan Democracy*. Polity Pressar, Cambridge, UK.

Kokotsis, Eleanore (1999). *Keeping International Commitments: Compliance, Credibility, and the G7, 1988–1995*. Garland, New York.

Kornhauser, William (1966). *The Politics of Mass Society*. Free Press, Glencoe, IL.

Korten, David. (1995). *When Corporations Rule the World*. Kumarian Press, West Hartford, CT.

Korten, David. (1999). *The Post-Corporate World: Life after Capitalism*. 1st ed. Berrett-Koehler, San Francisco.

Laird, Ian A. (2001). 'NAFTA Chapter 11 Meets Chicken Little'. *Chicago Journal of International Law* vol. 2, no. 1, pp. 223–229.

Leary, Virginia (1997). 'Nonbinding Accords in the Field of Labor'. In E. B. Weiss, ed., *International Compliance with Nonbinding Accords*. American Society of International Law, Washington DC.

Lee, Jacob S. (2001). 'Expropriation under Mexican Law and Its Insertion into a Global Context under NAFTA.' *Hastings International and Comparative Law Review* vol. 23, p. 385.

Lee, Thea (1999). Interview with Jonathan Graubart, Washington DC. 10 June.

Leyshon, A. (1992). 'The Transformation of Regulatory Order: Regulating the Global Economy and Environment'. *Geoforum* vol. 23, pp. 249–267.

Leyton-Brown, David (1976). 'The Multinational Enterprise and Conflict in Canadian-American Relations'. In A. B. Fox, A. Hero and J. Nye, eds., *Canada and the United States: Transnational and Transgovernmental Relations*, pp. 140–161. Columbia University Press, New York.

Linger, H., F. Burstein, A. Zaslavsky, et al. (1998). 'Conceptual Development of an Information Systems Framework for Improving Continuity in Epidemiological Research'. *European Journal of Epidemiology* vol. 14, no. 6, pp. 587–593.

Lipschutz, R. D. (1992). 'Reconstructuring World Politics: The Emergency of Global Civil Society'. *Millennium* vol. 21, p. 389.

Lipset, Seymour Martin (1959). *Social Mobility in Industrial Society*. University of California Press, Berkeley.

Liverman, D. M., R. G. Varady, O. Chavez, et al. (1999). 'Environmental Issues along the United States–Mexico Border: Drivers of Change and Responses of Citizens and Institutions'. *Annual Review of Energy and the Environment* vol. 24, p. 607.

Lorenzi, N. M., R. T. Riley, A. J. Blyth, et al. (1997). 'Antecedents of the People and Organizational Aspects of Medical Informatics: Review of the Literature'. *Journal of the American Medical Informatics Association* vol. 4, no. 2, pp. 79–93.

Lougheed, Peter (2000). 'Major Forces Shaping a New Canada'. *Calgary Herald*, 1 December. p. A33.

Lowry, Andrew (1992). 'North American Free Trade and the Environment'. *Business America* vol. 113, no. 21, pp. 22–24.

Lujon, Bertha (1999). Interview with Jonathan Graubart, Mexico City. 16 March.

MacCallum, Raymond (1997). 'Evaluating the Citizen Submission Procedure under the North American Agreement on Environmental Cooperation'. *Colorado Journal of International Environmental Law and Policy* vol. 8, no. 2, pp. 395–422.

Maclaren, Virginia (1996). *Developing Indicators of Urban Sustainability: A Focus on the Canadian Experience*. ICURR Press, Toronto.

Magraw, D. and Steve Charnovitz (1994). 'NAFTA's Repercusions: Is Green Trade Possible?' *Environment* vol. 36, no. 2, pp. 14–27.

Mann, Howard (2000). 'Assessing the Impact of NAFTA on Environmental Law and Management Processes'. Paper presented at the First North American Symposium on Understanding the Linkages between Trade and Environment, 11–12 October. Washington DC. <www.cec.org/programs_projects/trade_environ_econ/pdfs/mann.pdf> (December 2001).

Mann, Howard (2001). *Private Rights, Public Problems: A Guide to NAFTA's Controversial Chapter on Investors Rights*. International Institute on Sustainable Development and World Wildlife Fund, Winnipeg.

Mann, Howard and Konrad von Moltke (1999). *NAFTA's Chapter 11 and the Environment: Addressing the Impacts of the Investor-State Process on the Environment*. International Institute for Environment and Development, Washington DC.

Mapp, W. (1992). *The Iran-United States Claims Tribunal: The First Ten Years*. Manchester University Press, Manchester.

Markell, David L. (2000). 'The Commission for Environmental Cooperation's Citizen Submission Process'. *Georgetown International Environmental Law Review* vol. 12, no. 3, pp. 565–574.

Marrett, L. D., B. Theis, M. I. Baker, et al. (1998). 'Challenges of Developing a Cervical Screening Information System: The Ontario Pilot Project'. *Cancer Prevention and Control* vol. 2, no. 5, pp. 221–227.

Marshall, R. J. (1991). 'Mapping Disease and Mortality Rates Using Empirical Bayes Estimators'. *Applied Statistics* vol. 40, no. 2, pp. 283–294.

Mayer, Frederick (1998). *Interpreting NAFTA: The Science and Art of Political Analysis*. Columbia University Press, New York.

McCarthy, D. B., D. Shatin, C. R. Drinkard, et al. (1999). 'Medical Records and Privacy: Empirical Effects of Legislation'. *Health Services Research* vol. 34, no. 1, pt. 2, pp. 417–425.

McDonald, C. J., J. M. Overhage, P. Dexter, et al. (1998). 'What Is Done, What Is Needed, and What Is Realistic to Expect from Medical Informatics Standards'. *International Journal of Medical Informatics* vol. 48, no. 1–3, pp. 5–12.

McKinlay, J. B. (1979). 'Epidemiological and Political Determinants of Social Policies Regarding the Public Health'. *Social Science and Medicine* vol. 13A, no. 5, pp. 541–558.

McKinney, Joseph A. (2000). *Created from NAFTA: The Structure, Function, and Significance of the Treaty's Related Institutions*. M.E. Sharpe, Armonk, NY.

Medyckyj-Scott, D. (1993). 'Designing Geographical Information Systems for Use'. In D. Medyckyj-Scott and H. M. Hearnshaw, eds., *Human Factors in Geographic Information Systems*, pp. 87–100. Belhaven Press, London.

Mendelsohn, Matthew and Robert Wolfe (2001). 'Probing the Aftermyth of Seattle: Canadian Public Opinion on International Trade, 1980–2000'. *International Journal* vol. 56 (Spring), pp. 234–260.

Metropolitan Toronto (1995). 'State of the Environment Report: Metropolitan Toronto'. Metropolitan Toronto Planning Department, Toronto.

Mettee, T. M., K. B. Martin, and R. B. Williams (1998). 'Tools for Community-Oriented Primary Care: A Process for Linking Practice and Community Data'. *Journal of the American Board of Family Practice* vol. 11, no. 1, pp. 28–33.

Middlebrook, Kevin (1995). *The Paradox of Revolution: Labor, the State and Authoritarianism in Mexico*. Johns Hopkins University Press, Baltimore.

Moore, Molly (1998). 'Mexican Farmhands Accuse U.S. Firms'. *Washington Post*, 3 December. p. A36.

Morales, I. (1999). 'NAFTA: The Institutionalization of Economic Openness and the Configuration of Mexican Geo-Economic Spaces'. *Third World Quarterly* vol. 20, no. 5, pp. 971–993.

Moscarella, J. P., E. Hoyt, R. Cavanaugh, et al. (1999). 'Electricity in North America: Some Environmental Implications of the North American Free Trade Agreement'. In Commission for Environmental Cooperation, *Assessing Environmental Effects of North American Free Trade Agreement (NAFTA): An Analytic Framework (Phase II) and Issue Studies*, pp. 259–384. Commission for Economic Cooperation, Montreal.

Mouri, Allahyar (1994). *The International Law of Expropriation as Reflected in the Work of the Iran-U.S. Claims Tribunal*. Nijhoff, Dordrecht, Netherlands.

Mumme, Stephen and Pamela Duncan (1996). 'The Commission on Environmental Cooperation and the U.S.-Mexico Border Environment'. *Journal of Environment and Development* vol. 5 (June), pp. 197–215.

Munton, Don and John J. Kirton (1996). 'Beyond and Beneath the Nation-State: Province-State Interactions and NAFTA'. Paper presented at the annual convention of the International Studies Association, 17 April. San Diego.

'NAFTA Report Cites Dana Corp. in Small Step for Justice in Mexico' (1999). *PR Newswire*, 22 March.

Nagel, John (1997). 'NAFTA: Mexican Labor Group Calls for Action Following Victory in Maxi-Switch Campaign'. *Daily Labor Report*, 28 April. p. d12.

Newell, Peter (2000). *Climate for Change: Non-State Actors and the Global Politics of the Greenhouse*. Cambridge University Press, Cambridge, UK.

North American Agreement on Labor Cooperation (1998). 'Review of the North American Agreement on Labor Cooperation'. <www.naalc.org/english/publications/review.htm> (December 2001).

North American Free Trade Agreement (1994). *NAFTA Text*. CCH Incorporated, Toronto.

Norton, Roy (1998). 'Posture and Policymaking in Canada-U.S. Relations: The First Two Multroney and Chrétien Years'. *Canadian Foreign Policy* vol. 5 (Winter), pp. 15–36.

Nye, Joseph (1976). 'Transnational Relations and Interstate Conflicts: An Empirical Analysis'. In A. B. Fox, A. Hero and J. Nye, eds., *Canada and the United States: Transnational and Transgovernmental Relations*, pp. 367–404. Columbia University Press, New York.

O'Dwyer, L. A. and D. L. Burton (1998). 'Potential Meets Reality: GIS and Public Health Research in Australia'. *Australian and New Zealand Journal of Public Health* vol. 22, no. 7, pp. 819–823.

Office of Health and the Information Highway (1998). *Virtual Integration for Better Health: From Concept to Reality*. Health Canada, Ottawa.

Ontario Social Development Council and Social Planning Network of Ontario (1998). 'The Quality of Life in Ontario, Fall 1998'. Ontario Social Development Council, Toronto.

Orbuch, Paul and Thomas Singer (1995). 'International Trade, the Environment, and the States: An Evolving State-Federal Relationship'. *Journal of Environment and Development* vol. 4 (Summer), pp. 121–144.

Organisation for Economic Co-operation and Development (1993). 'Trade and Environment'. <www.olis.oecd.org/olis/1993doc.nsf/linkto/ocde-gd(93)99> (December 2001).

Organisation for Economic Co-operation and Development (1994a). *The Environmental Effects of Trade*. Organisation for Economic Co-operation and Development, Paris.

Organisation for Economic Co-operation and Development (1994b). 'Methodologies for Environmental and Trade Reviews'. <www.olis.oecd.org/olis/1994doc.nsf/linkto/ocde-gd(94)103> (December 2001).

Organisation for Economic Co-operation and Development (1996). *Trade, Employment, and Labour Standards: A Study of Core Workers' Rights and International Trade*. Organisation for Economic Co-operation and Development, Paris.

Organisation for Economic Co-operation and Development (2000). 'Joint Working Party on Trade and Environment: Methodologies for Environmental Assessment of Trade Liberalisation Agreements'. Report of the OECD Workshop, 26–27 October 1999. <www.olis.oecd.org/olis/1999doc.nsf/linkto/com-td-env(99)92-final> (December 2001).

O'Riordan, Tim (1998). 'Sustainability Indicators and the New Democracy'. *Environment* vol. 40, no. 9, p. 2.

Ostry, Sylvia (1997). *The Post-Cold War Trading System: Who's on First?* University of Chicago Press, Chicago.

Ostry, Sylvia (2000). 'Making Sense of It All: A Post-Mortem on the Meaning of Seattle'. In R. B. Porter and P. Sauvé, eds., *Seattle, the WTO, and the Future of the Multilateral Trading System*, pp. 81–94. Harvard University, Kennedy School, Cambridge, MA.

Ostry, Sylvia (2001). 'The Future of the World Trade System'. Symposium on the 50th anniversary of the Institut der deutschen Wirtschaft Köln. Berlin.

Parkin, Andrew and Centre for Research and Information on Canada (2001). 'Trade, Globalization, and Canadian Values'. The CRIC Papers, April. <www.cric.ca/pdf/cahiers/cricpapers_april2001.pdf> (December 2001).

Parkland Institute (2001). 'Advantage for Whom: Declining Family Income in a Growing Alberta Economy'. Parkland Institute, University of Alberta, Edmonton.

Partnership for Health Informatics/Telematics (1999). 'Canadian Health Data Model (Draft)'. Canadian Institute for Health Information, Toronto.

Patel, V. L. and A. W. Kushniruk (1997). 'Human-Computer Interaction in Health Care'. In J. H. van Bemmel and M. A. Musen, eds., *Handbook of Medical Informatics*, pp. 473–493. Springer-Verlag, Heidelberg.

Pearce, Clyde C. and Jack Coe, Jr. (2000). 'Arbitration under NAFTA Chapter Eleven: Some Pragmatic Reflections Upon the First Case Filed against Mexico'. *Hastings International and Comparative Law Review* vol. 23, p. 311.

Pembina Institute (2001). 'The Alberta Geniuine Progress Indicator Accounts: A Blueprint for the Way We Really Live'. Pembina Institute for Appropriate Development, Drayton Valley, AB.

Pettigrew, Pierre S. (1999). *The New Politics of Confidence*. Stoddart, Toronto.

Plagiannakos, T. (2000). 'Will Free Trade in Electricity between Ontario, Canada, and the U.S. Improve Environmental Quality?' Paper presented at the First North American Symposium on Understanding the Linkages between Trade and Environment, 11–12 October. Washington DC.

Potter, Edward (1994). Letter to U.S. National Administrative Office. U.S. Council for International Business. 31 August, on file with U.S. National Administrative Office.

Price, Daniel M. (2000). 'Chapter 11: Private Party vs. Government, Investor-State Dispute Settlement: Frankenstein or Safety Valve?' *Canada-United States Law Journal* vol. 26, pp. 107–114.

Price, Daniel M. (2000). 'Some Observations on Chapter Eleven of NAFTA'. *Hastings International and Comparative Law Review* vol. 23, nos. 3–4, pp. 421–429.

Privacy Commissioner of Canada (1999). *Annual Report 1998–99*. Minister of Public Works and Government Services Canada, Ottawa.

Program on International Policy Attitudes (2000). 'Americans on Globalization: A Study of U.S. Public Attitudes'. Program on International Policy Attitudes. <www.pipa.org/OnlineReports/Globalization/contents.html> (December 2001).

Promoting Calgary Inc. (2001). 'C-Prosperity: Regional Diagnosis'. Promoting Calgary Inc., Calgary.

'Province's Halt of Privatization Plan Ends Looming NAFTA Complaint' (1996). *Inside NAFTA*. 25 December, p. 14.

Public Citizen (1995). *NAFTA's Broken Promises*. Public Citizen, Washington DC.

Public Citizen (1998). *School of Real-Life Results: NAFTA Report Card*. Public Citizen, Washington DC.

Putnam, Robert and Nicholas Bayne, eds. (1987). *Hanging Together: Co-operation and Conflict in the Seven-Power Summit*. 2nd ed. Sage Publications, London.

Putnam, Robert, Robert Leonardi, and Raffaella Nanetti (1993). *Making Democracy Work: Civic Traditions in Modern Italy*. Princeton University Press, Princeton.

Ramroop, S. and R. T. Pascoe (1999). 'Processing of Spatial Metadata Queries with Federated GISs'. 11th Annual Colloquium of the Spatial Information Research Centre, University of Otago, Otago, New Zealand.

Raustiala, Kal (1995). 'The Political Implications of the Enforcement Provisions of the NAFTA Environmental Agreement: The CEC as a Role Model for Future Accords'. *Environmental Law* vol. 25, no. 1, pp. 31–56.

Raustiala, Kal (1997). 'The "Participatory Revolution" in International Environmental Law'. *Harvard Environmental Law Review* vol. 21, no. 2, pp. 537–586.

Redefining Progress (1995). 'The Genuine Progress Indicator: Summary of Data and Methodology'. Redefining Progress, San Francisco.

Redefining Progress (2001). 'Community Indicators'. <www.rprogress.org/projects/indicators/> (December 2001).

Regina Urban Environmental Advisory Council (1997). 'State of the Environment 1997: Sustainability and Waste Management'. Regina Urban Environmental Advisory Council, Regina.

Regional Municipality of Halton (1997). 'Halton Quality of Life: First State of the Environment Report for Halton Region'. Regional Municipality of Halton, Oakville, ON.

Regional Municipality of Hamilton-Wentworth (1994). 'State of the Environment 1994 Update'. Regional Municipality of Hamilton-Wentworth, Planning and Development Department, Hamilton, ON.

Regional Municipality of Peel (1995). 'State of the Environment: Atmosphere Report'. Regional Municipality of Peel, Brampton, ON.

Regional Municipality of York (2000). 'Our Environment, Our Home: York Region State of the Environment Summary Report 2000'. Regional Municipality of York, Newmarket, ON.

Reinert, K. A and D. W. Roland-Holst (2000). 'The Industrial Pollution Impacts of NAFTA: Some Preliminary Results'. Paper presented at the First North American Symposium on Understanding the Linkages between Trade and Environment, 11–12 October. Washington DC. <www.cec.org/programs_projects/trade_environ_econ/pdfs/Reinert.pdf> (December 2001).

Richardson, Sarah (2000). 'A 'Critique' of the EC's WTO Sustainability Impact Assessment Study and Recommendations for Phase III'. Commissioned by Oxfam GB, World Wildlife Fund-European Policy Office, Save the Children, and ActionAid. <www.oxfam.org.uk/policy/papers/wto/wto6.htm> (December 2001).

Rios, Maria Estela (1999). Interview with Jonathan Graubart, Mexico City. 12 August.

Risse, Thomas and Kathryn Sikkink (1999). 'The Socialization of Human Rights Norms and Domestic Practices: Introduction'. In T. Risse, S. Ropp and K. Sikkink, eds., *The Power of Principles: International Human Rights Norms and Domestic Change*. Cambridge University Press, Cambridge, UK.

Rodrik, Dani (1997). *Has Globalization Gone Too Far?* Institute for International Economics, Washington DC.

Roos, N. P., C. D. Black, N. Frohlich, et al. (1995). 'A Population-Based Health Information Systems'. *Medical Care* vol. 33, no. 12, suppl., pp. DS13–29.

Rose, Carol M. (2000). 'Property and Expropriation: Themes and Variations in American Law'. *Utah Law Review* vol. 2000, no. 1, pp. 1–38.

Rosen, M. J. (1999). 'Epidemiology and Risk of Pulmonary Disease'. *Seminars in Respiratory Infections* vol. 14, no. 4, pp. 301–308.

Rosenberg, Gerald (1991). *The Hollow Hope: Can Courts Bring About Social Change?* University of Chicago Press, Chicago.

Rosenfield, P. L. (1992). 'The Potential of Transdisciplinary Research for Sustaining and Extending Linkages between the Health and Social Sciences'. *Social Science and Medicine* vol. 35, no. 11, pp. 1343–1357.

Ruggie, John (1983). 'International Regimes, Transactions, and Change: Embedded Liberalism in the Postwar Economic Order'. In S. Krasner, ed., *International Regimes*. Cornell University Press, Ithaca.

Rugman, Alan M. (1999). 'Negotiating Multilateral Rules to Promote Investment'. In M. R. Hodges, J. J. Kirton and J. P. Daniels, eds., *The G8's Role in the New Millennium*, pp. 143–157. Ashgate, Aldershot.

Rugman, Alan M. and John J. Kirton (1998). 'Multinational Enterprise Strategy and the NAFTA Trade and Environment Regime'. *Journal of World Business* vol. 33, no. 4, pp. 438–454.

Rugman, Alan M. and John J. Kirton (1999). 'NAFTA, Environmental Regulations, and International Business Strategies'. *Global Focus* vol. 11, no. 4.

Rugman, Alan M., John J. Kirton, and Julie A. Soloway (1997). 'Canadian Corporate Strategy in a North American Region'. *American Review of Canadian Studies* vol. 27 (Summer), pp. 199–219.

Rugman, Alan M., John J. Kirton, and Julie A. Soloway (1999). *Environmental Regulations and Corporate Strategy: A NAFTA Perspective*. Oxford University Press, Oxford.

Runge, Ford (1999). 'Feedlot Production of Cattle in the United States and Canada'. In Commission for Environmental Cooperation, ed., *Assessing Environmental Effects of North American Free Trade Agreement (NAFTA): An Analytic Framework (Phase II) and Issue Studies*. Commission for Economic Cooperation, Montreal.

Sally, Razeen (2001). 'Looking Askance at Global Governance'. In J. J. Kirton, J. P. Daniels and A. Freytag, eds., *Guiding Global Order: G8 Governance in the Twenty-First Century*, pp. 55–76. Ashgate, Aldershot.

Sampson, Gary P. (2000). *Trade, Environment, and the WTO: The Post-Seattle Agenda*. Overseas Development Council, Washington DC.

Sampson, Gary P. and W. Bradnee Chambers (1999). *Trade, Environment, and the Millennium*. United Nations University Press, Tokyo.

Sandrino, G. L. (1994). 'The NAFTA Investment Chapter and Foreign Direct Investment in Mexico: A Third World Perspective'. *Vanderbilt Journal of Transnational Law* vol. 27, no. 259, p. 276.

Saul, John Ralston (1992). *Voltaire's Bastards: The Dictatorship of Reason in the West*. Penguin, Toronto.

Schrecker, Ted and Jean Dalgleish (1994). *Growth, Trade, and Environmental Values*. Westminster Institute for Ethics and Human Values, London, ON.

Scoffield, Heather (1999). 'Ottawa Stifling Hearings, Groups Say: Environmentalists Claim NAFTA Side Agreement Undermined by Secrecy in BC Hydro Case'. *The Globe and Mail*, 8 March.

Scollay, Robert (2001). 'Regional Trade Negotiations in the Asia-Pacific Region: Assessment of Current Trends and Implications for the FTAA and the WTO'. Working paper prepared for the Inter-American Development Bank.

Sepulveda, Alicia (1999). Interview with Jonathan Graubart, Mexico City. 16 August.

Sforza-Roderick, Michelle, Scott Nova, and Mark Weisbrot (1999). 'Writing the Constitution of a Single Global Economy: A Concise Guide to the Multilateral Agreement on Investment'. <www.globalpolicy.org/globaliz/econ/oneecon.htm> (December 2001).

Shahar, Y. and M. A. Musen (1996). 'Knowledge-Based Temporal Abstraction in Clinical Domains'. *Artificial Intelligence in Medicine* vol. 8, no. 3, pp. 267–298.

Shaw, Martin (1994). *Global Society and International Relations: Sociological Concepts and Political Perspectives*. Polity Press, Cambridge, UK.

Sierra Club and S. Holbrook-White (2000). 'NAFTA Transportation Corridors: Approaches to Assessing Environmental Impacts and Alternatives'. Paper presented at the First North American Symposium on Understanding the Linkages between Trade and Environment, 11–12 October. Washington DC. <www.cec.org/programs_projects/trade_environ_econ/pdfs/sierra.pdf> (December 2001).

Sjoberg, C. and T. Timpka (1998). 'Participatory Design of Information Systems in Health Care'. *Journal of the American Medical Informatics Association* vol. 5, no. 2, pp. 177–183.

Smyser, W. R. (1993). 'Goodbye, G-7'. *Washington Quarterly* vol. 16 (Winter), pp. 15–28.

Sohn, L. B. and R. R. Baxter (1961). 'Responsibility of States for Injuries to the Economic Interests of Aliens'. *American Journal of International Law* vol. 55, no. 545, pp. 553–554.

Soloway, Julie A. (1999). 'Environmental Trade Barriers under NAFTA: The MMT Fuel Additives Controversy'. *Minnesota Journal of Global Trade* vol. 8, no. 1, p. 55.

Spencer, Robert, John J. Kirton, and Kim Richard Nossal (1981). *The International Joint Commission Seventy Years On.* Centre for International Studies, University of Toronto, Toronto.

Stead, W. W., R. A. Miller, M. A. Musen, et al. (2000). 'Integration and Beyond: Linking Information from Disparate Sources and into Workflow'. *Journal of the American Medical Informatics Association* vol. 7, no. 2, pp. 135–145.

Steinberg, Richard (1997). 'Trade-Environment Negotiations in the EU, NAFTA, and WTO: Regional Trajectories of Rule Development'. *American Journal of International Law* vol. 91, no. 2, pp. 231–267.

Stone, Christopher D. (1994). 'Defending the Global Commons'. In P. Sands, ed., *Greening International Law.* New Press, New York.

Stone, V. (2000). 'Environmental Air Pollution'. *American Journal of Respiratory and Critical Care Medicine* vol. 162, no. 2, pt. 2, pp. S44–47.

Sustainable Calgary (1998). 'State of Our City Report 1998'. Sustainable Calgary, Calgary.

Sustainable Calgary (2001). 'State of Our City Report 2001'. Sustainable Calgary, Calgary.

Sustainable Seattle (1995). 'Sustainable Seattle State of Our City Report'. Sustainable Seattle, Seattle.

Szasz, Paul C. (1999). 'General Law-Making Processes'. In C. C. Joyner, ed., *The United Nations and International Law.* American Society of International Law and Cambridge University Press, Cambridge, MA.

Thérien, Jean-Philippe and Sébastien Dallaire (1999–2000). 'Nord-Sud: Une Vision Du Monde en Mutation'. *La revue internationale et stratégique* vol. 36 (Winter), pp. 21–35.

Theuringer, Martin (2001). 'International Macroeconomic Policy Co-Operation in the Era of the Euro'. In J. J. Kirton, J. P. Daniels and A. Freytag, eds., *Guiding Global Order: G8 Governance in the Twenty-First Century*, pp. 173–187. Ashgate, Aldershot.

Torres, Blanca (1996). 'Redes y Coaliciones en el Proceso de Negociacion y Aprobacion del Tratado de Libre Comercio de America del Norte'. In A. Borja, G. Gonzalez and B. J. R. Stevenson, eds., *Regionalismo y Poder en America: Los Limites del Neorrealismo*. CIDE, Mexico City.

Trakman, Leon E. (2001). 'Arbitrating Investment Disputes under NAFTA'. *Journal of International Arbitration* vol. 18, no. 4, p. 385.

Tuck, S. (2001). 'Fewer Canadians Support Free Trade'. *The Globe and Mail*, 5 February. pp. A1, 6.

Tufte, E. R. (1997). *Visual Explanations*. Graphics Press, Cheshire, CT.

Twigg, L. (1990). 'Health-Based Geographical Information Systems: Their Potential Examined in the Light of Existing Data Sources'. *Social Science and Medicine* vol. 30, no. 1, pp. 143–155.

Ullrich, Heidi K. (2001). 'Stimulating Trade Liberalisation after Seattle: G7/8 Leadership in Global Governance'. In J. J. Kirton and G. M. von Furstenberg, eds., *New Directions in Global Economic Governance: Creating International Order for the Twenty-First Century*, pp. 219–240. Ashgate, Aldershot.

United Nations Development Programme (1999). *Human Development Report 1999*. Oxford University Press, Oxford.

United Nations Environmental Programme (1999). *Environmental Impacts of Trade Liberalization and Policies for the Sustainable Management of Natural Resources: A Case Study of Bangladesh's Shrimp Farming Industry*. United Nations Environmental Programme, Economics and Trade Unit, Nairobi.

United Nations Environmental Programme (1999). *Environmental Impacts of Trade Liberalization and Policies for the Sustainable Management of Natural Resources: A Case Study of Chile's Mining Sector*. United Nations Environmental Programme, Economics and Trade Unit, Nairobi.

United Nations Environmental Programme (1999). *Environmental Impacts of Trade Liberalization and Policies for the Sustainable Management of Natural Resources: A Case Study of India's Automobile Sector*. United Nations Environmental Programme, Economics and Trade Unit, Nairobi.

United Nations Environmental Programme (1999). *Environmental Impacts of Trade Liberalization and Policies for the Sustainable Management of Natural Resources: A Case Study of Romania's Water Sector*. United Nations Environmental Programme, Economics and Trade Unit, Nairobi.

United Nations Environmental Programme (1999). *Environmental Impacts of Trade Liberalization and Policies for the Sustainable Management of Natural Resources: A Case Study of the Philippines' Forestry Sector*. United Nations Environmental Programme, Economics and Trade Unit, Nairobi.

United Nations Environmental Programme (2001). *Reference Manual for the Integrated Assessment of Trade-Related Policies*. United Nations, New York and Geneva. <www.unep.ch/etu/etp/acts/manpols/rmia.htm> (December 2001).

United States (2000). 'Position of the Government of the United States of America on Legal Issues Relating to Submissions on Enforcement Matters and Preparation of Factual Records under Articles 14 and 15 of the NAAEC'. 27 March. Unpublished, on file with Christopher Tollefson.

United States Department of Labor (2001). 'Status of Submissions'. 19 September. <www.dol.gov/dol/ilab/public/programs/nao/status.htm> (December 2001).

United States National Administrative Office (1994). *Public Report of Review.* 12 October.

United States National Administrative Office (1998). Public Hearing on Submission 9702. 18 February.

United States National Administrative Office (1999). 'Report'. 28 April.

United States National Administrative Office Hearing (1994). 12 September.

United States Trade Representative (1993). 'The NAFTA: Report on Environmental Issues'. <www.ustr.gov/environment/nafta93report.pdf> (December 2001).

United States Trade Representative (1997). 'Study on the Operation and Effect of the North American Free Trade Agreement'. 1 July. United States Trade Representative.

United States Trade Representative (1999). 'Accelerated Trade Liberalization in the Forest Products Sector: A Study of the Economic and Environmental Effects'. <www.ustr.gov/releases/1999/11/forest.html> (December 2001).

United States Trade Representative (2000). 'Draft Environmental Review of the Proposed Agreement on the Establishment of a Free Trade Area between the Government of the United States and the Government of the Hashemite Kingdom of Jordan'. <www.ustr.gov/environment/nafta93report.html> (December 2001).

United States White House (1999). 'Executive Order: Environmental Review of Trade Agreements'. <www.ustr.gov/environment/execo.htm> (December 2001).

Vagts, D.F. (1978). 'Coercion and Foreign Investment Rearrangements'. *American Journal of International Law* vol. 72, no. 17.

Valacer, D. J. (2000). 'Childhood Asthma: Causes, Epidemiological Factors, and Complications'. *Drugs* vol. 49, suppl. 1, pp. 1–8, discussion pp. 43–45.

Van Duzer, J. Anthony (1997). 'Investor-State Dispute Settlement under NAFTA Chapter 11: The Shape of Things to Come?' *Canadian Yearbook of International Law* vol. 35, p. 263.

van Oers, J. A. M. (1993). *A Geographic Information System for Local Public Health Policy*. Van Gorcum, Assen, the Netherlands.

Velasco, Elizabeth (1998). 'Trabajadores Agricolas Denuncian Explotación en E.U.' *La Jornada*, 3 December. p. 41.

Victor, David G. (1997). The Use and Effectiveness of Nonbinding Instruments in the Management of Complex International Environmental Problems. Proceedings of the Annual Meeting-American Society of International Law.

'Vital Trade Round' (2001). *Financial Times*, 2 August. p. 20.

von Furstenberg, George M. and Joseph P. Daniels (1991). 'Policy Undertakings by the Seven "Summit" Countries: Ascertaining the Degree of Compliance'. *Carnegie-Rochester Conference Series on Public Policy* vol. 35, pp. 267–308.

von Moltke, Konrad (1997). 'Institutional Interactions: The Structure of Regimes for Trade and Environment'. In O. R. Young, ed., *Global Governance: Drawing Insights from the Environmental Experience*, pp. 247–272. MIT Press, Cambridge, MA.

von Moltke, Konrad (2000). *An International Investment Regime? Issues for Sustainability*. International Institute for Sustainable Development, Winnipeg.

von Moltke, Konrad (2001). 'Misappropriation of Institutions: Some Lessons from the Environmental Dimension of the NAFTA Investor-State Dispute Settlement Process'. *International Environmental Agreements* vol. 1, no. 1, pp. 103–123.

Wackernagel, Mathis and William E. Rees (1996). *Our Ecological Footprint: Reducing Human Impact on the Earth*. New Society Publishers, Gabriola Island, BC.

Wagner, J. Martin (1999). 'International Investment, Expropriation, and Environmental Protection'. *Golden Gate University Law Review* vol. 29, nos. 1–3, pp. 465–538.

Wallace, Cynthia D. (1982). *Legal Controls of Multinational Enterprise*. Nijhoff, The Hague.

Wallace, Don (2000). 'State Responsibility for Denial of Substantive and Procedural Justice under NAFTA Chapter Eleven'. *Hastings International and Comparative Law Review* vol. 23, p. 393.

Walzer, Michael (1995). *Toward a Global Civil Society*. Berghahn Books, Providence, RI.

Waring, Marilyn (1999). *Counting for Nothing: What Men Value and What Women Are Worth*. 2nd ed. University of Toronto Press, Toronto.

Weiler, Todd J. (2001). 'Metalclad v. Mexico: A Play in Three Parts'. *Journal of World Investment* vol. 2, no. 4.

Weintraub, Sydney (1994). 'Current State of U.S.-Canada Economic Relations'. *American Review of Canadian Studies* vol. 24 (Winter), pp. 473–488.

Weintraub, Sydney (1997). *NAFTA at Three: A Progress Report*. Center for Strategic and International Studies, Washington DC.

Weiss, Edith Brown (1999). 'Understanding Compliance with International Environmental Agreements: The Baker's Dozen Myths'. *University of Richmond Law Review* vol. 32, no. 5, pp. 1555–1589.

Wellens, K. C. and G. M. Borchardt (1989). 'Soft Law in European Community Law'. *European Law Review* vol. 14, no. 5, pp. 267–321.

Weston, B.H. (1975). '"Constructive Takings" under International Law: A Modest Foray into the Problem of Creeping Expropriation'. *Virginia Journal of International Law* vol. 16, no. 103, p. 107.

'Why Exactly Does This NAFTA Commission Exist?' (2000). *The Globe and Mail*, 23 May.

Whyman, William E. (1995). 'We Can't Go on Meeting Like This: Revitalizing the G-7 Process'. *Washington Quarterly* vol. 18 (Summer), pp. 139–165.

Williamson, John (1990). *The Progress of Policy Reform in Latin America*. Institute for International Economics, Washington DC.

Williamson, John (1993). 'Democracy and the "Washington Consensus"'. *World Development* vol. 21, pp. 1329–1336.

Willison, D. J. (1998). 'Health Services Research and Personal Health Information: Privacy Concerns, New Legislation, and Beyond'. *Canadian Medical Association Journal* vol. 159, no. 11, pp. 1378–1380.

Wirth, David A. (1994). 'Reexamining Decision-Making Processes in International Environmental Law'. *Iowa Law Review* vol. 79, no. 4, pp. 769–802.

World Commission on Environment and Development (1987). *Our Common Future*. Oxford University Press, Oxford; New York.

World Health Organization (1986). *Ottawa Charter for Health Promotion*. World Health Organization, Geneva.

World Health Organization (1997). *The Jakarta Declaration on Leading Health Promotion into the 21st Century*. World Health Organization, Geneva.

World Trade Organization (2000). *Special Study: Trade, Income Disparity, and Poverty*. World Trade Organization, Geneva.

World Wildlife Foundation Canada (2000). 'Canada's Draft Environmental Assessment Framework for Trade Negotiations: Comments by WWF Canada'. 6 October.

World Wildlife Fund (1998). *Developing a Methodology for the Environmental Assessment of Trade Agreements*. World Wildlife Fund International, Gland, Switzerland.

World Wildlife Fund (2000). 'Living Planet Report 2000'. <www.panda.org/livingplanet/lpr00> (December 2001).

World Wildlife Fund and Fundación Futuro Latinoamericano (2000). 'International Experts Meeting on Sustainability Assessment of Trade Liberalisation'. <www.panda.org/resources/publications/sustainability/iem/> (December 2001).

World Wildlife Fund International (1999). 'Initiating an Environmental Assessment of Trade Liberalisation in the WTO'. Vol. II. <www.panda.org/resources/publications/sustainability/wto-papers/initiate.html> (December 2001).

Wortley, Ben Atkinson (1959). *Expropriation in Public International Law*. Cambridge University Press, Cambridge, UK.

Yergin, Daniel and Joseph Stanislaw (1998). *The Commanding Heights: The Battle between Government and the Marketplace That Is Remaking the Modern World*. Simon and Schuster, New York.

Young, Oran R. (1994). *International Governance: Protecting the Environment in a Stateless Society*. Cornell University Press, Ithaca.

Young, Oran R. (1998). *Creating Regimes: Arctic Accords and International Governance*. Cornell University Press, Ithaca.

Young, Oran R. (1998). 'The Effectiveness of International Environmental Regimes: A Mid-Term Report'. *International Environmental Affairs* vol. 10, no. 4, pp. 267–289.

Index